Why Normandy Was Won:
Operation Bagration and the War in the East 1941-1945

How Stalin and the Red Army contributed to the success of the Allies at Normandy

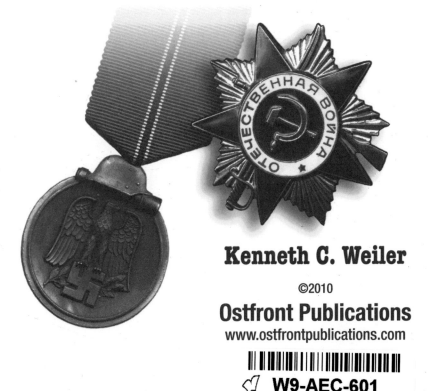

Kenneth C. Weiler

©2010
Ostfront Publications
www.ostfrontpublications.com

Why Normandy Was Won: Operation Bagration and the War In The East 1941-1945

Kenneth C. Weiler

Published by:

Ostfront Publications, LLC
P.O. Box 453
Hanover, PA 17331-7763, USA
kweiler1@comcast.net
www.ostfrontpublications.com

Library of Congress Cataloging-in-Publication Data

Weiler, Kenneth C.

Why Normandy Was Won: Operation Bagration And The War In The East 1941-1945/ Weiler, Kenneth C. - 1st Ed.

Includes bibliographical references and index.

LCCN: 2009939880
ISBN 978-0-9825779-0-5 (pbk)

1. Soviet Union-History-World War-1939-1945.
2. World War 1939-1945-Campaigns-Eastern Front. I. Title
D764.W 2010
940.54

10 9 8 7 6 5 4 3 2 1

Printed in the United States of America

*To my wife Sally, whose patience and support
made this book possible*

Credits

Cover Design: Proforma Graphic Concepts

Front Cover

>   M35 Heer Stahlhelm Wehrmachtadler, authors collection.

Back Cover

>   *Winterschlacht im Osten 1941/42*, authors collection.

>   *The Order of the Patriotic War*, 1942, 2nd Class, authors collection.

Acknowledgements

This work would not have seen the light of day had it not been for a number of people who have shared my interest in the subject and the importance of adding it to the historical record. Among these people is Dr. Hugh Scott, MD, RADM, MC, USN Ret. Admiral Scott's generous contributions of advice in the early days of this book and his of time, knowledge and perspective and his constant reminders to "stay on target" were most helpful for a new author. Marc Charisse, Editor, The Evening Sun, Hanover, PA (*www.eveningsun.com*) for his editorial support, gentle chastisement to keep me accurate and keen advice in many areas of the manuscript; David Glantz for his help in providing direction for the manuscript in its early days; Dan and David Badolato of Proforma Graphic Concepts (*www.proforma.com/graphicconcepts*) for their insightful cover and book design, Don Canapp, Sr. "The Computer Guy" for his excellent work creating my website (*www.ostfrontpublications.com*), Aasland Kjetil Gammelsrud (Finland) for his review of Chapter IX and his advice and suggestions for improving it. Tom Houlihan at *www.mapsatwar.com* for his generous cartographic support. Andrea Anesi at *www.anesindexing.com* for her superb work constructing the index, and Barbara Huston of Poist Photographic Studio, Hanover, PA (*www.poiststudioandframeshoppe.net*) for her creative author photo. Finally, and most importantly, my father, Charles G. Weiler, (U.S.M.C., K Company, 25th Marines, 4th Div. ,World War II, Saipan) for his instilling in me a life long sense of the importance of a nation's history, especially it's military, its contributions to its citizens and an appreciation of the sacrifices it makes for its people.

Praemonitus praemunitus

Contents

Contents - continued

Why Normandy Was Won: Operation Bagration and the War In The East 1941-1945

Adolf Hitler
(1889-1945)

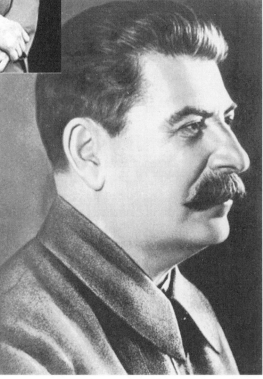

Joseph Stalin
(1879-1953)

"Introduction"

I n the opening days and weeks of the Allied invasion of Europe at Normandy in June 1944, the ether crackled and sparked across the English Channel with situation and intelligence reports coming into SHAEF (Supreme Headquarters Allied Expeditionary Force) operational headquarters in Portsmouth at Southwick House, 75 miles south of London. These reports from the combat units in France contained the typical information a commander would expect: Battle progress, enemy force predictions, friendly and enemy casualties, unit readiness and morale, supply status, especially fuel, and many bits of military minutiae that painted the picture of life in the front lines.

However, among the thousands of reports, certain unusual items begin to appear. At first, just an odd mention or oblique reference. But as the invasion progressed into late summer of 1944, these references and mentions become more and more frequent. These references had to do with the nationality, racial and ethnic make-up of enemy units encountered and captured with increasing frequency. Specifically, the reports described the German prisoners of war – or to be more accurate, the lack of ethnic Germans in the units encountered. A number of the prisoners captured in these opening weeks in Normandy were anything but the Aryans of the master race of Hitler's Germany, his so-called supermen. What the Allies discovered was enemy infantry and panzer troops from all over Western and Central Europe, including Dutch, Danish, Norwegian and some French. But what specifically caught the Allied command's interest was that many of the soldiers fighting for the Germans, were far from their home countries, mostly from Eastern Europe and Central Asia.

Among these captured soldiers from far away were former Russian Army Russians, Cossacks from the steppes of the Volga, men from Turkistan, the Caucasus and the far-flung portions of the Soviet Union. There were even Indians[1], as well as Thais from Indochina. What were the Germans doing

---

[1] These troops arrived in the west in 1943 - 44 and were mainly from captured British Commonwealth units in North Africa. For more on the locations, activities and relationships with the local inhabitants of these units see *Eastern Troops in Zeeland, The Netherlands, 1943 - 1945* by J. N. Houterman, Axis Europa, New York, 1997.

relying on men from such far away regions, most whom, by the way, had willingly surrendered to the Allies at the first opportunity? How had these men come to be in the German Army, some of them in the Waffen SS, the supposed cream of Germany's land fighting units? The Germans were about to confront the most dangerous threat to its land forces in Western Europe, a force that had to be defeated and destroyed quickly and these men were to provide the edge in this decisive struggle? What was needed was the best Germany could muster. However, not only were there no longer adequate numbers of Germany's best and brightest; most of them were not even in France for this momentous battle. Where were they? They were deep into the Union of Soviet Socialist Republics or Russia, confronting a far greater and closer threat to the German homeland.

This is the story of the vast Soviet attack against the German invader in the summer of 1944 in western Russia and the impact it had on the Allied success on the beaches of Normandy and the war in Europe. The narrative has a broad sweep, from the fields and meadows of Belorussia to the rocky shores of Normandy. It will attempt to describe the conditions of the two armies involved – the German Wehrmacht and the Soviet Russian Army, also known as the Russian Army. Along the way it will address a number of problems and challenges (political, economic, meteorological, organizational) each combatant encountered and how successful they were in overcoming them. Some of these problems have been discussed and debated before and they are well known and others will be new.

Operation Bagration was not only the largest operation on the Eastern Front, it was the largest operation of the war. It was the single event that destroyed the personal and material fabric of the German Army in the East, killing or capturing more Germans then either the battles of Stalingrad or Moscow. Operation Bagration was the offensive that demonstrated that the Russian Army had reached tactical and operational parity with the German army in the east. In all aspects of war fighting; planning, security, communications, execution and quantity of arms this was the battle that riveted the Germans, holding them in place and preventing their possible transfer of men and material to France.

Originally my intent was to describe the relationship, direct or otherwise, of the Russian attack against Germany's Army Group Center, an operation known as Operation Bagration in western Russia, and the impact this had on the western Allied success in northwest France in Normandy. However, during the writing and research for this narrower focus, I discovered a lack of knowledge of operations in Russia during World War II in general, and Operation Bagration in particular. With this in mind, the purpose and scope of the book changed. I decided it to enlarge it, hopefully adding to the body of military knowledge of these events and to inform the general public about the less familiar contributions made by the Red Army to enhance and ensure the Allied success at Normandy. The work is not intended to be a purely academic treatment of the events in France, Russia and eastern Poland, as my goal is ease of readership – understanding and information for the historian and the general public alike. The military historian who seeks more specific detail and information should consult the works cited and continue their study.

The primary focus of this work is the events on the other side of Europe, the Eastern Front, which ensured Allied success in Operation Overlord, the code name for the invasion of Western Europe. No one can appreciate the outcome of the Second World War without a basic understanding of the decisive role played by Soviet Union. The focus will be on the Eastern European member of the Allied coalition, the Union of Soviet Socialist Republics, which I will refer to as the Russians or Soviets[2] interchangeably for the sake of brevity, convenience and ease of reference, and their war with the European Axis allies. I will also use American and/or English spellings of geographical features as well as military unit designations.

I will also attempt to answer the questions of how and why Russian activity on the Eastern Front directly affected the Allied invasion of Western Europe. What was the state of Germany, and its armed forces, (the Wehrmacht) at the time of the invasion? How did they arrive at this condition? What if the Soviets had concluded a peace agreement with Germany by 1942? What was the German economic and industrial situation in June 1944, and that of the Russians? What was the immediate and long-term impact of Operation Bagration – the Russian attack against the German Army Group Center in June 1944 – on the outcome of the war in Europe? Finally, I will attempt to demonstrate the importance of the Russian Front to the success of the western Allied landings in France in World War II.

[2] The reference to Russia is a synonym for the U.S.S.R. and the use of the term Russian refers to all Soviet citizens, irrespective of their national or ethnic identity or whether or not they were a members of the Communist Party. The same interchangeability will be used when referring to the land forces of the U.S.S.R. as either the Red Army, Russian Army or the Soviet Army, which became the official title of the army in 1944.

Americans, in particular, tend to be afflicted with historical 'tunnel vision' and it is especially acute in regard to knowledge of the eastern European theater. As I have learned over the years, many Americans, especially those under 30, are wholly unaware that there was a war going on in Russia, Poland and Germany from 1941 to 1945! For some western Europeans and many Americans, the war in the East remains an unclear and baffling sideshow. This is a serious omission in the story of the Second World War, as the Allied success in Normandy was heavily dependent on the Soviets. They were the only land force in Europe fighting the German Wehrmacht and its Axis allies for most of the war.

There are many who have voiced the opinion that the Soviets alone could have defeated the invading Germans, without a Western front. This is an interesting, if not biased view of the contributions made by the U.S., Britain, Canada, and the other members of the Allied coalition. A strong position indeed, but one not without some merit and I will attempt to describe in some detail the Soviet industrial efforts to defeat the Wehrmacht, with or without western assistance. This observation is buttressed by David Lloyd George, Britain's distinguished statesman by his comment early in the German invasion of Russia that "the outcome of the entire war now depends on the U.S.S.R." He was not far off the mark. This sentiment was echoed by Sir Stafford Cripps, the British ambassador to Moscow who in July 1941 complained to his government that it was "underestimating the enormous and absolutely vital importance of the Eastern Front to Britain as our one insurance against the future".

The works cited and the references used are all currently available, with only a few exceptions, and most published in English. The reader will notice a number of works translated from their original German. This is because of the wide availability of American and German source materials in the marketplace, libraries and archives since the end of the war. Only a few Russian works have been consulted, because of the scarcity of translated material as well as the high political content, historical bias, or purely ideological slant many of these materials contain. I hope that as time passes more Soviet era material is translated and becomes available, not only for the historian but the general readership as well. In addition, it is the unbiased writings and recollections of the average Russian soldier and officer that need attention. Too little of this writing currently exists and as this generation passes into history their stories will sadly be lost.

Probably the biggest omission in the examination of the war in the East is a comprehensive analysis of the crisis year 1944. Many notable authors, historians, and scholars have touched on or alluded to this important nexus. But they have been just that – a short foray into the topic and a just as quick retreat. There is a growing body of memoirs and battle descriptions by the men, both officer and enlisted man alike. But each of these is a micro focus of the thousands of individual personal, technical, and political episodes and do not provide an interconnected, comprehensive analysis of why this theater of the war was *the most important* and the month of June 1944 was so critical to Germany losing the war. The study of the Eastern Front and its relationship to the Western theater has not been addressed and some might even say it has been neglected, and I will hope to remedy that here.

The author has diligently researched all of the material presented here, attributed sources and cited materials in a format generally accepted by most commercial publishers and academic institutions. The inclusion of the sources; maps, charts and footnotes on each page, while an outdated style, was chosen to facilitate 'readability' and understanding of the material presented, without the needless and bothersome chore of flipping back and forth to the rear of the book to read the footnotes. Should inaccuracies or omissions occur, it is hoped that the reader will forward his or her observations to the publisher and/or author for inclusion or correction in future editions.

This is several books in one: A military history, first and foremost; a social history; a political analysis and commentary; and an economic review. In addition to the primary focus of how the fighting in Russia guaranteed the success of the landings in Normandy and the subsequent breakout into Western Europe. I will also take several 'side trips' in the story of the war in the East, discussing how the war affected Germany and Russia in ways other than what happened on the battlefields. Evaluations of the economic, political, social and racial aspects of the war have been included, some at great length, to give the reader a greater sense of the disaster the German campaign was, not only to the two protagonists but also to most of central and eastern Europe. These forays are not meant to sidetrack the story but quite the contrary, to embellish and engage both amateur and specialist and make the picture of the destructive nature of the war in the East clearer, especially for the general reader.

The evaluation and study of the importance of the Soviet impact on the Normandy invasion is not intended in any fashion to devalue or diminish the efforts and sacrifices the western Allies made beginning on 6 June 1944. The entire purpose of this work is to bring to the attention of the reader, especially the U.S. reader, the complete picture of what was happening before and during the moments the first assault boats landed on the rough beaches in Northwest France. This is the missing link in the narrative; the rest of the story of what was happening some 1,300 miles to the east.

In addition to illuminating the war in the East for the Western reader, this study will examine the operations of two armies under totalitarian governments, undergoing dynamic change under the severe pressures of time, environment and economy which make the Second World War in the East unique. There has been adequate study made of the Western armies engaged in combat, which observed the rules of engagement, such as the Geneva Convention, fair play and honorable surrender. The totalitarian nations engaged in the East observed no such niceties; the grand sweep of this truly unique theater and the encompassing winner-take- all nature of the conflict is what makes this war such a compelling subject for study.

Since embarking on this work I have conducted a survey of my own, a personal and very unscientific verification of the lack of American awareness in this aspect of the war. I visited as many mass market bookshops, bookstalls, book conventions and smaller bookstores as possible along my journeys, mainly in the United States, seeking anything published about the World War II in the East. In each I made a stop in the history section and if the emporium was large and specialized enough, the military history section. I carefully traced the titles of all the works presented, searching for any and all works on the Eastern Front. The titles dealing with Normandy, Guadalcanal, Iwo Jima, the battle of Stalingrad, Saipan, Berlin, and Pearl Harbor were all present. If I'm fortunate, a few of the more popular works on the Eastern Front make their appearance, such as David Glantz's *Stumbling Colossus* and *Colossus Reborn*, Erickson's 'Road' series, Seaton's *The Russo-German War 1941-45*, the popular Carell's *Hitler Moves East* or *Scorched Earth*, Clark's *Barbarossa*, Werth's *Russia at War* and Catherine Merridale's *Ivan's War*. Considering the vastness and importance of the Eastern Front these stand out as isolated exceptions – mentions and references to a place and time that seems to have been forgotten or worse, entirely overlooked. They hint at something larger except for these few exceptions no comprehensive work presents itself to answer the question, 'what happened here'? What is this Eastern Front? Why is it important and what does it have to do with the rest of the war in Europe, especially the Allied success in Normandy? In the popular world of mass-market book selling, the Eastern Front is almost a non-entity and its absence is all the more conspicuous by the presence of just these few names.[3]

Part I lays out the building blocks of the story of the impact of the Eastern Front on the Western Theater. It will provide a look at the military systems of the two nations and the armies they built and managed, as well as a look at what life was like in each of them. In addition, a brief look at the relationship of the Union of Soviet Socialist Republics and the Western Allies will be presented and an examination of the political and economic as well as the military aspects of this relationship will be discussed.

Part II will address the war in Europe, with an emphasis on central and Eastern Europe and the developments in Germany, Poland and the U.S.S.R. in particular. A discussion of the war between Germany and her Axis allies against the Soviet Union will be conducted with a focus on the three campaign seasons leading up to the subject year of 1944.

Part III will concentrate on the year 1944 and the dramatic reversals suffered by Germany in Russia and will culminate in the discussion of Operation Bagration in June 1944 and its effects on all the combatants as well as the consequences this battle had on Germany and Russia. It discusses the connection to and the impact of the Soviet 1944 offensive on the Allied landings in Normandy.

[3] A recent example of omissions or oversights regarding the Russian area of the European Theater is the map on page 199 of the recently published *The World War II Desk Reference* (Grand Central Press, 2004). The map referred to is entitled "Major Engagements in the European Theater of Operations" and lists by place and date the most familiar, to western eyes, battles and engagements of the war in Europe. However, there are some glaring omissions and all have to do with events in the east. For example, the first battle of the war in Europe, the invasion of Poland in September 1939 is unnoted, as is the invasion of Russia in June 1941, the winter counteroffensive in front of Moscow of December 1941 and, of great importance to us here, Operation Bagration, June 1944. These omissions are all the more confounding and confusing as the authors *did include*, for example, the smaller and more minor operation: the relief of the surrounded German units at Korsun in January-February 1944. In the description section of the same chapter, the Moscow winter counteroffensive *is* listed and briefly described (Moscow, Russia 'Winter 1941-42') but still no Bagration, in fact, Bagration is mentioned only *once* in the entire 572 pages!

A more recent example of the American ignorance of the war in the east comes from Edward Wood's *Worshipping the Myths of World War II* (Potomac Books, 2006) where he states that during his research his conversations revealed only "a vague idea of the contributions of the U.S.S.R. to Allied victory…"

Chapter I looks at the establishment of the German army, its history, formation and organization and components. Chapter II Is a mirror of the first chapter with the subject being the Russian Army. Chapter III Discusses life in Germany during the war to give the reader a feel for life under Hitler in a totalitarian setting under the stress of a losing war. Chapter IV Is another mirror chapter, this time with Russia, its people, government and life in the "workers' paradise" as the focus. Chapter V widens the picture of the war in Europe with the addition of the Western Allies and the war from their prospective. Chapter VI Takes a closer look at the two nations at war and what their relationships were with each other and their preparations for war. Chapters VII, VIII, IX and X trace the course of the war from 21 June 1941 when Germany attacked Russia in Operation Barbarossa to the Spring of that fateful year 1944. For the readers not familiar with the war, this will provide the context for Operation Bagration and its support for the Allied invasion at Normandy. Chapter XI begins the core subject of the book, the preparations for Operation Bagration and the situation in the East at that time. Chapter XII discuss the planning, outlooks and threats and opportunities by both sides for the summer campaign of 1944. Chapter XIII discusses the Allied and German preparations to launch and defend against the amphibious landings. Chapter XIV is the discussion of the battle itself and what transpired for both sides. Chapter XV is the most central chapter of the book discussing the results of Operation Bagration, not only for the Germany army in the East but its impact on the operations in Normandy and, eventually in all of Northwest Europe. Also discussed is the entire reshaping of central and eastern Europe at the conclusion of the war with the fall of Berlin in the Spring of 1945. The arrival of the Soviet Union as a world military power, its new relationships with their wartime Allies in the West and what the new balance of power would be in Europe.

The German invasion of Russia was not the first invasion of this vast land. Two others were attempted and both failed. The warnings of the last attempt by the French under Napoleon serves us well and sets the stage for what follows. The memoirs of General de Caulaincourt, Duke of Vicenza was Napoleons Ambassador to Russia's Tsar Alexander. It serves as the best foreshadowing for what was attempted by Germany 129 years later. The following conversation between the Duke and the Tsar is of interest:

"If the Emperor Napoleon makes war on me, it is possible, even probable, that we shall be defeated, assuming that we fight. But that will not mean that he can dictate a peace. The Spaniards have often been defeated; but they are not beaten, nor have they submitted. But they are not so far away from Paris as we, and have neither our climate nor our resources to help them. We shall take no risks. We have plenty of room; and our standing army is well organized, which means, as the Emperor Napoleon has admitted, that we need never accept a dictated peace, whatever reverses we may suffer. What is more, in such circumstances the victor is forced to accept the terms of the vanquished... I shall not be the first to draw my sword, but I shall be the last to sheath it. The Spaniards have proved that lack of perseverance has been the undoing of all the States on which your master has made war... People don't know how to suffer. If the fighting went against me, I should retire to Kamchatka (sp) rather than cede provinces and sign, in my capital, treaties that were really only truces. Your Frenchman is brave; but long privations and a bad climate wear him down and discourage him. Our climate, our winter, will fight on our side. With you, marvels only take place where the Emperor is in personal attendance, and he cannot be everywhere..."[4]

Finally, this is a specialized, interpretative as well as a comprehensive history. Crucial events and personages are discussed; the significant events receive their due. However, this work also is an attempt to provide analysis of this pivotal event and not just to relate the lists of numbers; numbers of tanks[5], artillery, men and aircraft and to read again the timeline of events. The war in the East was a war of quantities and endurance, and the numbers are staggering. Discussion and debate of these numbers has been done before and perhaps will continue for years to come.

---

[4] *At Napoleon's Side in Russia, The Classic Eyewitness Account, The Memoirs of General de Caulaincourt, Duke of Vicenza* by Armand de Caulaincourt, Enigma Books, New York 2003, p. 5.

[5] The terms "tank" and "panzer" will be used interchangeably, however the latter will usually be used to describe German armored fighting vehicles.

PzKw VIE "Tiger" I. Germany's first heavy tank. Note anti-boarding barbed wire attached along the hull sides.

Part 1:

1935 - 1941

Background and Context

to Operation Barbarossa

Russian T-34/76 with crew and infantry riders

Chapter One:
The Wehrmacht

This chapter discusses the creation of the new German Army up until and including the early days of World War II. It is not a complete picture of the Army, but a selected view of it for the preparations for the invasion of Russia. Our discussion will dwell mostly on its unique background and history that was the genesis of what became the world's foremost military force for most of war. It will not answer every question one has about the German army, only that portion that answers the questions of how it got to be the army that almost destroyed the largest land army in the world in 1941.

In the Beginning

In September 1939 Germany stunned the world with a kind of warfare that had never been seen before. In place of the tramping of thousands of marching infantry and lumbering artillery, expected by the world's nations, along with a sedate enough pace that war could be fought with map pins on large maps in generals' offices that could be moved with thought and leisure. This was not to be that kind of war, the day to day progress of the panzers and motorized units could only be accurately tracked by an equally new news medium, radio. The few television sets and movie house newsreels only intensified the breakneck pace of this new form of war. To more fully understand how this new and improved war making originated, it is important to understand that army that developed it.

The birth of the modern German Army can be traced to or about the time of the Great Elector, Frederick William I (1640 - 1688) in the mid 17th century. He was the one most responsible for the development of a unique military style, that of a "German" way of war that can be distilled to include the following methodologies: a war of fluid movement *bewegungkrieg*, flexible command *auftragstaktik* and aggressive attacking, which became identified closely with the Prussian army which, two centuries later, became the modern German method of operations, popularly known as the Blitzkrieg.[6]

Robert M. Citino in his 2005 work, "The German Way of War"[7] presents a fascinating development of how Germany's Prussian military forbears developed a *kurs und vives* approach to war, a short and lively campaign style that a small nation like Prussia had to conduct, due to its smaller population, physical size, and economic limitations. It was this operational style that we see in all of Germany's 1939-1941 campaigns in the Second World War. As long as Germany was able to prosecute this short and lively style, which they called *Bewegungskrieg* and more popularly known as *Blitzkrieg*, to knock out its opponent quickly and without significant losses, things went well for it. However, when locked in the mortal stranglehold that Russia became for Germany, the weaknesses of her smaller economic infrastructure and population could not sustain such an effort, her magnificent army notwithstanding.

The use of the name *Wehrmacht* (armed forces) is a generic one and not specifically related to National Socialist or Nazi origins. Article 47 of the Weimar Constitution, approved in 1919, stipulated the Reichprasident as commander-in-chief of all Wehrmacht in the Reich. However, in popular usage the use of the term Wehrmacht has come to be identified with the forces of the Third Reich during World War II. One of the more noticeable changes in identification of the Wehrmacht's new equipment was the use of a stylized version of the Balkenkreuz, the straight-armed version of the flared armed black and white iron cross of World War I.

The pride and joy of the Prussian, then later the German nation was her land army. Structured along conventional military force tables, with the battalion, regiment, division, corps and army being the primary organizational units with combinations of these units (especially the armies being combined into army groups as the assignments dictated). In addition, special purpose commands *sonderkommando* were organized to undertake unique or short-term assignments.

---

[6] During the inter-war period (1918-1939 Europe) as the concept of blitzkrieg was unknown, the Germans referred to their developing theory of rapid and flexible movement of units simply as "mobile operations".

[7] *The German Way of War, From the Thirty Years' War to the Third Reich* by Robert M. Citino, University Press of Kansas, 2005, p.270.

Following the end of the "Great War" in 1918, the restrictive clauses of the Versailles treaty stipulated for Germany a land force of no more than 100,000 men and no offensive weapons such as tanks, heavy artillery, an air force of any kind; U-boats and conscription were abolished. In 1935, Hitler repudiated the Treaty and began to re-arm Germany and the name of the organization was changed from *Reichswehr* to the older *Wehrmacht*.

From an initial 21 infantry divisions of about 18,000 men each formed into 3 army groups in 1935 this force by 1945 grew to more than 239 infantry divisions controlled by a dozen army groups of varying strength, from as little as a few thousand men per division to full authorized strength, which in 1945 was about 12,000.

Equipment

Although much attention has been devoted to the *panzerwaffe*, as Germany's tank force is known, it was her ground troops, her infantry, that was the real combat power in her army, as it is in any nation's fighting forces. However, Germany, more than most, emphasized the importance of her infantry in preparation for war. The tough training regimen, termed 'hardness training' was based on the old axiom that 'sweat saves blood'. The end result of this rigorous training was to bond the men in a unit together to achieve a sense single-mindedness, or *einstazbereitschaft*.

The newest element of the new Wehrmacht's ground forces was its tank, or in German, its *Panzer* divisions. Although not the first military to include armored vehicles in its military, Germany was the first to make them an independent force, supplying them with organic artillery, engineering, communications, motorized infantry and supply units. In addition, the application of air power in the form of ground attack aircraft supplied by *Luftwaffe* made this a very formidable development. The 6 panzer divisions included in the invasion of Poland in September 1939 grew to 38 panzer division-sized units by April 1945.[8] This number did not include 18 motorized or mechanized divisions.[9] The number of panzers in each division varied as to number and type but ranged from a high of

---

[8] This number includes the seven SS *panzer* divisions. In the closing months of the war, several *panzer* 'divisions' were formed but never reached division-sized strength. They also differed in that instead of assigning them numbers they were named. These were *Panzer Divisions Kurmark, Clausewitz, Donau, Schlesien, Thuringen, Westfalen, Kurland, Holstein, Munchenburg and Juterbog.*

[9] In March 1943 the designation was changed from Motorized to *Panzergrenadier*.

over 300 in the invasion of Poland in September 1939 to a low of 52 vehicles in June 1942. The number of tanks in a division was as low as a few dozen in certain situations during the war.

To highlight one of the these *panzer* weapons and its effect in battlefield operations, we will look at what is probably the most famous of all the *panzers*, the heavy main battle tank *Tiger*, technically known as the *panzerkamphwagen Mark VI Tiger*, fortunately abbreviated to *PzKw Mk. VI*, or just *Tiger*. Although perhaps the most famous of Germany's panzers during the war, it was not the most numerous or even the most typical but best illustrates the strengths and weaknesses of Germany's mechanized forces.

The use of *the Pz.Kw. VI Tiger* was first introduced into combat by Army Group North outside Leningrad in 1942. The Soviets were to feel the sting of the *Tiger* more frequently than the U.S. and British forces as the bulk of the Panzerwaffe was deployed on the eastern front, especially the heavy tank battalions or *Schwere Panzer Abteilung*, popularly abbreviated in the literature as, *SchwPz Abt.* followed by the battalion number designation.

The Tiger was a powerful but fragile[10] and expensive tank (299,800 Reichmarks) that relatively few were built (1,355 out of 24,450 *panzers* produced, 5.5%) and as such they were grouped into units no larger than battalion size and placed under corps or army command. Due to Germany's weakening industrial capabilities, (no more than 100 *Tigers* were produced per month) especially after August 1944, there were never more than 15 *Schwere* (heavy) *Panzer* battalions at any one time in the field, and their vehicle readiness counts varied widely. In the field they were deployed to assist attacking front line *panzer* divisions in providing extra punch for an offensive or, in defensive combat, dispatched to threatened sectors to lend support, patch holes in the line or to contain or destroy enemy breakthroughs.

Fragile or not the *Tiger* was to develop a reputation all its own amongst the allies, Western and Russian. Amongst the U.S. and Commonwealth forces the cry of "Tiger!" would be cause enough for a halt, or even a

---

[10] The fragility of the Tiger was in her engine/transmission system. The engine fitted to the Tiger was underpowered and put the transmission under strain shortening its lifespan. Coupled with the high fuel consumption, special travel and combat tracks and slow road and cross country speeds, the Tiger required careful planning for its deployment.

retreat. In Russia, during the battle of Kursk, for example, Soviet anti-tank gun crews, with the 45mm anti-tank guns saw their shells bounce off the thick armor of the Tiger, and, some went insane with fear.

Despite their limited availability, August 1942 to May 1945, Tiger (both Tiger I and Tiger II models) crews claimed over 9,850 destroyed Allied tanks, again mostly Russian tanks. One unit, the 13th Company of the panzer regiment *Grossdeutschland*, destroyed 100 tanks with a loss of just 6 of their own. The record, however, is held by the *SchwPz Abt. 503* destroying some 1,700 Allied tanks.[11]

Following the army in popular and historical prominence would be the Navy, renamed the *Kriegsmarine* in 1935. Hobbled initially by the strictures of the Versailles treaty, the Navy was marginalized later by the Anglo-German Naval Treaty, which restricted the size of Germany's surface fleet to 35% of Great Britain's. While largely outside the scope of this work, suffice it to say Germany's navy went to war far sooner than her admirals wanted -- some say as many as five years too early -- and hence found her nautical powers underdeveloped and unable to challenge the eastern hemisphere's main nautical power, England, and later in the war, the United States.

While developing a modern, albeit small capital-ship fleet (most popularly known by the battleship Bismarck) and an equally modern submarine fleet known at the *U-Bootwaffe*, both surface and subsurface fleets were hampered by geography, technical deficiencies in electronic sensors and the political will to utilize these weapons properly.

Germany's newest and most independent military arm was her air force, the *Luftwaffe*. Almost entirely a creation of the Nazi party and headed by the number-two man in the government, Herman Goering, the *Luftwaffe* never entirely lived up to the great promise of its early conquests. From 1939 to 1942 it was the major air force on the continent, with only the British Royal Air Force challenging it for supremacy. With the expectation of short and lively battles with Germany's enemies, the long-range arm of the *Luftwaffe*, the multi-engined bomber force, was never adequately developed; her enemies' major political and economic centers of importance could be reached with the medium-ranged twin-engined machines then in production. Although Germany developed a few long range bombers (Heinkel He-177A and later versions of the Junkers Ju-88) technical

[11] *World War II Data Book, Hitler's Secret Weapons 1933-1945, The Essential Facts and Figures For Germany's Secret Weapons Program* by David Porter, Amber Books, 2010, p. 51.

problems with engines, rushed design and competition for scarce materials, fuel, trained pilots and factory floor space and the need for fighters to defend the Reich made long range bombing, especially after 1943, a declining priority. This lack of foresight in proper program management for the long-range bomber force was to hamper Germany's ability to strike at the distant targets of her newest enemies, the Soviet Union and the Allied ocean convoys far out in the Atlantic.

To provide the manpower to these labor-hungry organizations, the nation was organized initially into seven military districts, or *Wehrkreis* in 1938. The use of *Wehrkreis* districts originated in 1919 during the Weimar Republic and its purpose was to recruit, draft and train soldiers for the division(s) originating in their *Wehrkreis*. By 1943 the number had expanded to nineteen, the newest districts coming into being with the occupation of Austria, Czechoslovakia (Bohemia and Moravia), and the western Polish areas now known as *Generalgouvement*. The *Wehrkreis* was also responsible for the continued flow of replacements to their divisions. Initially managed by the *Oberkommando der Heers* (OKH, Army High Command) in 1933, the Home or Replacement Army, created in 1938 was better able to manage the recruitment and replacement system.

The Germany Army, known as the (*Heer* in German) was raised in 'waves', based on the age year of the male population. This was conducted by the *Wehrkreis* under the supervision of the Home/Replacement Army; during the existence of the Third Reich 38 waves were raised. The organization of the *Wehrkreis* consisted of a *Korps* and a Deputy or Training component. On mobilization the *Korps* was activated and sent to the front with its division(s) while the Deputy or Training component remained in the *Wehrkreis* and conducted unit training. The training cadre usually consisted of Great War (1914 - 1918) veterans, older officers and non-commissioned officers who, because of age, were not up to the rigors of campaigning. However they became a very competent training organization.

One of the greatest propaganda victories of the war was the German success in convincing the world that the *Wehrmacht* was a mighty mechanized or at least motorized force. Nothing could be further from the truth. The real transport mainstay of the 'modern' German armed forces was the horse. From the very beginning of the war, the invasion of Poland in September 1939, the German propaganda machine was intent on introducing the world to a new form of warfare, the *Blitzkrieg*, and a German army that moved on wheels and tracks. The reality was something else. With the exception of reconnaissance units, eleven panzer and the few motorized divisions, rail, horse, bicycle and foot moved the bulk of the *Wehrmacht*. The illusion of fully mechanized, modern and efficient armed forces was one of the feats that Germany did a splendid job in portraying. However, this new motorized army did not spring completely from the fertile minds of Joseph Goebbels propaganda ministry, it was developed over a period of years in secrecy and in foreign lands. It was not the number of tanks and planes that made the Wehrmacht so deadly in the opening years of the war; it was the differences in doctrine and organization.

Help From Russia

Prior to 1933, unable to design and build a modern army, Germany concluded a secret treaty with the new U.S.S.R. in 1922, the Treaty of Rapallo, to develop and share military technology. This agreement allowed the Reichswehr to build secret bases deep in the interior of the new Soviet Union. One for the development of panzer tactics was situated at Kazan, (450 miles east of Moscow) another dealing with aviation issues was located at Lipetsk (232 miles southeast of Moscow) and a chemical warfare center was constructed at Tomka[11] (475 miles southeast of Moscow). An interesting element in the location of the secret training centers was the consideration of local German-speaking people who could be used to work on the bases in the many support functions.

The issue of secrecy in this exchange was extensively observed between the two nations. Cover or bogus economic offices located in both capitals and no military uniforms were permitted to be worn by the exchanged military officers. The cover and deception efforts went so far that when, on one occasion, a German died in Russia, his body was shipped back to Germany in a crate labeled machine parts (or some similar ruse).

As was to be clear a decade later, the exchange between the two nations was not always a fair one. The Russians complained that the Germans always seemed to find an excuse to delay the shipment of tools or equipment, or suspend the training class of one skill or another, and generally foot-drag on their part of the exchange. However, as the clandestine relationship entered the early 1930s, the Germans began to withdraw from the bases as the Nazis came to power. The Inter-Allied Military Control Commission

---

[11] The complete list of sites of German military development and training: Smolensk, Fili, Tula, Lipetsk, Kazan, Trotsk and Saratov.

stated in 1930 that Germany could now be considered disarmed and withdrew its inspection staff primarily from the industrial regions. With the Allies no longer looking over Germany's shoulder, it brought its armament program into the open. In 1933 the agreement with Russia was ended. German Gen. Kurt von Hammerstein-Equord, the Reichswehr commander, stated, "We will work with Moscow as long as the West is not prepared to accept Germany as an equal. The relationship with Moscow is a pact with the Devil -- but we have no choice."[13]

The New Methodology

What made the Germans seemingly invincible from 1939 to 1942 was the employment of their weapons. For the first time in history they were employed together, in mass and suddenly, without warning in what today would be called a combined-arms weapons system; in short, the *Blitzkrieg*. The key difference in the German system, in addition to the infantry, air and artillery arms was that the supporting elements, such as bridging, supply and transportation were also motorized. All were able to keep pace with the armored formations and all under the command and control of the division commander, another new innovation. The ability of a unit the size of a division to have these assets at its disposal allowed far greater flexibility and exploitation capabilities than ever before. In earlier conflicts these assets, especially air and heavy artillery were available only at higher-level formations (corps and army) and thus prevented the quick response demonstrated by the Wehrmacht. These were novel and new theories that although known and recognized before the war by more forward-thinking Allied theorists, the more innovative and younger German military was quicker to grasp, understand and implement these daring theories and willing to risk putting them into use. Eventually the Allies learned this weapons integration by watching and doing and became adept at it, adding some modifications and alterations to fit their own organizational needs.

This new form of warfare had a secret component to it, the high level of German individual and unit training. The technological superiority, the skilled tactical prowess and massed strength were all good and necessary but it was the high morale of the German soldier that was the real secret to German military success. However successful the *blitzkrieg* methodology

---

[13] Claus-Jürgen Müller, *Das Heer und Hitler: Armee und Nationalsocialistisches Regime, 1933 - 1940,* Stuttgart, 1969, p. 46.

became it was expensive and the other arms, especially the navy, suffered as their budgets were reduced to finance the rapidly expanding *panzerwaffen*. This claim to productive capacity and steel allocations was to be a feature contested element in the German management of the war. In addition to the expense, the panzer division was an amazingly complex organization consisting of over 3,500 motor vehicles of all kinds. Its headquarters establishment coordinated all aspects of the divisions operations including transport, rations, maintenance, medical, personal health, field post, fuel, recreation and religious affairs and pay.

The brunt of the losses during the war was borne by the Heer, as the ground Army was known. Some 13,000,000 German men and women served in the Wehrmacht from 1935 to 1945. Of this number, 5,700,000 became casualties with 1,600,000 killed.

Finally, the 1935-1945 period would bring to its highest level of development another unique aspect of German history, that of the German General Staff. This unique military management body and/or system was to find its greatest authority and influence in the Third Reich as well as, for the first time, experience the severest curbing of its power and influence under Adolf Hitler.

Formed in the days of Frederick the Great, and reaching a level of deadly efficiency under Moltke the Elder (1880-1891) the German General Staff was to find fertile ground and its ultimate form in managing the men and machines of the Wehrmacht. The coordination of high technology, industrial production, personal and institutional discipline and a supply and logistical organization second to none made Germany the most effective military in the world. It was an organizational model that all the armies of the world would eventually emulate, at the very least to remain competitive and at best to survive in a hostile Europe.

Therefore, in August of 1939 the German Wehrmacht was ready to unleash her new field force against her neighbors, first to the east in Poland, and then, in April 1940, to the north on Denmark and Norway, and later that same spring to the west on England, France, the Netherlands, Belgium and Luxembourg. The savagery, speed and surprise of the attacks was to stun the world and a peaceful Europe, still seemingly paralyzed by the memories of the destruction, stalemate and the millions killed and maimed in the 'Great War'. Germany's former enemies went to extraordinary lengths to avoid another conflict. However, a vindictive, polarized Germany was hell-bent to regain her pride, her place in Europe's sun, and most importantly to her, seek the living space (*lebensraum*) she felt she needed.

From the early operations in the West it was quite apparent this was not only a new German Army, this was a new army, period. This army, designed and created in the laboratory of military theory was an exciting and threatening distillation of everything that was new in arms and armament. Given birth by the new and reckless German state and when unleashed and tested against its neighbors found to be frighteningly effective. In the Spring of 1941 this is the army that so worried Joseph Stalin, and most of it was moving towards Russia.

Chapter Two:
The Union of Soviet Socialist Republics and the Russian Army

"Your ideas are beautiful but only in theory: In practice, they can only be thrust upon people with tanks and brute force like yours, Comrade Colonel!

Lecture from a Czech resident of Prague to a Russian Colonel of the 35th Guards Tank Division, 1968.

The Russian army was a force in transition at the outbreak of war in the summer of 1941. This chapter will discuss three aspects of the other combatant, the Russian army, its soldiers and their equipment and training as well as unique and personal traits that made it identifiably Russian. The second aspect will be a discussion of Russian military theory and the men and their thoughts were of what future wars would be like. It will also dispel the notion of the Western view of what has been characterized as the Russian monolithic approach to war. This section will touch on what these original thinkers had planned for the new communist Russian army. Finally, the *Ezhovshchina* or the purges of the military leadership in the years leading up to the German attack will be discussed and the effects it had on the command and decision making ability of the field commanders. Also, a more extensive look will be made of 'Ivan', the Russian soldier, as he was popularly known, more so than German 'Fritz', as so little, until recently has been written about him.

The Early Days

From 1918 to 1920 a vicious civil war raged across this vast land now known as Russia, but early in the 20th century, known as the Union of Soviet Socialists Republics. Pitted against the Bolsheviks' "Workers and Peasants Red Army" (also known as the Reds and still later known in its official title, Red Army of Workers and Farmers (RKKA)[14]), was the Tsarist loyalist forces, known as the "Whites". As in most civil wars, the struggle was ruthless, cruel and frequently involved women, children and the elderly in the fighting as the various factions of Red and White armies ranged across the land.[15] During the civil war, Leon Trotsky, the People's Commissar, was the first head of the Red Army, and commanded the Army from an armored train, equipped with machine guns, artillery, a printing press, a radio for broadcasting and a flatcar for his Rolls-Royce command car. The armored train also carried a brass band to maintain the morale of the troops he visited. Indeed, the Communists saw war as the engine that powers social and historical change, pushing aside weaker societies that blocked the view and the road to the workers' paradise.

---

[14] 23 February is observed as the birthday of the Red Army.

[15] One method the Reds used to apprehend White enemies was to examine their hands, soft hands meant 'burzhui' and were shot on the spot at checkpoints. In an attempt to conceal their past the Whites responded by soaking their hands in alcohol to check the skin and then to rub dirt into the cracks. In addition to soft hands, anyone wearing a white color, a sign of the intelligentsia, could also be shot on the spot by a revolutionary soldier, who would not face legal proceedings.

By 1941 at the top of the military command structure was the STAVKA[16], a headquarters that was established by Joseph Stalin, an early member of the Communist party in Russia and now General Secretary. In the early part of the war, the STAVKA consisted of seven or so members: Stalin as Supreme High Commander, Vyacheslay M. Molotov, Foreign Minister, Klimenti E. Voroshilov, a Marshal of the Soviet Union and member of the Politburo and State Defense Committee, Boris M. Shaposhenikov, a Marshal of the Soviet Union, Chief of the General Staff, Simeon K. Timoshenko, another Marshal of the Soviet Union, field commander and former People's Commissar of Defense, Simeon M. Budenny, a Marshal of the Soviet Union and field commander and Georgi K. Zhukov, Colonel General, field commander and former Chief of the General Staff.

Ivan

The foundation block of the Russian Army was its soldier, the rifleman, the common man of the Russian Army or as he was frequently referred to, a *frontoviki*. They made up the mass of the Russian Army and an attempt should be made to understand the things that meant most to them and their units and their comrades.

The quality of life for the common soldier in the Russian Army during World War II was about the same as that of his civilian counterpart, tedious, regimented and monitored. As in any army one of the most important items to any soldier was what he ate. His rations were simple and monotonous (the staple being porridge[17] from rye flour, wheat flour was rare, coarse bread and tea), and during combat, it was usually altogether missing. Despite propaganda to the contrary, the political officers and unit commanders (the typical joint command structure of the Russian Army), frequently had to intervene with higher headquarters or locals for sufficient rations. Because of the frequently chaotic and limited nature of Russian army logistics it was often difficult to obtain food on a regular basis. Occasionally the units had to rely on the populace behind the lines, however the newly liberated towns and villages warmly received the Russian Army and, even when they shorted themselves, tried to provide something for the soldiers, which they called a "grandmothers ration".[18] This was observed only in the former Russian provinces, and this local largesse ended when the Russian Army entered the western Ukraine and the Baltic nations, where the locals hid

---

[16] Not be confused with the GKO.

[17] The Russian *frontoviki* called it "shrapnel".

themselves and their food from the 'kastaps', the slang name for Russians in Ukraine, usually in the *Bandera*[19] areas, blaming the lack of food on the *Schwabs* (one of the Russian terms for Germans) taking it. However tedious and unbalanced his fare all during World War II, the Russian soldier was almost always hungry until the rear-area support and transport caught up with him.

An occasional source of the hunger experienced by the *frontoviki* was the avaricious theft of his officers, both political and military. Theft of foodstuffs was epidemic in the Russian Army, even in 1944, one of the peak years of Allied Lend-Lease food shipments. The unfortunate Russian Army soldier was at the very end of a long supply line that, in the case of Lend-Lease supplies, that might have began in the fields of Kansas. However, when these precious supplies arrived in Russia they were often pilfered all along its length. By the time anything arrived at his mess, it may have been used for barter and sale by Russian Army and *polytruk* officers, even including those of general-officer rank.

To offer just one example in the First Ukrainian Front, a major general in June 1944 sent to Moscow the following supplies, with the intent of bribing higher officials: 267 kilos of pork[20], 125 kilos of mutton, 114 kilos of butter, five live goats, 1,959 kilos of sausage, 2,100 kilos of biscuits, 890 kilos of boiled sweets, 563 kilos of soap, 100 winter coats, 100 greatcoats, eighty fur vests, 100 pair of valenki (the common felt boots) and 100 pairs of (leather) boots.

It is difficult to fathom theft on such a grand scale with spies at all levels of the Russian Army, especially the politruks who were charged with the welfare of the men as one of their primary responsibilities. Sufficient to say that these very men charged with the care of the soldiers were part and parcel of the theft problem. One can speculate as to the urges and causes of such misappropriation of supplies -- safe to say that years and decades of want and neglect in the socialist system were being satisfied.

---

[18] The difficulty of supplying adequate amounts of food to the fighting soldier reached its most shocking level during the fighting for and around Leningrad. Local German counterattacks recovered bodies of captured German soldiers that were missing portions of their bodies, although their missing uniforms were found nearby undamaged. The conclusion: cannibalism.

[19] Bandera was a famous Ukrainian anti-Soviet resistance leader.

[20] A kilo is equivalent to 2.2 pounds.

The hardy nature of the common soldier of the Russian Army has been commented on a number of times and the variety of peoples and cultures that made up the Russian Army has never ceased to be of interest to the Western reader. For example, consider the following during the last days of the war in Berlin:

> "An anonymous woman diarist saw an endless supply column pulling up outside (her apartment): well-fed mares with foals between their legs; a cow mooing to be milked. In the garage opposite, they were already setting up a field kitchen. Other observers noted wagonloads of pigs and sheep. The Soviet troops had trekked like this for over 1,000 miles, bringing much of their food with them, on the hoof, including camels to carry the load."

In attempt to secure adequate stocks of food, units in the pre-war period took to running farms to grow their own. Frequently used as punishment duty because of the heavy labor involved, it at least afforded the unit fresh, if not abundant, foods.

Health, Welfare and Recruitment

Sanitation was another important item that was also frequently missing for the Russian Army rifleman. Dedicated billets were only available in the larger military bases or near cities. This was especially true during the advance into eastern Poland to assume the positions of the new Russo-German partition of that nation. This resulted in units occupying whatever shelter was available, including schools, warehouses, public buildings, offices and farm buildings. This resulted in a lack of adequate bathing and cleaning facilities and an increase of infestations of lice and related maladies caused by poor sanitation. This poor sanitation extended to the unit mess facilities and added to the woes of the fighting men and women.

As in Germany, the Soviets used a military-district system to raise manpower for the Russian Army. In 1918 six military districts were created to provide sufficient men for the new Russian Army. These were Yaroslavsky, Moskovsky, Orlovsky, Belomorsky, Uralsky, and Privolzhsky. Prior to the German invasion in June 1941 there were six districts combined into one Front. However, after the invasion the number of these districts increased dramatically, reaching a high of 33 in the later part of the war.

The above amply illustrates the contradiction that was the Russian army. A nation that just a few decades before was seen as backward and stunted was now developing and producing the most modern weapons from rocket artillery to cutting edge tank design and technology. Yet, turn a corner or move down the column a little and one might see soldiers grazing cattle and harvesting crops to feed themselves. The most modern and ancient, all used and understood at the same time. A blend of cultures and history that makes this army unique.

Equipment

The Russian soldier went without many of the accepted personal items and comforts his enemy had and was far removed from those enjoyed by his western allied friends. As the Russian Army went without the extensive logistical 'tail' of most other modern armies the battlefield soldier in the Russian Army made do in a most sparse manner. Few had blankets issued, so he used his greatcoat as his blanket, usually sharing it with a fellow soldier in colder weather, one man's foot in each sleeve and a head in each other's arms, sleeping close for warmth. When one turned, both turned. The remainder of the cold-weather clothing was *valenki, vatnik* (padded jacket) and pants, the now easily recognizable Russian winter hat or *ushanka*, with ear flaps, and canvas three-fingered mittens, configured to felicitate firing one's weapon.

Grooming was kept simple, which meant that face and scalp were usually shaved and cut closely or completely, as was the fashion in Russian military circles prior to the war. When not wearing the standard issue M36 steel helmet with small crest and slight ear fairing, the soldier's headgear was usually a curved, brimless field cap or *pilotka* and many were issued the distinctive pre-war peaked *budenovka*, usually with a large red star sewn on the front.

If combat conditions permitted, he slept in his underwear and dressed on waking. A most unusual aspect of his uniform issue was what passed for socks. He was issued with a large handkerchief-like cloth called a *portyanki* that served as his socks, being wrapped around the feet.[21] Conventional socks were also used, but were usually provided by relatives, as well as civic groups that would knit them and send them to the front. His footwear was remarkably similar to the German jackboot in summer and a felt version in winter. Although not consisting of an all-leather construction, the uppers were made from a treated canvas, only officers having the all-

---

[21] Later in the war when supply difficulties and shortages mounted, German soldiers also resorted to foot wrapping when their socks wore out, called 'fusslappen'.

leather summer boot. The boots issued to the Russian soldier were issued a size or two larger than his actual foot size to provide insulation space for winter use. Later, these boots would be made from felt that offered excellent insulating qualities. Compare this to the parade ground fit of the Wehrmacht solder with no space to insert additional insulation material or even a replacement winter boot, also the now famous photos of Germans wearing their thin summer boots wrapped with rags or wearing impossibly large straw overshoes (worn during sentry duty), a desperate attempt to stave off frostbite.

Ivan's basic uniform was issued in summer and winter weights and was found to be made of almost any material or fabric available. One popular source was the millions of yards of cotton twill sent to the Soviet Union as part of Lend-Lease shipments. His mess kit was a small pot and spoon found anywhere, but the most popular mess tins were captured German ones: A kidney-shaped affair, the eating utensil, an oversized spoon, either brought from home or found in the field. It was a comforting thought to any Russian Army soldier that when he was eating out of a German mess kit, a German wasn't.

Personal time, when it was available, was spent doing what most soldiers the world over and throughout time have done -- sleep, maintain their personal and combat equipment, write letters home, search for food[22], strong drink and sex to forget the war for a while.

When left to himself, the Russian soldier enjoyed the crude, (by western standards), Russian *makhorka* tobacco. Cigarette (*papirosy* in Russian) smoking for the Russian soldier was a rough-and-ready affair as no prepared cigarettes were provided, just the bulk tobacco. The paper used to roll his field cigarettes was from any source close at hand; several popular sources were the divisional newspaper and even pages from books. When tobacco supplies were interrupted, alternate materials were tried, such as leaves and herbs. So important was the supply of tobacco to the troops that it was even flown to the encircled Leningrad soldiers as essential supplies. German cigarettes were eagerly sought as the Russian Army pushed the Wehrmacht back. As light and flimsy as cigarette paper is, more than 900 tons were sent via Lend-Lease shipments. Perhaps someone can calculate how many cigarettes can be made from this amount of paper.

---

[22] Food was such an importance in the conduct of the war in the east that it made up 14% of Lend-Lease shipments or almost $6 billion USD.

The Russian soldier also made use of captured enemy material. It was not unusual to see Russian soldiers wearing German boots, smoking German cigarettes, drinking German beer and wine (a good amount of it from France), and firing German weapons, especially the MP38 and MP40 *machine pistole* (similar to the Russian PPSh submachine gun,) and, later in the war, using the *Panzerfaust*[23] anti-tank rocket weapon. Russian officers, especially at company level and lower, preferred the German Walther pistol to the American Colt-45 look alike Russian made TT-33 as it was accurate, small and there was always plenty of ammunition available for it. Also, German weapons were not always better. An interesting comment regarding the German 'stick' or 'potato masher' hand grenade was that it was inferior to the Russian F-1 and RDG-33 models (the Russians called them "sausages"). The larger German grenade was difficult to carry and was considered 'weak'.

The condition of his clothing bordered on that of the refugee. By the early summer of 1944 his greatcoat was torn and patched but the items most needing attention and replacement or repair were his well-worn boots. There is frequent mention of searching the battlefield (before the locals arrived) and obtaining the good-quality German leather boots, especially in summer.

His relationship with his superiors, communist dogma notwithstanding, treated him little better than a farm animal. Punishment was severe, brutal and frequent, especially in the first year of the war. He literally was a face in a crowd, one who could be and was, replaced easily and frequently[24]. The value of the common soldier of communist Russia lay in his numbers and willingness to do what he was told without question, even if it was almost certain that obeying would result in his death. There is an old Czarist saying that it takes 20,000 dead men to train a general. If it was true for Imperial Russia, it would also prove true in communist Russia. The leadership of the Russian, Ukrainian and the other central Asiatic peoples, from various

---

[23] The use of the *panzerfaust* rocket weapon was not all German against Allied. Large quantities of the weapon were captured during the clearing of Pomerania by the 1st and 2nd Russian Byelorussian Fronts and were used against the German relief force to free the city of Kustrin on the Oder river which was surrounded and cut off. It accounted for almost a quarter of all Russian tank losses.

[24] Glantz, in his *Stumbling Colossus*, (*Stumbling Colossus, The Red Army on the Eve of World War* by David M. Glantz, University Press of Kansas, 1998) states that at the beginning of the war, there was a better than 60% chance that within six months the Russian soldier would either be dead or in captivity.

tribal chieftains, to Czarist leadership to the Soviets, is a long history of harshness and frequent cruelty; and this was extended to the common foot soldier by his commanders.[25]

In a final gesture of crass indifference, should the Russian soldier be killed in combat, no attempt was made to notify his loved ones back home. It was understood by these hardy people: If your soldier does not come home when the war is over, he is dead.[26] This lack of interest in the welfare of the rank and file by the Russian Army command was one of the reasons many Russian soldiers originally joined the Communist Party -- the party administration, much more efficient then the Russian Army's, notified the next of kin of the death of their loved ones. As a result, the Russian Army was a rich source for new Party recruits.

In the opening months of the war, the presence of thousands of dead that littered the battlefield had a deleterious effect on Russian Army morale. In December of 1941 Lev Mekhlis, head of the Main Political Propaganda Directorate of the People's Commissiariat of Defense ordered that all dead be promptly buried with appropriate respect and decorum. However less than a year later compliance with this order was spotty. The equipment and weapons of the dead were to be carefully recovered, but bodies were being pitched into open trenches or shell holes. Special attention was given to recovering overcoats, tunics, hats, sweaters, pants, boots, and gloves. A burial party was not given credit for its work unless they presented the guns of the dead for evidence.

The harsh history of Russia had one positive effect on her military; it made for a very tough, tenacious and hardy people and a very durable soldiery. The Russian infantryman has frequently been called the "the only Russian secret weapon" of the war, his ability to be supplied with less and do more with it was the envy of the world. His peasant background made him at home on the land; he took easily to military training and was possessed

---

[25]Regarding the value the Red Army put on its soldiers, consider the following conversation. In a meeting late in the war, General Zhukov would make the frank admittance to U.S. General Eisenhower that "...When we come to a minefield, our infantry attacks exactly as if it were not there. The losses we get from personnel mines we consider equal to those we would have gotten from machine guns and artillery if the German's had chosen to defend that particular area with strong bodies of troops instead of minefields." From Bundesarchiv-Militararchiv RH2-2625.

[26] The 29 October 2002 edition of *Pravda*, article "Remains of Red Army Soldiers Found in Novgorod Region" stated that the Russian Army's "Dolina" expedition has discovered and reburied over 60,000 soldiers, officers and men, since 1998.

of a terrible determination to beat back the Fascist invader. Accounts from German sources of the ability of Russian soldiers to quietly endure incredible suffering and deprivation became commonplace and generated a level of grudging respect, if not understanding.

The Waffen SS units attached to the Wehrmacht had similar opinions of Russian soldier. Generally their comments were that the Russian rifle soldier was tough and tenacious under almost all circumstances but he was badly led and supplied, especially as it pertains to food. He could be tough and stubborn in one engagement and then without notice or provocation, run away on another.

Russian Military Theory

One of the more enduring misrepresentations of pre-war Russian military development is that of the massive, simple-minded steamroller mentality and lack of originality and flexibility in tactical and strategic thought. Although these new tactics were occasionally practiced during combat by the more enlightened generals, unfortunately the reality of chaos and confusion, lack of experience and training in the first year of the war, however, is quite different.

In the 1920's and early 1930's the Russian Army had some of the foremost and gifted military theoreticians in the world. Men such as Mikhail Frunze, Mikhail Tukhachevsky, N. E. Varfolomeev, Lapohinsky, S. I. Molikov, E. A. Shilovsky, Alexander Svechin, V. K. Triandafilov and Dmitry Karbyshev all contributed to the concepts and development of modern warfare, especially as advancing technology was affecting it. These men were advancing such ground-breaking ideas as combining infantry, tanks, artillery and aircraft[27]; defense in depth, flexible defense, the strategic reserve; such radical ideas as total mobilization of the entire nation for war, utilizing all facets of a nation's strength: military, economic and political. Their forecasts of what future wars would look like were not encouraging in the least; one even suggested that in a future war, there would be more civilian casualties than military, such would be the total involvement of the new form of modern war.[28]

---

[27] Shortly to be known as 'combined arms'. On selected occasions, such as the invasion of the Soviet Union commando or special forces units such as the Brandenburgers and paratroops, as used in the west were added to the attacking force.

[28] For a more complete discussion on Russian military theory see *Thunder on the Dnepr, Zhukov-Stalin and the Defeat of Hitler's Blitzkrieg*, Bryan Fugate and Lev Dvoretsky, Presidio Press, 1997.

The subjects and topics under discussion ranged all across the military, economic and political spectrum. For example, in 1934 Tukhachevsky suggested a method other than using the railroad to transport troops to the front be found because air power, with its far reaching attacks on rail lines would certainly render that previously swift and reliable means obsolete. The solution was to prepare positions in depth before the outbreak of hostilities. Others debated the role of nations waging wars with allied nations, called "coalition nations", and the cooperation required to be successful. Shimansky, in his article "Strategic Reserves", discussed the need for a nation to fully mobilize, even against a weak opponent, in order to lend the character of a national effort in the war, in which everyone is united in the outcome. Although not an original idea, the Revolutionary French had used conscription in the 18th century, however this was an interesting viewpoint considering that all wars heretofore had been fought between professional armies and rarely involving civilian populations.

It is of interest to think what these great military thinkers could have done with their newfound theories had they been allowed to fully develop them. However, in the mid 1930's Stalin was determined to bring the Russian Army, especially its command structure, under tighter control of the Communist Party. His deepening paranoia resulted in the deep and far-reaching command and leadership purges of 1936-1938.[29]

One of the results of the purges, the one that concerns us here, was the death of the development of Russian military theory. The net result of the loss of so many leaders in the Russian Army was to stop any thought outside that of the Party line. The loss of such interest in and intellectual curiosity of military theory was a tragic loss to the Russian Army and military science in general, and when combined with the loss of the trained and talented leadership, the loss of the new thinkers was equally tragic and was to have a profound and direct effect on combating Germany just a few years later.

A final word on Russian military theory. If the development of Russian military theory was an internal affair, help with the practical, tangible aspects came from a most unusual source -- Germany. In the wake of the Great War, Germany cast about seeking ways to guard and defend herself in her most vulnerable period, the years from 1919 to the rise of National Socialism in 1933. Restricted by the Treaty of Versailles, Germany's

[29] The military purges of the 1937-1940 period are also known as the "military-Trotsky plot".

Reichswehr sought ways and means around the covenants and restrictions. It is ironic that these two nations, now so sorely in need of one another, would be archenemies just a few years hence.

Purge!

In 1936 Stalin, as mentioned above, suffering from yet another bout of personal and managerial xenophobia, began a systematic review and restructuring of the military. It was known in the West as the 'purge' (the *Ezhovshchina* in Russian) and roughly divided into political and military spheres, the former from 1936 to 1938 and the latter from 1936 to 1940 or 1941.

The incomprehensibility of the destruction of the leadership of the Russian Army on the brink of invasion by its archenemy Germany and continuing afterwards by Stalin in one form or another borders on insanity. Such was his phobia of remnants of Tsarist and Western influences. The purges were an ongoing process of 'cleansing' the Russian Army that was begun back in the Russian Civil War and Stalin saw no need to suspend the actions of the investigating committees and courts until this greater threat to the bastion of world communism was eliminated. It is estimated that from 1937 to 1941 a total of 54,714 officers in the Russian Army had suffered some form of persecution, from censure to execution.

The purge-hobbled STAVKA was the staff that actually ran the war from the Russian side. In addition to the members listed above, Stalin would add participants to the nightly meetings as he desired or the situation required. The nightly meetings began around 9:00PM and often went on until one or two in the morning, and occasionally till dawn.

The high price for failure in the Russian system caused the meetings to be tension filled sessions. Russian General S. M. Shtemenko reports of several attendees suffering from nervous disorders in anticipation of the meetings and taking early retirement for illness caused by the stress. The nervous tension and the fear it caused is just another example of life in Stalinist Russia; it was Stalin's style of management based on the stresses caused by the war and the Communist system in general which operated on a fear[30] system to maintain control of all aspects of Russian life. However, the level of fear and stress was acute at the highest command levels.

---

[30] It is interesting to note that, as do other nations when classifying their confidential information into secret and top secret (*sekretno* and *sovershenno* respectively in

The scope and dragnet of the purge was unlimited. The most significant figure caught in its web was the Russian Army Chief of Staff and Vice-Commissar for War M. Tukhachevsky. Arguably the most brilliant mind in the Russian Army, Tukhachevsky was the victim of a double threat against him, both from the highest levels in Russia and Germany, Stalin and Hitler.

His alleged 'crime' brought against him in Moscow originated in the 1920's during the Russian-Polish war. During the offensive against Warsaw, Tukhachevsky, his command in desperate need of support against a Polish attack, requested help from Stalin, then a political commissar under Russian General Budenny's Southern Front, and it was denied him, rather using the forces to advance on Lemberg. The lack of support prevented the Red Army from capturing Warsaw and Tukhachevsky blamed the failure on Stalin. Stalin neither forgave Tukhachevsky or forgot the accusation.

The second source of Tukhachevesky's downfall was from Germany. SS *Obergruppenfuhrer* Reinhard Heydrich, chief of the S.D. or *Sicherheitsdienst*, the SS Security Service, was informed of the accusations against Tukhachevsky and saw an opportunity to ferment internal intrigue within Stalin's government and, perhaps, seriously impair his relationship with the Red Army command. In February 1937 forged documents incriminating Tukhachevsky and several other senior Russian Army officers, were sold to contacts of the NKVD and presented to Stalin. The plot and trial against Tukhachevsky was a foregone conclusion. Between Stalin's vengeance and the German forgeries, Tukhachevsky was found guilty and condemned to death and was executed on 11 June 1937. His loss to the Russian Army was to be keenly felt in the war to come.[31]

The quality of new purge-approved Russian Army officers was abysmal, especially in the first year of the war; few of them had ever been to a military academy or school. It was common for Russian officers to be convicted of ordinary crimes without permanent impact on their careers. They served short sentences and were returned to their units. Ample supplies of men and poorly trained officers, the latter frequently obtaining their positions via political connections, were used lavishly because of the abundant,

---

Russian), only Russia has an additional level of security classification, known as *strogaya konspiratsiya* or extreme secrecy. The use of the word konspiratsiya or 'conspiracy' is noteworthy and typically soviet.

[31] *The Tukhachevsky Affair* by Victor Alexandrov, Prentice-Hall, 1963.

almost limitless Russian manpower supplies.[32] This inflexible method of warfare, with the objective of accomplishing everything through the use of human or material mass, is the most inhumane and costly possible.

The training programs for both German and Russian was intense and vigorous. The days were long, the food usually inadequate and the beds hard. For the Soviet soldier, the training, especially in the first two years of the war, was cut short and he was moved into a combat unit for the remainder of his training. The German soldier usually had the opposite experience. His training was very thorough and exact with all the toughness expected in the German Army. However, as the war deteriorated for Germany training for recruits after 1943 became shorter and briefer.

One of the aspects of the 1936 -1939 purge of the Russian Army leadership that is seldom commented on was the lingering effects of the aftermath of the purge. Specifically, how it affected the thinking and independence of the surviving officer corps and the operation of the smaller organizational units; divisions, brigades and battalions. With another, albeit smaller, wave of arrests in April, May and June 1941 to remind them, fear of any independent action, order, thought or activity that caused unwanted attention from Stalin or his security organs was enough to cause most unit leaders to err on following the German "non-provocation" orders issued by Stalin resulting in the destructive paralysis of command in the vital opening weeks after 22 June 1941.

June 1941

The "non-provocation" orders from Stalin were instructions issued to the army which would prevent any hostile action by commanders or soldiers in the field regardless of what the Germans did, without express, written instructions from Stalin. Stalin was terrified in provoking or providing the Germans with an excuse to commence hostilities before he felt the Russian Army and the nation was ready. Military historian Roy Medvedev wrote, "Never has the officer corps of an army suffered such losses in any war as the Soviet Army suffered in this time of peace."

---

[32] One wonders if the robot-like massed infantry charges or the ability to withstand extreme temperatures had anything to do with the 200 grams of vodka issued to each front line soldier. See Order of State Committee of Defense Decree, 22 August 1941(562cc).

An example of the Russian Army's unpreparedness can be demonstrated by examining the 251st Rifle Division, part of the second reserve army ordered created on 14 July 1941, formed in the city of Kolomna.   Its commanding general Khomenko wrote:

"The division was sent to 30th Army on foot, under strength, and 'totally lacking in cohesiveness'. Before dispatch, the representative of the MVO (mobilization organ) reassured the division commander that all shortages would be made up at the concentration region. Khomenko described the arriving division's state:

"1. The division was forced to arrive on foot, and it lacked a number of subunits (artillery, chemical company, etc.) It had no material support units, since the personnel of these subunits moved on three trains and arrived in the division's operational area only at the beginning of August. To date, some of them have still not arrived:"

"2. The division has not succeeded in forming and putting together rear service organs;"

"3. Party and Komsomol organizations have not been created in some units and subunits;"

"4. An overwhelming number of divisional personnel were mobilized from reserves. The entire division has only about 400 cadre soldiers from the NKVD;"

"5. In the haste of formation, horses were improperly distributed. Artillery horses were left behind, and... for this reason, artillery horses were received as reinforcements only after the artillery regiment was loaded on trains;"

"6. Haste of formation led to subunit commanders not knowing their subordinates and subordinates not knowing their commanders, and, as a result, discipline in divisional units was poor;"

"These and a series of other instances, which related to the 251st Rifle Division, led to the fact that the division entered battle unprepared, badly executed the missions assigned to it, and suffered heavy losses".

"Khomenko could have been writing about all of the reserve armies because his detailed description suited them all. Within two months, most of the reserve armies that barely escaped the brutal battles around Smolensk, Demidov, and Elnia and along the Sozh River would be destroyed. In the fall it would take two more mobilized waves of these partially trained and poorly equipped reserve armies to finally halt the German thrust at the gates of Moscow."[33]

In the early months of the start of Operation Barbarossa, German advances were also aided by numerous instances of Russian Army units rebelling against Russian authority, especially those units raised and stationed on newly acquired or non-traditional Russian territory, such as Ukraine. Karel C. Berkhoff in his "Harvest of Despair" provides the following:

"The question arises why the German armed forces were able to advance so quickly. One reason was that Stalin had ignored countless warnings of an imminent attack. Thus the Russian Army in the western regions had hardly any maps and too few arms when they needed them most. But more important than any lack of insight or preparation was desertion and unwillingness to fight. Despite the threat of the death penalty for desertion, massive numbers of soldiers abandoned their posts. Almost all drafted Ukrainians from western Volhynia and eastern Galicia left the army, and the remaining Russian Army soldiers near the Soviet border-mainly members of the Communist party and its Komsomol from central and eastern Ukraine -- faced sniper fire from locals. In central Ukraine, enormous numbers of reservists evaded their mobilization. Largely in vain, authorities tried to arrest deserters by blocking all of the roads."

The Russian army, as was the German one four years later, was made up of many different ethnic peoples from all corners of Russia. An example of what this lack of cohesion can do to command and control functions of an army is illustrated here. It also demonstrates the unpopularity of the communist government for many of the men from these areas. "Pihido (a Ukrainian native) saw a large group of Russian Army soldiers of various ethnic backgrounds who had just been captured in the Kiev encirclement. Because they were guarded by lenient Slovaks, they could talk to locals

---

[33] *Stumbling Colossus, the Red Army on the Eve of World War*, by David Glantz, University Press of Kansas, 1998, p. 220. Used with permission.

who approached them. 'All of them complained about a terrible chaos in the army. The Russian Army soldiers were always hungry and had to beg or steal. There was no underwear, no soap, many had lice. Footwear was mostly broken; they had to fight barefoot or with rags wrapped around. There were no blankets.' Most also complained that they had been left to their own devices: only sergeants or lieutenants from the reserves were with them. Most important of all, it became apparent to Pihido and others that the Russian Army soldiers did not *want* to fight. From all around came comments like 'They want us to die for them-no, we are not as stupid as they think.' 'They sucked our blood for twenty-five years, enough already!' 'They left our children without bread, to starve to death, but force us to defend Stalin and his Commissars.' A soldier from Siberia said, 'About two hundred of us got together. We decided to force our way back, at all cost, toward the Germans. We armed ourselves with submachine guns and grenades and moved toward the Dnieper. Twice we had to force our way through with grenades, for the (army) commissars tried to turn us back to 'our people.' We killed them and moved on. That's how we reached the Dnieper. Here we gave our weapons to the Germans and they moved us to the Right Bank (the German occupied bank)."[34]

These examples indicate the level of resentment, unrest and unpreparedness of the Russian Army in the early days of the invasion. The conscription of non-Russians into the Russian Army in the rapid period of expansion without the time to properly train, blend and inculcate Russian and Communist dogma into these newly made soldiers gave rise to the early reports of mass surrenders, defections and led to the German belief of the success of the Blitzkrieg. It probably accounts for the 'hit and miss' quality of Soviet units mentioned in many German action reports. These truly were the darkest days for Russia. Despite these language and political differences, the majority of the Russian army was made up Russian speaking natives and they would be the chief defenders of the Party and Russia in the trying weeks and months to come.

The second most area of wasteful military expenditure is one of equipment and animals. The vast encirclement battles in the first three months of the invasion trapped large amounts of tanks, guns, vehicles of all kinds, ammunition, food and general supplies. Such were the qualities and

---

[34] Reprinted by permission of the publisher from *Harvest of Despair: Life and Death in Ukraine Under Nazi Rule* by Karel C. Berkhoff, pp 12-13, Cambridge, Mass.:The Belknap Press of Harvard University Press, Copyright 2004 by the President and Fellows of Harvard College.

quality of captured equipment that the invading Germans were impressed enough to turn it around and use it in their own units against their former owners, especially artillery, anti-tank guns, the T-34 medium tank and the hardy Russian pony to pull supply sleds during the cold winters.[35]

With respect to the Russian Army political influence the Communist Party's control reached all the way down to the individual Russian Army soldier, in the form of the commissar or *Politicheskii rukovoditel* (Political officer).[36] In addition to the organs mentioned above, the commissar had a number of vital tasks to accomplish in his assigned unit, among them: Communist Party education, discipline of the troops, ensuring their proper care, recruitment of new Party members, ensuring strict compliance with issued orders, identification of suspicious persons and enforcement of all rules. Those who failed to toe the line could wind up in a punishment battalion.[37]

The Party's mistrust of any powerful organization, even its own Russian Army; was such that each unit from company size on up had an assigned commissar.[38] He accompanied the commanding officer of his unit wherever he went, stood with or near him as he issued orders or addressed the troops so the troops understood his importance and power by his proximity to their commander, and in combat ensured that there was no faltering, change of plans or retreat without orders. The order had to be signed by both men or it was invalid. The power of the Commissar was absolute and his word was law. This power frequently rankled his equal in the Russian Army, but commanding officers who dared challenge their commissars were few and far between. The power and influence of the commissar was such that in the German's invasion plans for Russia, the commissar was singled out for especially harsh treatment; if captured, immediate execution.[39]

---

[35] An interesting perspective on waste during wartime,but in the Allied armies from the perspective of a French civilian see, *The Normandy Diary of Marie-Louise Osmont, 1940-1944* by Marie-Louise Osmont, Discovery Communications, 1994, p. 79-80.

[36] The informers in the Red Army, who worked for the Special Department of the KGB were known as *stukachi.*

[37] Post-war documentation indicates that 422,700 men died in Red Army punishment battalions during the war. This number exceeds the entire killed and missing losses of the United States in the war of 404,100.

[38] The position of 'commissar' is not new to the Red Army. There have been such positions in the British Army in the form of 'chaplains' in Oliver Cromwell's New Model Army, "Representatives on Mission" in the French Army during the Revolution and 'imperial magistrates' in the Russian Army during the Russo-Japanese War.

In the conduct of the war, Stalin managed his most senior military officers, the marshals, based on their individual abilities. He never forged close ties with any of them and hence owed them no favors. It can safely be said the higher the rank of the officer, the greater their popularity and fame the greater was the danger that they would fall prey of Stalin's paranoia.

Life in the Russian Army in times of peace was a trying experience for the new recruits, in war under Stalin, recruit as well as officer, found it to be an exhausting and deadly experience indeed. In the initial 12 months of the war, the most significant achievement of the Soviet military leadership may very well be that of instilling a greater fear of his Russian Army command than of the German invader.

Reorganization

Intelligence arriving from spy rings in the West and from observations of the Axis build-up in the former polish border regions in June 1941 found the Russians in the midst of a major structural, deployment and partial mobilization reorganization. The looming threat from Germany was hardly a time for an major reorganization of the one element that Stalin's communist government would need to defend Russia, the military. Despite this mortal danger, the reorganization proceeded apace as well as the redeployment of a major portion of the Western and Southwestern Front units out of their prepared positions, frequently referred to as the Stalin Line and into the newly occupied eastern Polish areas, without benefit of secure communications, supply, defense coordination and the hostility of the Poles that comes with being an invader.[40]

The case for the Soviet restructuring of the Russian Army and the consequent confusion in the opening weeks of the invasion has been somewhat overstated. The chief impact of the restructuring was primarily managerial and organizational. The actual units and formations, even when not supplied and staffed to their new TO&E (Table of Organization and Equipment, the authorized amount of men and equipment for a given sized unit) strengths exceeded their German equivalents. For example the revised TO&E strength of a Soviet tank division was 375 tanks; in the German panzer division anywhere from 135 and 209; a Russian Army rifle

---

[39] Such was the importance placed on these officers that they were held to a high level of responsibility. Should their unit be found retreating without orders in combat the commissar was shot first; then the commanding officer. The absence of an appeals process is duly noted.

[40] *Stumbling Colossus, the Red Army on the Eve of World War.*

division was to have 1,204 machine guns, its German counterpart 486. As these numbers demonstrate, even with a less than full organizational complement, the Soviet combat units would have, in many instances, been comparable to German strengths. However, in the first months of the war very few Russian divisions were up to authorized strength. The real German advantage was in organization, training and experience, together with the negative effects of Russian reorganization and the resulting dislocation and redeployment, especially with the acquisition of the new western Polish territories as well as the loss of experienced senior officers.

Despite the larger number of weapons in the newly reorganized Russian rifle divisions, the situation the new tank units was even more troublesome. The new Russian mechanized corps was to have over a 1,000 tanks contained in two tank divisions. Unit deployment of an organization of this size occasionally required barracks and depots scattered over a space some 45 to 55 miles, what is even more questionable is how was a commander of a unit of this size to communicate with his subordinate units when they had few or no radio equipment? Photos of the period show Russian tank commanders holding signal flags to indicate maneuver and situation information. It would not be until 1943 that Russian tank and mechanized units began to be equipped with radios, courtesy of Western Allied Lend-Lease aid.

One final aspect of the Russian Army must be addressed and that is the patriotism of the average *frontoviki*. Much has been made of the use of communist party commissars and NKVD security units in maintaining discipline in the ranks, but comparatively little has been written about the native patriotism of the Russian soldier.

In the early days of the German invasion, the occasions of mass defection, abandonment of positions and disobeying orders was more the cause of disorganization, poor or incompetent leadership rather than lack of zeal and love of country. The typical Russian soldier was just as patriotic as was the British, American, Japanese and German soldiers. What is frequently misconstrued or miswritten as a hatred of Russia was actually the reaction of many years of poor economic management of the economy, abuses of power by communist party cadre and other flaws of the system that the individual was giving vent to. As the war progressed and the true nature of the German plans for the Slavic *untermenschen* became clear, with the *einsatzkommando* squads going about their deadly work, the choice of governments was an easy one to make.

Chapter Three: The German Home Front

France, Spain and England are countries
with an army. But Prussia!
Prussia is an army with a country.

Anonymous

This chapter will describe what life in wartime Germany was for the average Heinz and Heidi and the millions of *gastarbiter* foreign workers forced or induced to work in German homes, factories and mines. What was daily life like? What did they eat, wear and play? How did they shop and what was available to buy? What was their health like? How did it suffer under the privations of war? What was life like under Allied bombing? It will also look at the sources of information, news and propaganda in a fully managed society. Finally, with the demands of wartime production, what did they do for a living? Where did they work? For how much and for how long? What was the entertainment? To meet the needs of increased weapons demand, Germany induced and enslaved millions of laborers in the occupied countries. Where did they come from? Where did they live? How were they treated? This will be an extensive and detailed look at life in Nazi Germany to fully acquaint the reader with and provide background for understanding how the Germans mobilized for war.

What was the impetus of the people in allowing its government to restrict many of their rights and privileges and lead them on the road to second destructive war in the same century? Finally, why did these same educated, refined and civilized people follow their government down that road to perdition, especially after 1944 when the signs of impending defeat were all around them? Was Germany doomed to continue repeating, war after war, generation after generation, its military hypnotic fixation? This chapter will attempt to answer these and many more questions.

Volk and Reich

Germany began the war in 1939 after several years of full employment and after the civilian standard of living had reached its highest level in German history. In the early years of the war, what became known as the "soft war", civilian consumption remained high. Germans continued to try for an economy of both guns and butter. The German people entered the period of the war well stocked with clothing and other consumer goods. Germans frequently used the term "prewar quality" when comparing items of lesser quality manufactured during the latter part of the war. Although consumer goods became increasingly difficult to obtain, Allied studies show that fairly adequate supplies of clothing were available to those who were bombed out until the last stages of disorganization in 1945.[41] Food, though strictly rationed since 1939, was nutritionally adequate albeit monotonous, and available until 1944 when shortages of all kinds appeared. The German diet had about the same number of calories as that of the British.[42]

However, by 1944 daily life for the average German was becoming unbearable, especially if one lived in or near the major cities. It was a little more tolerable out in the countryside, which did not attract the hoards of Allied bombers and where one usually had better access to food. As a poll taken after the war revealed, if one were not a Jew, Communist, or other 'undesirable' and "kept their heads down", domestic life in Hitler's Germany was just tolerable -- just. Shortages of consumer goods did not begin to appear until 1942. From this time on the domestic economy made greater use of bartering, black-market purchases and political connections to obtain what was needed.[43]

---

[41] At the height of the Allied bomber attacks against the major cities, the Germans maintained mobile disaster convoys that constantly roamed the nation, issuing clothing, shoes and food.

[42] *The United States Strategic Bombing Survey, Summary Report, European War,* September 30, 1945.

The first three years of the war seemed to be characterized by the semi-official attitude of "As much normality as possible, as much war as necessary". However by late 1943 the slide to total war made this feeling and lifestyle all but impossible.

The German Wartime Diet

One of the most intrusive elements into German domestic life was the advent of food rationing. Every major combatant, Allied or Axis, utilized food rationing as a means to equitably distribute scarce or high status (red meat, sugar, chocolate, coffee) foods, ensuring that all segments of the population could access these precious and scarce commodities.

In September 1939, food rationing was instituted in Germany and there were seven color-coded cards representing major food groups. Lines outside food stores and shops came commonplace and ration coupons on their color-coded cards (purple, fruit; white, sugar; yellow, dairy; pink, cereals; blue, meat; orange, bread and green, eggs) were required. The major staple of the German diet, potatoes remained un-rationed until November 1942 and the eighth card, brown, was issued. Also, coal was rationed, starting in early 1940.[44]

To alleviate the fuel shortage for heating and cooking a coal composite was manufactured to supplement or replace the hard or anthracite coal (known a "stone coal") and soft or Lignite "brown" coal. Many German families cooked with wood during the summer months, which was still plentiful early in the war, saving the precious coal ration for the winter heating. The manufactured "brown" coal was ground, mixed with water and compressed into brick sized blocks (or briquettes) and burned in that form. Even the coal dust from the "stone coal" was not wasted. The

[43] Germany was not the only combatant nation where obtaining adequate amounts of food was a problem. In 1942-1943 American petroleum drilling workers in England living on standard British food rations started to become undernourished to the point that it was affecting drilling performance in the field. It wasn't until in desperation the head of field drilling operations applied to SHEAF quartermaster for permission to purchase additional food that the men returned to full health and work performance improved. See *The Secret of Sherwood Forest* by Guy H. Woodward and Grace Steele Woodward, Red River Press, 1973, reprinted 2003 for additional details on British domestic food supplies.

[44] For an in depth study of German wartime agricultural organization see *Labor Organizations of the Third Reich*, Chapter 5 The Reichnährstand, by J.R. Angolia and David Littlejohn, R. James Bender Publishing, 1999.

dust was mixed with wood chips, rags, newspaper and water and blended together. When it reached a clay-like texture it was formed into baseball size balls and dried in the sun. This burned well and gave off a reasonable amount of heat.

The decline in food available to the German home front in 1944 despite rationing caused the Gestapo to begin inspections, searching for theft rings, stamping out black market profiteers and hoarding. Inspections by the local authorities became more frequent as officials were concerned that military supplies were being siphoned off for civilian use. In the first few months of 1945 food became so scarce in Cologne the Roman Catholic cardinal issued a blanket absolution for stealing food, "if it was for the purpose of feeding and preserving self and family".

With the daily food ration reduced in mid-1942, the hunt for food became a vital part of daily activities. The best off were the farmers who were exempt from rationing, coming under the government category of self-sufficient families. The city dwellers had it the worst, being the farthest from the countryside and its farms and wholly dependent on a fair and efficient distribution system. To provide adequate bread, a staple of the German diet, additives were put into the mixtures at the bakeries to make up for the shortage of flour, including wood saw dust, husks, ground cobs, shells and the like.[45]

One growing chore of the typical German was known as "hamstering". This was not quite black market purchasing, even if one could afford it, but also not quite evading normal food distribution outlets. It was nothing more than going directly to the source of the food, the farms. On weekends and holidays, families would pack baskets and hike off into the country and offer to purchase food directly from the farmers. It was a combination KdF hike for the exercise and the need to procure fresh food to supplement declining ration provided amounts.

As the war progressed, finding food became more and more of a challenge and began to occupy a greater part of the working day. Examples of the populace doing whatever it had to do ease the pain of hunger were many. One woman exchanged her large precious heirloom dining room table for fats, meat and a number of prepared foods, telling her family that one had to do what one had to do. Bartering and scavenging became routine – it is

---

[45] Conversation with Dr. Volkmar and Karin Kreibich, Seeheim, Germany, summer 1990.

said that a woman traded her wedding gown for a sack of sugar and then traded the sugar for a stack of shingles to repair a hole in the roof caused by an Allied bomb.

As the war progressed, especially by the winter of 1944, the average diet consisted of potatoes, bread, sausage and cabbage and even then the quality and quantity of these meager foods declined. Rare was the German who by 1944 had anything remaining from the pre-war period to enjoy, such as wines, gourmet items or anything imported, especially from outside Europe. Fruit became a rarity; chicken and fish available only on occasion and coffee, especially after 1941, almost impossible to obtain.

By 1944 the trains bringing food into the cities became more and more sporadic because of Allied air interdiction prompting civilians to take even greater risks. In one example, a train carrying sugar was stalled by Allied air attack. When word reached the nearby residents of Leipzig, some mounted their bicycles and pedaled out to find it. When they did it was already swarming with looters. When one young girl managed to load a 100-pound bag of sugar onto the handlebars of her bicycle, she was caught in a follow-up Allied fighter-bomber attack. Ignoring the machine-gun fire all around her she pedaled on, ruining the tires of her bicycle as she arrived home with her prize. The sugar was sufficient to keep her family going for several weeks, using it for both cooking and barter.

The food shortage was artificially created, however unintentionally, by the government stockpiling food for military usage, releasing it to civilian consumption just before spoilage set in. This also contributed to the declining health of the average German by the almost empty nutritional value it then had. This was a remarkable change in a nation that from the rise of the Nazis to power in 1933, had conducted numerous campaigns to improve public health. These campaigns combated smoking, excessive consumption of alcohol and the promotion of a more 'natural' diet consisting of whole-grain breads, fruit and vegetables. The encouragement of government and domestic science, and research into public health supported and was constantly concerned with the maintenance and improvement of the German "germ plasm", a concept connected to Nazi racial theory. Today this would be described as human DNA. To construct the German master race, the public was constantly reminded that "you have the duty to be healthy". This was a basic tenant of Hitler Jugend (the government organized and sponsored German youth organization) education; hence the emphasis on physical fitness in most of the HJ's camps, meetings and exercises. Those who disregarded their health were compared to Jews and the other "undesirables" in German society. The government also conducted a vigorous war against cancer, which included banning such food additives as coal tar colorants, especially the yellow dye that was added to enhance butter's appeal. Food was to be considered a precious national resource and its production, processing, distribution and consumption were closely monitored. The government also used food distribution as a weapon, especially against Jews and Gypsies, who were considered "waste eaters".

This is a significant observation of the decline of general health of a nation that had previously enjoyed one of the highest standards of health in Europe. Nazi nutritionists stressed the importance of a diet free of petrochemical dyes and preservatives. Many Nazis were environmentalists; many were vegetarians. Species protection was a going concern, as was animal welfare. Goering barred vivisection in all scientific work, noting the "unbearable torture and suffering in animal experiments" and he threatened to commit to concentration camps "those who still think they can treat animals as inanimate property." [46] Nazi doctors worried about overmedication and the overzealous use of X-rays; they cautioned against an unhealthy workplace and the failure of physicians to be honest with their patients (allowing momentous exclusions, of course, for 'racially unfit' or undeserving).

The growing scarcity of food led the government to attempt to extract the last morsel of nutrition of every consumable and to develop food substitutes and replacements. For example, attempts were made to utilize the 40 million kilograms of cattle blood discarded during slaughtering; nutritionists calculated that it was the equivalent of 100,000 head of cattle weighing 500 kilograms each.

By 1945, posters and billboards in Berlin appeared advising the populace how to augment their diets with readily available food sources, such as using pieces of clothing pulled through the water to catch frogs. In a few instances, riots erupted when factory and office workers who did not have the 'luxury' of time to wait in lines found things unavailable on shopping

---

[46] These statements are ironic in that Goering appointed himself the *Reichjaegermeister* or National Hunting Master.

days. Case in point were those with "Muki" cards, ration cards for mothers with children, which entitled them to proceed to the front of the food lines and purchase what they wanted.

One hope of German military expansionism was to satisfy their growing need for food by conquering Europe's prime agricultural regions, such as the Ukraine. However the gross inefficiencies of the German byzantine bureaucratic organization insured that only a fraction of the productive fruits of these occupied places reached the Reich. For example, only fifteen percent of the Reich's food during the war came from the occupied countries.

German Health

The difficulty in obtaining sufficient and different kinds of food was making an already deficient diet increasingly dangerous to the average German's health. A foreign visitor late in 1943 noticed the effects of this diet on the teeth of the general public. They were decaying quickly and without adequate infusions of different foods to balance the diet or vitamin supplements, if their health continued to get worse as the war dragged on. One dentist said that if the decay continued for another year no one would have teeth. For those that saw their dentists, the dentists themselves were having difficulty obtaining dental supplies of all kinds. The few physicians left in society were unable to stem the decline of the state of German health. Many had been inducted into the military and a number in Germany's pre-Nazi medical profession consisted of a relatively significant portion of Jews who had been forced to flee the country, had been arrested or were dying in concentration or death camps.

Indeed, the loss of skilled members of the German health and commercial establishments was recognized early on by Hitler himself. In 1935 an order was issued from Hitler suspending attacks on Jewish businesses by the NS-Hago (*Nationalsocialist Handwerks-, Handels- und Gewerbe Organization* or National Socialist Handicraft, Commercial and Business Organization) because of the economic depression these same Jewish shops were providing much needed employment for German workers.[47]

The loss of key medical professionals and medical supplies led to a growing increase of disease, especially tuberculosis and sexually transmitted diseases. The former was a result of the lack of proper heating from the cut

---

[47] *Labor Organizations of the Reich*, p.32.

backs in heating coal in the cities as well as the long hours waiting in lines, riding the available unheated tram cars and working in unheated factories and plants. The increase of sexually related diseases was blamed on the breakdown in morality because of the Nazi inspired cult of youth and the absence of parents and relatives working in the war industries leaving the youth unsupervised and to their own entertainment.

In addition to declining dental health, this same visitor noticed that many Germans were constantly sick. The bad diet, stress from the bombing, bad war news, loss of friends and family, long working hours in semi-heated offices and factories were all having their effect on the general well being. Civilians were thin, starting to get threadbare, gaunt, and took offense at the slightest provocations. This was most apparent, he observed, in the public places such as shops, trams and restaurants.

Here's an example of how one woman coped:

> "Right after New Year's in 1940 I got a card from the labor bureau. I had to report for compulsory service. The girls felt very sorry for me when I resigned from the printing plant, because I was being sent to a munitions plant.[48] Instead of going to work late in the afternoon, I had to be at the plant-way out in Allach -- at 6:00AM, which meant I had to leave the house before five to get there on time. The women had to work a twelve-hour shift, and when we came home, completely worn out, the shops were closing or had already closed, or if they were open, they had nothing left by the time we got there. And prices kept going up, even though the government said it had frozen prices. Before the war you could buy margarine for 63 pfennings a pound. Three months later, in the winter of '39-'40, it cost 98 pfennings! And I had to count every pfennig. In the printing plant I earned 42 marks a week, but out in Allach, the women doing compulsory service got only 35 marks; and 6.50 of that went to transportation, 4.90 for the cafeteria, and 90 pfennings a week for the Winter

---

[48] With the growing shortage of labor, the government reluctantly began recruiting women into the labor force. One job that the women attempted to avoid at any cost was assignment to an armament factory. The absentee rate was higher than average and the factory management and local officials began to describe the situation as *Frauenflucht* or the flight of women. The excuses used were numerous, from the need to care for children, to the need to repair bombed housing, to waiting on lines for food and other essentials.

Aid, a state run charity. After I had paid my rent and utilities I had barely one mark a day left for everything else -- food, laundry, clothing, repairs. And I couldn't earn anything on the side, because in the evening I was just too tired to clean offices, as I'd done earlier. When I finally got home after shopping, I could have fallen asleep standing up. Luckily we didn't have night air raids that first year, or I probably would have collapsed; many women in our plant did later on. They couldn't take the pace, especially the older ones, and that wasn't surprising when you consider how badly we ate."[49]

The above was the domestic and employment situation of a single woman in western Germany during the early period of the war, albeit a somewhat more precarious situation than that of a married couple or extended family. Fast forward the calendar to 1944, add day-and-night bombing, loss of loved family members in the fighting and bombing, increased demands by the war industries, increasing shortages of almost everything, especially the essentials and one can only marvel at the stamina, fear, courage, dedication and survival skills of the average German worker.

As strained as the domestic conditions became, especially in 1944, the government attempted to provide support to German families in the form of subsidized women household workers recruited from the occupied countries to the east as well as an official organization, the *Deutscher Frauenhilfsdienst* or German Women's Help Service. This organization, a component of the DAF (*Deutsche Arbeitsfront*) the German Labor Front, made up of young women of high school age was to provide assistance in the form of shopping for working women, minding children in a Kindergarten to helping farm families during harvest season.

As the war progressed, money in Germany began to lose its value for two reasons, as everyone who could was working long hours, and in some cases receiving extra or bonus pay leaving little time for shopping.[50]   Secondly, as the war cut off the supply of many raw materials, or these materials were

---

[49] *In Hitler's Germany, Everyday life in the Third Reich* by Bernt Engelmann, Pantheon Books, New York 1986 p. 177. Reproduced with permission.

[50] Working hours increased as the domestic economy was converted into a war economy. Average working hours increased from 32 in 1932 to 50 in 1942. *World War II Data Book, The Third Reich 1933 - 1945, The Essential Facts and Figures For Hitler's Germany*, by Chris McNab, Amber Books, 2009, p.54.

diverted to war production, consumer goods slowly disappeared, especially luxuries. Clothing and rubber products of any kind were especially difficult to obtain by 1944. Shoes began to be made with wooden soles, and new clothing appeared made of low-quality fabrics that quickly wore out and were harsh to the skin. The wooden shoes caused many Germans to complain of sore and blistered feet as walking had become commonplace with the confiscation of private automobiles and shortage of fuel, the destruction of public transport systems and the diversion of what was left to the war effort. The shortage of leather for shoes was such that in 1942 the Hitler Youth was asked to go barefoot during the summer to conserve the remaining precious shoes.

Although more an inconvenience in the United States and more so in the other allied nations, the availability of food in Germany took on a serious, almost major war effort by the government to control. A healthy male population was essential to raising and maintaining a strong military and Germany struggled all through the war to preserve it. As did the Allies, a reliable and nutritious supply of food was essential to the morale of the people and directly contributed to the war effort.

Rest, Recreation and Diversion

To keep morale up, people attended lectures, popular music concerts and most popular of all, cinema. (In 1939 there were 492 theaters and opera houses in Germany.) There were more than 7,000 cinemas in Germany and the Propaganda Ministry went to great lengths to keep them open despite the shortages and the bombing. Radio was another popular pastime in that mostly pre-television era. The average German listened to the radio for four and a half hours a day, and music, mostly classical, was constantly broadcast to keep everyone cheerful.

Morale was not taken lightly by the Nazi government, especially after the February 1943 Stalingrad disaster in Russia. Hitler was quite sensitive to the need to have the loyalty and affection of the people behind him and the Party from its earliest days went to great lengths to ensure public, and more specifically worker, contentment. The public mood was regularly polled and reported to the highest government officials by the SD, the security service (*sicherheitdienst*) of the SS.

The principle agency for orchestrating this campaign of workplace enhancement, public harmony and happiness was the *Kraft durch Freude Gemeinschaft* or the National Socialist organization "Strength through Joy".

Known most widely by its initials, *KdF* was a component of the German labor organization or *Deutscher Arbiter Front* and as most workers were part of the *DAF* they were already enrolled in the *KdF*.

The *KdF* was the Nazi party's benevolent face to the German people. It was basically a government organized nationwide tourist planning and entertainment agency. Its primary focus was to provide structured, restful and educational vacations to all working Germans, especially those of the lower working classes who would not otherwise be able to afford such holidays. For example the *KdF* provided world-class luxury cruise [51] vacations to the Atlantic, Baltic, and Mediterranean coasts. In addition to the cruises, the *KdF* organization provided concerts, day trips, retreats, tours, theater, art exhibits and related artistic and cultural events. However when the popularity of these excursions grew and the blue-collar workers began to intrude on the popular resorts of the rich, these establishments began posting signs that they did not cater to the *KdF* trade. This was also the same organization that attempted to put every German family into the seat of an automobile, the aptly named *KdF* wagon or Strength through Joy Wagon that was mercifully shortened to the Peoples Car or *Volkswagen*. [52]

With the outbreak of war in September 1939, the assets of the *KdF* organization were impressed into the war effort and its many concert halls, kitchens and related support facilities curtailed the entertainment aspects of their charter and began assisting the bombed-out, displaced and visiting soldiers and refugees.

---

[51] At one time the *KdF* operated seven cruise liners, which, in 1938, took 7,000 vacationers to the Norwegian fjords; other popular locales were on the Iberian Peninsula. The workers eligible for the cruises were usually productivity winners and model employees. When the war broke out these vessels became military transport, hospital and barracks ships, one of which, the *Wilhelm Gustloff* had the misfortune of being torpedoed in January 1945 with the largest loss of life at sea during the war.

[52] The contract provision for the installment payment plan for the *KdF* car was as strict as they were unrealizable. The 990 Reich-Marks the car was to cost did not include a mandatory 200 additional Marks for insurance, all at a rate of 5 Marks per week, a rate at which no worker would ever see a car. Should the worker need to cancel his *KdF* car contract, if he was permitted, it would cost him a 20% penalty against the refunded amount on which no interest was paid. To demonstrate that the *KdF* management never had any intention of delivering these "workers autos" and which was in reality a forced savings plan without interest, the final insult to the German worker was that all the cars would be delivered in one color, a shade of "deep grey blue" which would make military use of these vehicles quite easy.

The *KdF* organization and the events it offered were generally popular, despite its overwhelming appeal to and catering for Germany's working class. It provided recreational opportunities that millions heretofore could never had afforded or experienced. By and large it was the most popular of all of National Socialism's programs. To demonstrate the popularity of the *KdF* programs some 59,000 entertainments (hikes, lectures, clubs), 12,400 operas, 20,000 plays, 11,000 variety programs and some 8,000 night club-type performances were presented. In all the DAF spent 11% of its budget on *KdF* activities.

White, Gray and Black Information

A great part of the information obtained in war is contradictory, a still greater part is false, and by far the greatest part is of doubtful character.

Clausewitz, On War
Chapter VI, Information in War

The various ministries of the government controlled almost all information and entertainment available to the average German. As the war progressed and turned badly for them, the means and methods by which this information was received became more tightly controlled.[53]

The primary source of this daily information was the Ministry of Propaganda, headed by Joseph Goebbels. His ministry, the Ministry of People's Enlightenment and Propaganda (*Reichsministerium fur Volksaufklarung und Propaganda* or RMVP) and its chief component dealing with the arts, the Reich Chamber of Culture (*Reichskulturkammer* or RKK), controlled and approved what was broadcast over the airwaves, screened in movie theaters, seen on stage and printed in the press.

Most of the independent newspapers that did not report what was considered favorable or published information in any way contrary to the Party line were brought under strong pressure to conform or risk closure.

---

[53] As the newsreels became more strident and less newsworthy and credible, the public began to wait outside the theater or in lobbies until the feature film started. To counter this, Goebbels instructed the theater owners to close and lock the doors to the theater once the newsreels began.

The *Deutsches Nachrichtenburo* (DNB) was the official German news source, issuing press releases, and articles to the national and international press. By the beginning of the war in 1939, almost every newspaper [54] was thoroughly under the control or owned by the government publishing firm Eher Publishing.[55]

In the early days of the war the articles and stories were fairly accurate as to what was happening in Europe and the world in general, (which was fairly safe to report), as these were the halcyon days of German military expansion. Of course certain subjects were heavily biased, such as anything that had to do with the Jews, communists, gypsies or other like 'undesirables.'[56]

As the war progressed and especially by early 1944 the German media became so unreliable, vague or false in its reporting that the information became almost meaningless and most people, in secret, made fun of its content and delivery. To find out what was actually happening in the world the citizens of Germany chose to listen to foreign broadcasts, also known

---

[54] Kennedy in *The Library of Congress World War II Companion* quotes "two-thirds of the nation's newspapers" p. 809.

[55] Although they were voices of the NSDAP, the following were the official newspapers of various components of the Party: The SA read *SA Man*, HJ read *Der Hitler Jugend*, the SS read *Die Schwarze Korps*, the SD and Police read *Die Deutsche Polizei*, the official voice of the NSDAP was the *Volkischer Beobachter*, the officials in Berlin read *Der Angriff* and at the end of the Third Reich, there was in Berlin *Der Panzerbar*. "Signal" magazine, the best selling magazine in occupied Europe, was read widely by and published by the Wehrmacht. It appeared bi-monthly in 20 languages and, in 1943, had a peak readership of 2.5 million.

[56] The German government went to great lengths to insure that the word and message of the Nazi Party was clearly received. Initially the German government offered a low cost radio affordable for even the meanest segment of the population. Station selections were limited but for those who never possessed such a device before this was not a problem. For those who could afford more there was an embryonic form of television. Known as the *Fernsehempfanger FE 1* this simple receiver provided a small viewing screen and limited quality control features but was a significant step forward in the progression of real-time message transmission. The first television broadcasts began on 22 March 1935, a full year before the British began their broadcasting program, generally accepted to be the pioneers of television service. Of interest to us here was that Germany took its television to occupied France and from 1942 until their retreat in 1944 broadcast live programming from the captured French transmitter atop the Eiffel Tower. During the war the transmitters in Berlin and Paris broadcast television programs for wounded soldiers. In occupied France at this time there were an estimated 500 French made receivers and additional German sets in French hospitals.

as "black radio", which was forbidden[57]. The foreign broadcast of choice was the British BBC (British Broadcasting Company) from London. Even in the darkest days of the Blitz of London in the summer of 1940, the BBC broadcast what was really happening, even when the news was bad for the Allies, thereby winning the trust of its listeners. However, if the Gestapo or any of the German controlled police forces in German-occupied Europe caught anyone listening to a foreign broadcast the result was usually a long prison sentence (5 years) and, near the end of the war, death. To ensure 'funk' (radio) discipline, the government assigned radio wardens *funkaufseher* to ensure listening compliance. This listening compliance covered all work places in the Reich; during a government announcement one could not leave an office or workstation until the broadcast was completed. The most popular receiver was the *VE 301 Volksempfaenger*, made popular as it was the most inexpensive, made all the more popular as one could pay for it in installments if one could not afford its cost outright.[58]

For the truly disadvantaged, for the public spaces such as train stations, market spaces and the like, and most rural inhabitants, there were loudspeakers. By the end of the 1930's there were more than 5,000 speakers in place throughout Germany. All important announcements were easily identified as Minister Goebbels preceded each message with, at first, martial music. But as the war drew on, and especially as it turned against Germany the martial music was slowly replaced by the classics, especially Wagner and Beethoven.

In the summer of 1942 when the Allied air attacks -- especially the RAF night carpet bombing of the western German cities -- were beginning to cause mass disruption and civilian deaths were mounting, a device was available to the public that was attached to the common table radio, called the *drahtfunk* or cable radio. With the radio kept on, this attachment produced a repetitive ticking sound, very much like someone striking a hollow piece of wood. When an Allied bomber raid was detected approaching, the sound changed to metallic pinging. This pinging was intended to catch the attention of the listeners to the imminent official announcements of the distance and direction of the approaching bombers. By mid-1943 as the

---

[57] From: *Die Entstehung der Verordbung uber ausserordentliche Rundfunkmassnahmen* vom 1. September 1939.

[58] This unit became popularly known among the people as *die Goebbelsschnauze* or Goebbels Nose. For more information on black radio and its variations, see Sefton Delmer and the uses of white, gray and black radio.

attacks were becoming constant and more destructive, most families took turns sitting or working near the radio to listen for the change in sound to alert everyone to the impending attack and warn them to seek shelter. There was also a version that provided broadcast announcements to various districts threatened by attack, such as 'Achtung! Achtung! Drahtfunk! Enemy planes approaching PQ 161!' The alpha-numeric referenced a map coordinate.

Allied Strategic Bombardment: Life in the LSR

Long before the Russians or the western Allies had set foot in Germany, the Allies were inflicting serious damage to Germany's ability to wage war through the strategic bombing campaign[59]. By mid 1943 when the Allied air attacks against the cities began to assume their height, many families were displaced by the destruction of their apartments and homes. Because of this growing destruction everyday items like cooking utensils, light bulbs, small electric appliances and shoelaces became prized items.

The Royal Air Force, after some costly daylight raids early in the war, reverted to a strictly nighttime campaign over Germany and the occupied countries. In 1942 the Americans began arriving in force in southern England in the form of the 8th Army Air Force. By mid-year this growing air armada began daylight raids over occupied France with the new heavy multi-engined Boeing B-17E "Flying Fortress" and Consolidated B-24D "Liberator". This growing might, the U. S. bombing during the day and the R.A.F. at night, was to slowly reduce German towns, villages, cities, factories, farms, bridges, canals, roads and airfields to rubble. By the end of the war Berlin suffered 24 major bomb attacks, destroying 33% of all housing. The major cities of Frankfurt, Nuremberg, Munich, Cologne, Dusseldorf, Hamburg and Dresden suffered similar or greater amounts of damage.[60]

The use of shelters for protection from aerial bombardment was an accepted civil defense procedure and had proved itself on many occasions. However, R.A.F. bombing, included a mix of high explosive and incendiary bombs, and an improved method of dropping and aiming these on cities and

---

[59] For an excellent treatment of the Allied strategic bombing campaign, see *Death From the Heavens, A History of Strategic Bombing* by Kenneth P. Werrell, 2009, Naval Institute Press.

[60] After the devastating air raid on Coventry in November 1940 this level of destruction was called by the British 'Coventration'.

built-up areas made the aerial attack a much more devastating event than ever before. The firestorms reduced the safety of the shelters, and in many cases the occupants in them were in greater danger than those outside. As residents of London and Moscow had learned before them, it was occasionally safer to risk staying home than the possibility of entrapment in the shelters.

One survivor of the bombing in the capital describes the experience of a friend attending a dinner:

> "We became so used to the presence of death that when she went to a dinner party in Berlin after an air raid, she realized that while eating, a short distance away rescue workers were hearing the faint knocking of trapped people in a collapsed building. What surprised her afterward is that they went on eating and drinking and making polite conversation as if the horror next to them did not exist".[61]

In the first raid on Hamburg alone, about one third of the houses in the city were destroyed and German estimates indicate 40,000 to 80,000 people killed. No subsequent city raid, until the February 1945 raid on Dresden[62] shook Germany, as did the July-August 1943 raid on Hamburg. By 1944 the RAF had dropped 676,000 tons of bombs on Germany compared with 16,000 in 1940. German officials were concerned that if this were to be the fate of German cities, then it was just a matter of time before Germany was forced out of the war. With the inability of the Luftwaffe to defend the Reich, this became almost a certainty. With the exception of cities and towns in the far eastern portion of Germany and the occupied countries, one city after another was laid to waste by the nightly visits of the RAF Bomber Command.[63]

The neighborhood cellar bomb shelters became the new living rooms of the cities of the Third Reich. So important had they become to survival they soon became the center of daily life. As the war progressed into 1944 the

---

[61] *The Home Front: Germany* by Charles Whiting, Time-Life Books, 1982, p. 148.

[62] The number of claimed dead in the Dresden raid of 13 February 1945 have been numerous and wildly fluctuating, the highest of 350,000 to 400,000 by Axel Rodenberger in 1952 in his *Der Tod von Dresden*. Although now thoroughly discounted by subsequent evidence and documentation, especially after the fall of the East German government in 1989, the most reliable and current figure is an estimate of 25,000 to 40,000. This figure comes from Friedrich Reichert an official of the Dresden City Museum and best sums up the estimates from several sources.

likelihood of the nightly attacks was taken for granted, especially in Berlin, which became a favored target for both the RAF night and the USAF day bombers. People prepared foods to take with them into the shelters, informal clothing became the norm with some women donning turbans in place of hats which became too much of a bother in the close confines of most shelters. To get preferred places in the shelters people began lining up at shelter entrances at sundown to be the first ones admitted.

When the blackout was proclaimed in September 1939 a minor fashion item came into vogue that of wearing one or more luminous buttons on coats and jackets. This along with white painted curbs and steps helped those walking about at night in the darkened city streets.

As the bombing increased in intensity the shelter dwellers learned to adapt to the new atmosphere created in and near the shelter. When bombs exploded nearby, people kept their mouths open to equalize air pressure to protect their eardrums and took short breaths when the air ducts were sealed to conserve precious oxygen when the many fires started outside. The cellar dwellers became used to the pressure/vacuum/pressure/vacuum experience of being bombed. As the heat inside the shelter increased, people dipped bedclothes in water and draped them around themselves to ward off the heat and covered their eyes against bomb flashes. They also became experts at identifying the type of bombs and knowing when they were dropping. They learned to distinguish U.S. from British bombs by the sound of their whistling or lack of it and other identifiable sound characteristics and learned what the bomb dropping patterns were so as to duck ones head in time.[64]

[63] *The United States Strategic Bombing Survey.*

[64] The traffic in bombing terror was not all one way. Beginning 13 June 1944 and ending gradually in September the same year 8,892 V-1 (A-2 or FZG-76 *Flakzielgerat* or anti-aircraft target device in German nomenclature) flying bombs were launched at greater London and other English cities. Of these 3,531 reached British soil, 2,419 landing in the London Civil Defense Region causing 6,184 deaths and 17,987 severely injured. To cause additional confusion, the Luftwaffe painted the short wings of the V-1 with the alternating white-black-white-black identification bands used by the Allied air forces.

The same month the V-1 threat tapered off, the first V-2 (A-4) landed in London, 8 September 1944, however this supersonic ballistic missile arrived silently and its speed was so great no radar image was noticed. The British, initially unaware what was causing these large explosions, soon learned to their dismay that these were the ballistic missiles identified earlier from photographic intelligence flights over Peenemunde, Germany. Quickly realizing that there was no defense against these faster than sound projectiles, the War Ministry informed the public that the unknown explosions were from gas mains.

In the larger cities with their more frequent raids, the people were able to identify by sound the kind of bomb dropping on them.

> ". . . every bomb had its own peculiar sound. If there was a rustle like a flock of doves flying up, it was bundle of small stick bombs breaking apart, with each stick finding its own target. If there was a short, sharp explosion, it was a 12-kilogram fire bomb, which could spread fire eighty meters in all directions. If it was like a bucket of water splashing in the street, it was a 14-kilogram liquid fire bomb, which could spread liquid rubber and benzine fifty meters around the impact area. If it cracked like an explosive bomb when it hit, it was either a 106-kilogram bomb that threw out rags soaked with benzine or heavy oil or a 112-kilogram fire bomb, which covered nearby houses with a thousand 'cow cakes" of benzol and rubber. And there were still, of course, the explosive bombs and mines, which tore out the doors and windows to provide air to feed the flames and surpassed the effects of an earthquake, so that those in the cellar thought of themselves as perched in the heart of a volcano."[65]

In an attempt to 'fire proof' their homes, some citizens, each evening in anticipation of the nightly RAF raids, began to fill every container with water; bath tubs, sinks, buckets, pots to make fire fighting as quick and efficient as possible. In addition, some enterprising owners prepared a mixture of lime and water to form a paste and applied to their roofs to retard burning.

To add to the danger and dread of the allied attacks were the bombs that did not explode -- at least not right away. The Germans called them *zeitzunder*, meaning delayed action, and *blindganger* or "blind walker" bombs, or duds. Both kinds added to the time and risk by the bomb disposal units and the gangs of POWs used to clean up after the raids to return the town or city to normal, or what passed for normal in Germany in 1944 and 1945.

The forced company of the shelters forged a certain pride in the suffering experienced by the bomb shelter occupants. Even when the government began evacuations to the country and small towns, many returned illegally

---

[65] *Under the Bombs, The German Home Front 1941 - 1945* by Earl R. Beck, The University Press of Kentucky, 1986, p.61.

for a number of reasons, chief among them were the scorn resulting from class and social differences between the German city and rural dwellers,[66] but most commented when asked what they missed most was the camaraderie and deep friendships that were formed in the shelters.

One of the many ways to pass the seemingly endless hours of boredom and terror was to guess the final destination of the approaching allied bomber stream:

> "The raids seemed continuous, and every German listened in to the hourly *Luftlage* (air situation) broadcast by all stations. As soon as a bomber formation penetrated the Reich, a special transmitter would give its exact location, strength, altitude and direction. Germany was divided into alphabetically designated areas, with corresponding first names assigned to each area. Although the map was supposed to be secret, each household had a charted copy for itself, to enable the family to make advance preparations, or to pass the time playing the game of 'Bertha, Bertha'. There was a red formation, a blue one, and a green one, red 2, blue 2 and so on, and bets were made as to the over which they would make their swoop. . . At 'Gustav Friedrich' (the end of the game, 'Gustav Friedrich' being the code name for Berlin) you packed your bag, and joined in the national tide flowing to the shelters: Berlin would be sounding the alert in ten minutes."[67]

What made the RAF raids so destructive was their ability to jamb German early warning radar sets. This was begun in 1943 by using metallic strips cut to the width and length of the radio frequencies of German radar sets, especially the *Freya*, *Mammut* and *Wasserman* early warning devices and later the *Wurzburg* and *Giant Wurzburg* sets. So much of this material was dropped in and near German cities that the strips were used as substitute tinsel for Christmas tree (*Tannenbaum*) decoration.

---

[66] The strains caused by the forced sharing of shelters in the small town and villages of the Reich caused a number of outbursts between those seeking shelter and those required to provide it. The villagers called the women from the cities "bomb wenches" and the city dwellers in turn described their rural 'hosts' as those who "eat like kings but live like pigs". In summary, this was a very unpopular program and the urban residents, regardless of the risk, found any means possible to return to threatened homes in the cities.

[67] *The German Home Front, 1939-1945* by Terry Charman, Philosophical Library, 1989, p. 193.

Firestorm!

The cities of Dresden and Hamburg were the largest locations of a new man-made phenomenon known as a 'fire storm'. This is where the mix of incendiary and high explosive bombs were used to break apart the buildings and the fires ignited by the incendiary bombs combine and create an immense conflagration generating powerful drafts that had the strength to suck people into them and were impossible for the fire brigades to fight. When a firestorm was created, city *Luftschutz* (air-raid wardens) were instructed not to send the people to the shelters, but to order an evacuation. This had to be decided early enough to give the population time to get clear of the built-up city areas. If delayed too long the draft of the fires would grow too strong, initially sucking in small movable objects. But as the vortex grew, roofing materials, even trees and people would be drawn into them, especially smaller, lighter people such as women and children. The fierce blowtorch-like fires created extremely high temperatures. There are reports of street asphalt becoming liquid and canals, lakes and fountains in the inner cities boiling. The letters 'LSR' marked on major buildings indicated the location of a *Luftschutzraum* or air-raid shelter in the buildings cellars.[68] These turned out to be of little protection during a firestorm. Even with thick steel doors on some of the better shelters, the intense fires sucked the oxygen from these rooms to asphyxiate the people inside and the great heat warped and buckled the steel doors making them inoperable and literally cooked those trapped inside. After a raid, the Germans did not attempt systematic recovery of all bodies or even of all trapped persons. Those who could not readily be removed from the rubble were left.[69]

The advent of the firestorm, with its greedy need for oxygen and the intense heat it created, made all but the most sophisticated shelter a tomb. The rescue personnel in Hamburg, Lubeck, Dresden and other cities that experienced firestorms stated that many days had to pass until the cellars,

---

[68] Also, a two letter code was painted in phosphorescent paint next to the entrance, such as VR, VL, HR or HL. They were the directions to the air raid shelter in the basement or cellar of the structure. The letters stood for "*Vorne Rechts*" meaning "front right" or "*Vorne Links*", "front left", etc. A darker, humor intended version was also making the rounds in the larger eastern cities near the end of the war, meaning *Lernt schnell Russisch*, or Learn Russian Quickly.

[69] For a graphic and moving account of the effects of the destruction of the German cities and the psychological impact on the victims see *On the Natural History of Destruction* by W. G. Sebald, The Modern Library, New York, 2004.

where the shelters were located, had cooled enough to allow the rescue personnel to enter them. When they did, no survivors were discovered and the people who sought shelter there were found in positions that made them seem to be asleep, their faces blackened from the lack of oxygen and the effects of the intense heat. The clothing they wore was completely dissolved by the heat, disintegrating at the slightest touch. Another, lesser known danger but just as deadly to the shelters was flooding from burst water mains.

After the creation of the first firestorms, especially when it was observed how defenseless the Germans were in the face of them, the firestorm became the desired end-product of every attack. However, the defenders were not entirely helpless, especially in the early stages of the attack. Heretofore, the residents of the cities were advised to seek safety in their basements and bomb shelters and not to emerge until the 'all clear' signal was sounded, usually from an electrically powered siren.

In the 4 December 1943 attack on Leipzig, a number of residents, contrary to instructions, emerged from their shelters prior to the completion of the attack and before the 'all clear' was sounded and began to fight the fires. This early and extensive anti-fire measure directly contributed to prevent the formation of the firestorm, the joining of the thousands of small fires together into the giant, oxygen- hungry furnace. This localized measure was spontaneous and not an organized effort and the city authorities and fire fighting officials were not enthusiastic in having untrained and unprotected civilians standing on precariously sloped medieval rooftops with a garden hose in one hand and a bucket of sand in the other fighting fires. However, it was just this effort that prevailed over the formation of the firestorm. The R.A.F. in time learned to suppress local fire fighting efforts, organized or not, by spacing the arrival of their bomber streams. This spacing served several functions, among them kept the attacking aircraft safely spaced apart, allowed the fires and bombs to break-open the structures and permit the firefighting equipment and firemen to appear. The later arrival of follow-up bombers caught the fire fighting brigades in the open and their destruction allowed the formation of the firestorm to progress unhindered, a clever, deadly and efficient calculation.

Frederick Taylor in his "Dresden" puts the question of what Germany was expecting out of World War II?:

> "This is perhaps the great, still-unanswered question about Germany and the German people between 1933 and 1945. With the vast material and spiritual riches of places like Dresden at your disposal, why place all that at risk by launching a ruthless, in large part genocidal, attack on the rest of Europe? Whatever the Nazi ideologues might say, Germany did not lack *lebensraum*. Did anyone really expect the world to fight back while wearing kid gloves, in order not to damage Germany's artistic treasures or kill German civilians?"[70]

This multiple approach to the conduct of the air war against Germany by the Allies was to have a significant effect. The Germans both at home and in the field could no longer expect the periodic respite to renew and refresh its armies and rebuild its homes and factories. The 'round-the-clock-bombing' by the Allies meant that the factories and shops supplying the fighting forces as well as the dwellings that housed the workers that worked in them were all disappearing in firestorms that were reducing the cities and towns of the Reich to ashes. The beauty and history of Germany's ancient cathedrals, monuments, buildings, towns, cities and universities were being lost forever. Eventually, the last link between the source of supply and the fighting front would be broken; that of the roads, bridges and canals by the new type of Allied aircraft, the long range fighter-bomber that, beginning in 1944 was to roam the Reich at will.[71] With this last link under attack, the final attempt at strangling the German war effort began.

The RAF and U.S.A.A.F.[72] raids on Hamburg, like the German raids on London three years earlier were more a political weapon than a military one. By that I mean they were terror raids, raids that had as much psychological intent as a military one. True, they were justified in that burning out huge sections of London, Hamburg and Berlin deprived workers of housing and whatever armaments plants located within them, but there was always the element of 'We got Hamburg last night, it's your city tomorrow night!' to

---

[70] *Dresden, Tuesday, February 13, 1945* by Frederick Taylor, Harper-Collins, 2004, p. 411.

[71] These machines were primarily the Lockheed P-38J, Republic P-47D and the North American P-51C and D model fighter aircraft.

[72] U.S.A.A.F. United States Army Air Force. This is what United States Air Force was known as before 1946.

keep the average resident preoccupied and sleepless. By the autumn of 1944 the Allied air attacks against targets of all types in the Reich became so numerous, one factory worker was heard to say, "Today we have finished rebuilding the plants and tomorrow the bombers will come again".[73]

De-Housing Germany

In addition to the widespread death, disruption and loss of productive capacity additional burdens were placed on the German economy. For example, according to German records injuries from aerial weapons moved from third largest source in 1942 to first largest source in 1944 and 1945. Personnel wounded by air action suffered, as a rule, multiple wounds and shock, resulting in longer periods of hospitalization and convalescence than wounds suffered from military action.[74]

After the war, the loss of habitable housing was crippling the Allied Occupation Authorities administration of defeated Germany. Douglas Botting adds the following:

> "Fifteen million urban Germans had fled from the cities to escape the bombings. Of those who remained, five million had been made homeless, and their number was more than doubled by the millions of refugees who had fled from the Russian Army in the east, or were still being expelled from western P o l a n d , Czechoslovakia and other parts of Eastern Europe. All of these people competed for what little shelter remained. The best of the undamaged houses were requisitioned by the Occupation armies, messes and offices, and their German inhabitants were turned out into the street. The majority of Germans in the smaller towns also were living in squalor and penury, often in condemned quarters, and usually in a state of severe overcrowding. In Germany as a

---

[73] As Britain did during the Blitz of 1940, Germany evacuated large numbers of children from the major cities threatened with air attack. Known as the *Kinderlandverschickung* or KLV program, from 1939 to the end of the war in 1945 approximately 3 million children and young people were sent to 5,000 camps in the rural areas. Ranging in size from 18 to 1,200 'campers' with the ostensible purpose of removing the future of the Reich from harm's way, the children were under the supervision and training of the Hitler Youth organization, and exposed to a wide range of disciplines from benign elementary education to strident and often brutal SS theology all wrapped in a tough physical fitness regimen. For a firsthand account of this tragic part of life in the Third Reich see *A Hitler Youth in Poland* by Jost Hermand, Northwestern University Press, 1997.

[74] *The United States Strategic Bombing Survey.*

whole, 10 people were now living where six had lived before, and some places were worse than others-in Dusseldorf the average living space was reduced to four square yards per person."[75]

Botting goes on to give an example of this loss of housing for one family:

"On your way from Dusseldorf to Aachen you come upon what is perhaps the most ruined town in Germany, Julich which is 93 per cent destroyed. We began to walk among the rubble. A minute later we came upon a stovepipe sticking out of the ground. It took us a little time to find the entrance to what was clearly some kind of underground dwelling, a narrow incline tunneled into the earth. The cellar consisted of two tiny rooms housing seven people. Six of them were in what I suppose must be called the sitting room, which was about the height of a man; they could just cram into it-the parents, two adult sons, and two younger children (the seventh was out). In the adjoining hole you could just make out a dim hell of wooden beds and dirty bedclothes. They had neither water nor lavatory; for excreting they used either a pail or, more commonly, the rubble outside. The clothes they stood up in seemed their only possessions." [76]

Even the secret anti-Hitler Jewish support groups were having trouble finding refuge for hiding their escaping charges. No one wanted to see any more city folks, it was always the same old story, there was already too many looking for housing after the bombing intensified in 1944.

In an attempt to mitigate the distress and discomfort of the displacement of German families from their bombed out homes, the German occupation government in France looted the homes of Jews of furnishings (Jews who had been arrested or fled the arrival of the German occupation). In Paris alone, furniture was removed (stolen is more accurate) from over 47,000 houses and apartments and shipped to Germany.[77]

The shortage of housing in industrial regions of Germany threw another task onto the already overburdened plate of the German Labor Front or

---

[75] *The Aftermath: Europe* by Douglas Botting, Time-Life, 1983, p. 51.

[76] Ibid.

[77] From the 1943 Rosenberg documents used as evidence provided at the Nuremberg Trials, 1946.

Deutsche Arbeitsfront (DAF). During the preparations for war, Germany had been ignoring its growing housing squeeze, especially in residential housing, and the growing numbers of volunteer foreign and slave laborers needed a place to live in Germany and her occupied nations. Add to this challenge the net reduction of available housing due to allied bombing and extreme measures were necessary.

Robert Ley, chief of the DAF, and already in charge of post-war housing plans, was now assigned the task of Reich Dwelling Commissioner or *Reichwohnungskommissar*. He was now tasked with attempting to either build or find housing for the growing labor force in Germany as well as the "de-housed" native Germans. With building materials all but impossible to obtain, especially for such non-war critical uses as dwellings, he instituted a campaign called the "Voluntary surrender of insufficiently used living quarters". The plan was as follows; the local representatives of the *DAF*, with a special local dwellings warden (*Ortsheimstattenwalter*) leading the way, supported by party representatives, ascertained which apartments or other living quarters were too big for their present inhabitants or otherwise inadequately used. They examined at the same time the possibilities of remodeling such quarters and proffered their advice to the owners who were, in this and other ways, "invited" to help the war workers and their families of "front fighters" to obtain a new home.

The use of terror as an instrument of war has never been a successful weapon; it is instructive that one recalls the lessons of the past: two in particular. When the Luftwaffe began its terror campaign over London that fateful summer of 1940, the population's will to resist was not reduced or broken; quite the contrary, it was hardened. A similar result occurred with the firestorm in Hamburg in May 1943, with the antagonists reversed. Terror as a weapon has seldom proved itself of any value. No war, battle or siege was ever decided based on terror alone, as the above examples illustrate. Terror itself has much in common with nuclear weapons; it is the fear of their use that constitutes their real value.

Before we leave the question of attacks on the major cities of Germany is the question of civilian order and discipline. It was noted that during the German Blitz in the summer of 1940, there was evidence on numerous occasions of widespread looting of the dead and property after bombing raids. Such instances of the breakdown of law, order, and decency were not limited to London and other allied cities visited by the war.

In Germany, as the Wehrmacht retreated before the onslaught of the victorious allies and before order could be re-established by the occupying forces, there was an almost universal tendency to loot anything that would provide shelter, protection and sustenance for the survivors of the ravaged areas of the remains of the Third Reich. A popular misconception is that the highly disciplined Germans with their great respect for law and order would never stoop to such primitive and base actions to maintain their lives; however, the opposite was the reality. The assumption that one nation would loot while another would refrain from such activity when both were faced with the same conditions and challenges is unrealistic and grossly misunderstands human nature.

All across war torn Europe, from Stalingrad in the east to London in the west, the looter was as much a part of the war as was the civilian, soldier, sailor, or airman. Left to their own devices and with the possibility of escaping punishment for theft, articles of value left unprotected will be taken or stolen, whoever is defining the term at the moment of its removal. No nation involved in the war was immune. In the closing days of the war in Vienna, Austria the prim and proper Viennese were observed looting anything that wasn't nailed down. In the western part of the Reich in Frankfurt-am-Main, the *gauleiter* (district leader) ordered the men to leave the city, a precaution not only to avoid destruction from street fighting, but to reduce the chances of looting. Many did leave, happy to avoid having to die for a losing cause, and some did not, sitting out the end in air raid bunkers and cellars. In between bouts of American artillery fire, the remaining residents went on a looting spree plundering the property of those who had left.[78]

In retrospect, as the Germans discovered after their bombing raids on London, Rotterdam and Stalingrad, un-targeted, mass carpet bombing of civilian residential districts did not cause the populace to revolt and sue for peace, it disrupted and delayed but did not materially reduce wartime weapons production. What the Allies fail to observe was their own reaction to being bombed: it will not have the desired result on the people being targeted. It has, in fact, the reverse affect, to harden their resolve, to support the powers that be, to bind them even closer together in their determination to not only survive but to fight back. The pre-war aerial

---

[78] *The U.S. Army in the Occupation of Germany 1944-1946*, Earl F. Ziemke, Center of Military History, United States Army, Washington, D.C., 1990.

bombing theories came to be just that, theories. There was no input into the bomb load/bomb mix/number of aircraft equation of the psychological aspect of being bombed. There could not be, with the exception of the air raid on Guernica during the 1936-1939 Spanish civil war, there was no other model to use to evaluate this type of warfare.

Arbiter, the Search for Labor

A growing concern for average Germans, especially in the later war years were the fate of loved ones in the Wehrmacht and the availability of food and housing, especially during the colder months. Later would come concerns over order and discipline on the home front, especially with the growing presence of millions of 'guest' laborers, which in smaller towns and villages occasionally outnumbered the local German population. As the military situation deteriorated for Germany, and as more and more industries that were exempt from military conscription were required to provide recruits, the forced use of foreign, 'guest', and slave laborers increased and, as the Allies closed in on Germany from the east and west, an uprising by these workers was a growing worry.

The growth in the number of these workers reflects the all-encompassing nature of the war as it overwhelmed Germany. For example, in 1936 only 220,192 foreign or *gastarbiter* workers were registered in Germany; in 1937 - 265,689; 1938 - 375,078; 1939 - 939,386; 1941 - 3,506,000, 1942 - 4,665,000; 1944 - 7,615,970.

The shortage of labor was nothing new to the Reich and was in existence before the war. As early as 1936, the foreign labor portion of the German agriculture sector was at 25% and rose to 43% a year later. By March 1944 there were some 5 million[79] foreign workers in Germany, more than 800,000 in Berlin alone, from some 26 countries, releasing an equivalent number of German men to fight on the Eastern and Italian fronts. In the Spring of 1939 the German civilian labor force was a little more than 39 million, by the same time in 1945 it was approximately 28 million.

As the demand for labor for the war industries grew, the conspicuous exemption of party workers from both the military draft and war work created a growing animosity. In December 1942, Bormann arranged a secret deal with the military that party officials born after 1900 would be

---

[79] *The Oxford Companion to World War II* gives this figure as 7,126,000 (Oxford University Press, 1995).

given a six month period of service at the front after which they would
be returned to party duties, regardless the dire situation of the nation,
party activities were paramount to anything else and everything else
was secondary.

"The 1941 campaign and the winter stalemate had so depleted
German manpower reserves that new sources had to be tapped.
This meant that thousands of workers would have to be drawn
from war industry and agriculture, while at the same time the
output of the armaments industry had not only to be maintained
but also sharply increased to make good the enormous material
losses of the fall and winter. To replace the workers thus lost to
industry, Hitler ordered the integration of 6,000,000 workers
from the occupied countries into the German economy, of which
1,600,000 were to come from the east, 1,200,000 of these from
the Ukraine. Fritz Sauckel, Plenipotentiary for the Allocation
of Labor under the Four-Year Plan, was placed in charge of
the program, with the authority to issue instructions to all top
authorities in the Reich and in the occupied territories. All
prisoners of war were to be integrated into the armament and
nutrition industries, and additional workers were brought in from
the occupied countries. As far as possible these civilian workers
were to be recruited on a voluntary basis. If quotas could not be
filled in this manner, a program of forced labor 'in its severest
form' would be instituted. In addition to this manpower for
industry, 400,000 to 500,000 young girls were to be sent from
the east for domestic duties in German homes. The keynote for
the treatment of these workers was struck in Sauckel's original
program. They were to be 'fed, sheltered and treated in such a
way as to exploit them to the highest possible extent at the lowest
conceivable degree of expenditure'".[80]

"Foreign workers were divided into four main categories. First
there were the 'volunteers', mostly from Western and Northern
Europe, who were free to live out of barracks and move around
the city as they pleased during their time off. Next came the
forced laborers from all over Western Europe, followed by the

---

[80] *The Soviet Partisan Movement 1941-1944,* by Edgar M. Howell, Department of the army
Pamphlet, No. 20-244, August 1956.

Ostarbeiter, workers conscripted from Eastern Europe in general and from Poland in particular -- more than half of all civilian foreign workers in Germany were Poles, who wore the letter 'P' sewn on to their clothes. These workers were confined to barracks and camps, and were marched to and from work each day."

The transport of the *Ostarbeiter* to Germany was also conducted with the least possible expenditure. The request by *Reichminister* Sauckel for more human transport conditions to include uncrowded wagons, food and water and heating in winter went unheeded. An organization set up under a Dr. Otto Braeutigam under Rosenberg's ministry known as the central relief agency for the eastern workers or the *Zentralstelle Ost* (ZAVO) reported that as many as 5 percent of the eastern laborers arriving in the Reich were in such poor condition that they were sent to a special return camp in Berlin-Blankenfelde for return to Russia.[81]

At the bottom of the heap were Soviet prisoners of war, who were kept strictly segregated. Non-officer prisoners from other countries were made to work, but in jobs that were not directly connected with the German war effort, in accordance with the Geneva Convention. Soviet prisoners, officers and men enjoyed no such protection. They were given the heaviest, dirtiest and most dangerous tasks, for example in the armaments industry, mines and steelworks, where they were frequently worked to death.

Contact with workers from Western Europe was frowned upon, however contact with workers from Eastern Europe, primarily Poles and Russians was strictly forbidden. German workers were instructed to keep a clear distance from the Poles, reminding them that the mixing of Polish and German blood was a racial crime; that those who treated them as friends were putting their own fellow countrymen on the same level as alien races, and that it is a fact established by experience that any soft treatment weakens their will to work. Government authorities were especially incensed about the fraternization between French *gastarbiter* and German women, who seemed to have a weakness to their amorous advances.

In the early days of the war when a German victory seemed imminent there was some eagerness for going to work in Germany, but as the war went on and the losses mounted and when word of the declining standard of

---

[81] *The House Built On Sand, The Conflicts of German Policy In Russia 1939 - 1945* by Gerald Reitlinger, Viking, 1960, pp.268-269.

living and the increasingly harsh measures used to increase war production in Germany made its way back to their home countries, combined with poor living conditions and harsh treatment, the mood changed and most foreigners came to find that going to work in Germany was the same as a death sentence.

> "The campaign stressed many supposed benefits of working in the Reich. One was simply 'getting to know Germany.' *Reichkommissar* Koch promised that those working there (as well as those migrating to southern Ukraine for agricultural work) would be the first to receive land in Ukraine once the time was ripe for land distribution. While in Germany, the workers would earn a good wage and receive free housing and medical care. Each month, part of their wages would be deposited in a personal savings account, which they could access on their return. Dependent relatives in Ukraine would receive financial support as well. Moreover, the workers would learn skills that would later secure them good jobs back home."[82]

The campaign to recruit workers in the east, especially in Ukraine was mildly successful, as the German civil authorities induced the Orthodox Church leaders to promote the effort and lend it credibility. However as the Germans suffered reverses in the field, especially after their failure at Stalingrad, the pool of volunteers to work in Germany dried up. This reluctance had a number of sources, among them the fear that Germany would now not win the war and the return of the Soviets and possible repercussions. In addition, there were the increasingly harsh and cruel methods of 'recruiting' and the negative reports from injured or otherwise incapacitated workers from Germany.

The German dragnet for labor became wide and indiscriminate. Of interest is the following report from several of the labor camps in Berlin in 1943 regarding the treatment of the *Ostarbeiter*:

> "Despite the official rations *Ostarbeiter* are entitled to, it has been reliably established that the meals in the camps are as follows: In the morning, half a liter (a little more than a pint) of turnip soup. At lunchtime, on the worksite, one liter of turnip

---

[82] *Harvest of Despair*, pp 253-254.

soup. At night, one liter of turnip soup. Also the Ostarbeiter are given 300 gr. (about 10 oz.) of bread per day. In addition, they receive, per week, 50 to 75 gr. (about 1.8 oz.) of margarine, about 25 oz. of meat or meat products, which are distributed or withheld according to the whim of the camp leader. Large amounts of these rations get corruptly distributed. But the biggest scourge in the camps is tuberculosis, which is spreading rapidly among minors … sick workers are not even isolated … sick workers are forced to remain at work by beatings. I am not aware of the reason why the German authorities imported a large number of children from the Eastern Territories. It is a fact, however, *that many children between the ages of 4 and 15 are in the camps, and that they have neither parents nor relatives in Germany. The food they receive is the same turnip soup the adults receive.*" (Italics added for emphasis)[83]

With the large numbers of slave laborers working in Germany by 1943 it was possible to develop a typical *Ostarbeiter* profile, and the result is quite surprising. The typical worker in Germany from the east was an 18 year old schoolgirl from Kiev. This startling result is because of the large number of females imported into Germany to perform domestic duties in German households, especially the women from Russia because of their low cost.

The subject of the employment of German women in the labor markets, especially in the war industries, was an example of confused Nazi management policy. Hitler's prudish standards as they related to women continued to prohibit the Reich's labor organizations in recruiting them in any labor activity outside of traditional women's occupations. The inconsistency in the applications of these prohibitions is demonstrated by his willingness to import hundreds of thousands of Polish and Ukrainian women and girls for labor to free German women from their domestic chores, then imposed a year-long duty requirement in the Women's Labor Service the *Deutscher Frauenarbeitsdienst*. Germany could have increased its labor pool by 20 to 40 percent by permitting the entry of women.

By 1944 the German economy had no alternative to the *Auslandereinsatz* (employment of foreigners). It was this large influx of cheap or free labor that enabled the German armaments industries to surge to record production that same year.

---

[83] *The Oxford Companion of World War II*, Oxford University Press, Oxford, England, 1995, p. 461.

The sectors utilizing these laborers reflect those that were either most easily replaced in the German economy or reflected the most arduous and dangerous jobs. For example, agriculture used 2,747,238, metals 1,691,329, construction 478,057 and transport 378,027. It requires little imagination to realize that had not Germany secured this supplemental workforce the war effort would have been severely impacted and the output of farm and factory alike greatly reduced. These workers accounted for some 40% of the nation's workforce and in some of the armaments plants foreign workers made up 90% of the work force.

But while these workers aided the war effort, it was not without cost. With the employment of foreign workers inside the Reich rapidly growing and as many of them, especially from Poland and Russia had to be segregated from the native Germans, a nationwide system of containment was established. At one time as many as 20,000 camps were in existence (500 in Berlin alone), from local street corner camps to military sized barrack containments for the largest arms manufacturers. Added to the cost and time spent constructing these camps was the number of Germans involved in their administration, at the peak some 500,000 were involved in the direction, management and supervision of the foreign and slave workers.

In addition to the utilization of foreign labor in the German war and domestic economy there was the use of Allied prisoners of war. Whether in compliance with the provisions of the Geneva Convention or not, the number of these captured soldiers and airmen grew. Initially just a modest 348,000 in 1940, the number grew to the astonishing number of 1,831,000 by 1944.

The nations that provided these workers, voluntary or not, also reflect the eastern trend as providers of cheap or slave labor. With the exception of France, the majority of foreign labor was located east of Germany, with the Soviet Union, Poland and Czechoslovakia, in that order, providing the bulk. Indeed, the large populations of these nations had a direct bearing on the numbers. For example in 1944 the Soviet Union provided 2,758,970, Poland 1,688,080 and Czechoslovakia 280,000.

A complicating factor in procuring labor from the East was that two competing organizations were draining the same labor pool, the Plenipotentiary for Labor Recruitment under Fritz Sauckel and the Economic Staff East and the powerful *Reichskommissar* for the Ukraine, Erich Koch. Koch was primarily interested in preserving the labor in the Ukraine to meet the increasing demands for Ukrainian wheat and other grains. The competing organizations are another example of the multi-jurisdictional confusion, intentionally or not, that typified Nazi occupation policy.[84]

Despite these significant numbers, the need for labor grew and by 1944 drastic methods were used. The heavy-handed manner in which the Germans implemented their perverse racial and ethnic policies in the East was clearly demonstrated by the manner in which foreign labor was 'recruited'. Although volunteers were originally called for, almost immediately local administrations were put under considerable pressure to fill minimum quotas as quickly as possible. This led to numerous abuses almost from the start. Both male and female workers were literally pulled from their beds or picked off the streets and assembled without being allowed to pack clothing, blankets or food. Families were indiscriminately split up. Many were marched long distances in severe weather, and then crowded into cattle cars and locked in without adequate provision for feeding or sanitation. Many, drafted without regard for physical qualifications and unfit for labor services from the beginning were returned from the Reich in deplorable condition. Such a practice had a very depressing effect on the morale of both the drafted workers and the population left behind. This feeling was intensified by the spectacle of public beatings and the burning of whole villages for failure to comply with demands for filled labor quotas. Families were held in ransom for conscripted workers who escaped to the forests. The entire population became widely stirred up and quickly came to regard the transports to the Reich as similar to exile by the Soviets to Siberia. Fear soon gripped large areas of the Ukraine and numbers of the natives left their villages for the forest country seeking the protection of the partisans, greatly increasing and strengthening these bands. Soviet propaganda gave wide play to the whole program and the open German substantiation had an almost immediately visible effect of cutting volunteering to near zero and increasing the powers of resistance of both the Russian Army and the irregulars, in particular the Partisans.

The average German citizen's fear of internal revolt or uprising by the foreign slave workers and allied prisoners of war was not unfounded. In 1943 alone the precursor to the *Volksstrum*, the *Stadt und Lanwacht*

---

[84] By 1943 there were the following organizations and ministries dealing with labor in Germany: General Plenipotentiary for the Employment of Labor (Sauckel); the Ministry of Labor (Seldte); the Labor Front (Ley) or the Reich Labor Service (Hierl).

captured 6,556 prisoners of war (both escaped from prisoner of war camps and airmen shot down over the Reich), 12,346 foreign workers that did not report for work and 1,345 criminals.

Despite the millions that were dispatched from the east to work in Germany, their value would never be a great as the volunteer workers from other nations, especially the West. The fact that they were forced and slave labor was reflected in their productivity, which was significantly lower than the prevailing standing in a given industry. Anti-Slavic attitudes, poor and insufficient food, poor housing and almost non-existent medical care all contributed this expensive, ambitious and inhuman program.

Nazi Germany, the Organized Life

One aspect of the war with Germany that some may not appreciate or realize was the extensive nature of the German government's regulation, organization and militarization of everyday life for the average German before and during the war. In the attempt to create a true peoples community or *volksgemeinshaft* the Nazis spared no effort or expense. To insure compliance and obedience, not a difficult chore for most Germans, the government literally organized every aspect of public and most private functions of the people. There were at least sixty-four distinct uniformed organizations in Hitler's Germany, ranging from nationwide bodies such as the *Reichsarbeitdienst* (National Labor Service) and the National Railway Service through volunteer organizations such as the German Red Cross, down to specialized groupings such as the *Deutschen Falkenorden* and the *Deutscher Jagerschaft*, organizations responsible for falconry and hunting and the national stud farms in East and West Prussia, officials of which had their own unique rank insignia.

To cite a few examples of this militarization, the employees of most government jobs wore military styled uniforms, from ministerial officials such as Propaganda Minister Joseph Goebbels, to political organizations such as the Nazi party's *Sturm Abteilung* or Storm detachments, the SA. Children were included as well; boys from ages 10 to 14 wore the uniform of the *Deutsche Jungvolk* and later that of the militarized boy scouts, the *Hitler Jugend* (Hitler Youth, ages 14 to 18). Girls joined the *Jungmadel* (Young Maidens) and the *Bund Deutscher Madel* (League of German Girls) in the same age groups. The uniforms these children wore were as detailed and ornamented as those of the armed forces, complete with rank badges, regional (*Gau*) and specialist insignia, anniversary clasps and winter and summer weight versions. There were a number of veteran's organizations, all with their own insignia; a women's organization, the *Nationalsozialist-Frauenschaft*; and the *Lehrerbund*, the teacher's organization.[85] There were uniforms for the *Ostministerium*, the branch of government that oversaw the conquered Eastern territories, the *Reicharbeitsdienst*, the government labor service, the *Nationalsozialistches Kraftfahr Korps* (NSKK) the government transport service, the *Nationalsozialistches Fligerkorps*, the national flying organization, the *Gauwerksscharfuhrer*, the labor front Gau works leader, the *Reichnahrstand*, the farmers league, the railways, the tram drivers, an organization known as the *Reichbund Deutscher Kleingartner* or National League of German Allotment Growers or small gardeners, even the senior members of the Supreme Court had a military styled uniform and officers cap with their own unique *Reichsadler* or national eagle.[86] The list goes on and on, even retired civilian engineers and specialists that volunteered to return to work in industry as technical consultants, known as *TeNo's* for *Technische Nothilfe*, had their own uniform, frequently with their own dress dagger! These organizations, known as *wehermachtsgefolge* or armed forces auxiliaries were not part of the armed forces, but served such an important support role that they were given protection under the Geneva Convention and/or militarized.[87]

In addition to these organizations, there were frequently sports clubs attached, complete with rank badges, pins, armbands, shoulder boards, ribbons, caps, hats, berets and, of course, the ubiquitous steel helmet; some organizations used leather ones.

The list of political, sports and social organizations is truly dizzying in its comprehensiveness. It becomes hard to find a portion of German society from 1933 to 1945 that was not identified by a military styled uniform of some kind, which just may be the point of it all: a comprehensive all encompassing way of life, a new way of life. In the study of group dynamics

---

[85] Dr. Alfred Vagts in his *Hitler's Second Army* (Infantry Journal, Washington, D.C., 1943 p. 3) states "Early in 1939 it was estimated by the association of all German tailors that every third German at that time wore a uniform, either of the Army or of some Nazi society."

[86] For an informative and colorful guide to German military and NSDAP insignia and uniforms see *German Insignia of World War II* edited by Chris Bishop and Adam Warner, Chartwell Books, Inc. , 2002.

[87] See *Organized Labor of the Reich* for an extensive selection of German labor organizations and their documents, uniforms, awards and badges.

in psychology, individuals seeking personal identity frequently identify with certain groups. To clearly establish an identity, one must make these groups distinct, and a uniform accomplishes this task quite well. The use of military features in the design of the uniform, emphasis on regimentation, rank, position, all appealed to the German preference for order and stability and contributes to the subconscious preparation for supporting or entering armed military service. No other nation seems to have grasped the symbolic importance of the uniform in society to garner the dedication, bonding, and herd mentality not only in solidifying its power over the populace but to earn the love and sense of belonging of the people in doing so. In a nation like Germany, where love of order is a national mania,[88] the uniform was the reminder that one was a part of the national group, a contributor to the cause, a talisman to show the entire world where one's allegiance lies. With a nation almost completely garbed in uniforms, the uniform became a visual reminder of where the power lies and the national duty that was required by everyone. In short, the entire nation was in preparation for a major sacrifice of some kind, a girding of the national loins, a showdown with destiny, the *Gotterdammerung* of the Nazi world.

National And Domestic Security

Germany, like Russia, had its security services to insure domestic compliance and the Nazi's hold on power. The most famous of these organizations was the state within a state, the SS or *Schutz Staffel*. Under Heinrich Himmler, its Reich Central Security Department or *Reichssicherheitshauptamt* (RSHA) under the command of *Obergruppenfuhrer* Reinhard Heydrich had the most impact on the average German. Four organizations under the RSHA were charged with security; the Secret State Police or *Geheime Staatspolizei*, *Gestapo* for short; the *Kriminal Polizei* or *Kripo*; the External *Sicherheitsdienst* or *Ausland* SD intelligence department, and the *Inland* SD for Internal intelligence. These four organizations provided intelligence information to the German leadership and exercised control of the domestic population through appeals to love of country and native loyalty or, conversely, by fear and force.[89]

---

[88] In a poll taken after the war, the respondents were asked to list the three biggest worries they had about life in the nation. The number one worry was "lack of public order".

[89] As mentioned earlier, these were the organizations providing written reports on the health and welfare of the German civil population during the war and were avidly read by the Nazi leadership.

The *Gestapo* had no restrictions as to its arrest powers and maintained an army of informers and spies to be its eyes and ears in every corner of Germany. For example, each apartment building had its *Gestapo* informer who reported any unusual or suspect activity. In 1939 it had approximately 20,000 spies and agents and by mid-1943 over 100,000. The fear of *Gestapo* attention alone was enough to maintain a largely compliant populace right up until the closing days of the war. Whether communist or Nazi, the net effect of these security organizations was the same, control over all aspects of life in Germany and Russia; and later the occupied and conquered countries through fear and intimidation.

Perhaps the best example of Nazi philosophy attempting to shape the future of the German family was Himmler's SS program for increasing the number and Aryan quality of German children. Known as the *Lebensborn* or Spring of Life program, or formally, the *Lebensborn Eingetragener Verein* organization, starting in 1935 this was a series of birthing 'homes' that pregnant women could apply for having their children born there. There were from ten to thirteen homes established throughout Germany staffed by nine to twenty-two nurses. The quality of life was very good at the homes, frequently better than the living standards of their parent's or their own family homes. The homes themselves were obtained from a number of sources but large estates expropriated or 'donated' from wealthy Jews was the usual source. The newborn child was then cared for by the *Lebensborn* organization, which supervised the adoption of the child by approved SS or Aryan families. Existing records indicate the number of these children born in Lebensborn homes were relatively few, no more than 7,500 to 8,000. In addition to the domestic program, Himmler authorized the forced removal, or kidnapping, of children in occupied countries if they were determined to be of Aryan stock. As many as 200,000 to 250,000 children were abducted from their parents and brought to Germany. Tragically, very few, from 25,000 to 40,000 were ever returned to their native countries or found their way home.[90]

A little known horror of the *Lebensborn* program, largely overlooked because of the extermination of adults in the death camps, was the killing of some of these abducted children. Children that were older or resisted Germanisation (or *eindeutschung*) were put to death at the Kalish

---

[90] Bleuel, H. P. *Das saubere Reich: Theorie und Praxis des sittlichen Lebens im Dritten Reich*, Bern u. a. 1972, S. 192.

concentration camp in Poland. Himmler thought that leaving these children of Aryan stock with their families would be such a threat to the future of the Reich they were better dead. Such was the program by which New World Order was going to pursue to insure the 'purity' of the New Europe.

The New German Way Of Life

The advent of the *National Sozialistische Deutscher Arbiter Parti* (NSDAP) a wing of the National Socialist German Workers Party, also known as the Nazis was for many thousands of Germans a way of life. So encompassing, so completely dominating many aspects of everyday life had the Party become that many Germans consciously or not traded some or all of their own identity and adopted that of the NSDAP as their new one. As discussed above, so much of German life was organized, all facets of public and private life, that it was almost impossible to escape the intrusion of some aspect of the Party.

At the very highest ranks of the Nazi structure were the 'true believers'; this is the very top tier of German leadership, Hitler, Bormann, Hess, Goebbels, Goering, Himmler and others. At lower levels of government, state and regional (*Gau*) the loyalty of officials and party members was just as fervent and dedicated. So closely had Hitler become identified with Germany, the Germans and the Party it is almost impossible to separate one from the other. In the years of the Third Reich, many Germans combined all three persona and became one with the nation.

What the Nazis created was a new form of government best described as a political religion, National Socialism. This new political phenomenon, these 'religions', which includes communism, deal with profound layers of human experience, most often suffering. These 'see all', 'know all', and 'control all' societies were a once-upon-a-time unfulfilled dream of various theoretical utopianists. However, the arrival of the technological state enabled these new 'theorists', Hitler, Rosenberg, Stalin, Lenin and Marx, to name the most pertinent to our examination, to move from the theoretical to the feasible. To unite the nation, each year, the Party organized a themed gathering or rally somewhere in Germany, usually at a politically significant site closely connected with the history of the movement. The appreciation of the many sacrifices that were asked by the Party and 'der Fuehrer' was demonstrated at these rallies. These rallies were massive events requiring many months preparation and planning, and costing hundreds of thousands of scarce marks. Combining theater, church, worship, entertainment, physical and youth indoctrination and spectacle, the annual rallies brought all elements of the German 'family' together in a classless, mainly outdoor communion. This was the church service; the Mass, the meetinghouse even of the Party. The Party did not miss any opportunity to demonstrate the strength and splendor of National Socialism.

Loyalty to Hitler and the party was for some total. In the last days of the Reich as the Allies closed into the heart of Germany, many party functionaries committed suicide rather than allow themselves to be captured. So completely Nazified had some in the very top become that not only would they kill themselves, but the in case of Goebbels, he had his six children poisoned and he and his wife had themselves shot by SS guards.

So what was daily life like in Nazi Germany? As in most other things, it depends. It depended upon who you were, where you lived, how old you were, what you did for a living, what religion you practiced, how loyal and patriotic you were, and countless other valuations and variations. Perhaps one can understand the Nazi rise to power in Germany using the following analogy.

The setting is the depression ridden 1930's in the United States. Imagine, if you will, if the head of one of the New York mafia families ran for and won election to the Presidency of the US. Everyone likes the 'can do' energy of the mafia, the ability to break the log jams in government, eliminating crime, making the dollar worth something, appointing capable people with a 'get the job done' practicality, finding people a good paying job and making the trains run on time. Initially, polite society was embarrassed by the crude behavior, the bullyboy excesses of the street fighting mob, and later a little worried about the more sinister 'hit' men.

The Germans, unlike most Americans, were willing to give up much personal freedom for domestic calm and strict observance of law and order. They are used to and expect their government to 'take care' of them, e.g. health care, unemployment insurance and similar social programs, subsidized or government provided day care, etc. In return for this benevolent parental government they are expected to be loyal, faithful, and obey.

When things became most uneasy, as in the treatment of the Jews and the restrictions on the church, it was too late to voice protests and to do so was considered unpatriotic, illegal and, even worse, un-German. Add book burning and, in comparison with what else was going on, it was the preferred method of deportment to understand that what you were seeing and experiencing was your German governments efforts to make a better Germany for you by ridding it of these degenerate and burdensome peoples; finding room for a 'new Germany'; eliminating perverted art and entertainment forms and other similar 'improvements'. So, one could always find an 'approved' book to read, an 'approved' composer to listen to and an 'approved' movie to watch. After what the Germans went through during the end of the Great War and the global depression, a full dinner plate, a steady job and regular pay was more than enough for most to ignore what was happening down the street.

Chapter Four:
The Russian
Home Front

"...The Russians saved Western civilization in
the thirteenth century by taking the brunt of the
Mongol onslaught. And look what it cost us!"

Russian history student, 1981

This is the companion chapter to the previous one, with the subject changing to Russia. How was the communist state created? Who were the principle figures and personalities? What were the Russian people like? Who were they? What was life like under German occupation? How was the government organized? What was its impact, demands and requirements of the average Russian? Who was Stalin and what was he like? What were the state security organs, how did they operate and what did they do? The Russian war economy will be examined at length and the impact of the Allied Lend-Lease deliveries will be examined as well.

Brave New World

By the date of its invasion by Germany in June 1941, the Union of Soviet Socialist Republics was almost 24 years old and was still feeling the effects of its violent birth in October 1917. With a desire to kill 'the infant while still in its cradle' at the end of the Great War several western nations attacked or supported an attack on the new nation, including the United States, Britain, Finland and Czechoslovakia to rid the western democracies of the communist threat. The effort required by the new government to defend itself, suppress internal dissent and eliminate the remnants of the former government was great and exhausting; it was not until the early1920's when, with the exception of a few distant regions in the far east, the Communist Party firmly established itself, from the Polish border to the Pacific ocean, 8,250,000 square miles, 11 time zones and 6,000 miles across.

By the mid 1930's the U.S.S.R. was a nation in the throes of rapid industrialization. The Communist Party was determined to bring to this giant, largely agricultural nation, its promise of peace, bread and land. Ruling a land rich in natural resources, the Party began to push the new state into the family of industrialized nations, a titanic effort that was succeeding, after a fashion. This land, then around 100 million people, occupies the largest landmass on the planet. The number of nations, peoples, languages and religions dwarfed every other.

The initial challenge to the Party was to meld these disparate groups into a coherent nation. The difficulty was that a number of them, especially the southern and central Asian Islamic regions and the three northern Baltic nations had no interest in joining the new atheistic Communist Soviet Union, which led to terrible bloodletting as the government's main weapon; the new Russian Army and the Party security units fought, shot, starved, banished and imprisoned the recalcitrant nations and peoples into line.

Most of the country, especially the lands east of the Urals were undeveloped and unsettled, but teemed with natural resources: timber, gold, oil, tin, aluminum, natural gas, diamonds and coal to name the most plentiful and valuable. It was not unusual for someone traveling in this giant area not to see another human for weeks. The drive to industrialize began under the Czar but really took off under the communists, using a series of "5 Year (economic) Plans" to bring this about. The transition from a farm economy to a factory economy was not easy. Forced relocations of workers either to or from industrial and farm occupations was common, and the drive to collectivization caused much disruption to long established lifestyles, beliefs, traditions and systems; the crushing of the *Kulak* peasants in the Ukraine is but one example, however extreme.

Despite the richness of the natural bounty, poor management, bureaucratic bungling, and simply bad decision-making caused much of the produce of the farms and products of the factories and mines to be wasted. For example, a shortage of bags for the potato crop at harvest caused much of it to be left on the ground to rot; irregular electricity service at a collective dairy caused the milking machinery to stop and thousands of gallons of milk to be lost and livestock injured; the wrong kind or wrong amount of seed corn was shipped to a collective farm in the Ukraine and planting was held up until the correct seed was received and planted, resulting in most of the crop being lost due to frost by the late planting, the arrival of winter and the late harvest, especially a problem in this cold region.

With some of the richest soils in the world, the famous *Chernozem* soils in particular, that stretch from the Ukraine to beyond the Urals,[91] with proper management the Soviets could have been an exporter of foodstuffs, energy, and all manner of finished goods instead of being dependent on foreign imports and capital. The waste and inefficiency of the Soviet economy has become the stuff of legend and was an excellent example how not to run a country. The loss of much of this bounty meant that long lines formed at food stores in cities, people in towns and villages went hungry, or were poorly clothed and shod and the quality of life in general was less than it could have been. It was once said that several small nations could live off the waste that the Soviet system in Russia generated, for when it came to resources, the nation wanted for nothing. Efficiency was never a significant trait of Russia or communism or socialism, and Russia in the 1930s and 40s was an excellent example.

At the bottom of Soviet life was the peasant, the landless farmer, beneath the *Kulak* class. Most lived in various levels of poverty, having the barest necessities of life. In his "Harvest of Despair" Karel Berkhoff describes a

---

[91] *USSR Agriculture Atlas*, Central Intelligence Agency, 1974.

series of visits in the Ukraine by Hans Koch, Wehrmacht *Fremde Heere Ost* (OKH's intelligence service for the Eastern Front) officer and had the following to say about the peasants he saw there:

> "Hans Koch met about six hundred village elders within two months that fall (1941). None of them he considered better dressed than the poorest vagrant in Germany. Most "Soviet" peasants wore rags, and the lucky owners of shoes still tended to go barefoot so as to save them for the fall and winter. In general, the peasants owned almost nothing. "Over and over," Koch found, "the impoverished   population visits the battlefields to look for a piece of belt, a discarded ammunition holder, a piece of cloth. The houses of Jews who fled (or were murdered) are ransacked for remaining goods or clothes as if by termites. A single worthless scrap or utensil is very rare here." Once in a peasant family's place, Koch lit his kerosene lamp. The woman of the house whispered to her grown-up daughter, "I haven't seen such a lamp since my wedding." Peasants used what they called "Stalin's lightning": a can or exploded artillery shell filled with a piece of linen and any kind of fuel. Standing near such a lamp for more than a few minutes was rather risky." [92]

The disappearance of the Soviet cooperative farm manager with the arrival of the German occupiers was to have a direct impact on farm and garden management. Many years under the communist system had all but robbed the individual of any independent thought or enterprise:

> "In some regions harvesting had already started on a Soviet order and simply continued during and after the Germans arrived. Some of these harvesters dressed in black, so as to be less visible to Soviet planes that attacked the fields. But in the many localities where no Soviet order to harvest had been issued, hardly anybody took the initiative. Itinerant *Banderites* found that even though the crops were ripe, the peasants did not get to work. "This was the case wherever we went. The reason for this stagnation was that there was nobody to 'order.'" The Germans also found that the peasants were "generally willing to work" but awaited orders. This inaction indicated the influence

---

[92] *Harvest of Despair*, p. 116.

of the Soviet system, under which nobody took responsibility for anything out of a fear of being denounced as a saboteur. Thus the harvest in Dnieper Ukraine started late in 1941 and generally only after *Banderites* or Germans asked for it. If the Ukrainian peasants would not get to work, the Wehrmacht told them in a posted announcement, "you and your family will go hungry." Another poster warned that "laziness" would bring "only famine and poverty."[93]

The terrible waste and mismanagement was carefully shielded from Western eyes and the Russian people themselves, although it was widely suspected. The system of central planning was based on attaining production goals, not necessarily meeting quality standards.[94] The best of the production went to the Party leadership and the upper portion of Soviet society and the mass of the people had to make do with shoddy, poor quality goods that remained, when they were available. Complaints were not well received as complainers were considered an enemy of the state and punishment was sure to follow. This could be in the form of loss of access to better housing, schools, preferred food and luxuries and if the complainer persisted in his or her annoyances, a visit to the Gulag was almost certain.

However, life at the lowest levels of Russian society did improve slightly if only because of German occupation management or the lack of it. Food production was higher and the distribution of it more market oriented, based on traditional supply and demand forces. The private garden plots were expanded and the incentives of profit and sufficiency returned. However, this was to be a short lived scenario as soon as the fortunes of war shifted back to the Russian forces, the specter of the return to Soviet methods and control loomed.

Ivan and Svetlana

As so little is known in the West about the ordinary citizen of Stalinist Russia as compared to his extensively examined counterpart in Germany it is appropriate to take a moment here and examine in detail their lives and see what made them Russian.

---

[93] Ibid, p. 119.

[94] Lenin himself said that that "...in the end productivity is the most important single factor in the victory of (the) new economic structure. Plan fulfillment is of paramount importance."

This lack of knowledge of life in the U.S.S.R. in the 1930's and early war years is because of the intense insularity that was life in this giant nation. The control of all forms of information, foreign travel, and especially foreign visitors by the government meant that any and all information originated in controlled and prepared form from a central source, and that it was carefully shaped and molded to fit into the ongoing dogmatic world constructed by Stalin and his propaganda organs.[95]

The source of most official Soviet information was the two governmental organizations *Tass* for press releases, articles and news within the USSR and *Novosti* which provided the same for the foreign press. Due to official policy that kept the nation cut off from the free flow of news and information from the rest of the world, Novosti correspondents compiled reviews of foreign news for official review in Moscow to determine its suitability for domestic consumption. The two most prominent domestic newspapers in the USSR were *Izvestia* (Truth) and *Pravda* (Peace) for the civilian public and *Krasnaya Zvezda* (Red Star) for the military.

The average Russian knew very little of the outside world, especially those born from the mid-1920's and later. They were educated in a state system that fed them a never-ending stream of propaganda; that their nation was surrounded by "capitalists" with enemies all around as well as within. Their comforts were few, there were never enough of even the basics, they were managed by a bloated centralized government, whose only concern was to protect the Party and that meant pouring almost limitless resources into the armed forces.

> "There was still widespread hardship, to say nothing of resentment of the collectives and the harsh working conditions. The soldiers who would fight at Stalingrad and Kursk were born into a Soviet system and knew no other. Though older people might never be reconciled to the new world, and younger ones might joke and make cynical remarks, the language and priorities of Soviet Communism provided the war generation with the only mental world they knew, not least because the

[95] The lack of information of life in everyday U.S.S.R. during the first half of the 20th century, and especially during the Stalin period, is slowly ending. For an excellent description of private life during this period see *The Whisperers, Private life in Stalin's Russia* by Orlando Figes, Metropolitan Books, Henry Holt and Company, New York, 2007.

alternatives were excluded. Even the offspring of peasants, the most resentful section of the population, had no opportunity to develop a different political outlook, or at least not on a public scale. Children's training began the moment they stepped through the door of nursery school. As future Soviet citizens, they would start to learn about the revolution as soon as they could pick out the Cyrillic letters forming Stalin's name. Where once their grandparents had chorused extracts from the Psalms, these children learned lessons on the triumphs of electrification, science and Communist morality. They also learned to be grateful that their elementary schools existed in the first place, for it was the Soviet regime, they were told, that cared to cultivate their literacy." [96]

Take for example the experience of one Kirill Kirillovich, an officer in training, in the late 1930's:

"...Students attended the usual classes, but there were extra sessions in the evenings and at weekends, when they were sent on exercises. Most children did that kind of thing, Kirill explained, remembering the militaristic spirit of the 1930's, but we did more of it. Mainly training with rifles. They also worked particularly hard at mathematics and at German, as if in conscious preparation for the war that everyone expected they would have to fight. We knew it was coming, Kirill confirmed. Every newspaper and wall poster warned Stalin's people about Fascism, and so did every broadcast speech that talked about the world. We saw the films. There was one I remember, the title was something like 'Professor Mamlok.' It was about what people would suffer under Fascism. It told us exactly what Hitler would do if he were in power here. We knew, he added, about the Jews in Germany." [97]

The emphasis of invasion and occupation by a determined Germany even at this early date is interesting and instructive. It is as if Stalin was preparing the nation for an eventual confrontation with the German threat even when he himself denied the reports of German intentions with the military buildup on the new Russian-German border in the former Poland.

---

[96] Merrydale, Catherine, *Ivan's War*, Metropolitan Books, New York, 2006, pp. 167.

[97] Ibid, p. 37.

Big Brother

What characterized and made life in the U.S.S.R. distinct from life anywhere else was the establishment of institutional suspicion and fear. Unlike in Germany where the forces of social control (*Gestapo, Ordnungspolitzi, SA, SS,* etc.) preferred to rely on personal and national discipline first to ensure the necessary social control (and later fear and repression), the Party in the Soviet Union through its internal organs of state security utilized suspicion, fear[98] and mistrust as the ruling element to do the same and a formalized version known as the "self criticism" exercises. The planned or desired end result was a populace that often after years of party imposed discipline would, in time become self-disciplined, thereby ensuring national loyalty. The Soviets periodically "examined" their party members to ensure not only loyalty but also dogmatic knowledge, the ultimate goal of every member becoming a potential example and recruiter. However dedicated, both nations operated on a basis of eternal vigilance, always watchful for any deviation from the party line and for any threat, real or perceived.

Like her arch-enemy Germany, Russia under the communist banner was a totalitarian society with extensive and overlapping police, security and intelligence organizations dedicated to ensuring that no one stepped out of line, all anti-communist influences and ideas were suppressed and all threats against the Party and state were identified and eliminated. However, unlike Germany the large number of security organizations, their extensive reach, power, resources and complexity is truly bewildering.

A brief examination of the Soviet security organizations as it affects our understanding of the USSR in the Second World War will provide an example of these all-pervasive organs, their affect on the nation and the military. Two organizations in particular will amply demonstrate their formation and style, the powerful NKVD (later to become the KGB), especially its Special Departments and one of its later developments, the sinister SMERSh.[99]

[98] It is interesting that the Russian word for fear *strakh* is pronounced and almost spelled the same way to refer to members of the U.S. military that are exceptionally disciplined and organized, known as strak.

[99] For an excellent description of all Soviet security organs see *Stalin's Secret War, Soviet Counterintelligence Against The Nazi's 1941-1945* by Robert W. Stephan, University Press of Kansas, 2004.

[100] An adage attributed to NKVD successor, the KGB was "Just give me the man and I will give you his crime".

In 1934 the OGPU (*Obed'enniy Gosudarstvennoi Politicheskii Upravlennie* or Combined State Political Directorate) was transformed into the GUGB (*Glavnoe Uptavlenie Gosudarstvennoe Bezopasnosti* or Main Directorate of State Security), which was brought under the new organization, NKVD (*Narodnii Kommissariat Vnutrennykh Del*, or Peoples Commissariat of Internal Affairs) at the beginning of the war with Germany. This marked the beginning of Soviet state security's most powerful and autocratic period. All key aspects of internal and state security were now subordinated into one body under one leader, in 1938 this was Lavrentii Beria.[100]

In its founding year, February 1941, the NKVD consisted of the following organizations. The security organizations that make up the NKVD and a separate security department, the NKGB are vast and changed frequently during the war:

The number of internal divisions of this one organization will amply illustrate the Soviets xenophobic guard against subversion: GUGB (Chief Directorate of State Security), GUPVO (Chief Directorate of Frontier and Interior Troops), GULag (Chief Directorate of Camps), and GUM* (Chief Directorate of the Militia). As if this extensive organization wasn't enough, in 1939 the GUPVO branch was divided into six more Chief Directorates: GUPV (Chief Directorate of Frontier Guards), GUKV (Chief Directorate of Convoy Troops), GUVOVPGO (Chief Directorate of Troops for Guarding Industry and State Facilities), GUZhV (Chief Directorate of NKVD Railroad Troops)[101], GUInzhV (Chief Directorate of NKVD Engineer Troops) and GUIntV (Chief Directorate of the NKVD Intendants Service).[102]

* Not to be confused with the GUM department store in Moscow.

[101] As of 21 June 1941 there were 8 NKVD Railway Guard Troops *divisions* (italics added for emphasis) and 5 brigade-sized units, spread across the U.S.S.R. Their function was to exert firm control on the railway network in their areas of responsibility during the mobilization period, secure effective shipment of military materials to the frontline troops and provide the maintenance of the railways in the occupied territories. Each of these divisions had four rifle regiments, their own armored train, artillery and anti-aircraft support.

[102] The center of NKVD activity in Moscow was the largest building in Lyubianka Square the former Czarist era Rossiya Insurance Company. The prison and interrogation rooms located in the basement have become quite famous as was the courtyard where the executions were carried out in the early days of the 1920's. The noise of the shots were blotted out by several trucks racing their engines from which the mufflers had been removed. In 1922 the American newspaper reporter George Seldes reported seeing in this same basement the former insurance company's advertising signs, encouraging Russian citizens to insure themselves against untimely death, two of which read, "Insure your life NOW" and "Protect your wife and children when you are gone-insure NOW".

This bewildering array of security organizations was not a Soviet monopoly. Nazi Germany had just as many security and policing bodies, some of the more unusual are the *Forstschutzpolizei* or Forestry Police, *Deichpolizei* or Dyke and Dam Police, *Postschutz* or Post Office Police, *Flurschutzpolizei* or Agricultural Police and *Jagdpolizei* or Game Police.[103]

At the beginning of the war, the NKVD established its own field troops called Line Divisions, separate from the Russian Army, these combat units, complete with their own artillery and armored units, were made up of 47 ground and 6 naval Frontier Guards Regiments, and 11 other NKVD combat Regiments containing approximately 100,000 men. These units were formed into 15 division-sized units. In addition Destroyer Battalions *Istribitelyniy Battalon*, responsible for hunting down enemy agents and parachutists were formed and the notorious Blocking Detachments *Zagraditelniy Otryady* formed from GUPV (Frontier Guards) units whose task it was to insure Russian Army units followed orders and did not retreat[104]. During combat any Russian Army soldier caught 'advancing' to the rear was almost certain to be arrested and frequently shot immediately.[105] At the battle of Stalingrad the NKVD was responsible for the execution of over 13,300 Russian Army soldiers for a series of offensives, including desertion, failure to obey orders and the most popular collective catchall category "counterrevolutionary crimes against the State". The NKVD was to be kept busy right up to the end of the war enforcing draconian discipline, in 1945 alone over 134,000 officers and men suffered the maximum punishment, which included over 250 senior officers.

---

[103] See *World War II Data Book, The Third Reich 1933 - 1945, The Essential Facts and Figures For Hitler's Germany.*

[104] It is of interest to note that during the disastrous 1939 - 1940 'Winter War' with Finland, to 'encourage' the Red Army troops to advance and obey orders, leather whips with ball bearings were used on them by their officers and their *politruki*. They were found by the Finns by the dozens after the battle of Suomussalmi in December 1939. For en excellent study of this tragic event see *The Winter War, Russia's Invasion of Finland, 1939 -1940* by Robert Edwards, Pegasus Books, New York, 2008.

[105] A function of the NKVD was to provide security for the Soviet labor camps (GULags). When hostilities broke out, they were to insure that the prisoners were evacuated rather than let them fall into the hands of the enemy; if they could not be evacuated, they were to be executed. As many NKVD units were impressed into rifle units to fight, the fate of the prisoners was a sad one.

[106] One example of this internal banishment which is of particular interest to us in this study is that of the Volga Germans. Invited to Russia by Catherine the Great to settle and develop the vast stretches of Russia, especially the border regions of the south and east, a group of Germans seeking better land to farm and induced by generous

Banishment, Deportations and Executions

The tasks assigned to these security organizations and their extensive reach into everyday life in Soviet Russia was quite unlike anything before it or since. One of the more odious assignments was the punishment of whole populations that had run afoul of Soviet aims, thought, policy or which simply un-nerved Stalin. The usual punishment for these 'crimes' was internal banishment or expulsion. In 1944 650,000 Crimean Tatars, Chechens and Ingush were exiled to Central Asia. These actions involved almost 100,000 NKVD, NKGB and SMERSh troops and workers to assemble, transport and settle the targeted peoples, all conducted during the height of the war.[106] It is also of interest to note that all exiled peoples with men in the Russian Army could not be recommended for the award of Hero of the Soviet Union, an additional disgrace to be suffered by those Stalin mistrusted.

By the conclusion of the war Beria, with his expert on deportations, Mikhail Suslov, had expelled 1,500,000 people. Stalin even agreed to the over 400 medals Beria wanted to award his hard working NKVD units. In the unheated freight wagons used to transport the victims, over 25% of the people being expelled died on route or shortly after arrival in such far away locations as Kazakhstan, the Ural region and frigid Siberia.[107]

tax benefits and religious tolerance, settled in the lower Volga river valley. With the arrival of the Second World War and the approaching of the seemingly unstoppable German armies in 1941 Stalin uprooted and transported all 400,000 of them from the Volga German ASSR (Autonomous Soviet Socialist Republic) in August. However with the Russian counteroffensive at Stalingrad in November of that year no unit of the Wehrmacht ever occupied any of the former German Volga lands. Even today the Volga Germans were never returned to their former lands and property. Not the death of Stalin, or any of the later Communist leaders wanted to go on record as bringing the Germans back together again.

To demonstrate the Russian fear of the Germans and also to justify future actions against them it is interesting to note what happened in August of 1941. The Red Army dropped paratroopers disguised in German uniforms into the villages of the Volga Germans to test their loyalty by asking them to hide them. If they were responded positively they were executed. In addition to the paratrooper test was a house search. The searchers were looking for swastika flags, the very same flags handed out by Russian authorities to celebrate the 1939 Russo-German pact. Such was the impact on the innocents of the rapid change of fates and alliances of their governments.

[107] Stalin was not the only one to move large segments of his population around. In three years 629,000 ethnic Germans were resettled from outside the Reich with an eventual 400,000 to come. During the same period 365,000 Poles were moved into the General Gouvernement and 295,000 French citizens were evicted from Alsace, Lorraine and Luxembourg. With the exception of the Germans, one can assume the others were all forced resettlements.

One of the threats to Soviet security was the political prisoners being held in jails and prisons in the path of the German advance. Initially they were to have been transported to secure areas in the east, but the rapid German progress in the early weeks and months of the invasion made this difficult. The *Luftwaffe* with almost complete freedom of the skies was active interdicting rail and road networks as well as heavy Russian military use made moving the prisoners, in many cases, impossible.

When word leaked out that the NKVD was under orders not to let any of the prisoners fall into the hands of the German's or allowed to be freed, fear of mass executions spread and local nationalist movement paramilitaries began to move to the prisons to prevent what they feared might happen to the inmates.

Despite their attempts to forestall the executions thousands were shot in their cells or in prison courtyards, including women and children. Russian NKVD units such as the 13th NKVD Escort Troops were said to have murdered over 20,000 in prisons in Lvov, Tarnopol, Dubno and Kolomyja. However, in a few cases, such as in Sarny, local nationalist forces managed to intervene and prevent the NKVD units from their deadly work and held the prisons until the arrival of German advanced units.

In addition to the life and death fight against the Wehrmacht, the continuation of the terror against its own citizens and the large deportation operations in the south, the Soviet economy was showing the strain. In November 1944, which in western Russia should have been at the conclusion of harvest season, just the opposite was occurring: famine. Apparently the attention to greater perceived threats had distracted the managers of the U.S.S.R. from the basics of running the nation.

The Man of Steel

The psychological and emotional make up of Joseph Stalin has been studied and commented upon by many sources, one of the more interesting and pervasive was Stalin's fear for his personal safety. Unlike Hitler, Joseph Stalin has not received as much examination until recently and for this reason I will dwell on him and his life. This fear was so intense he seldom[108]

---

[108] One of the front visits was in August 1943 during the Red Army counter-attacks after the Germans cancelled their offensive around Kursk. However, he did not visit this active front, he went instead just west of Rzhev to the Kalinin Front. He approached as close to the front as the small village of Khoroshevo, Beria preventing him from going any closer. He stayed in the home of an old woman, and when leaving attempted to

visited the troops in the field, much less visit units at the front lines, even in the later stages of the war when his armies dominated the battlefield. His preference was to remain in the Kremlin, managing the war from the safety and security of Moscow, dispatching orders and generals and receiving reports. Compared to his rival, Hitler visited his Wehrmacht several times during the war in the east, even once during the declining stages of the campaign, in 1943.[109]

Stalin the man, his personality, moods, strengths and weaknesses is succinctly captured by Simon Sebag Montefiore in his "Stalin, The Court of the Red Tsar":

> "Stalin was already famous for his Sphinxian inscrutability and phlegmatic modesty, represented by the pipe he ostentatiously puffed like a peasant elder. Far from being the colorless bureaucratic mediocrity disdained by Trotsky, the real Stalin was an energetic and vainglorious melodramatist who was exceptional in every way."

> "Beneath the eerie calm of these unfathomable waters were deadly whirlpools of ambition, anger and unhappiness. Capable both of moving with controlled gradualism and of reckless gambles, he seemed enclosed inside a cold suit of steely armor but his antennae were intensely sensitive and his fiery Georgian temper was so uncontrollable that he almost ruined his career by unleashing it against Lenin's wife. He was a mercurial neurotic with a tense, seething temperament of a highly strung actor who revels in his own drama-what his ultimate successor, Nikita Khrushchev, called a *litsedei*, a man of many faces. Lazar Kaganovich, one of his closest comrades for over thirty years... left the best description of this "unique character": he was a "different man at different times... I knew no less than five or six Stalins."

---

pay her for his stay, found he had no money, nor did anyone in his party, so he gave her a few personal keepsakes. There is no record what these were. Stalin noticed when arriving in the village that there seemed to be no villagers around. When pressed, his NKVD chief admitted that the village had been emptied of its inhabitants, with the exception of a few elderly residents and replaced with a *division* (italics added for emphasis) of NKVD troops.

[109] Berdichev, 5 August 1941; Vinnitsa, 25 August 1941; Uman, 26 August 1941; Vinnitsa, 16 July 1942 and Zaporozhye 17 February 1943.

"...We now know that he talked (constantly about himself, often with revealing honesty), how he wrote notes and letters, what he ate, sang and read. Placed in the contest of the fissiparous Bolshevik leadership, a unique environment, he becomes a real person. The man inside was a super-intelligent and gifted politician for whom his own historic role was paramount, a nervy intellectual who manically read history and literature, and a fidgety hypochondriac suffering from chronic tonsillitis, psoriasis, rheumatic aches from his deformed arm and the iciness of his Siberian exile. Garrulous, sociable and a fine singer, this lonely and unhappy man ruined every love relationship and friendship in his life by sacrificing happiness to political necessity and cannibalistic paranoia. Damaged by his childhood and abnormally cold in temperament, he tried to be a loving father and husband yet poisoned every emotional well; this nostalgic lover of roses and mimosas who believed the solution to every human problem was death, and who was obsessed with executions.[110] This atheist owed everything to priests and saw the world in terms of sin and repentance, yet he was a "convinced Marxist fanatic from his youth. His fanaticism was "semi-Islamic", his Messianic egotism boundless. He assumed the imperial mission of the Russians yet remained very much a Georgian, bringing the vendettas of his forefathers northwards to Muscovy.""

"He was a self-creation.[111] A man who invents his name, birthday, nationality, education and his entire past, in order to change history and play the role of leader, is likely to end up in a mental institution, unless he embraces, by will, luck and skill, the movement and the moment that can overturn the natural order of things. Stalin was such a man. The movement was the Bolshevik Party; his moment, the decay of the Russian monarchy. After Stalin's death, it was fashionable to regard him as an aberration but this was to rewrite history as crudely as Stalin

---

[110] In this same work we see Stalin's preference for death as a solution for all problems large and small, also as an example and warning for all to observe. In 1918 during the revolution when assigned by Lenin to Tsaritsyn, the southern Russian city on the Volga later to become famous as Stalingrad, he quickly demonstrated his determination to restore order and discipline in the city and region by shooting civil or military offenders, suspected or real. In summary, no man, no problem.

did himself. Stalin's success was not an accident. No one alive was more suited to the conspiratorial intrigues, theoretical runes, murderous dogmatism and inhuman sternness of Lenin's Party. It is hard to find a better synthesis between a man and a movement than the ideal marriage between Stalin and Bolshevism: he was a mirror of its virtues and faults."[112]

Stalin rarely drank, his mind was always clear. He had no objection to anyone else around him taken to strong drink; indeed he was able to make use of this human weakness by keeping track of the careless word or deed from those around him. The flask that was maintained for him at the various state, political and military functions was always filled with water, the clear liquid that everyone else assumed was vodka. He was always in control of himself and everyone else.

Should we wonder of the coincidence of Stalin's birthday, 21 December, the period marking the least amount of daylight, the darkest time of the year? Perhaps there is a connection with this gloomy time of the year, in an officially atheistic Soviet Union, a time of darkness, depression and his paranoid personality?

An example of Stalin's neurosis and paranoia can be seen in his reaction to NKVD and SMERSh reports of the Russian Army occupation troops growing fond of the soft life of guard duty, American bubble gum, jazz, jitterbug records and German beer and wine. In addition to these physical comforts unknown in Russia at this time was the developing 'softening' of the rigid division between officers and their men. The silence of the guns and bombs and the loss of fear of assignment to the *shtrafniki*, the punishment battalions, was leading to a certain blending, a familiarity between the officers and the men they commanded. This was unnerving to Stalin, a sign of western infection pervading the defenders of the motherland. This exposure to western capitalism would destroy all the years of Marxist-Leninist education and sacrifice.

---

[111] An anecdotal story is oft told of Stalin scolding his son Vasily for using his father's name for personal gain. "I'm a Stalin too," he pleads to his father. "No you're not," replied his father. "You're not Stalin and I'm not Stalin. Stalin is Soviet power. Stalin is what he is in the newspapers and the portraits, not you, not even me!" Such was how Stalin saw himself, the symbol, rather than the man, of the nation.

[112] *Stalin, The Court of the Red Tsar* by Simon Sebag Montefiore, copyright © 2003 by Simon Sebag Montefiore. Used by permission of Alfred A. Knopf, a division of Random House, Inc.

"...The longer Soviet troops remained in Germany, the less they cared for Moscow's (NKVD, politruks and special departments) homilies and threats. A culture developed among the old hands. Drink, women, secrets and hard currency were its main constituents. Eighteen months after the peace, it was clear to Stalin's officials that almost no veterans could be allowed to remain abroad. Their influence was too liberal, too damaging to the regime of discipline and ideological rigidity... By the spring of 1947, the Soviet military authorities in Germany had come around to the view that all soldiers with two or more years of service on German soil (which meant all combat veterans), as well as anyone who had worked closely with candidates for repatriation, should be sent home without delay. They were to be replaced by more reliable, younger, less capricious types. The *frontovik* was fine for winning wars, but authoritian military rule demanded people with the souls of bureaucrats."

The sense of fear that permeated Russia under the communists, especially the Stalinist form, was deep and systemic. The dread of making a careless statement or expressing an opinion contrary with state policy drove many people, historians and academics especially, to practice a type of intellectual denial. Hanna Arendt in her *Origins of Totalitarianism* published in the late 1940s described the nightmare of life in such a society, which applies to both Russia and Germany:

"People were killed under totalitarian rule by dint of absolute historical or racial laws, without anger or utilitarian calculation. Suffering was determined by categories, divorced by anything done by the individual victims, whose ranks could be redefined and replenished almost ad infinitum. The need for constant alarms and enemies virtually guaranteed inflation within the economy of terror."

As one can clearly see Stalin was fighting a sort of two front war, one with the German attackers and the other the barely controlled native populations and the still yet to be purged anti-communist element, a similar situation as Germany experienced but different in source and scope. These latter were referred to by Stalin's security forces as the "unreliable element" and was just as dangerous to him as the German invader and both was fought at the same time. The postwar records and recollections of the atrocities committed by the NKVD in the western Russian cities threatened by the German advance make for depressing reading.

As in the deportations and internal banishments, Stalin was not going to permit anyone who was a threat to him or to his régime to escape the clutches of Soviet power and as we have seen, even when in doubt as to a person's 'reliability' including children, death for them was a better alternative than escape. It brings the insanity of the war in the East to a new level of brutality and senselessness and echoes the German final solution.

With the Russian Army desperate to maintain pressure on the still dangerous Wehrmacht, Stalin saw fit to divert valuable rail transport, men and time, and continue his punishment of whole peoples by expulsion to far-flung wastelands to the east. It can be assumed with the western allies providing newer and better quality infrastructure in the form of engines, wagons, rails and motor trucks, he had the luxury of conducting internal business as usual, Communist style. Nothing was too much of a burden if it posed even a remote threat to the State.

Stalin learned early the lesson of the internal destruction of the Tsarist army in the First World War, the affects of political and morale subversion and was not about to let this happen to him and his Russian Army. He immersed himself in everything military, attending to every small detail, the use of the commissar network to be his eyes and ears. The Russian version of the German SS was the NKVD and performed many of the same functions: Reliability in combat, a counterweight to the army, answerable only to the Party. The meddling of the political officer in the day to day functioning of the army is by now well understood, given the fear, doubt and lack of initiative it inspired. It was costly, wasteful and cumbersome but it ensured Stalin that the army would not be a threat to him and his hold on power.

The Culture of Fear

Part of life in the Soviet Union was based on a culture of denunciation, the constant vigilance of enemies real or imagined. It became the almost natural tendency to denounce, it was a companion with a pervasive national mistrust and distrust of almost everyone, including ones family members. Since the purge of the mid 1930's Russia had been a nation without a sense of trust. It was as if trust was replaced by vigilance and suspicious observance.

As one can see from this brief look into the world of Russian state security organizations during the Second World War, the xenophobic nature of such states in which their comfort and security rests on stamping out all thoughts, actions and deeds determined to be a danger to the leadership, no expense was too great, no numbers too big and no matter too small to escape the attention of these organizations.

Unlike Russia's archenemy Germany, the nature of the Russian security system has a distinct character to it that positively identifies it as communist and perhaps, uniquely Russian as well. As mentioned earlier, in comparing the two organizations an interesting difference becomes apparent in that in the German setting the various security services viewed the population as German first (primarily ethnic German's) and as National Socialists second. The implicit understanding was that a native born German would be unlikely to subvert their Fatherland and an understanding was established that all suspicious or anti-German activity should and must be reported to the authorities out of loyalty to the Fatherland. One was always considered German first and everything else second, a distinctly national, racial or tribal rather than a political difference.

The Soviet version, on the other hand, was to trust no one. The approach the communist internal security services took and the Party in general used was to assume that one was guilty until proven innocent. One was suspect until proven trustworthy. It was a system that was founded on the age-old Russian characteristic of cultural and social xenophobia of everyone, native born as well as foreigner, of multiple levels of checks, counter-checks and verifications that everyone and everything is an enemy and can never be fully trusted. It was a system of which the Party was first and everything else second. Examples of this fear and non-stop mistrust[113] are amply demonstrated by Stalin's internal exile policy, the purges of the late 1930's[114] and even extended to the isolation and incarceration

---

[113] During the development of the JS-1 and JS-2 heavy tanks, on 8 August 1943 the prototypes were driven from the factory outside Moscow through the streets of the capital and into the Kremlin for an inspection by the Soviet leadership. Here they were examined by Stalin, Molotov, Voroshilov, Beria and several others. No record exists on what resulted from the inspection by the leadership, however one interesting detail survives. For the purposes of the display all the crewmembers with the exception of the drivers were replaced by NKVD officers.

[114] See *Stalin, The Court of the Red Tsar*, pp 228 – 235 for additional information on the stunning number of arrests, expulsions and murders during the "Terror" of 1936 – 1939.

of Russian Army POW's from German prisons, many sent directly from prisoner of war camps to the GULags in the Far Eastern regions. Their families and loved ones never knew that they had been rescued, freed and re-imprisoned by their own nation.[115] The Soviet national neurosis was feeding upon itself.[116]

Stalin, at the conclusion of hostilities, was presented with an updated map of the Union of Soviet Socialists Republics. Going from west to east, he was able to justify all the seized lands within the Russian historical perspective of loss and denial. Losses suffered under the Tsars, under the post-Revolution Civil War, to the Poles in the 1920's, to the German's in the 1940's. The new Russia was entering the height of her power and influence in post World War II Europe. The devastated regions provided Stalin with the justification for additional national sacrifice to rebuild and restore, this time with the assistance of millions of German and German-allied prisoners of war. Also included were millions who fell afoul of the NKVD for whatever reason and were sentenced to long terms in the Gulags and the massive infusions of western Lend-Lease machinery and infrastructure support.

The treatment of Russian citizens at the end of the war requires comment if only to demonstrate that for the average Russian, however remotely involved in the war, the suffering did not end with the last German soldier killed, captured or pushed west. The last brick falling in the fighting in Berlin was the signal for another round of suffering for this nation for whom suffering was becoming an all too noticeable component of their national patrimony.[117]

---

[115] The interned number of returning Red Army POW's killed by Stalin after the war range from a low of 500,000 (Harff and Gurr) to a high of 5,000,000 to 6,000,000 (Davies). **http://users.erols.com/mwhite28/warstat1.htm**

[116] Old habits die hard. At the conclusion of the Czechoslovak invasion in October 1968, whole divisions which occupied regions in Czechoslovakia and were suspected of being tainted by western influences were dispatched immediately to the Chinese frontier.

[117] An example of the suffering that was sustained by the Russian citizen during the war can be demonstrated by the amount of food provided to the people by the Soviet government. Food was allocated by caloric value based on ones occupation, or lack of it. Among those receiving the least were dependents who received 780 calories per day, followed up the scale by workers in medium industries 1,387 to 3,181. For workers in moderate to heavy industries to workers in heavy industries (mining, steel, tank production) starting at 1,913 to workers performing the heaviest tasks, 4,418. From U. G. Chernyavskii, *Voina I prodovol'stve. Snabzhenie gorodskogo naseleniya v Veliuyu Otechestvennuyu voiny 1941 – 1945* Moscow: Nauka 1964.

The last year of the war, 1945, and the immediate post war years, Stalin again began another xenophobic round of purges, murders, exiles, expulsions and imprisonments of his population.[118] However, in this new phase, it was to include the most powerful men in the country, and the leadership of the victorious Russian Army. Stalin's psychotic need to eliminate any threat to his person, power and influence had to eliminate or at least subdue the one group that could threaten his hold on the nation: the military.

In 1945 the victorious Russian Army was the darling of the public and the nation and was finally accepted as an equal, especially among the western nations. It came out of the war vastly more powerful then when it entered the fight and this was too much for an unstable leader like Stalin. In his topsy-turvy world of power, threats and dangers to his control, this was unacceptable. To him the war was an interruption to business as usual, the Soviet quest for quashing any threat to expanding the nation and the Party and its influence. During the period 1941-1945 he needed the leadership that his generals and marshals provided to win victory over the German invader. When the threat to the nation and the Party was gone, the need for such strong, influential men was also unneeded. As such, Stalin approached this as just another matter of statecraft. The requirement for this particular tool was gone and so they would be dispensed as necessary. It was nothing personal, just business, Soviet style. Actually Stalin had come to like and enjoy the company of his military leadership, especially Zhukov, the brusque outspoken savior of Leningrad, Moscow and Stalingrad, and the conqueror of Berlin. Knowing Stalin's state of mind, anyone that could lay claim to such accomplishments was a threat indeed.

With the removal or diminishing of the influence of the wartime military leadership,[119] it was time to address the threat to the rank and file and the common citizen of the nation. During the war huge numbers of Russians had come under the influence, direction, or had in some shape or form, come in contact with the enemy or some form of Western influence. In Stalin's eyes everyone but the most trusted security organs was contaminated by these

---

[118] Estimated Russian civilian deaths after the war, 2,000,000 to 4,000,000.

[119] The Russian Army, like its former enemy, the German's, was, in part, saved by the oncoming Cold War. With the resumption of mistrust of the West, the Red Army had to maintain its size and strength in the coming war against the West. Germany, as the new confrontation state with the newly formed Warsaw Pact had to be supported, remain intact to defend Western Europe against the newly energized Russian dominated East, especially after the detonation of the first Soviet nuclear device.

contacts and had to be separated from the general population, quarantined if you will; interrogated and their level of 'exposure' to Western thought, ideas and influence evaluated, removed or crushed. Stalin would permit no information to enter his Russia without his shaping and preparing it for delivery.

The ostensible return to Soviet 'business as usual' as the threat from Nazi Germany receded can be demonstrated by the following from *Stalin, the Court of the Red Tsar*:

> "Beria arrested 931,544 persons in the liberated territory in 1943. As many as 250,000 people in Moscow attended Easter church services. He delivered the phone intercepts and informer reports to Stalin who read them carefully... the message was clear: liberalism and ill-discipline threatened the State. The costs of Stalin's victories were vast: almost 26 million were dead, another 26 million homeless. There was a famine raging, treason among the Caucasian peoples, a Ukrainian nationalist civil war, and dangerous liberalism among the Russians themselves. All these had to be solved with the traditional Bolshevik solution: Terror."

"Before they turned to terrorizing Russia proper, Beria and the local boss, Khrushchev, were running a new war in the Ukraine where three native nationalist armies were fighting Soviet Forces..."

The suffering continued. Stalin negotiated with the Western Allies at Yalta regarding how the final national boundaries would look and ordered the NKVD to regain every Russian who had left the Soviet Union, for whatever reason: voluntarily, prisoner, and fugitive. To him they all failed his first test: they allowed themselves to be captured and did not die for the Motherland. To him they were already legally liable for the maximum punishment, death. However, the need for large amounts of cheap or slave labor undoubtedly saved many thousands from a bullet in the back of the head, the preferred NKVD execution method;[120] they were instead

---

[120] For more on this gruesome method, see *Death in the Forest, Story of the Katyn Forest Massacre* by J.K. Zawodny, University of Notre Dame Press, 1962. Jonathan Brent, in his *Inside The Stalin Archives* (Atlas & Company, New York, 2008, p. 232) suggests that Stalin, convinced that with the German and Soviet occupation, Poland would never rise and therefore need not worry about the discovery of his authorization to murder the Polish army officers. This work is also an excellent source for an inside look at what *is* Stalin.

sentenced to long terms in the Gulag, the mines or construction sites, rebuilding the shattered regions of the western USSR as slave laborers, known as Zeks[121].

Among the most unfortunate members of Russian society at the conclusion of the war were the wounded soldiers. The insensitive treatment of those who lost a hand or limb frequently led to suicide rather than live as a cripple. Those who were quadriplegic were derisively called 'samovars'. The treatment was so bad that none were allowed to live in Moscow; they were loaded onto trains and shipped to towns and villages above the Arctic Circle. Apparently the sight of wounded veterans was uncomfortable.

Due to the need to prepare for any confrontation with the West, now the new enemy, Stalin continued the national state of emergency and thereby his draconian control methods to bring Russia into its deserved place in the superpower sun. He realized that with regards to technology Russia was still behind in the race for world domination and nothing short of a total, national effort was going to do it, especially when the United States detonated the first nuclear device over Japan. This just confirmed Stalin's direction and methods on the road to success.

The level of vindictiveness exhibited by Stalin and his organs of control and security is nothing short of incomprehensibility. It is easily arguable that the true victims of the war were the Jews and Russian peasants. Hindsight of the activities of both the Germans and the Russians in Poland and Russia provides a truly astonishing montage of suffering, horror, separation and death to these largely simple and harmless people that defies understanding. It is Poland's geographic misfortune to lie between two aggressive super powers. For the Russian peasants, it truly was an unfortunate accident of birth.

This detailed look into the world of the Soviet Union, the Russian Army and its security organizations is intended to establish a sense of what life was like in the Soviet Union and in the Russian Army. But if more than just a 'taste' of life in Stalin's Russia is desired, it is hoped that by describing in detail the police and security forces it will be plainly evident this was a government that never placed any trust or faith in its citizens. Stalin once said, "If you have to choose between Party and individual, you

---

[121] Zek is a shortened version of the Russian word for prisoner, Zachlyuchennyi.

should choose Party because the Party has the general aim, the good of many people but one person is just one person."[122]

Short of outright contempt, the Soviet citizens were given the most shallow and superficial inclusion into the decision making process and they were at the total mercy of a system that pretended to value their worth and labor but in reality went to any length to squander their efforts. Given the slightest pretext the Soviet system confiscated what little property and freedoms they possessed and replaced them with empty promises. For the workers and peasants their moral values and religion was subverted, and ultimately their lives wasted; for the masters of the Kremlin this was not too great a price to pay for safeguarding the Party. What we see in Russia in the early 1940's is a ruthless totalitarian system under attack by its arch enemy and desperate to defend itself. To ensure that the State and Party survived nothing was considered too extreme or radical to protect it.

Russian War Production, Relocation and Allied Lend-Lease

The Russian economy from the early 1930's to the end of the war and beyond produced an astounding amount of weapons from the largest military industrial complex in the world. However small the Soviet domestic consumer economy was, the Soviet Union was the largest producer of tanks and field artillery during World War II. As the Russian Army was the Communist Party's guarantee to power, it was in their interest to keep it well supplied, armed and under control. Even with the hurried relocation of significant amounts of industry to the east in 1941 and again in 1942, the Soviets managed to produce 98,300 tanks[123] and self-propelled guns, 19,830,000 rifles, 525,200 guns and mortars and 122,100 aircraft, no small achievement. Stalin once said that the war was going to be won by production. The following is from Erickson's "The Russian Front":

"While the next three months would prove critical (September, October and November 1941), the economic war had been put on a sound footing. Before November, the Soviet Union had lost between 50% and 66% of its productive capacity in coal, pig iron, steel and aluminum, along with a quarter of its engineering capacity. The industrial output of the country had been halved."

---

[122] *Stalin, The Court of the Red Tsar* by Simon Sebag Montefiore, Alfred A. Knopf, New York, 2003, p. 6.

[123] Of these, some 53,000 were the T-34 series machines.

"In 1942, as the Wehrmacht bit deeper into Russia, there had to be a second wave of evacuations, the largest industrial migration in the world.[124] Well over 1,900 plants were moved eastwards, and an aircraft factory within seventeen days of being relocated, was producing its first aircraft."[125]

Granted, this production was obtained with the assistance of the western Allied nations in the form of the Lend-Lease program.[126] Russia had adequate supplies of the chief raw materials, such as coal, oil and iron ore and out produced western allied nations, most notably the U.S., in such minerals as nickel, manganese, chrome, pyrites and magnesium ores. However, the loss of major mining and manufacturing regions such as the Donbas, Ukraine and parts of Leningrad and effects of the dislocation and evacuation of the industries and their workers in the face of German advances in the first two years of the invasion caused reductions in domestic arms production that, with the exception of a few metals, never again reached the pre-1941 levels.

---

[124] See map *The Dispersion of Soviet Industry* from *Chronological Atlas of World War II* by Barrie and Frances Pitt, MacMillan, London, 1989, p. 70.

[125] Bob Carruthers and John Erickson's comments notwithstanding, John Fischer in his book *Why They Behave Like Russians* (Harper Brothers, New York 1946) states the following, pp. 11- 12, "Incidentally, nearly all the destruction was done by the Germans. *I was surprised to find that neither the Soviet's famous scorched-earth policy nor its removal of factories to new sites beyond the Urals was carried out on anything like the scale which the outside world had been led to believe.* (Italics added) The great Dnieper dam, for example, was only partly crippled when the Russians abandoned it; the power plant was untouched, and except for a relatively small center section the dam itself was left intact. The Germans soon had it repaired, although they were never able to put its electric current to much use. When they finally were forced back from the river, they razed the dam to its foundations and blew up all nine of the giant turbines. Similarly, most of the Ukraine's industrial plants, including its largest steel mill and the big Kharkov tractor factory, fell into German hands almost undamaged. *The Russians succeeded in moving only the lighter machinery to the East; consequently the new wartime industrial centers in Siberia were built up, in the main, not from "refugee factories" but with American Lend-Lease equipment".* (Italics added). John Fischer traveled extensively in Ukraine and in several Russian cities in 1946 as part of the United Nations Refugee Relief Agency (UNRRA) as such he had firsthand knowledge of conditions there at that time and his observations warrants careful consideration.

[126] Amongst the many commodities shipped to the Russians during and after the war, was food, mostly in bulk form such as cereals. Starting in 1943 one of the more popular items was Spam, the ready-to-eat processed meat product in a can. Several sources have commented that at critical times during the war, this was the single most important item that kept the Red Army fed. It is also reported that the average Red Army soldier found it delicious. The Russians nick named the little blue cans 'second fronts' (vtoroy front myaso). After the war, Nikita Khrushchev stated that "Without Spam, we wouldn't have been able to feed our army". Gottlob Bidermann's German Pak

With this loss of access to a significant portion of their pre-invasion raw materials and manufacturing capacity, the Soviet Union was heavily dependent on Allied Lend-Lease shipments, especially in the early war years, 1941 to 1943. For example, the western Allies provided raw materials as well as finished goods to the Soviets, such as high-octane aviation fuel (59%), railroad rails (92.7%), steam locomotives (81.6%), rail cars (80.7%), and aluminum (55.5%). This was in addition to large quantities of trucks, Jeeps, communications equipment and other vital items.

With the Allies supplying critical aid in the form of ores, bulk and semi-finished steel, machine tools, copper, and logistical and transportation equipment such as cars, trucks, railroad rolling stock, railroad equipment and steam engines, this permitted the Russians to concentrate on the purely military items of rifles, sub-, light, and heavy machine guns, pistols and, most importantly tanks and artillery, which were more effective than allied equipment of the same type, while the Allies supplied the transportation and communication infrastructure.[127] With this support the number of tanks and guns the Russians produced is staggering. No other allied nation, the U.S. included produced weapons in these quantities. The Russian tanks produced were the impressive T-34 series of medium tanks and the KV and the JS series of heavy tanks, arguably the best all round fighting vehicles of the war.[128]

As the Russian Army were sustaining heavy losses in the opening months of the German attack the Russian industrial sector was in the process of one of the largest movements of industrial equipment in history,

---

(anti-tank) unit recalls over-running a Russian engineer unit laying mines. After killing a number of the Russians and dispersing the rest, they ransacked the Soviets supply carts and vehicles, finding a number of small cans of meat marked "Oscar Mayer-Chicago". A second popular food item was a powdered egg food, which came to be called "Roosevelt eggs" (Rosevelt yaitsa).

[127] It is interesting to note that in the initial months of Allied Lend - Lease Aid a good portion of the equipment sent to the U.S.S.R. was almost unusable. Early U.S. and British tanks could not stand up to Russian winters and the latest German models, and manufactured clothing was not practical for Russian use. It was as if the Allies were so desperate to keep the Russians fighting it was a case of 'send them something, anything, just keep them fighting.'

[128] There is an anecdotal story that Soviet officials inspecting a German tank plant prior to the invasion (during the German-Soviet technical exchange period, a component of the Treaty of 1939) repeatedly asked to see the heaviest tank in production as they refused to believe that the PzKw Mk. IV was indeed the heaviest, given that it was some 5 tons lighter than the T-34/76A, the new Soviet *medium* tank (Italics added for emphasis).

attempting to transport its industrial infrastructure out of the reach of the fast moving German panzer units, an unprecedented transportation feat

The newly developed industrial regions, especially those east of the Ural's was to become the keystone of the Russian war economy. The area was far enough from Luftwaffe interference and was rich in natural resources. The immediate problem was the lack of existing infrastructure, adequate communication networks and skilled workers. The first winter in these new industrial zones was a harsh one, worker accommodation was crude and in some locations nonexistent, they washed, ate and slept next to their machines while the factory was literally built around them as they worked. One worker was criticized by her boss as not getting the correct measurements of the artillery shells she was making on her lathe. She said she was trying but the snow on her machine made it hard to see them clearly.

The chief problem with Russian industrial production and its protection was that many of the war related factories and plants were located in the western regions of Russia, Ukraine and a few in the newly occupied Baltic and Polish areas. There was much discussion in 1940 between Stalin and his industrial department heads about the risks to these resources if left in place. With the threat to Russia coming from the West, the need to address the safety of Russian war production was a serious concern, however Stalin was not about to disrupt this vital production in the midst of the military reorganization and its new weapons just beginning to come off the assembly lines. At the urging of the military, none of these important sites should be located West of the 1939 border.

Barrie and Frances Pitt in their "The Chronological Atlas of World War II" capture the immensity of the task:[129]

> "Appreciation of the danger (of German capture) came early, and quite astonishing feats of reorganization were launched. Vast armor plate mills were shifted bodily from Mariupol to Magnitogorsk; entire steel mills from Zaporozhie and the tube rolling plant from Dniepropetrovsk were transported beyond the Urals, while Kharkov's tank-engine plant, it's mammoth jigs loaded onto the trains while German shells crashed around the railhead, went to Chelyabinsk. Heavy machine works at Novo Kramatorsk, including a 10,000 ton press, were stripped down in five days under German bombing and shipped to the Southern

[129] *The Chronological Atlas of World War II*, p. 70.

Urals, while 498 factories traveled eastwards in 80,000 trucks from Moscow itself. The bulk of the Kirov factory was evacuated from Leningrad and sent all the way to Sverdlovsk, a further 92 plants had been brought out during August and September and, on Stalin's direct orders, more was ferried across Lake Ladoga and so to the east even after Leningrad had been virtually sealed in."

"Between July and October 1,500,000 trucks and 915,000 railway wagons had shifted over 1,000 plants eastwards – 455 to the Urals, 210 to western Siberia, 200 to the Volga and over 250 to Kazakhstan and Central Asia, together with the men to rebuild the factories, install the machinery and then run it. From Leningrad nearly 20,000 scientists and technicians were flown out to Sverdlovsk, Chelyabinsk and Kazan, in all over 100,000 men accompanied this Diaspora of Soviet industry."

"The achievements were prodigious. Aircraft factories in Saratov began production even before the roofs were on, and 14 days after the last jigs were in place the first MiG fighter rolled out; ten weeks after the last teams of engineers left Kharkov the tank works produced the first 25 T-34's. By April 1942, the corner had been turned."

"Despite the biting cold and rudimentary shelter the new factories produced over 4,500 tanks, some 3,000 aircraft, 14,000 guns and over 50,000 mortars during those winter months. They were to play a vital part in the battles immediately ahead."

The listing of numbers of plants, mills, factories and shops disassembled, loaded and transported eastwards is the easier of the tasks the Russians faced in the first two years of the struggle. What is less discussed is the workers and their families that went with the plants and factories.

At its peak over twenty-five million people accompanied their factories eastward. The task of balancing the need to remove the workers or the threatened factories first ahead of the German advance determined the priorities of the moves. Eventually it came down to this: when your plant moved, you moved. The incredible effort of planning the moves in coordination with the desperate need to move military men and equipment to halt the Germans is one of the unknown success stories of the war in the East and deserves its own examination.

However heroic the disassembly and loading of the various manufacturing plants and factories was, once on the carriages and rail lines, there were additional problems and difficulties. The massive requirements of supplying and transporting the military to the fighting front, the evacuation of civilians, especially women and children as well as the industrial relocations to the rear caused massive rail traffic snarl-ups on the tracks and sidings. In January 1942 the average haulage was down 50% compared to peacetime. Nearly 3,000 carriages were standing idle for lack of locomotives, 66% of them loaded with evacuated material. Frequently the snarls were solved only when the trains were over-run by the advancing Germans, or the bottlenecks were finally broken and the trains began to move east.

All told about 12.5% of the productive capacity in the western regions was evacuated in time. While seemingly a low figure, considering the number of the industrial plants in the threatened areas this was a sizable number of factories indeed, and as the most vital war industries were given priority for evacuation a significant number of the most important were saved.

The combined effects of increased Russian production and Allied Lend-Lease arms and material shipments can be demonstrated by the following almost forgotten German counteroffensive in south-central Russia in the autumn of 1943. By late October the Red Army had advanced along the northern coast of the Sea of Azov severing contact with the German forces defending the Crimea, now cut off. Hitler, frustrated that the seasonal rains had not yet started to help slow the Russian offensive, decided to risk a limited offensive and ordered an attack from what became known as the "Nikopol bridgehead" south to the 75 mile wide Sivash, the series of swamp and land connections to the Crimea, especially at Perekop, the traditional and best paved gateway into the Crimea to reestablish a connection with the German's forces trapped there.

Commencing on 15 November the attack was led by one of the Waffen SS's best units, the 1st SS Panzer Division "Liebstandarte Adolf Hitler" led by one of his oldest Nazi fighters Sepp Dietrich. After initial success the delayed rains finally began and the attack slowly ground to a halt, never reaching the coast or Perekop. However even during this relatively short advance, the German's killed 20,000 Russians, destroyed or captured 603 Russian tanks, 300 pieces of artillery and 1,200 anti-tank guns. When the result of the operation was reported to Hitler, reflecting the astounding military production effort of the Soviets, he exclaimed, "Where will it end!" The German propaganda minister Goebbels recorded in his diary, "The Soviets have reserves of which we never dreamed in even our most pessimistic estimates".

As ambitious as the western aid to the Soviets was, it was not the first time the west came to the aid of the Communist regime. Near the end of the Russian civil war in 1921, there was vast areas of famine in Russia, such that Lenin authorized Maxim Gorky to seek help from the west for food supplies to correct a serious error in agriculture policy of extorting grain from the peasants. The then U.S. president Herbert Hoover responding the request established the American Relief Administration (ARA) and began supplying tons of foodstuffs to Russia. By mid-summer of 1922 the ARA was feeding approximately eleven million Russians per day. Support was also provided in the form of agricultural management, especially seed to assist in preventing future famine.

As would be the case in 1945, the new Bolshevik government never publically acknowledge the generosity of the United States. In a stunning example of thanklessness of foreign assistance that was to become all too common under Stalin, the Soviets that organized the ARA relief were imprisoned and Gorky was dismissed from his position. Another example of Russian xenophobia.

For The Motherland!

For the Russian workers left behind, there is an interesting report made by the German SD (*Sicherheitsdienst*) or Security Service in September 1941:

> "...the workers of Kryvy Rih, the center of the Soviet iron industry, were "very loyal" and wanted nothing but work and a higher wage. This generalization was accurate for most of Dnieper Ukraine's workers, most of whom had been unable *or unwilling* (italics added) to evacuate. The retreating Soviet authorities had left behind as many as 80 percent of the unskilled workers who had worked in the iron industry in the Dnieper bend. As noted earlier, workers in Kryvy Rih had attempted to prevent the destruction of the factories. Unlike the wait-and-see attitude so common among peasants at that time, they and the remaining engineers restored and reopened their places of work without any German signal or help."[130]

---

[130] *Harvest of Despair*, pp. 152 – 153.

"Ukraine's light industry underwent a more independent development. As Fedir Pihido described the situation at the sugar refineries: "The roar of the battles had not yet faded and the Germans had barely arrived, when the factory workers and employees crept out of the holes where they had been hiding from the Bolsheviks as deserters, and got together to reconstruct their factories. The German commissars watched and wondered where all this was coming from." Many employees took out machines and parts they had hidden in wells, ponds, under heaps of scrap iron, and cases in the ground, and by 1942, with little or no German assistance, most of the town-based factories were up and running. There also developed new professional associations, such as one of engineers in the Kiev region that secured for itself a ten-year lease of all the brick, cement, and ceramics factories."[131]

There is also an interesting reference to the loyalty to the Communist Party of the average Ukrainian worker:

"At first the Germans were in no rush to hire and demanded guarantees that job candidates were reliable and at the very least had not been in the Communist party or Komsomol. Thereafter many Germans realized that such membership had not been based on any real conviction. Although in Dnipropetrovsk Communists had to wear brassards, at the H. Petrovsky Metallurigical Factory, whose workers the SD found "very diligent, reliable, and absolutely loyal to the enterprise," the main engineer was a man known as a former party member... ".[132]

The relative success of the evacuation of the Russian war industries has been addressed in dedicated works by other authors and to explore this massive, dramatic and fascinating undertaking here is beyond the scope of this work, however, it is important it be understood that the success of this giant moving program may have been enhanced by wartime propaganda, as John Fischer pointed out earlier.

---

[131] Ibid, p. 155.

[132] Ibid, pp. 152 – 153.

[133] An interesting, if anecdotal, example of Soviet reluctance to recognize western, especially U.S. aid via Lend-Lease was the answer given to a visiting British officer from a Soviet officer about the Jeep vehicles they were using. When asked where they came from, the Soviet officer replied that they were made in Russia. When the Soviet officer was shown the English writing on the dials on the dashboard, he smiled and replied, that

Allied Support

The workday was brutal for the typical Soviet factory worker, 12 hours a day and as much as 18 hours on Sunday. This applied to women and children as well. In a detonator factory, one worker said women and children worked side by side, they piled boxes and crates on top of each other so the little hands could reach the lathes.

As the Germans were to do a year later, Russia also turned to its prisoner population to fill the gaps on the production lines, mines and farms. Somewhere in the vicinity of a million prisoners were put to work, directly or indirectly for the war effort.

To demonstrate the Allied commitment to Russia and her importance in the fight against Germany, the Allies made huge transfers of raw and finished materials to the Soviets. Over the war period, and as late as 1946, the Allies sent 811 merchant vessels with materials of all kinds to Russian ports, the German U-Boats sinking 58 of them. At the off-loading ports of Murmansk, the British had to supply air cover to protect the port and even supply cranes that could unload the heavier items; the largest Russian crane could only lift 11 tons.

Although the Russians produced a large number of tanks during the war, this production effort was seriously disrupted in 1941 and again in 1942 with the relocation of plants and factories to the East. The Allies, especially Canada provided several thousand thanks during these years to supplement depleted Russian stocks until the relocated factories came back on line. During the course of the war the Western Allies shipped an immense amount of raw and finished materials to Russia. One of the most important was explosives and explosive material. For example the Allies shipped over 103,000 tons of the chemical Toluene a key component in TNT, providing a third of all explosive material used by Russia. This additional material alleviated an ammunition shortage in the most critical early years of the war.

At the conclusion of the war the following materials had been delivered to the Russians: 22,206 aircraft, 351,700 light and medium trucks, 78,000 Jeeps,[133] 15 million pairs of boots, 380,135 field phones, 40,000 field radios,

these vehicles were originally built for export. Also, the stenciled lettering usually found on all U.S. military vehicles was occasionally left on the Lend-Lease vehicles shipped to Russia. A common belief was that the letters "USA" stood for Ubiyat Sukinsyna Adolfa, roughly translated to mean Kill the Son-of-a-Bitch Adolf.

125 million miles of telephone cable, 107 million square yards of cotton cloth, 4,500,000 tons of food stuffs, 49,000 tons of leather, 35,170 motorcycles, 1,981 locomotives, 11,155 freight cars, 12,755 tanks, 8,701 tractors and 361,903 heavy trucks. It was this material that kept the Russians in the war and clearly helped them win it as Lend-Lease consisted of 7% to 10% of total Russian military production, depending on the source quoted.[134]

With the west now beginning to deliver all manner of material support to the desperate Soviets, this was not the first time western aid arrived in Russia. In the late 1920's Sergo Ordzhonikidze, Stalin's commissar of heavy industry invited western manufacturing firms to come and design, produce and build new factories in Russia, chief among them was Austin, General Motors and Ford. Austin built a huge complex at Nizhni Novgorod and Ford built plants to produce its Model A and Model AA light trucks. Later, agricultural plants producing tractors we constructed at Stalingrad and Kharkov. In addition to vehicle and farm production was plants built to produce semi and finished metals, such as the steel mills built by Arthur McKee and Company of Ohio at Magnitogorsk, which had to be up and operational in eight weeks!

Red Production

Jason Long, in his exhaustive study of Soviet wartime armaments production has this to say on Soviet tank production:[135]

> "Soviet production of armored vehicles was far more disrupted by the invasion than was the case with artillery production. It was more centralized in locations that were further west than Stalin would have wished in the fall of 1941."

> "A new generation of armored vehicles was just being fielded by the Soviets based on their experiences in Spain, Finland and the Far East as well as German successes (in France) when the Germans attacked. The primary conclusions were the needs to increase armor thicknesses, to prevent engine fires and the ability to operate in extremely low temperatures."

---

[134] *A German-Soviet Military-Economic Comparison*, Arvo L. Vercamer, http://feldgrau.com, 2002.

[135] *Forging the Red Star, An Examination of Soviet Armaments Factories and Their Production*, http://members.tripod.com/~Sturmvogel/sovWarProd.html.

[136] An interesting and seldom mentioned defect of the T-34 was the occasional spontaneous explosion of its internal (later models of the T-34 were equipped with

"The T-34 was designed to withstand 76mm shells at ranges over a kilometer and 37mm shells at any range. A new diesel engine was adopted since diesel fuel has a far higher flash point than ordinary gasoline and is thus much less likely to explode. Its sloping armor was adopted to maximize effective armor thickness for a given weight. Due to the international situation it entered production in 1940 before all the bugs were worked out. The Kharkov and Stalingrad Tractor Factories were forced to use components from older tanks to meet their production quotas in the early part of their production runs and the new engine and transmissions that were used still had to have the bugs worked out. More T-34's may have been lost to mechanical failure than to enemy action in 1941[136]. Stalingrad was responsible for 42% of all T-34's produced up until the German attack in August 1942.[137] A total of 35,120 T-34/76's were built during the war."[138]

One aspect of tank production that has frequently been overlooked is the issue of serviceability. Both combatants stressed production of new vehicles over that of the production of spare parts and maintenance components to keep the vehicles in service. The historical literature is littered with references to broken down, abandoned and crew-destroyed vehicles, many due to the lack of proper maintenance and availability of spare parts to perform this important component of keeping a vehicle, its crew and its parent unit in action. The Russian Army was able to address this issue only in the last stages of the war and the Germans, due to their strained economic circumstances, never adequately did. As an example, in the opening months of Barbarossa, Russian tank serviceability rates were as low as 27% in some units. Both nations were primarily concerned with the establishment of new combat units and the rebuilding of combat depleted units, usually to the detriment of the spare parts inventory.

In 1943 the Russians took a page from the Germans operating manual and using captured PzKw Mk. III tank and StuG Mk. III (*sturmgeschutz* or assault gun) vehicles to create the SU-76i, a Russian assault gun carrier,

external fuel tanks as well) empty diesel fuel tanks (?), which usually destroyed the vehicle.

[137] The Kirovskiy and Izhorskiy factories, located in Leningrad, were evacuated to Chelyabinsk, along with a portion of the Kharkov Diesel Factory, and the combination was called Tankograd (Tank City).

[138] *Forging the Red Star.*

mounting a 76mm gun. About 200 of these conversions were produced from vehicles captured in and around Stalingrad in early 1943.[139]

Not only are the production quantities themselves a point to be proud of, the quality of these weapons was excellent as well. Great efforts were made to reduce the amount of time and of materials required to produce the weapons.[140] The 76mm USV divisional gun, for example was redesigned to make it more suitable for anti-tank use and to simplify its manufacture. The hours required to manufacture this gun went from 1029 in 1942 to 475 in 1944, and the parts required to assemble one went from 2080 to 719. The decline in hours required to manufacture the 76mm gun is a perfect example of the learning curve in manufacturing, though it is suspected some of the steep decline in 1944 is attributable to sophisticated machine tools supplied through Allied Lend-Lease.[141]

This production sophistication and determination enabled the Russians to produce over 188,000 pieces of anti-tank, field and anti-aircraft artillery during the war[142], an incredible feat of manufacturing and the chief reason the Russians were able to create artillery divisions (an in 1944 Corps sized artillery units) with massive numbers of guns per division.

Despite prodigious feats of weapons production, the issue of quality control as it pertains to engine, transmission, fit and finish and crew comfort seems to be a secondary consideration:

> "One characteristic of Western armored fighting vehicles that is little discussed by the Soviets was that the reliability of Western tanks allowed then to drive on long past the time that Soviet tanks had to be returned to the factory for a total mechanical rebuild.[143] Soviet vehicles were purposely designed with short mechanical lifetimes. In combat this mattered little when the

---

[139] In an attempt to find a solution to destroy the heaviest German vehicles the Russian Su-152 assault gun which mounted a 152mm main gun, was introduced in the spring of 1943 and a few saw combat at Kursk in July. The crews nicknamed it the *Zvierboi* or "Animal Killer" for its ability to destroy the German Panther, Tiger and Elephant tanks and assault guns.

[140] In 1941 the Germans captured approximately 5,000 of these excellent weapons and about 3,000,000 rounds of its ammunition. With another 3,000 captured in 1942, the Germans now had sufficient stock to equip its anti-tank guns and *panzerjager* units with the weapon. The Germans were so impressed with the 76mm gun that they manufactured ammunition for it when captured stocks ran low.

[141] *Forging the Red Star.*

[142] Ibid.

life expectancy was measured in days. But in training units this reliability of Western tanks was a godsend since they needed far less maintenance than Soviet tanks.[144] Even in combat units this characteristic was useful, why else would the 1st Guards Mechanized Corps convert *from* the T-34/85 *to* (italics added for emphasis) the U.S. made M-4 Sherman, a tank with a smaller gun and thinner armor?"[145]

This action on the part of Russian tank commanders reflects the findings of U.S. and Russian tank testing commission at the Aberdeen Proving Ground, Maryland in 1942. The final suggestion by the commission was the need to bring the Russian tanks (T-34/76 and KV-1 were tested) up to American standards of reliability and simplicity of operation as soon as possible.[146]

The question of maintenance and engine/transmission life expectancies of Soviet tanks is an important one and has a direct bearing on the ability of the Russian Army to engage and pursue the enemy. The recommended maintenance for tank engines was 250 to 300 hours for the T-34, 200 to 250 for the JS series tanks. The average travel distance for one tank engine hour is 6 to 8 kilometers. The intervals between maintenance for the T-34/85 was 250 hours, however the crews and/or unit commanders frequently pushed that to 320 to 350 hours during mobile operations.

The issue of engine/transmission reliability of the early T-34's is captured in photographs taken during the opening weeks of the German invasion. In one of the more popular photographs a disabled T-34 is shown on one

---

[143] In late 1941, 18% of the Red Army's front-line strength in armored vehicles was replaced monthly.

[144] Evgeni Bessonov in his *Tank Rider, Into the Reich with the Red Army* (Greenhill Books, London, 2003) frequently mentions the poor fighting condition of the T-34 variants, even as late as the winter of 1944. He mentions situations covering all aspects of T-34 usage including poor running condition as well as vehicles with inoperable main guns, etc. The fact that these vehicles were kept at the front with the advanced elements of the Red Army says something else about the ability of the Russian forces to keep up with the damage inflicted by almost around the clock combat as well as basic maintenance.

[145] *Lend –Lease Armored Fighting Vehicles*, Jason Long, **http://members.tripod.com/~Sturmvogel/SovWar Prod.html**.

[146] It appears that reliability standards had not improved too much with the passage of time. In the 1968 invasion of Czechoslovakia orders from Russian Army high command were issued to push off the road any vehicle that broke down or could not move. Soon several hundred tanks, personnel carriers, artillery tractors, even vehicles containing top-secret cipher equipment rolled down the steep roadsides.

of Lvov's main thoroughfares with a spare transmission strapped to its rear deck. The inference is that not only was the installed transmission not reliable but the ability of the crew or the unit maintenance section to have a ready replacement is questionable.

In addition to the mechanical reliability of the T-34 was the question of training and vehicle distribution to the fighting units. In the midst of the chaotic reorganization taking place in the four western military districts facing the Germans, training and crew vehicle familiarization was also just as chaotic.

Consider the following regarding the status and methodology of crew tank training in the pre-war and early war periods:

> "...Training was normally organized in worn and torn training vehicles in order to save operational hours of maneuver tanks (the front line combat units), which was real nonsense. As a result, the new vehicles, which were more advanced and had significant improvements from the tanks of the early series, were kept in garages, unused. Whereas it was insane to use BT-2 tanks to train crews of BT-7 tanks, using old T-26 vehicles in training crews of T-34s was complete absurdity! For instance, by 1 December 1940 the tank forces of the Red Army had only 37 T-34 tanks in service. It is only natural then that propertraining was impossible under the circumstances. By 1 June 1941 a total of 832 T-34 tanks were deployed in the western military districts, but of these only 38 were in use, the remainders were sealed for long term storage! As a result, no more than 150 T-34 tank crews had been properly trained to operate the vehicles by the time the war started."[147]

Regardless of the few shortcomings of the early T-34's[148], the vehicle was a masterful achievement by both the Soviet military and Soviet manufacturing. The T-34 represented to the Red Army and the Russian people nothing less than a war-winning weapon; it had all the advanced features of the most modern armored fighting vehicles, and introduced several new ones. It truly symbolized the communist victory over Nazism.

---

[147] *T-34 Medium Tank (1939 - 1943)* by Mikhail Baryatinskiy, Ian Allen Publishing, 2007, p. 60. Reproduced with permission.

[148] Affectionately known or nick-named "tridtsatchetverka" among the Russians.

It was manufactured in the widest possible quantities which suggested its value and the great devotion of the war workers and military to its success. By the conclusion of the war over 34,780 T-34/76 models, 22,559 T-34/85 models were built (not including the thousands of self-propelled guns built on the T-34 chassis), an impressive feat of military production by any standard.

While the Russian military became well supplied to defeat the Germans, the average Russian was coping with shortages of all kinds. With the desperate condition of Soviet industry, civilian goods manufacture was almost shut down. The everyday items from hats, pants and shoes to pots and pans had to be made locally, bartered or traded for. For example, in 1944 the production of shoes was down 93%, cloth 86% and clothing 90% and if this wasn't enough to cope with, gross agricultural production declined by 63% in 1943.

Unknown to the Germans, the U.S.S.R. contained within it four major industrial zones. The Moscow zone, the Donets Basin, the Urals and the Kuznets basin, located in western Siberia. *Fremde Ost* identified two at the outset of the war, (Moscow and the Donets zones) and became aware of the third (the Ural) by early 1942. The remaining zone in the Far East was discussed within German intelligence but they had no hard data as to its size and related industries to prove its existence; as such it was dismissed by Hitler. Unfortunately it was to be this last zone that enabled the Soviets to weather the dark days of the summer of 1942 when the second industrial relocation program was put into action (the first was the previous summer, 1941) and arms production was at its lowest.

An additional element unknown to the Germans was the stockpiling of strategic materials prior to the war. This factor, in conjunction with the undisrupted industrial zones in the Urals and the Far East, was to enable the Soviets to keep the Red Army supplied, if just barely, and operational until the relocated industries established themselves, begun production, recruited and trained new armies and started receiving the quantities of Lend/Lease goods that began to arrive in 1942 in quantity via Murmansk, Iran and the Far East.

The attempt to summon forth Russia's patriotic past notwithstanding, Stalin was not about to rest on historic memory and goodwill of the people to fight, starve, die and work to exhaustion. Along with the responsibilities of maintaining internal order, Lavrenti Beria was also involved in the war effort. As part of the Soviet hierarchy, he assumed oversight of war production, especially vigilant for any signs of slowing or softening of worker effort and output. Everyone in the plants and offices and institutions directly or indirectly connected with armaments and munitions was gripped by dreadful fear. Beria was no engineer. He was placed in control for the precise purpose of inspiring deadly fear.

The awarding of medals and decorations by the Soviets during the war was quickly discovered to be a great morale and production motivator. The numbers of medals struck and awarded during the war for both military and civilian achievement are nothing short of incredible. During the 1941 – 1945 period the Soviets awarded over 11,000,000 medals, awards and decorations. And it was done quickly too. The U.S. Army often took as long as six months to process individual awards, the newly motivated Red Army, as little three days.

Unlike its western counterparts Russia saw its workers as a war Front of its own. Medals and awards were awarded to those factories and plants exceeding their production quotas and their participation in the war was no rear area effort run by the civilian sector but closely allied to the fighting fronts.[149] There is ample photographic evidence of the workers contributing their hard earned wages to purchase a tank or airplane, their best wishes and greetings painted on the turret or fuselage and sent it to the front along with a delegation of workers that built it.[150]

To demonstrate the importance Stalin put on industrial effort in modern war, he once lectured the Politburo that, 'Hitler's generals, raised on the dogma of Clausewitz and Moltke, could not understand that war is won in the factories'. There is evidence that the Soviets put as much emphasis and importance on the armaments worker as on the front line soldier. There are ample photographic records of factory workers wearing medals who never went near a battlefield. This had many benefits for national morale,

---

[149] The awards for exceptional labor efforts are as follows, followed by the number awarded: Medal For Assiduous Labor Effort In the Great Patriotic War of 1941 - 1945, Est. 8,000,000; Medal For Outstanding Achievements in Labor , 7,000,000; Order of the Red Star, 2,860,000; Order of the Red Banner of Labor, 800,000; Medal For the Restoration of Iron and Steel Industries of the South and Medal For the Restoration of the Coal Mining Industries in the Donbas, 115,600; Order of Honor, 66,000; Gold Hammer and Sickle Medal, 19,000.

[150] The two most popular slogans were: "For Stalin!" and "For the Motherland!"

to directly include the worker in the fight and not as a distant participant who only heard and read of the war and their efforts via propaganda and the occasional factory visit by a wounded soldier.[151]

In addition to the above factors was the comparison of the economies of the two nations involved in this gigantic battle. The Soviets ability to turn out prodigious quantities of war material was based on two factors, one of which the Germans would never be able to compete with and that was the overall size of the Soviet economy. The GNP of the U.S.S.R. was simply larger than Germany's[152]. Second, and of critical importance was Stalin's firm control of what his now militarized economy produced. From the moment of the invasion in June 1941 all production was directed to producing war material. All consumer goods production and importation was halted. By contrast, Germany for a variety of reasons did not assume full wartime production status until January 1943! Even then, compliance was spotty until later that same year.

Such was the Soviet military economy by 1944 that Germany had no hope of ever achieving productive parity. As early as 1941 the Soviet military industrial economy was experiencing what Seaton describes "paying the penalty of overproduction", if an economy the size of the Soviet Union's was overproducing arms, obsolete or not in 1941, the portent for Germany for an easy time in Russia was dim indeed. A prudent leader, bent on attacking his most deadly foe would spend whatever time and resources were needed to carefully evaluate his enemy's ability to design, produce and field weapons. The callous contempt for anything Slavic, eastern or communist tainted and clouded German planning, at one time the world's most experienced, capable, most astute military command in the world. If Russia, home of world Communism was the deadly threat it was made out to be in Germany, it was not reflected in the amount of planning and consideration given Barbarossa, or Case Barbarossa, to give it its full title. The largest land invasion in modern times was given less thought to its unique conditions of manpower requirements, fuel needs, climate, distances and time than was devoted to the invasion of the much smaller,

---

[151] Peter Tsouras in his fine book *The Great Patriotic War* (Greenhill Books, 1992, pp 8,9) shows aircraft designer Sergei Ilyushin in uniform and an elderly rifle designer Fyoder Tokarev wearing medals.

[152] Allied Lend-Lease added to 5% to Soviet resources in 1942 and 10% in 1943, 1944. From *The USSR and Total War: Why Didn't the Soviet Economy Collapse in 1942?* by Mark Harrison, Professor of Economics, University of Warwick, 2002.

weaker nations invested earlier. The underestimation of Russian abilities, military as well as industrial under the command of Soviet communism was a major error; based on a military that preferred operational expertise to logistics and accurate intelligence.

The relationship between the western Allies and the Soviets was almost from the start a contentious one. The Russians were constantly demanding more of what the Allies could deliver, better quality than what they did send her and when the shipments did arrive, it was never soon enough. Considering Russia's enormous sacrifice in men and material it is hard to argue with her being too demanding or fickle. However, at the beginning of the Third Protocol of the Lend-Lease agreements in 1943 there is the first instance of U.S. resistance or questioning of the requests by the Russians regarding the aid. The era of imminent threat to the survival of the Soviet Union had passed and the Allies, especially the British and later the U. S. were beginning to wonder, especially in light of major increases in Russian weapons production of all kinds, just what were the Soviets doing with all this material, especially the most requested items, aircraft. This matter and a number of issues such as basing of Allied (U.S.) bombers on Russian territory for shuttle bombing runs and the requests of the latest Allied aircraft technology (especially the U. S. made Norden bombsite) to Russia contributed to the growing tensions between to the two nations. Add these military and supply disagreements to the growing ideological and cultural differences and what we have is the real beginning of the Cold War.[153]

Russian household consumption was badly affected by rearmament in 1940, however it was severely impacted in 1941 and even more in 1943 and 1944. Living standards fell to 40% below pre-war levels as millions were overworked and malnourished and worker mortality rose significantly. Much analysis has been done by economists regarding the solvency of the Soviet economy and how it survived, especially in the first two years of the war. These studies have addressed all the nominal aspects of economic analysis including supply, demand, production, investment, opportunity costs, payoffs and choice. Under all these classical elements of economics

---

[153] The issue of cordial inter-allied relations was amply demonstrated by the concern in the Kremlin council about what would happen if the west halted the flow of goods to the U.S.S.R. especially that most desirable item, the American truck, the Studebaker. It was praised by both private and general for its reliability and toughness. Along with Soviet trucks it carried the Soviet *Katyusha* rocket launcher and was the prime mover for soviet artillery from 1944 on.

the Soviet economy should have collapsed-under a western model that is. However under a demand economy one has to factor in state imposed discipline, that is, who will work at what job producing what article for what price. When this aspect is no longer up to the worker or consumer to make a choice, the answer of why the Soviet economy did not collapse is more easily understood. Commissars were not only limited to supervision and performance of the Red Army in the field, there was the civilian worker equivalent that prowled the factory, plant, shop and mine all insuring the effort and result of their labor went to the greater glory of the Soviet state. One final aspect to Soviet munitions production should be kept in mind, that it survived by virtue of employing 60 percent of its women to work in the factories and in food production. A significant statistic in any economy.

The psychic damage of the invasion was so deep and lasting that even the victory over Germany four years later could not undo it. So secure had the Soviet nation become, so confidant in its military and its command, as well as in Stalin, and the Communist Party, which assured the population the sacred Russian soil would never be occupied by any enemy. As a whole, the shock of four years of occupation, starvation, brutality and death became a scar that, perhaps, may never heal.

The demand economy, especially under wartime stress of the Soviet Union allowed it to perform prodigious feats of production and economies of scale. However, the industrial tunnel vision of producing only what was needed to win the war was to have severe affects on the Russian economy after the war. With the Allies supplying many of the finished infrastructure goods and the Russian industries concentrating on weapons, all other needs, such as consumer goods, even those as basic as clothing and shoes was diverted to war production. The result was an economy so unbalanced that, after the war it would take decades to redirect it back toward a semblance of normality and many say it never did get there.

Attack! T-34/76 with supporting infantry aboard.

Chapter Five:
The Western Allies

"The U.S. Army... should expect to confront
11 or 12 million Axis soldiers in the European theater,
amounting to around 400 to 500 fully equipped and
splendidly trained divisions... The Allied powers would
therefore have to field 700 to 900 divisions...
approximately 25 million men."

"Writing the (Allied) Victory Plan of 1941"

"To American production: without which
this war would have been lost"

*- Joseph Stalin, toasting Franklin Roosevelt at the
Teheran Conference, November 1943*

This chapter will introduce the Western Allies and their contributions to the successful efforts to defeat Nazi Germany. It will look at the various military operations the United States and Great Britain undertook in Western Europe and North Africa in preparation for the landing in Northwestern Europe. Also a survey of the major weapons used by them will be conducted, examining their performance in combat.

The Grand Alliance

By the early months of 1944 the war in Western Europe was already into its fifth year. The dread reality of a two front war for the German-led portion of the Axis was about to become a reality; the only question that remained was where and when the second front would begin. The primary members of the Western Allies were China, France, Great Britain and its Dominions, and the United States. The Soviet Union, the other major member, made up the eastern Allied member.

The primary mission of the Grand Alliance, a term coined by British Prime Minister Winston Churchill, was the planning for and operational pursuit of the defeat of Germany, Italy and Japan. Initially contemplated was a strategy of economic blockade to wear down the German economy and when the proper moment arrived, attempt an invasion of the occupied area to combat and defeat the German army.

It was quickly realized that due to Germany's rapid and extensive victories and the amassing of large tracts of Europe, an economic blockade vis a vis that of World War I would not be feasible. The economic resources available to Germany were far more extensive than in the last war and an economic blockade would not only be ineffective; the ability to impose a blockade of such a vast area was impractical. Therefore, planning committees were established to chart the various strengths and weaknesses of defeating first Germany, and then Japan. As events turned out, the task became a simultaneous endeavor.

After several conferences, meetings and creation of several planning staffs a consensus was reached, that of a dual approach to the return to western Europe. The primary effort would be a landing somewhere in western France and a secondary, a large diversion, somewhere in the central Mediterranean.

In charge of the invasion planning effort was U.S. General Dwight D. Eisenhower with his headquarters in London. The choice of an American to lead the invasion effort was a direct recognition of the size of the personnel and materiel support contributed by the United States. The British were to be the other partner in the staffing and planning, with smaller contributions provided by the Canadians and even smaller contingents of Free-French and Free-Polish units.[154]

The allies soon came to an understanding that an invasion of occupied Europe against a largely undefeated German army could not be risked, as early as the U.S. originally wanted to invade. This was initially in 1942 and as a second choice, a year later in 1943. An agreement was reached to develop methods or moving, controlling and commanding large amphibious forces with several preliminary landings to gain experience.

The first was in North Africa with Operation Torch in November 1942, then in July 1943, at Sicily with Operation Husky and even later against several sites in Italy, Operation Baytown at the 'toe' of Italy and later that month Operation Avalanche at Salerno and finally Operation Shingle at Anzio. Each one more difficult, more elaborate and closer to the German homeland. By January1944 the Western Allies had developed confidence in their methods and had also trained and toughened their field armies to a level of confidence that would insure success in the largest and most important of all the invasions, that of France, the shortest and most direct route to Germany.

The Arsenal of Democracy

The last to arrive in the Allied camp and its second biggest member was the United States of America. After a decade of political wrangling as to the possibility of becoming engaged in another European war, the isolationist elements in the U.S. political family were silenced for good on the morning of 7 December 7, 1941 with the Japanese air and naval attack against the U.S. Pacific fleet port at Pearl Harbor in the Hawaiian Islands. The U.S. inclusion into a new World War was completed with the

---

[154] The fate of the Polish soldiers left in Poland was not as benign as their Free- Polish brethren. As the Red Army advanced into Poland new armies were formed from conscripted Polish residents. Those objecting to serving their new masters were forcibly drafted into the Red Army, albeit in units designated "1ˢᵗ Polish Army" etc. Those objecting faced reprisals by NKVD units against their families. They were never accepted as equals with the Red Army, being referred to as 'westerners' or *zapadniki*, former capitalists, and therefore suspect.

German declaration of war against the United States a few weeks later, in keeping with their agreement with the other members of the Axis, Japan and Italy[155]. It was ultimately seen as a politically foolish and strategically unnecessary move on Germany's part.[156]

With the U.S. firmly in the war, it now had to, almost from scratch, build an armed forces with which to combat the Axis. Having the good fortune of the protection of two large oceans to her east and west, and friendly neighbors to the north and south, the United States had the enviable geographical location of being separated by vast distances from her enemies. This allowed her the time and place in which to build and train her armies in almost complete peace and security.

With a two-front war to be fought, and with oceans to be crossed, the United States had the economic and industrial resources with which to build the might needed to fight two enemies. What was sorely missing was the experience in doing so, that which the British had accumulated the hard way, by trial and error. But acquired it she had.

With the good fortune and intelligence of having the right people in the right places, the allies were able to agree on what military to build, what the objectives were, creating a plan to accomplish the goals, who was going to command it, and how and when their objectives were to be achieved.

After several years of combat, the Western Allies realized that the quality and competence of the German fighting armies were first rate. The question remained how to fight this superb military machine. The strategic evaluations conducted by the Allies of the German enemy soon presented them with an answer and at the same time provide direction.

Captured German equipment and soldiers confirmed the assessments of Allied intelligence about German training and equipment design. Their findings revealed that German tanks, equipment, artillery and small weapons were state-of-the-art and compared with existing Allied weapons

---

[155] In 1932, the year F. D. Roosevelt was elected, the United States had the 16th largest military (138,000 men) in the world. The nations of Czechoslovakia, Poland, Romania, Spain, Turkey and Yugoslavia, to name a few, had larger armed forces.

[156] It has been widely recognized that the German declaration of war on the United States in December 1941 was a self-defeating invitation to engage the largest productive nation on Earth. It was a direct reflection of Hitler's opinion of America as a nation of shopkeepers, over sexed and jazz crazy mongrel peoples and one that was far away, both physically and psychologically.

and in several cases were superior. However, what was soon ascertained was they could not compete with was the quantity of this material required to fight a continent-wide war, which was soon to be confirmed shortly after the successful Allied invasion of France at Normandy. Echoing Stalin's observation that this will be a war of production, the Allies, the U.S. in particular, began to organize and construct the factories and design and produce the weapons to defeat the Axis enemy.[157]

The "arsenal of democracy" was not a shallow remark. The United States during the 1941 – 1945 period produced thousands of weapons of all kinds, many featuring the most advanced technical design. Furthermore, in 24 critical areas of raw materials and foodstuffs, the United States possessed and in quantity exceeded all other nations, allied and axis in but six.[158] In weapons production the numbers are equally impressive. With the exception of tank and artillery production, the United States out produced all other nations, allied or axis in the key areas of fighter, transport and bomber aircraft, trucks (lorries), machine guns and all types of naval shipping. As an example of the U.S. naval productive capacity, the United States produced 141 aircraft carriers of all types, the closest competitor, Japan, with 16.

Hail Britannia!

Frequently seen as the senior partner of the Grand Alliance, Great Britain formed the front line of the Allied efforts to return to Western Europe. As the primary nation to guarantee the support of Poland against aggressors, however unable to follow-through on its support, Britain nevertheless complied with its agreement and declared war on Germany in 1939.

By the time the United States was enveloped by the war in December 1941, England had been in the war for over two years, and had been actively fighting Germany on several fronts. The first clash with Germany was the April 1940 invasion of Norway, then later that year, in May/June, the invasion of France until forced off the continent at Dunkirk by a flawed Anglo-French strategy and audacious German mechanized and air

---

[157] For an even handed and interesting look at the war effort of all combatants, see *The Library of Congress World War II Companion*, Edited by David M. Kennedy, et al, Simon & Schuster, 2007.

[158] The productive measurement indices are: coal, oil, iron, copper, lead, zinc, tin, nickel, bauxite, manganese, tungsten, chromium, molybdenum, magnesite, sulphur/pyrites, phosphates, potash, rubber, wheat, rice, maize (corn), potatoes, sugar and meat.

movement. In July, Germany prepared to finish its offensive in the West with an invasion of Britain. However, the failure of the Luftwaffe to defeat Britain's Royal Air Force in the sky's over southern and central England ended German military activity for the next four years.

In the Spring of 1941 Great Britain and the Greek First and Second Armies encountered the Wehrmacht again in Greece, in April, where they were once-again out-maneuvered by the Germans and forced to evacuate by sea to the island of Crete in the central Mediterranean. The final humiliation of the BEF (British Expeditionary Force) and their Greek evacuees came a month later when the Germans, lacking sufficient naval presence in the central Mediterranean launched a bold airborne invasion of the island. In a battle that was touch-and-go for several days, the Germans once again out-maneuvered the British Commonwealth defenders and Greek allies forcing another a seaborne evacuation to North Africa.

Thus concluded British efforts to contain German aggression in the opening years of the war, with dismal results. The western Allies were forced off the continent and were soon expected to suffer the same result in North Africa with the loss of the Suez Canal, threats to oil supplies, and the drastic consequences that would entail on Allied resources.

In the 1940-42 period the British fought the Axis in the air with the Royal Air Force (RAF) and on the ground against the German Afrika Korps under the command of General Erwin Rommel and his Italian allies in Tunisia and Libya. After the U.S. invasion of the western portions of North Africa in Morocco in Operation Torch in November 1942 and the British offensive after the German defeat at El Alamain that the writing was on the wall for the Axis in Africa. By 11 May 1943 the end was reached at Menzel Temime on Cape Bon in Tunisia and 250,415 hard to replace German and Italian soldiers entered Allied captivity.

The conclusion of operations in North Africa set the stage for the continuation of the war into the southern reaches of Europe via Sicily and Italy and finally France.

Dieppe

Laying the groundwork for the Allied landing against a defended coast would require the development of new procedures, methods and devices that did not exist. Amphibious operations, with the arguable exception of airborne landings are the most risky of all military operational exercises.

The transition from ship to water to land exposes the attacker to numerous instances of vulnerability that do not exist in other troop movements. To minimize these risks, practice landings were planned and developed to familiarize the commanders and participating units with their responsibilities and areas of greatest danger.

During the Allied buildup for a future trans-channel invasion of Europe many factors and pressures came together during the discussions and development of just how the invasion could take place, where and with who. Among these was the desire of British Commonwealth troops to take an active part in the defense of Britain as well as the growing demands by Russia for a Second Front in the West to relieve German pressure on its forces, especially in the first two years of the German invasion.

In July 1940 British Admiral of the Fleet Sir Roger Keys was directed by the newly organized allied Combined Operations Command to undertake the development of a program of harassing raids against German occupied France designed to gain combat experience, probe the German defenses and their response times to a threat and to provide tangible evidence to the occupied nations that Britain was still a viable combatant and propaganda material for future use.

The French coastal town of Dieppe was selected for such a harassing raid and on 19 August 1942 6,000 Canadian and a few other Commonwealth troops were landed on the rocky beach. The planning for the raid was full of omission and errors and this was reflected in the many components that were missing or misunderstood and were crucial to ensuring the raids success. To address our interests in the raid here, suffice to say the raid was a failure. The landing was confused and half of the raiding force put ashore was killed or captured. One of the primary goals of the raid was to lure the Luftwaffe into action and inflict a significant loss on their shore based fighter strength. That was not achieved, the British lost 106 aircraft to the Luftwaffe's 48.

What the Dieppe disaster did provide was a clear need to not assume that an amphibious landing was simply putting men and their weapons into boats and rowing ashore. The complexities of timing, weather, geography, hydrology and enemy intelligence would all take a higher priority in the planning process. The transfer of many more thousands of men, equipment and the need to properly command them all in a major assault on Europe was to assume the major part of the Allied commands time and energy for the next two years. The road to Berlin was to be longer and fraught with more danger than anyone now thought.

The Lure of Technology

"One day a Tiger Royal tank (the Tiger II was frequently referred to by the western Allies as the Tiger Royal or King Tiger) got within 150 yards of our tank and knocked me out. Five of our tanks opened fire on him from ranges of 200 to 600 yards and got five or six hits on the front of the Tiger. They all just glanced off and the Tiger backed off and got away. If we had a tank like the Tiger, we would all be home today".[159]

With the Allies were firmly ashore in North-western France in the summer of 1944, their ships pouring a torrent of men, weapons and machines into the ever expanding bridgehead, by early July they finally came face to face with the 'best and the brightest' of German combat units. The Waffen SS panzer units, which heretofore had been posted at and were anticipating the landings 175 miles north-west near Boulogne-Calais in the Pas de Calais area, were now encountered during the grueling 'battle of the breakout' from the Normandy area into greater France.

This was not the first U.S. encounter with the panzerwaffen, as the experience in North Africa had provided a baptism of fire there two years earlier in 1942. However capable the Wehrmacht's 10th, 15th and 21st panzer divisions were in Tunisia (they served commendably under the 'Desert Fox' himself, General, later Field Marshal, Erwin Rommel), but for sheer blind obedience, zeal and ferocious tenacity, nothing matched fighting against the Waffen SS panzer and panzer grenadier units.

With the U.S. and its allies now in mainland Europe, they were for the first time matched against Germany's best. With this in mind comes the matter of Allied preparedness in men and equipment, especially weapons.

The technical quality of Allied armament in almost all respects had caught up and in most areas now exceeded Axis, even German, equipment. In the air there was the Boeing B-17, North American P-51, Supermarine Spitfire and PBY Catalina and Avro Lancaster, on the sea were the Missouri-class battleships, under the sea were radar-carrying submarines of the Seawolf class. On land were almost unlimited amounts of artillery and the accurate tools to direct it; the ubiquitous Jeep and the largest heavy truck fleet in the

---

[159] Conversation with Sergeant Clyde D. Brunson, report,
    2nd U.S. Armored Division, 1945.

world. However there was one glaring exception to Allied military quality, and that was the primary armored fighting vehicle, the main western Allied battle tank, the M4A4 'Sherman'.

In the area of main battle tank design and development, one item that stands out for closer examination and criticism is the U.S. M4 "Sherman" tank. German panzer design and development, especially their Mk's IV, V and VI vehicles, consistently outclassed all Western Allied tank designs during the war. The U.S., in particular, had three years (1939 to 1941) to watch what the Germans were producing and fighting with before the Japanese attack at Pearl Harbor. With the landings in Normandy, three years later, the U. S. had made no significant improvements on, or even considered replacing, their main battle tank, the M4 Sherman, which was designed in the late 30s and began to be issued to units in 1941. This reliable, fast but also high profile, quick to catch fire, under-gunned vehicle raises the question of is this the best the U. S. could do? The baptism of fire in North Africa, especially the early encounters with the German Tiger in late 1942, should have raised a series of warnings of its poor battlefield performance and the risk it posed to U.S. tank crewman and the outcome of Allied operations in the field. Amazing as it seems, these warnings went unheeded or ignored and the Sherman, in all its many variations was to remain in production, largely unchanged, throughout the war.

It is truly remarkable that the "arsenal of Democracy" could not produce a better main battle tank than the Sherman. The United States had none of the disadvantages of Germany with her scarce raw materials and labor, (a good portion of it forced, untrained or slave labor), day and night bombing of the factories and, limited fuel and oil supplies. On the contrary, it enjoyed all the advantages, such as captured machines to evaluate and examine, unlimited raw materials, the excellent design talent and facilities, first class casting and production facilities, testing and training ranges and the result is the Sherman? Perhaps the question should be rephrased to ask why the U.S. stayed with the Sherman, in light of the developments taking place in Russia and Germany after 1941. Fascinating and at the same time bewildering. The many years of self-imposed isolation and neutrality were having their affect.[160]

160 Actually, there was a serious attempt to install a larger, more effective main gun in the M4 Sherman, in late 1943. After field experience confronting the German 88mm antiaircraft gun in North Africa, the U.S. Armored Force Board planned to install the U.S. 90mm M3 anti-aircraft gun in the M4 Sherman in time for the planned invasion of Europe. The gun upgrade for the Sherman would have been a rather easy affair as the

The reason the U.S. stayed with the Sherman was the theory behind the design and deployment of the Sherman by the U.S. Chief of Staff George Marshall and General Leslie McNair. It was envisioned that the Sherman would be used as a tactical exploitive vehicle, not a tank versus tank fighter -- that was the role of the tank destroyer units also being formed. Unfortunately the practical vehicle that was needed had to do both and Germany recognized this a long time ago.

John Mosier, in his "The Blitzkrieg Myth" has this to say about Allied and, in particular, U.S. armor development:

> "[T]he Soviet Union had not made the mistake that the Germans (and the French, British and Americans) had made in tank development. ...the Soviet Union had already built fast, powerful tanks with potent guns. In fact the very excellence of the T34 has obscured the (other) accomplishments of Soviet tank designers in the 1930s."

> "As is well known, early Soviet tank designs derived from the experimental vehicles developed by the American inventor Walter Christie, the first man to build a truly fast tank. The story of American tank design is a sorry one, and nothing illustrates just how appalling it was than the rejection of Christie's designs. It was true that in his obsession with speed, Christie built tanks with numerous problems. But his basic suspension design, easily identified by the four to six large (road) wheels on each track, was the basis for all successful postwar tank suspension systems."[161]

Mosier goes on to describe the wisdom of the Russian use of the Christie suspension system, especially in attacking anti-tank obstacles. The Finns in 1939 had constructed 80 miles of anti-tank obstacles across the Karelian Isthmus. These consisted of the now famous 'dragons teeth', the large upright pointed stones or, later, the belt of four to five rows of graduated

90mm gun was already installed in the turret for the M26 Pershing heavy tank, which was just entering production. In fact Chrysler Engineering Corporation had modified an M4 with the new turret and would have had minimal disruption to Sherman production at the time. However, senior U.S. commands thought the gun would make the Sherman "too much of an unbalanced design", as well as not wanting to disrupt the M26 production schedule, amongst other objections. A mass produced 90mm M4 Sherman available for the Normandy invasion would have had a profound and perhaps decisive impact on the battle. See *M4 Sherman At War*, by Michael Green and James D. Brown, Zenith Press, 2007, pp 121 - 122.

[161] *The Blitzkrieg Myth* by John Mosier, Harper-Collins, 2003, p. 81.

height concrete pyramids. Tanks with the wider tracked large wheeled Christie suspension system could, if approached correctly, ride up and over these obstacles and proceed with their attack. The Allied narrower tracked small wheel leaf-spring systems could not negotiate these obstacles the same way and were much more prone to getting their tracks and/or road wheels jammed between the 'teeth' of the obstacle, stopping the tank, usually in a very conspicuous and exposed position, inviting destruction by the enemy. In addition, the Christie large road wheel system eliminated the need for return rollers, simplifying design and manufacture. There was also the advantage of limited road use on the rubber rimmed road wheels should the track be lost.[162]

The Christie system was eventually used in the Russian T-34 series (as well as the JS[163] series of heavy tanks and SU series of assault guns) of main battle tanks. Considering this was an allied weapon, it is interesting to ask the question why the western allies didn't request the plans and design information and produce the T-34 or close variants of it, for western use.[164] A few examples were sent to the U.S.A. for test and evaluation during the early years of the war, albeit they were the earliest versions, the "A" model, but this evaluation and resulting familiarity should have given the U.S. an inside look at what the foremost producer of tanks in the world of what was to come. Surely western or American technical specialists and engineers compared the Russian tank against their own, in particular the M4A1 "Sherman" and saw the numerous advantages the Russian vehicle offered. This would not only be a reasonable request by the western Allies, but an equitable one as well, as it was the Allies that were supplying the Soviet Union with the massive amounts of life giving raw and finished materials.

---

[162] The robust design of the T-34 is amply demonstrated in that it could even use captured German tank parts to keep them running. There is photographic evidence of a T-34 using German PzKw Mk. V "Panther" road wheels!
See: **http://armor.kiev.ua/Tanks/WWII/T34/tam4_02** (in Russian only).

[163] For the American readership the author has chosen to use the more familiar JS (Joseph Stalin) designation for the Soviet heavy tank series. The series is also referred to as the IS (Iosef Stalin) series of tanks.

[164] One question that has not been given the attention that it demands was the "surprise" appearance of the T-34 tank on the battlefield in the opening weeks of the invasion. Throughout the Russo-German pact period there was extensive exchange of military and economic missions to both nations, including inspection of either nation's armament production facilities. One would think that from August 1939 to June 1941 no mention, photographs or appearance of the T-34 was ever reported. Russia knows how to keep secrets.

A perfectly acceptable and politically correct answer of why the western Allies did not pursue collaboration in producing the T-34 was that the U.S. manufacturing plants were already tooled and into series production of the M4 and training units were already graduating their first classes and to change now, on the eve of war would be foolhardy at the very least. However, another possible answer lurks just off stage. Perhaps the western Allies were reluctant to admit their tank was inferior to the T-34? The capitalist tank the lesser of the communist tank?

The T-34 design in U.S. or at least western manufacturing hands could have speeded the development of a better, more reliable, more comfortable fighting vehicle than the strapped Russian manufacturing plants were capable of. The inclusion of power assist features, better interior and exterior communications systems, crew comfort and the ability to begin planning for an advanced version of the T-34, (what eventually became the T-34/85 series) or even an early JS series of vehicles. The Russian-American tank production/design connection was a missed opportunity that could have made the lives of U.S. and Russian tankers more comfortable, safer and longer.[165]

It was not until late in 1943 when the M10 "Wolverine" was introduced as well as the M36 tank destroyer with a 90mm gun, newer, more powerful vehicles to be sure, but still utilizing the same dated chassis of the Sherman with its high vertical profile, vertical side armor, rotary engine and gasoline fuel, which made the Sherman such a conspicuous, and to their crews, a dangerous target on the battlefield. The appearance of these new vehicles notwithstanding, they were usually collected into their own units (as did the Germans with their Tiger and super-heavy 'specialty' vehicles) and not integrated into the main tank organizations. This was the same year that the Germans introduced such advanced armored vehicles as the PzKw. Mk. V "Panther" and the *panzerjager* (tank hunter) *JagdPanther*.

Consider the following after action report from a Colonel in the U.S. Army in 1943 with regard to operations against the new German heavy tanks, the Pz.Kw VI "Tiger" I SdKfz 181:

"I have inspected the battlefield at Fais Pass in Tunisia, being with the force which retook it. Inspection of our tanks destroyed there indicated that the 88mm gun (with which the German

[165] See **http://www.battlefield.ru/library/archives/stat/stat7.html** for a detailed evaluation of the T-34/76 at the Aberdeen Proving Ground, Aberdeen, Maryland, 1942.

Tiger was equipped) penetrated into the turret (of the U.S. tanks) from the front and out again in the rear. Few gouges were found indicating that all strikes had made penetrations."[166]

Consider the following comments from a German crewman on a tracked artillery vehicle after fighting on several fronts:

"The German soldier of World War II felt no hatred for the individual French soldier, or the British Tommy, or the Ami (Americans), as we called them then. The French were pitied because of their lousy leaders and the fact that they were forced to fight with over-aged weapons; the British were respected as good fighters under lousy commanders, and the Americans, well we didn't really know what we should think about them; they were too new in the business of war. The Russians were hated with a red-hot passion because every one of us had seen what they did to German POW's. The tankers of the British Empire forces and the American tankers were looked at with pity, because they were sent into battle in "rolling coffins" that even a 50mm gun could and did blow away (destroy). All those of us who had been in tank battles felt sorry for them, because they had a lousy chance to survive. Only when they had a massive number of tanks on their side did they have a chance. Personal valor is fine, but at least your own people must give you a chance to survive. One PzKw V "Panther" against one M-4 ("Sherman") equals four dead Amis and a pile of rusting junk. Often, the Brits and the Americans were referred to as "the comrades with a different APO number".[167]

In defense of the Sherman were several compensating advantages over the German panzers: their speed, mechanical reliability and lower fuel consumption, to name the most significant. The western Allies early on realized that on a one-to-one basis engaging a German *panzer* after 1943 was risky. The solution to the problem all depended on cooperation and tactics. The Allied ability to mount greater numbers of Sherman's against

---

[166] **http://www.achtungpanzer.com/pz5.htm** *Panzerkamphwagen VI Tiger Aust. H/E Sd. Kfz. 181.*

[167] *WWII Tech, World War II History,*
http://www.geocities.com/Area51/Cavern/2941/articles.htm

their much fewer German counterparts gave a greater chance at success, also the ability to call for air and artillery support also helped to even the playing field for the U.S. and British tankers. This is why the weather played such an important part of Allied field operations during the war. During a European winter, the weather was anything but ideal for such operations; we need look no further than the Battle of the Bulge for an excellent example.

The roots of Allied, especially American, technical foot dragging can be found in its history, politics, national preferences, as well as an advantageous geographical location. Two major domestic wars were fought to, first its independence and some 95 years later to settle internal regional differences in a civil war. Without aggressive enemies on any of its borders, the United States was free to develop its economy, institutions and infrastructure without the burden of maintaining a standing military. Its first fore in a foreign war was a brief conflict with Spain in 1898 in a largely naval war which put the U.S. on the map as a world and economic power. The two world wars were another matter. The technical development of military weapons after 1900 would make the oceans smaller and bring the enemies closer. The threat to democracy and the generosity of the United States was impetuous in providing men and treasure to France and Britain in 1917 to fend off and destroy an aggressive Germany and twenty-three years later found itself again embroiled in war after being attacked by Imperial Japan in 1941. However slow to develop and use weapons, with the collective force of a united citizenry, the "sleeping giant" can awake and wreak vengeance on a scale unseen in history.

The island nation of Great Britain is primarily a maritime power and has always sought solace and comfort in its vast and modern navy in times of national danger. The Royal Navy was the hallmark of all navies and, until the latter part of 1944 when eclipsed by the United States Navy, was the largest and strongest in the world. The requirement to maintain a strong ocean force, in addition to the protection of the home islands, was also to protect its worldwide empire with its long and vulnerable water lifelines.

The British Army has always been a much smaller force than the Royal Navy. Its primary responsibility was to provide protection of an amphibious attack on the home islands and to provide command and control of its large commonwealth forces stationed in their home countries. The world wide depression had severe repercussions in Europe, and the military forces of all the nations felt the red ink of their nations budgets and Great Britain was no exception. With the scarred memories of World War I still fresh and the tight grip of the global depression at hand, the funds for development and expansion were absent until the late 1930's when the specter of war once again became all too clear. Unfortunately, the lack of technical development, especially in armored vehicles was to hinder the British Army such that it would have to depend on U.S. tanks and other armored vehicles to supplement its own meager inventory.

Where the Allies do excel is in aircraft and artillery. The introduction of the Lockheed P-38 "Lightening", the Republic P-47 "Thunderbolt" and arguably the best fighter of the war, The North American P-51 "Mustang" all met and eventually exceeded the performance of the German fighter aircraft, with the exceptions of the jet and rocket machines. The range, firepower, design quality, pilot training and unlimited amounts of fuel and base support made these the aircraft the scourge of the European skies. The Luftwaffe did produce advanced versions of the Bf-109 and the Fw-190 but the collapsing German economy, the demands of other fronts, fuel shortages and its effect on reduced pilot training and base support and repair made the Luftwaffe in Western Europe almost non-existent.

Allied artillery, especially the 105mm and 155mm field guns were the equivalent the German army fielded and with the possible exception of the Russian artillery, was the best in the war. What gave the Western Allies their clear across the board edge in artillery was their ability to provide it with almost unlimited ammunition, the quantity of guns per battery, it was superbly directed by both ground and air controllers and an increasing amount of it was motorized to keep pace with the armored units. German unit histories (*kriegstagebuch*) frequently mention the plentiful, deadly and accurate Allied artillery fire.

This trial by fire of new weapons and the lessons learned by the Allies how to use them was put into practice, first in North Africa in 1942/43, then in Russia and Italy in 1943 and finally in France in 1944. The application of Blitzkrieg tactics was no secret by 1943, and as soon as the Allies mastered the art of combining infantry, armor, artillery and air power into a single offensive weapon and coordinating it all, include the advantage of unlimited resources, and the Allied version became an unbeatable force.

Maps:
Situations and Plans

STAVKA Command Structure
August 1942 - February 1945

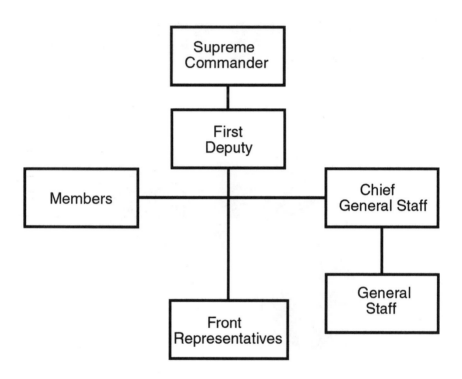

German Army High Command (OKH)
1942

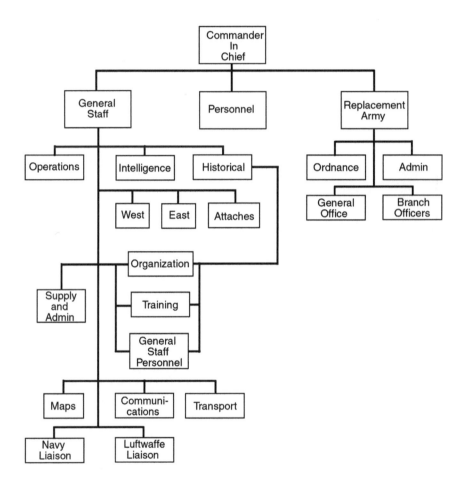

Situation: June 1941

Baltic Sea

ARMY GROUP NORTH
23 Infantry Divisions
3 Panzer Divisions
Air Fleet I

LATVIA

LITHUANIA

NORTH-WEST FRONT
20 Rifle Divisions
4 Tank Divisions

POLAND

ARMY GROUP CENTER
12 Infantry Divisions
9 Panzer Divisions
Air Fleet II

WEST FRONT
30 Rifle Divisions
8 Tank Divisions

BELORUSSIA

SLOVAKIA

ARMY GROUP SOUTH
54 Infantry Divisions
5 Panzer Divisions
Air Fleet IV

SOUTH-WEST FRONT
40 Rifle Divisions
16 Tank Divisions

UKRAINE

HUNGARY

AXIS ALLIES
14 Rumanian Divisions
2 Hungarian Divisions

SOUTH FRONT
12 Rifle Divisions
4 Tank Divisions

RUMANIA

Situation: June 1941

0   50   100 miles

The Marcks Plan

The Halder (OKH) Plan

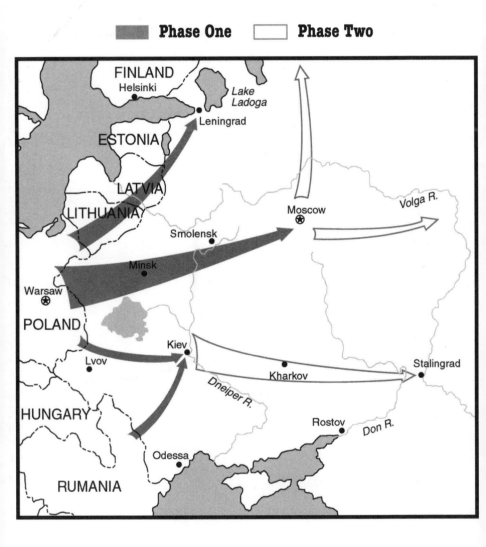

The Final Plan: Unternehmen Barbarossa

18 December 1940

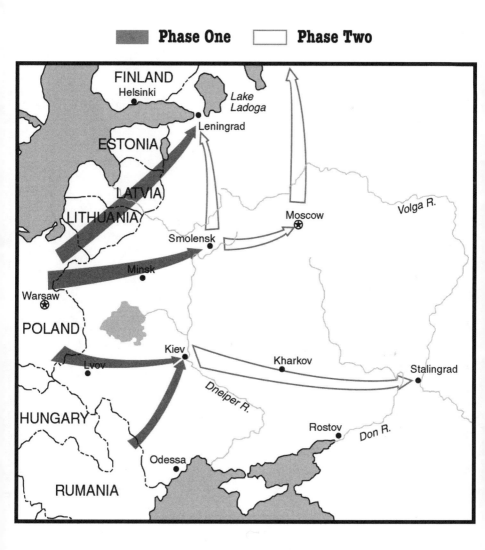

Phase One   Phase Two

FINLAND

Helsinki

Lake Ladoga

Leningrad

ESTONIA

LATVIA

LITHUANIA

Moscow

Volga R.

Smolensk

Minsk

Warsaw

POLAND

Kiev

Kharkov

Stalingrad

Lvov

Dneiper R.

HUNGARY

Rostov

Don R.

Odessa

RUMANIA

Normandy, France: The Overlord Area

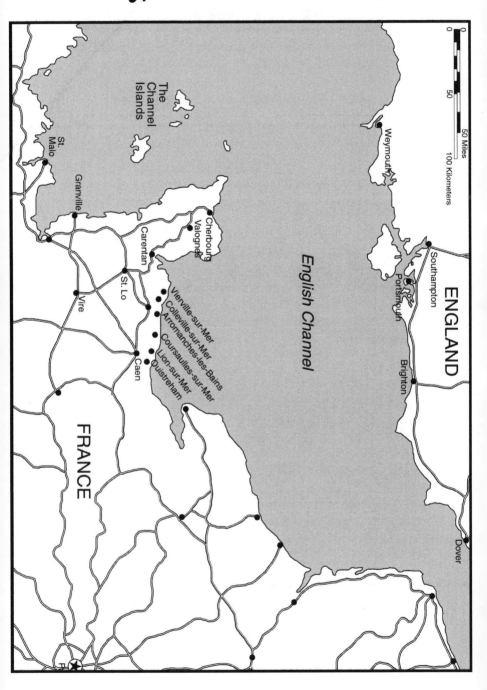

Operation Bagration Starting Positions

Operation Bagration Final Positions

Part 2:

1941 - 1943
Background and Context
to Operations
Overlord and Bagration

Two wrecked T-34/76 tanks. Post battle, Kursk, July 1943.

Chapter Six:
The Soviet Union and Germany on the Eve of War

When Barbarossa is launched, the whole world will holds its breath!

- Hitler

It's not enough to kill Russians, you have to knock them down

- Frederick the Great

This chapter will examine the war planning both nations conducted in the years leading up to the German invasion of Russian in June 1941. It will ask what were the problems they faced and how did they solve them. It will look at the various components of their plans, the reasons for the decisions made and what influences caused changes in these decisions and the eventual and final plans. The first look will be at the German invasion plans, the development of competing plans, who were the chief planners, the rationale and thought behind each one and which and why the final plan was chosen and by who. The same examination will be conducted for the Russian side of operations, offensive versus defensive plans, the impact of the 1939 treaty with Germany, the 'forward' positioning of Russian Army units and Stalin's paranoid desire for peace at any price.

German Attack Rationale

German National Socialism and Russian Communism were born about the same time in central Europe and for many of the same reasons; unstable, corrupt and incompetent governments or ruling aristocracies, hunger, economic dislocation, and civil unrest. The Communists were an early target of the young Nazi Party in the 1920's, especially of the *Sturm Abteilungen* or Assault Detachments, more frequently referenced as simply the *SA*, who almost daily fought a number of vicious street battles in Munich and Berlin with the Communists and Socialists.

The political, social, racial and economic differences between the two systems, are too extensive to discuss and enumerate here, save that Hitler early on considered communism and the home of its first government, Russia, his archenemy. Ultimately, he convinced himself and later Germany, that Russia and communism would have to be defeated for two primary reasons: to destroy the cradle of communism and its perceived threat to Nazi Germany, and to provide the space required by a growing Germany, for her *Lebensraum* in the East.[168]

The subject of an invasion or occupation of Russia has a long history in Germany. The growth of Pan-Germanism in the last years of the 19th century gave expression to gathering back into the fold such far-flung German communities as the Volga River Germans that had settled there under Katherine the Great, they and those in the Baltic provinces began to experience discrimination, and gathered together to live in closed communities for protection. This situation raised questions such as should they be brought back into the Fatherland or should the borders of the

---

[168] For an extensive discussion of the place Communism occupied in the Nazi mind, see *Mein Kampf*, by Adolf Hitler, Eher Verlag, 1925 and *The Rise and Fall of the Third Reich, A History of Nazi Germany*, William L. Shirer, Simon and Schuster, New York, 1960.

Fatherland be extended to embrace them? It is this second direction that began to develop in Nazi theoretical circles

There has been much debate as to the German claim that Germany had to attack Russia when they did or Russia would have attacked Germany anyway. All factions within Germany: OKW, OKH and Hitler agreed that Russia was preparing to attack Germany; it was only a matter of time as to when.[169] This finding was buttressed during the opening months of the campaign when a captured Russian general mentioned that he had been sent truck-loads of maps of Germany but had none of the terrain his units occupied. We have discussed the frequent Russian press and motion picture references to a struggle with Fascism and their frequent mentions that a war with Germany was inevitable and had been preparing for such a war. Stalin undertook to begin a massive war-oriented economic program back in 1929; in addition, Russia later admitted that it was not ready for war in 1941. The preferred start date was 1943

Hitler made anti-communism one of the building blocks of German National Socialism. In his book "Mein Kampf" there is frequent reference to attacking and defeating the Communist menace to the East and the need for the Germans gaining "*Lebensraum*" mostly at the expense of the eastern nations, principally Communist Russia. Stalin was keenly aware that Germany was Russia's ultimate philosophical and military enemy, no matter what alliances were concocted between them, and even then these were temporary 'agreements of convenience' that lasted until one or the other nation was prepared for war. As we have seen, it was Germany who in June 1941 was prepared first. If not fully prepared, at least it was motivated to move first.

James Lucas in his excellent study of the German soldier in Russia has the following to say about the conflict between Russia and Germany:

> "To this folk memory of genocidal battles fought in centuries past must be added a religious aspect of a crusade against godlessness which caused many young men from Western Europe[170] to enlist with the German forces. This idealistic, almost romantic concept of being a crusader may have been but brief. Nevertheless it cannot be denied that it existed and

---

[169] The Russian buildup in the Bialystok and Lvov positions undoubtedly gave rise to this scenario.

[170] Especially France, Holland and Norway, in addition to Germany's military allies.

was reinforced in the early days of the campaign by the action of villagers in the Ukraine who blessed the men in the vehicles marked with the black cross and who saw the German soldiers as a liberating, Christian host."[171]

With Hitler anxious to secure Germany's eastern border as plans for the invasion of France and the low countries proceeded, he instructed his foreign minister Von Ribbentrop to approach his counterpart in Moscow, V. M. Molotov to propose a military peace and economic treaty. Russia's third Five Year Plan required growing amounts of new technology and Germany was in need of raw materials which she was unable to obtain on the international market because of boycotts of the leading western nations due to the German laws regarding Jews and other minorities. An important component part of the treaty was the secret codicil which called for the division of neighboring Poland, which both Germany and Russia had conflicts with; Germany at the end of World War I with border incursions and for Russia it was the Polish - Ukrainian border battles in the 1920's.

The invasion of Russia was significantly influenced by the Russo-German Treaty of 1939. The launching platform for the German invasion was the new border roughly in the center of former Poland, just east of Warsaw. This new border, starting at Memel on the Baltic Sea and descending south, skirting the East Prussian border, briefly West around Bialystok, down the River Bug past Brest-Litovsk to a point north-east of Lvov, then West to the Carpathian Mountains along the Hungarian border, east to the River Prut following it to the Black Sea north of the Rumanian sea port of Constanta. This advanced the German armed forces hundreds of miles to the east, closer to Russian soil, and posed a number of defensive problems for the Soviets and their newly occupied portion of Poland.[172] In addition to the elimination of Poland as a nation and the physical joining of Russia and Germany, there were extensive economic components included in the treaty.

---

[171] *War on the Eastern Front: The German Soldier in Russia, 1941-1945* by James Lucas, Greenhill Books, 1991, p. 12.

[172] It is interesting to note that after the German invasion of Poland on 1 September 1939, German foreign minister von Ribbentrop urged his Soviet equal, foreign minister Molotov to have the Red Army begin its occupation of the previously agreed upon portion of eastern Poland. Molotov delayed and demurred for almost two weeks (8 September to 18 September), stating that the U. S. S. R. did not want to be seen as an aggressor. For additional insight see *Hitler and Russia, The Third Reich in a Two Front War 1937-1943,* by Trumbull Higgins, MacMillan, 1966, pp. 36-37.

The trade treaty spelled out in great detail what was to be included in the exchange of goods and technical information. Among the items to be sent to Russia were industrial and military goods. The military items included naval ships (the cruiser *Luetzow*), plans for battle ships, artillery, samples of the latest panzers, aircraft including the modern Messerschmitt Bf-109 and the Junkers Ju-88, explosive materials and formulas for chemical weapons. Industrial goods included machinery for the petroleum industry, railroad rolling stock, electrical generation equipment, machine tools, and generators. Material amounting to over 640 million Reichmarks (the Reichmark-U.S. Dollar exchange rate in 1940 being 1 RM was worth $.20).

With the grain now flowing into Germany from Russia, the traffic in the other direction was not quite so fast. The German trade mission, the body that managed the exchange with Russia, reported deliveries of military equipment to Russia were having an adverse impact on the ongoing equipping of new German divisions, part of the expansion of the Wehrmacht. In attempt to placate the Russians, Germany proposed sending consumer goods to Russia in lieu of the contract military goods. The Russians insisted on the original contract items.[173] It appears that washing machines and refrigerators had less appeal.

The Russian component of the treaty consisted primarily of raw materials and the quantities were extensive. One million tons of cereal grains, 1 million tons of oil, one million tons of soybeans, more than 100,000 tons of cotton, 500,000 tons of phosphates and large quantities of other vital industrial materials, all of them either scarce or non-existent in Germany.

What Germany was attempting to do was nothing less than the replacement of their overseas imports, no longer available because of the British naval blockade, with the agricultural and mineral wealth of Russia. In addition, agreement of the quantities of raw material to Germany by Stalin, without any negotiation of quantities, confirmed in Hitler's mind that Russia was able to provide these vast amounts of grains and petroleum and fixed the image of Russia as one vast larder for German exploitation, voluntary or not.[174]

[173] *The House Built On Sand, The Conflicts of German Policy In Russia 1939 - 1945* p. 194.

[174] During the German occupation of the Ukraine, the most productive portion of German controlled Russian territory, the anticipated quantity of grain was never what it was under Soviet management. German racial policies, conflicting administrative districts and political infighting all took their toll.

In the minutes of Politburo meetings in the Kremlin there is commentary by Stalin that the grain deliveries to Germany were not to be delayed for any reason. He gave orders to ensure the shipments were complete; if not, stocks from Ukraine's daily needs were to be used to supplement any shortages.

There has been much debate and discussion regarding the international surprise and outrage of the Russo-German treaty; however when the details leading up to the agreement are reviewed, the event should not have elicited such a response. In 1935 Russia signed an alliance with France while the Comintern published a call to all nations to confront Fascism. Further, in 1938 the Soviets called for a conference of nations opposed to German aggression, only to be ignored by both *France and Britain*. Finally, in 1939 there were negotiations by France, Britain and the Soviet Union to create a three-power alliance, ostensibly against Germany which came to naught.

It is interesting to note in the closing years of the 1930's that Russia recognized the threat and danger of an aggressive Germany would have against all the major European powers. Her efforts were met with little or no cooperation from the western powers. In view of this lack of cooperation and self-interest, and recognition of the threat Germany posed to them is it any wonder Russia went it alone and concluded the Treaty? With this hindsight, it is much less surprising. There may have been stark ideological differences between the two nations but the press of practical political questions superseded them. When the Western nations rejected Soviet overtures to an alliance to contain an aggressive Germany, what alternative did Russia have?

With the completion of the strategic survey on 29 October 1940 Germanys OHW Operations Division analyzed five major areas for consideration and inclusion into the planning of *Barbarossa*: enemy manpower, space, time, intelligence information and the objective. The following will show how they became the final plan.

---

[175] The vast expanse of the Pripet marshes covered some 65,000 square kilometers (480 kilometers wide and approximately 525 kilometers long) and effectively separated Army Group Center from Army Group South. The name of these vast swamplands can also be spelled Pripyet and, in Russian, *Poles'ye*. The marshy terrain channeled all mechanized transport onto rail lines and the few all-weather roads that were essentially raised causeways. The villages and towns were islands surrounded by swamp and shallow, brackish water.

Planning The Attack

As early as 21 July 1940 Hitler had directed the OKW to begin framing plans for a campaign in the east. On 29 July 1940, eleven months prior to the invasion, the first plans for an attack against Russia were committed to paper by Maj. Gen Erich Marcks; they were to be the first of several plans put forward for the campaign; most of the variations between them had to do with primary objectives, campaign progress milestones, force compositions, enemy strengths, supply and logistical requirements, comparisons of German and Soviet T, O and E's (Tables of Organization and Equipment), start dates, campaign length and the like. He labeled his plan Operations Outline East (*Operationsentwurf Ost*) and it consisted of material from Foreign Armies East (*Fremde Heere Ost*) the German intelligence gathering organization, geographical information from OKH, and even data gleaned from Soviet Marshal Mikhail Tukhachevsky, from his report of the Russian campaign in Poland in 1920.

What became known as the "Marcks Plan" envisioned two main drives into Soviet territory; the main drive out of central Poland towards the key cities of Minsk, Smolensk and finally Moscow. The second main effort was to be south of the Pripet marshes to seize Kiev[175]. The Black Sea coast and Leningrad sectors were to be secondary targets, to be addressed after the successful completion of the primary ones of Moscow and Kiev.

A second major plan was also produced, by General Halder. His plan submitted in December 1940 envisioned for the first time three major efforts: the two as before and the new third toward Leningrad. The once-secondary target under the Marcks Plan was now important enough that its attack force was strengthened at the expense of the southern effort toward Kiev.

The final plan kept the three-prong effort but shifted even more strength to the central and northern efforts, with Leningrad becoming the main target, Moscow falling to second place to be taken after the Leningrad effort. This was the plan that was accepted, which became Hitler's selection which he called '*Fall Barbarossa*', issuing his Directive 21 in December 1940.[176] German focus went from a central-southern direction to a northern-central one. The shift in direction was the correct one, but the final target, Leningrad was not. It seems that communist place names

---

[176] It is of interest that Hitler's directive did not discuss geographical objectives, just the destruction of the Russian Army and the prevention of attacks against the German homeland. It was the military planners that specified the terrain objectives.

were having an effect on Hitler's decision making even at this early stage. Placing Moscow as the secondary target in both army groups was ignoring this cities importance in the hierarchy of Russian government and life. This decision would also come back to haunt them.

The final objective of this plan was what has become known as the "A-A" line, a straight line connecting the cities of Archangel in the north and Astrakhan in the south. This terminus, if reached should knock Russia out of the war; it was the two cities, Archangel in the north on the White Sea and the southern end at the vast river delta at Astrakhan on the salty Caspian Sea, 1,600 miles from Warsaw and 2,000 miles from Berlin. It was an awesome undertaking for any army.

Campaign Objectives

One of the key objectives in the operational plan of the attack was the northern Russian city of Leningrad. It has been mentioned that this city caught Hitler's attention by virtue of its name, very similar to another city with a magnetic name for Hitler on the lower Volga. However, there was real economic and political reasons for including Leningrad in the original planning. Leningrad was a major manufacturing city as well as a warm water port with which supplies could be brought in to sustain the German offensive. It was far easier to ship heavy cargo such as tanks, artillery, fuel and ammunition by sea then over scarce road and rail nets. In addition, Leningrad was to point of connection with Germany's northern ally, Finland. A key component in the plan was to use the Finn's to seal off Leningrad from the north and by the Germans from the south. The Gulf of Finland and Lake Ladoga seal off the city from west and east respectively. Finally, there was the political aspect of capturing the city named after the architect of communism, Lenin, the birthplace of the revolution and the spiritual home of the Bolshevik's.

What is of interest was not making Moscow the main target of any of the German invasion plans. Granted Moscow was the farthest objective of the plans and would probably be the best defended of them all, but what seemed to escape the attention of the German planners was its importance to Stalin, its supreme status as Russia's military nerve center and to the Russian people. In addition to its administrative importance was its key position in Russia's Western rail and road transportation network. Finally, the city was one of the four largest manufacturing locations in pre-1941 Russia, all vital considerations in any military planning operation.

The third operational objective of the plans was the first city of the Ukraine, the city on the Dnieper River, Kiev. Located on the vulnerable West bank of this major water artery at the southern end of the vast Pripet Marshes, this would have been the main target of any German invasion plan and the STAVKA and Stalin knew it and it was accorded the military protection of 56 rifle divisions it deserved.

Nord, Mitte und Süd

It was recognized early on that the operational area of the invasion would increase in size; the front would lengthen as Western Russia is shaped like a funnel lying on its side, with the small end at the occupied Polish border and the wide end deep into Russia. The starting linear border was some1,200 miles in length, not including the Finnish attack areas in eastern Finland. As the area in which to wage the battle would get larger for the Wehrmacht, there would be no geographical features against which to 'pin' the enemy and defeat him, as the English Channel in France and the Low Countries provided in the west. The planned 'stop line' of Barbarossa, known as the "A-A" Line, is some 1,800 miles in straight line length, the wide end of the Russian 'funnel'. It was from this distance that it was considered impossible to bomb Germany.

The organization of the German attack forces for the invasion took the form of dividing the offensive units into three groups of armies, they were labeled Army Group North (In German *Heeresgruppe Nord*) with its ultimate objective of Leningrad. Army Group Center (*Heeresgruppe Mitte*) with its final objective of Moscow and Army Group South (*Heeresgruppe Süd*) with its intermediate objective of Kiev and its final objective of Stalingrad.

The forces assigned to the three army groups were reflective of the importance of their objectives, the distances to be covered and the Russian defenses expected to be encountered. Army Group North was allotted 26 divisions of which 3 were panzer divisions with one division in reserve and three security divisions. Army Group Center was assigned 51 divisions which included 9 panzer divisions and two divisions in reserve, its wider front and short line distance to Moscow qualifying it for the additional units. Army Group South was given 59 divisions with included 5 panzer divisions, with three reserve divisions.

An interesting inclusion in Army Group South was two of Germany's foreign allies, Rumania and Hungary. Rumania contributing 14 divisions and Hungary 2. This was to be the first time in a major German military operation that foreign combat units were used and would be commanded by their own officers. To the north the Finns, a ready ally of Germany after their defeat by the Russians in the Winter War in 1939/1940, with their Finnish Army Group, were set their own objectives to regain land lost during the 1939/1940 war. Their 15 divisions, buttressed with the addition of five German divisions under *Armeekorps Norwegen* operating from occupied Norway with Murmansk as their objective, two divisions in the Salla area of Finland with the shore of the White Sea south of Kandalaksha as the objective and one in the Lieksa area in southern Finland, on the northern end of the Finnish Army Group.

To support the three army groups, three *Luftwaffe Luftflotte* (air fleets) were assigned, one to each Army Group. *Luftflotte I* to Army Group North, *Luftflotte II* to Army Group Center and *Luftflotte IV* to Army Group South. As in the infantry and panzer assignments, the number per *Luftflotte* were apportioned accordingly as well. 1,280 aircraft were assigned to the three air groups, a combination of fighters, bombers and ground attack Stuka dive bombers. Although this number of aircraft was significant, it was less than the number used against the French and British in the West a year earlier. Those losses had not yet been replaced.

The postmortem of the Wehrmacht's performance in the French campaign brought to light a number of shortcomings and corrections needed prior to engaging the Soviets. Kershaw, in his *War Without Garlands* makes the case for improvements:

> "On 20 March 1941, he (Von Kluge) directed that training should concentrate on hardening the soldiers, since in Russia they would be without even the simplest comforts. Men and horses had to practice long-distance marches, be prepared to cope with chemical and biological weapons, and anticipate assaults, when they came, to consist of several and deep waves of infantry supported by tanks and artillery. German infantry weapon co-ordination would have to improve if ever they were to defeat such attacks. Soldiers needed to be tougher to cope with the inevitability of close combat and overcome their present aversion to fighting at night. The Russians, described as 'children

of nature' reveled in night combat. Despite shortcomings, the Red Army was better equipped than the Wehrmacht's previous victims. German soldiers would have to copy the Spanish and Finnish infantry precedents of attacking tanks with explosive charges. The coming war would not be conducted on roads as in the West; limitless space and massive forest areas would need to be reconnoitered and cleared. German headquarters staffs would now be vulnerable. Normal security precautions would not suffice. Headquarters personnel should become familiar with their side-arms and expect to use them. For some, it was daunting prospect."[177]

The western portion of the Union of Soviet Socialist Republics, the areas between Europe and the foothills of the Ural Mountains encompass a tremendous expanse of land by European standards. However, this area constitutes only a small part of this large nation, its remaining portion east of the Urals is even larger. If space and time make up one of the larger problems to overcome in an invasion of this country, the natural obstacles are just as intimidating.

A postwar study written by captured German generals supervised by U.S. Army historians had the following to say about the terrain in greater western Russia:

> "Northern European Russia proper, that is to say the swampy wood-land north and northeast of the Valdai Hills, is not suitable for mobile warfare, particularly not for large armored formations. The crucial blows of an offensive, therefore, have to fall in central and southern European Russia. In central European Russia lies the Smolensk-Moscow Ridge, a low glacial moraine whose western extension is known to the Germans as the Orsha Corridor (*Landbrucke von Orscha*). This is the watershed between the Black and Caspian Seas in the south, and the Baltic and White Seas in the north. Here are the sources of the Dneper, the Dvina, the Lovat, and the Volga. Access to this ridge is of paramount importance for any conduct of military operations in the western part of European Russia. But the western approaches to the Orsha Corridor are protected by a wide belt of swamps and forests

[177] *War Without Garlands, Operation Barbarossa 1941/1942* by Robert J. Kershaw, Sarpedon, New York, 2000, p. 21.

which extends from the Pripyat Marshes past Veliklye Luki and up to Leningrad. After breaking through this belt, an attacker still faces the watersheds of the Don and the Volga. Even if he has reached the Volga, an enemy coming from the west will find himself only in the outer ramparts of the Soviet domain; before him lie the Ural Mountains, and beyond them, Siberia."[178]

The problem of space and time was to be the chief unknown of the entire planning process. With the observation made above of the widening of the operational area, the Germans had one overriding requirement. The planned solution to the possibility of an endless pursuit of the Russian enemy was the maneuver elements of the Wehrmacht had to pierce the Russian formations and encircle and contain them to prevent them from falling back into the limitless interior steppes of the Ural range and central Asia. The Germans would be forced to bring the Russian armies to battle at or near the frontier areas, defeat them and advance without respite to the next objective. Should the Russian forces be permitted to fall back or be permitted to breakout from incomplete encirclements and regroup or retreat into the interior of the country, the prospect of an unlimited pursuit of an elusive enemy could occur.

One of the most interesting challenges to the Wehrmacht was that of the timely and efficient delivery of supply to the advancing forces. The items with the highest priority were fuel and ammunition. Understandably that would be a high priority for any army, especially an invading one. However, as past famous generals have observed an army travels on its stomach and the listing of food was not amongst the short list of priorities. In fact the German army was expected to live off the land during the invasion. When one considers that the German army of 1941 was the most modern of its kind at the time, this is an astonishing fact. Consider, the Wehrmacht was invading the largest nation on the European landmass, in an ever widening scope of operational area and it was expected to do their own provisioning in a hostile environment. Although initially greeted by some as liberators with bread and salt, the regional traditional greeting for visitors, the genocidal racist policies soon implemented by the SS and Einsatzkommando as well as the destruction of crops and food stores by the retreating Red Army made this a chancy prospect.

---

[178] *Terrain Factors in the Russian Campaign,* Department of the Army Pamphlet No. 20-290, July 1951.

It is on this point that much conjecture has occurred regarding the prospects of ultimate victory against Russia regardless of the amount of land occupied or the numbers of men killed or captured, tanks destroyed or guns seized. The Russians had the potential, as long as their political and military leadership remained intact and exercised even minimal control over their forces to continuously retreat deeper and deeper into the Asian mainland. This was the unthinkable fear of the German planners. Although the German planners feared a retreat, Russian doctrine was quite the opposite; to attack the enemy and carry the battle onto his soil. Despite the offensive stance, retreating is what transpired.

Military Intelligence

In identifying the size of the enemy the German operations group used the figure of 170 Russian divisions of all types plus the potential of almost unlimited reinforcements and replacements. Against this force would be 145 German divisions of all types. The advantage of numerical superiority was never an issue, the Germans had always known they would be outnumbered, but did not envision this to be an insurmountable difficulty. The Germans were counting heavily on the poor performance of the Russians, recently demonstrated against the Finn's in the 'Winter War' of 1939-1940,[179] the political purges of the 1936-1938 period and the overall lack of experience in combat, especially in the use and maneuver of large bodies of mechanized vehicles and units. There was also the element of deception in the German plan as to the attack, if, when and where it would fall.[180] But Soviet strength was wildly underestimated by the Germans. The

---

[179] The Germans paid especially close attention to the unfolding Russo-Finnish battles in the Karelian Isthmus and along the central border north of Lake Ladoga. A General Staff report dated 31 December 1939 had the following terse evaluation of the performance of the Red Army: "In quantity a giant military instrument. Commitment of the mass; organization, equipment and means of leadership: unsatisfactory. Principles of leadership: good - leadership itself, however, too young and inexperienced. Communications systems: bad. Transportation: bad. Troops not very uniform - no personalities. Simple soldier, good natured, quite satisfied with very little. Fighting qualities of the troops in a heavy fight: dubious. The Russian mass is no match for an army with modern equipment and superior leadership".

[180] It is interesting to note that Field Marshall von Braushitsch told Hitler in July 1940 that the campaign "would last some four to six weeks" and that "from eighty to one hundred divisions could do the job" and Russian strength was assessed as "fifty to 75 good divisions". The developing optimism was bolstered in January 1940 during the botched invasion of Finland by first three and then five Soviet armies of urgent demands by the Soviets to the Germans for huge amounts of military equipment and machinery to produce heavy artillery ammunition, all signs to OKH that the Red Army was in trouble.

actual number of Red Army troops in the western regions numbered some 2,900,000 and 5,370,000 throughout the U.S.S.R. This does not include 100,000 NKVD troops and such locally formed units as the Home Guard (*Narodnoe Opolchenie*), which was raised in the cities as needed as they became threatened. These units eventually totaled some 60 divisions.

The operational guessing game that became the German intelligence effort to determine how many Soviet divisions the Wehrmacht would encounter once Barbarossa was launched was echoed by none other than Hitler himself. In a conversation with his foreign minister von Ribbentrop in April admitted that he had little idea how many troops the Russians had and would only find out when the invasion was launched.

The German failure to properly evaluate the strengths, weaknesses and intentions of their Russian opponent was due in part to two factors; one the racial component that 'blinded' all things Slavic to German sensibilities and the other was the organic suspicious nature of the Soviet nation. It was this second element that the Germans found so difficult to penetrate. During the war a 66 mile zone immediately behind the front was managed by NKVD Frontier Troops in a series of guard posts, check points and citizens that were encouraged and frequently threatened to report all suspicious or unfamiliar people.

German wartime intelligence was constantly confounded by the impenetrability of Russian society from which the Russian army came from. Robert W. Stephan in his *Stalin's Secret War* describes Russia as a "counterintelligence state" in which the very fabric of Russian society was based on suspicion. Everyone was observed, accounted for, screened and examined on a regular basis as part of their daily activities. In such a society the introduction of a stranger or someone without the proper or incomplete documents was soon identified. It was no surprise then that according to postwar Allied interrogations of German intelligence officers who stated that up to 90 percent of their agents sent behind Russian lines failed in their assigned missions.[181] The lack of an effective intelligence gathering operation in the Soviet Union is all the more confounding as the Germans had such an advantage no other nation had. The secret clause in the Treaty of Rapallo added in July 1922 provided the Germans with bases in several locations in the heart of Russia for almost 15 years. It was a badly missed opportunity.

[181] *Stalin's Secret War, Soviet Counterintelligence Against The Nazi's 1941-1945* by Robert W. Stephan, University Press of Kansas, 2004, p. 53.

A significant component to the German planning of the invasion of Soviet Russia was its racial component. German military planners were subject to the Nazi party's racial influences in the evaluation of the Russian military. Hitler's boasting of Russia being nothing more than a rotten structure and all one had to do was kick in the front door and it would all coming tumbling down is noted. The Nazi subconscious opinion of the subhuman Russian Slavs also carried over into the comparatively brief intelligence work and evaluation of Russian military organization, its structure and its readiness levels. This uncharacteristically German attitude of the lack of extensive planning and evaluation of their soon to be Eastern foe was to have major consequences.

The aspect of time in the selection of the start date of the campaign as well as the length of it assumed an importance as never before. As the sheer scope of Operation Barbarossa was as huge as it is, the need to properly address the aspect of time was critical. The operational planners saw the May to October time period as the most favorable for the campaign and all significant combat and maneuver had to be concluded at the commencement of the muddy season and no later than the beginning of the dreaded Russian winter, usually arriving in European Russia by early November.

An important part of the planning process was the simulation of the operation in war gaming sessions; the OKW gamed-out an invasion for themselves. A lengthy game was conducted over three long sessions in late 1940. After the end of the third session, they had only reached to November of a hypothetical invasion launched at the beginning of a standard European campaign start date of late May/early June. By that stage of the game the Wehrmacht had 'destroyed' 240 Red Army divisions of all kinds, leaving an estimated 55+ remaining. A fourth and final stage was planned but cancelled because of the assurance of the game umpires and participants that any nation amassing losses of this magnitude would surely surrender or be incapable of further resistance. What is of further interest was the point reached at the end of the third game stage was a point just short of Moscow, outside of Leningrad and in the general area of Kiev. The end of the game session was approximately the same point that was reached during the actual invasion. When the German invaders reached the same point in November/December 1941 instead of the estimated 55+ remaining Red Army divisions there was actually 220 divisions remaining. If the fourth and final stage of the game had been played and the intelligence known of the ability of Russia to mobilize almost unlimited numbers of men would the Wehrmacht have invaded Russia and if the answer was yes, would they had been better prepared for an extended campaign? All the intelligence indicated a short one would be the case.

The matter of accurate information of the disposition and size of the Red Army has been an item of debate since the end of the war. The forward positioning of many units, especially motorized units, was caused by early differences of strategy within the Red Army command as to the mission of the Red Army in the eventual confrontation with Germany. The German planners saw this forward positioning for what it was; a stance that indicated the aggressive intent of Stalin. The last question the operational planners had was, 'would the Reds fight in the border areas or fall back into a retreating action as in 1812?' As was mentioned above, the need to prevent the Red Army from escaping the clutches of the panzer divisions was imperative for German success.

Signs of growing Russian military strength were available to the Germans. In March 1941 a visiting Luftwaffe delegation went to the Urals to see aircraft factories there and reported back to Berlin that large-scale modern aircraft production was underway.

As will be recalled, when the German General Staff was instructed to prepare plans for the campaign, the original plan of attack drafted by Gen. Marcks was for a two-pronged offensive, north and south of the Pripyat Marshes. Additional components of the "Marcks Plan" envisioned an offensive in four phases. The northern prong had the Dvina/Dneper River lines as the first phase, seizing Vitebsk and Rogachev. The second phase: Simultaneous advance to Smolensk and Pskov by the northern prong, as well as the northern wing of the southern prong. The third phase was to be the largest and grandest phase of the three. Phase three envisioned the seizure of Leningrad, Moscow and Kharkov. As this was the most ambitious of the phases it was assumed that by this phase Red Army units in the border regions would have been defeated and the move on Moscow, Leningrad and Kharkov be more 'mop up' than assault operations.

The fourth phase was a simple advance to occupy significant objectives and control the interior. This had the entire west bank of the Volga and Don Rivers as the final objective. It was thought that occupying an area this size would prevent the feared Russian bombing attacks on Germany, a key feature of the Marcks Plan.

It is interesting to note that the primary inclusion of the southern prong was to prevent a Russian attack on the Romanian oil fields, and not to occupy the food producing areas of the Ukraine, as were later plans. Marcks did not propose more than this effort, a secondary assist to the northern prong because of limited capacity of Hungarian and Romanian railroads; neither nations rail system would permit assembly of the forces necessary to become the main effort of the German offensive.

The Russian occupation of Bessarabia and Bukovina in 1940 and the danger to Romanian oil sources was a growing concern. The annexation of these lands were part of its portion of the spoils of the August 1939 German-Soviet agreement, the Ploesti oil fields were now only 120 miles from the Red Army, the source that supplied most of Germany's petroleum and made Hitler very uneasy.

General Marcks did include a cautionary note in his planning of the German invasion of the U.S.S.R. He stated that if the Russians did not sue for peace or completely collapse, the German forces would have to occupy a much larger area, perhaps all the way to the Ural Mountains. He did acknowledge that this would certainly eliminate any opportunity for the Russians to reorganize in the West and they might set up a new government in Asia and maintain a state of war for an indefinite period. This particular piece of information did not seem to stay Hitler's hand in continuing the planning and invasion of this giant nation.

The expansion of the Wehrmacht, especially the Heer after the French campaign, although subject to changing thoughts on force structure and size, was hurried, and never was fully completed prior to the attack on the Soviet Union. It is fascinating to see that Germany, on the eve of the largest invasion in modern times of the largest country in Europe was on the brink of *reducing* its armed forces.

"...In the midst of the French campaign, Hitler officially directed the army to reduce in strength to 120 divisions, while concurrently expanding its mobile elements to 20 panzer and 10 motorized divisions.

"The resulting demobilization provided the army with a reserve supply of weapons and equipment. Ten weeks later Hitler reversed the decision, calling for an *expansion* (italics added) up to 180 divisions, to pursue the Russian campaign. With only 11 months remaining to the invasion, time and energy were devoted to creating new units and operational planning. Any hopes of mobilization - motorizing infantry and artillery, introducing new weapons and standardizing tables of organization and equipment - were gone."

"Occupying Europe and garrisoning the flanks and rear of the proposed invasion led to the identification of commitments which the German General Staff assessed would require the army to field 208 *divisions* (italics added) by June 1941. There were other agencies also competing for the army's increasingly scant resources of manpower and equipment. Goering's Luftwaffe expanded its ground capabilities after the fall of France. On 8 November 1940 Hitler further ordered the expansion of the Waffen SS from two and a half to four divisions and the SS Regiment 'Leibstandarte' to a full brigade. This prompted army officers to complain the SS were a 'wandering arsenal' led by men who had never seen combat, and that these weapons would be better served by 'Third Wave' conscripted divisions of World War I veterans. At the end of August 1940, Hitler ordered the army to release 300,000 metal workers back into the armaments industry. To expand to 180 divisions, the army drafted the age groups of 1919, 1920 and 1921. They began basic training in August 1940. They would finish one month prior to the Russian campaign."[182]

Preparations

Robert Cecil, in his excellent treatment of the subject, *Hitler's Decision to Invade Russia*, 1941states the following:

"In the quarter-century between the withdrawal of Bismarck's guiding hand and the outbreak of the First World War it is possible to trace two mutually contradictory attitudes towards Russia, which we shall also find in Hitler's thinking. On the one hand there was the contempt for the Slavs and their administrative and technological incapacity... from this derived the conclusion, which the victories on the eastern front in 1914-18 tended to support, that Russia would fall an easy victim to German arms. On the other hand, there was the uneasy fear that this might not long continue to be the case; that Russia would eventually emerge into the modern world and that when this at

[182] *War Without Garlands*, p. 21.

last occurred, her immense resources of manpower would make her indestructible. At the beginning of the century, a German population of 65 million saw on its eastern borders a Colossus of 170 million, growing in numbers of three times the German birth rate. Germany lacked natural frontiers and, as the war-time blockade was soon to demonstrate, lacked the raw materials to sustain a long war."[183]

As early as March, a group of specially equipped high altitude reconnaissance aircraft[184] from the Luftwaffe's *Aufklarungsgruppe*[185] *Ob.d.L*[186] occasionally referred to as Aufklarungsgruppe "Rowehl" began conducting flights across the German-Russian demarcation line in east-central Poland in depths of up to three hundred kilometers (188 miles) into eastern Poland, Ukraine and western Russia. Photographing troop and equipment concentrations, road and rail networks and airfields, this information provided data for the maps soon to be needed by the field armies.[187] One fact that was ascertained from these flights was that in the event of war, the German oil supplies from Rumania would be in jeopardy from a Red Army not far away.

In addition to the high altitude flights over western Russia, the Baltic States, and the Ukraine for the purpose of gathering intelligence on Russian force dispositions, the Germans also set up radio interception or 'listening' stations. These stations were set up in Bulgaria, Romania, Hungary, Bohemia, Moravia, western Poland, East Prussia and Finland. However their potential was not realized, as the power of the radios was insufficient to reach any further than the Desna and Dnepr river lines, the Finnish border regions and the Baltic States. In addition to the radio data and over-flights, agents sent from Finland and Turkey contributed to the intelligence picture as well.

---

[183] *Hitler's Decision to Invade Russia 1941* by Robert Cecil, David McKay Company, Inc., New York, 1975. pp 17-18.

[184] These aircraft were Junkers Ju-86P-1 and P-2, two seat high altitude photographic reconnaissance machines. These aircraft are noteworthy for their extended wingspan, high altitude capabilities and use of diesel engines.

[185] Reconnaissance Group.

[186] *Oberbefehlshaber der Luftwaffe*. Air Force High Command.

[187] There is frequent mention of the inaccuracies of these maps as to key terrain features, roads, etc. Captured Russian maps were preferred as their accuracy was far superior to the German issue, and were reproduced with both Russian and German place names.

Additional intelligence was obtained from the *Brandenburger* Special Forces units which conducted clandestine operations in the border areas seeking terrain information. To demonstrate the intensity of German intelligence efforts into Russia by the end of 1940, 232 agents were apprehended and by the same time the next year the number captured increased twelve-fold.[188]

The numbers involving all aspects of Barbarossa were staggering. Never before had such military power been assembled against another country. The Wehrmacht fielded 3,000,000 men, 3,200 tanks, 7,500 pieces of artillery, all formed into 75 infantry divisions, 17 panzer divisions and 13 motorized divisions with 26 more infantry divisions, 2 panzer and 1 motorized division in reserve in Germany and France. Stretching for 100 miles behind the German start line were ammo, fuel stores and supply dumps of all kinds to fuel the initial 400-mile advance. 500,000 trucks, from East Prussia to Rumania would transport the invasion force forward, assisted by almost 600,000 horses,[189] an amazing panoply of armed strength. Contrary to popular myth, Germany never realized the dream of full military motorization; it largely fought a 20th century Second World War of and for petroleum with 19th century technology of horses and coal.

The Wehrmacht was actually short thousands of vehicles to equip not only its growing number of mechanized units, but its infantry divisions as well. To make up the shortage of vehicles the Wehrmacht needed which the German automotive industry was unable to provide, civilian vehicles were confiscated from their owners in Germany and in the occupied nations. Initially the loss of the family motor vehicle was a problem to the average German; however by 1942 due to rationing and shortages, the ability to obtain fuel for a private car was almost impossible anyway.

The obvious German preparations for the invasion of Russia make for absorbing reading. The over-flights are a case in point. With a nation so conscious of its internal security as was communist Russia, their forbearance of these German incursions is all the more remarkable.

---

[188] During the opening weeks of the invasion, during the NKVD execution of "unreliable elements" in the various prisons, in Proskuriv "...eleven were shot, along with thirteen German pilots..." These were most certainly from the secret Luftwaffe high altitude reconnaissance over flights.

[189] Stokesbury in his *A Short History of World War II* (William Morrow and Company, Inc., New York, 1980, p. 153) gives a figure of 625,000, three times as many as Napoleon.

Russian Planning and Doctrine

Russian military doctrine as formulated during the early 1930's was one of an offensive response to any enemy violation of Russia or Russian controlled territory. The soil of Mother Russia was seen as sacred and no enemy should violate it. As early as 1936 at a general staff meeting in Moscow chaired by Marshal T. Tukhachevsky to introduce the new Field Service Regulations a possible war with Germany was not only speculated but seriously considered. German Fascism was determined to be the most dangerous enemy of Russia and plans to either thwart German aggression or join in an alliance with Western nations to contain or destroy it was discussed.[190]

The doctrine adopted by the STAVKA was ridged and permitted little initiative or decision making at lower echelons of command. The comparison with German tactical field doctrine could not be more different, the Russian one was inflexible as the German was adaptable and supple. This form of military management, coupled with the fresh and ongoing purges of army commanders, sent a chill through the command and control structure insuring very few commanders made decisions without consulting their unit commissar or a superior authority. With field communication networks fragile prior to the invasion and, in many cases in the opening days and weeks of the invasion, disrupted caused catastrophic conditions when attempting to direct units during the opening weeks of the German invasion.

In early 1941 Stalin ordered Soviet State Defense Plan 41 to be implemented. It was this plan that organized Soviet doctrine to respond to enemy attacks by offensive action regardless of the actual tactical battlefield situation. It was this plan that dictated the forward deployment of two-thirds of the over 300 Russian rifle and tank units. However, complexities with the movement of many new units and communication and transport difficulties saw only a partial implementation of Defense Plan 41 and when Germany attacked in June, many units were under manned and under equipped, some having only their officer headquarters and staff operations in place and many of them were recently promoted out of military academies or from junior commands to fill the vacancies caused the rapid expansion of the Russian Army as well as to fill the gaps by the ongoing purges.

Kennedy in *The Library of Congress World War II Companion* refers to "more than 700,000" p. 397, also, Kershaw in his *War Without Garlands* (Sarpedon, New York, 2000, p. 9) cites an animal total of 750,000.

[190] *The Tukhachevsky Affair*, pp. 18-19.

What is little known or discussed in the western press until recently is the difference in opinion in the highest ranks of the Red Army and the Communist leadership in 1940-1941 of how the newly acquired Polish territory should be defended against what was expected to be the inevitable conflict with the newly victorious and powerful German Wehrmacht.

The acquisition of the eastern Polish territories in late 1939 posed two quandaries to Stalin.[191] With the newly acquired Polish territory, how to use it to best advantage to provide for the defense of Russia. To demonstrate ownership he had to position a significant number of Red Army units in these new areas. This had several advantages: indicating to the former owners who was now in charge, suppressing any internal or domestic opposition, and to demonstrate to the new neighbors to the west that the Russian government took the occupation of these areas seriously and intended to stay. However, massing troops in these areas put them dangerously close to attack and destruction should any hostilities develop with the Germans to the west. It was a very forward deployment of such a large number of units.

The forward positioning of these units in central Poland was in keeping with Stalin's and the communist party's offensive doctrine of carrying war to the enemy. The Party had optimistically conceived that when the Western nations were attacked by Germany, the workers would arise spontaneously and join in fighting the attacker. With Germany tied down combating the French and British as well as the Dutch and Belgian army's and their workers, these forward placed units would explode out of the Bialystok and Lvov positions and, as Stalin and the Party saw the script, bring the workers' paradise to all of Western Europe. Stalin had refused to consider any other strategy as he considered anything else to be defeatist and contrary to approved Party thought. After the just completed Red Army purges of 1936-1939 this was dangerous thought indeed.

When Germany turned west against Denmark and Norway in April of 1940, and against France[192] and the Low Countries a month later, Stalin was quite relieved that the Germans would now be fully engaged in the west, and a replay of World War I was about to occur. Hitler desperately wanted a treaty with England and her colonies so as not to have to launch

---

[191] Whereas the Germans would refer to their Polish acquisitions as *General Gouvernement*, Stalin referred to the Soviet occupied portions as "western Ukraine" and "western Belarus". Notice that both references brazenly extend the eastern border of Germany into the former Polish nation and the same to the west for the U.S.S.R.

an invasion. He was worried that his army would become embroiled in a chancy amphibious invasion of a nation that he saw as racial equals and therefore an ally, albeit one that did not recognize this. Becoming entangled in an invasion and fight for England would dash, or at the very least, greatly delay his long desired invasion of Bolshevik Russia, something Stalin was counting on so as to buy the time his armies needed to complete his military reorganization.

Forward positioning, despite its beneficial presence to the Soviet leadership, had serious tactical problems. Captured German combat reports describe finding groups of Russian tanks mired up to their turrets in mud, due to a lack of knowledge of the surrounding terrain. In hindsight, the Red Army would have been better off to remain in place within the pre-1939 borders, with their prepared positions, established communications and transportation connections, forward supply dumps and familiarity of locale than at the new border to position there screening, or trip-wire units. This would have had the advantages of eliminating the disruption of moving the fronts hundreds of miles west, suspending them, as it were, in unprepared or partially prepared positions in the face of the most dangerous enemy Russia ever confronted. However, hindsight is always so much clearer.

Stalin was convinced that Germany would direct most of its attack against economic targets, toward the south, to the Ukraine. Some of this decision was predicated on Russian experience in dealing with the Germans during the negations during the 1939 peace treaty. It was noticed and reported to Stalin the Germans were very interested in negotiating for raw materials, especially oil.

The pre-1939 Russian western defenses were the so-called "Stalin Line". These ran in north to south from the Baltic to the Black Sea. The OKH in its intelligence evaluation of Russia's western defenses described the Stalin Line as a dangerous combination of concrete, fieldworks and natural obstacles, tank traps, mines, marshy belts around forts, artificial lakes enclosing defiles, cornfields cut according to the trajectory of machine gun fire. Along a front of 120 kilometers, no less than a dozen barriers carefully camouflaged and proofed against light bombs and shells of 75 and

---

[192] The speed of the three week victory over France and the low countries conveniently hides the cost of the German success there: 25% (683 vehicles) of the panzerwaffe were destroyed or put out of action for various reasons, over 26,000 men were killed and 111,000 wounded and a curious 16,600 missing. It was hardly the effortless victory it frequently appears.

100 millimeters had been constructed and sited in skillfully chosen fire positions. Thousands of pine trunks masked ditches which the attacker could not discover until it was too late. About three kilometers behind, over stretches of ten or twelve kilometers, three ranges of pines had been driven more than a meter into the ground. Behind this obstacle stretched-out abatis made of trees sawn to within a meter of the ground, and whose tops, turned toward the enemy, had been entangled with barbed wire. Concrete pyramids strengthened this barricade.

With the unforeseen quick German victory in France and the Low Countries in July 1940, the entire military strategy of the Red Army in the western border regions was in jeopardy. It was now evident to key Red Army commanders that the German panzer units, secretly and quickly being transferred eastward could quickly cut off and destroy the exposed Bialystok and Lvov positions should war come. The loss of these units would leave only the unmechanized infantry, support services, internal security units and the assembling reserve echelon units defending Russia and her new Polish lands. The consequences would be grave and the outcome almost certain: destruction of the western border units and possible deep enemy penetration into Russia itself.

In addition to a defective deployment, there was the issue of the structure and equipping of the Red Army itself, then in the midst of major reorganization. An enemy on one's border is hardly the time to regroup; however the miscalculation of the length of the war between Germany and her western neighbors by Stalin the previous year placed the Red Army in a precarious position. In addition to the strategic situation, there were systemic problems in the reorganization as well as ample evidence of incompetence or gross negligence.

John Erickson in his *The Road To Stalingrad* describes an almost incredible series of poor decisions that were made in early 1941 regarding the reduction in production or cancellation of vital machine guns and anti-tank and field artillery guns. The leadership of the party and certain Russian Army generals seeking favor with Stalin or establishing their own areas of influence were responsible for mistakes that in hindsight are incomprehensible. With the growing body of evidence of the German build up in eastern occupied Poland becoming clearer by the week, these decisions seriously contributed to the poor performance of the Russian units defending against the German attack in June of the same year. For example, Marshal Kulik was of the opinion that small automatic weapons were of use only by police forces and had no place in the field army. The production of the versatile 76mm field and tank gun was stopped by Stalin with the urging of G. I. Kulik. Production of machine guns, anti-tank guns and similar arms also felt the effects of political indecision, all this at a time of the rapid expansion and reorganization of the Russian Army.

Given the above, one wonders what was on the minds of the political leadership, Stalin and the command of the Red Army. One can only surmise that Stalin went ahead with the cutbacks in weapons production as not to offend or constitute a threat to his non-aggression treaty with Germany. Even then, there were very obvious signs that Germany was growing interested in her eastern neighbors, with units of the Wehrmacht occupying or allied with Hungary, Rumania and Bulgaria, and large-scale activity in the Balkans. Add to this the now conspicuous daylight high altitude reconnaissance over-flights of the new border regions. These flights, deep into Russia itself, should have raised warning flags in a number of Soviet ministries and directorates; however, just the opposite happened. It was as if all eyes had become blind to the rising German threat, resting instead in the written comfort of the non-aggression treaty of almost two years earlier.

The situation of the Red Army units in the western defense positions was precarious. Letters home from newly assigned units to the newly occupied border regions in Poland indicated that their equipment was substandard, coming from First World War stocks, France and even the Russian Civil War. The age of the recruits was startling as well, recruited and trained in a hurry and their physical strength, discipline and skills were all deficient.

With this expectation, Stalin, following the recommendations of Generals D. G. Pavlov[193], G. I. Kulik, and Defense Commissar K. A. Meretskov placed a large number of the Red Army's new tank units in two forward locations known as the Bialystok and Lvov positions. This forward positioning of such expensive and valuable offensive units would expose them to great danger against a very competent German panzer force; their abilities amply demonstrated against the French, who had the largest and most modern land army in Europe. With almost the entire panzer force transferred east with the fall of France and the build-up for "Barbarossa"

---

[193] General Pavlov was selected by Stalin as an example of what happened to commanders who failed to stop the German attackers. In July he was arrested, tried and shot for treason.

now arrayed against them instead of the anticipated defensive infantry units, a major decision had to made and made soon, as unbeknownst to his generals Stalin, despite his denial, knew the planned offensive date against Russia (planned for May 1941) was rapidly approaching. What was to be done?

However, Stalin had two other generals that had a much different opinion on the disposition of the Red Army western units. Zhukov and Timoshenko wanted a more flexible approach to the engagement of any enemy, one that would consist of offensive and defensive strategy, not just Stalin's preference for the offensive. The proofs of the soundness of Zhukov's strategy were demonstrated in January 1941 in two secret and very important war games played in Moscow. Taking the part of the aggressor enemy or "the blues", he quickly destroyed the Bialystok position[194] and began an offensive against targets further east when the game was finally halted. In the second game the sides were switched and he defended against "the blues" or the attacking enemy, and his flexible defense not only halted the attacker but also allowed him to even launch counterattacks against them. This was enough proof for Stalin, and after a heated postoperative assessment of the war games, he replaced Meretskov with Zhukov as Red Army chief of staff. This is arguably the most important decision Stalin made in World War II, and saved Russia in the process. There was to be much work for the new Chief of Staff in the remaining five months before Operation Barbarossa began.

---

[194] In the first war game only a limited portion of the western border was considered and the southernmost forward position; the Lvov salient was not war-gamed.

Chapter Seven:
Issue Signal "Dortmund":
Operation Barbarossa
June 1941

"Had I known they (the U.S.S.R.) had that many tanks I would have thought twice about invading."

Adolf Hitler

"The acquisition of new soil was to be obtained only in the east"

Adolf Hitler

"A way of atonement is open to Germany. By combating Bolshevism, by being the bulwark against it, Germany may take the first step towards ultimate reunion with the civilized world."

Winston Churchill, 1919

This chapter will discuss the largest military invasion in Europe in modern history; the German 1941 invasion of Soviet Russia. The forces involved in the early morning attack will be reviewed and the complete German domination of the battle in the early months and the confused and disorganized Russian response to it described. It will look at the progress of all three German Army Groups, especially the extraordinary German advance in the north, a true *blitzkrieg*, to seize Leningrad and how close Army Group North came to taking it. Also examined is the controversial German decision of Army Groups Center and South to halt the attack against Moscow and to turn and meet at Kiev forming the largest double envelopment and one of the largest prisoner captures of the war. Finally we will see the final German attempt to take Moscow and examine how close they came to succeeding and the first major Russian offensive of the war to date, the winter counteroffensive in front of Moscow and its results and the unplanned German winter in Russia. In conclusion we will stop and look at the state and condition of the German Army in Russia after six months of non-stop campaigning.

Barbarossa

Little did the future Prime Minister of Great Britain, Winston Churchill, know what his words would lead to in the days after November 1918 when the victorious allies gathered at Versailles. In just a few short years, a desperately poor former corporal in the German army was to pen his own thoughts about what direction lay the destiny of Germany, and they were amazingly similar to those of Churchill.

When the first maps were unrolled in front of the German officers involved in the invasion of Russia, there was a quiet, stunned silence from most. Most anticipated another field exercise or a continuation of the invasion of Britain or the Vichy portion of France. When the word Russia was read on the maps and charts, all who were familiar with the earlier invasions of the almost invasion-proof country felt history repeating itself once again. After the shock had worn off and they devoted themselves to the detail planning of the operational aspects of the invasion, many requested copies of the noted author Armand de Caulaincourt's memoirs *At Napoleon's Side In Russia*. As Napoleon's ambassador to Russia, his Master of the Horse, Caulaincourt's record of the invasion and its tragic retreat of the Grand Armee is the most comprehensive and cautionary.

If anyone was going to show what had to change to be successful when invading Russia, Caulaincourt was the one to point the way.[195]

Sixteen days after the commencement of Barbarossa, the 4th Panzer Army of Army Group Center arrived at the banks of the Berezina at Borisov in the Byelorussian Soviet Socialist Republic. German General Günter Blumentritt was with the forward elements of the Army as he and his staff surveyed the opposite bank and the road beyond to Orsha and still further to Smolensk, for all appearances wide open, unguarded. As he stood there some in their party pointed to the river itself, more specifically to the river bottom pointing out rows of stumps of poles leading to the opposite side. Initially they were unsure what they were looking at, but soon realized that they were the remains of the last conquering army to pass this way. These stunted remains were the supports of one of two hurriedly built bridges constructed by French engineers in that harsh winter of 1812 to carry the frozen and dying remnants of Napoleon's retreating Grand Armee out of Russia.

Unbeknownst to this newest conqueror, now in all out assault on the last threat to German National Socialism on the European mainland, these 129 year old remains called out from their watery grave a warning to this newest of invaders a warning of the seeming ease during the mild weathers which quickly turn deadly with great suddenness.

Hitler and his famous *gefuhl* or power of feeling that he used to guide his decision making may have failed him in the planning of the Russian invasion. Originally the operational code name was to be 'Fritz' but he changed it to 'Barbarossa', he preferred the name of the ancient German emperor that united the German states and led them into Russia. However inspiring that choice was, he failed to heed the untimely demise of Barbarossa, who drowned in a stream. A fate filled omen indeed.

Frustrated with the cancellation *of Unternehmen Seelowe* or Operation Sealion, the planned amphibious invasion of England in the summer of 1940 and with the modest campaign assisting the Italians in North Africa progressing satisfactorily, there remained only one obstacle to the final conquest of all of Europe: The Union of Soviet Socialist Republics. For Hitler, especially, Russia and all it represented was a special case.

---

[195] During the approach to Moscow in 1941, so as not to influence and distract his staff, Hitler forbade them to read Caulaincourt's book.

The Attack

The German invasion of Russia began unannounced at the early hour of 0300[196] on 22 June 1941 with a thunderous crash of aircraft bombing, artillery, machine-gun and mortar barrages, and tank, truck and armored personnel carrier engines. Ignored were the traditional formalities of recalling ambassadors and exchanging ultimatums and issuing declarations, to Hitler a treaty was just so much ink on paper and was no defense against German contempt for protocol. From near the Arctic Circle on the Barents Sea in northern Finland, to the shores of the Black Sea in southern Rumania, Germany and her Axis allies unleashed the largest invasion of another country in modern times.[197]

The Wehrmacht on the morning of 22 June 1941 was the acme of military readiness. Fresh and rested and now combat tested from the flat lands of Belgium and Holland, the rolling meadows of France, and the hills of the Balkans, the German armies that struck the larger Russian Army was not to be equaled by any of the Allies until the latter stages of the war when the western Allied and the Red Army's finally matched its organizational levels of experience and proficiency. On the other hand the Russian Army, as has been mentioned and will be again, was in the throes of a massive reorganization, expansion, re-equipping and re-deployment and recovering from the leadership and command purges of three years earlier. If ever there was an award for an Army that was unprepared to defend itself and its homeland, the Red Army of late spring 1941 is arguably the best example.

The exploits of the Brandenburgers, the German special forces units, were keenly felt in the opening days of the invasion. Stalin prohibited the use of radio communications due to the threat of German interception, and thus forced the Red Army to rely on land line (wire) telephonic communications. As this was now the sole means of communication with all levels of command within and among the field units, the lack of pre-war security along the telephone lines themselves is amazing. It was only within the last few kilometers of the front the lines were buried. After that the lines were strung on the above ground telephone poles just as everyday

---

[196] The start times for the invasion varied from north to south, starting at 0300 and the final attack time 0330. However, initial German offensive action on the border in the Lvov area was reported as late as 0400.

[197] For OKW staff planning and troop assembly purposes, the western side of the Russian-German border was known as the 'Otto" line.

public telephone lines were. As telephones in the U.S.S.R. at that period were a rare commodity, (usually only party offices, post offices and towns and cities had telex and telephone offices), these lines were far and few between and it did not take much sabotage to sever communications to the front. All the pre-attack German Brandenburger sabotage units had to do was cut a few dozen meters of phone line, bury it, and until the cut was discovered, the units at the front were as far out of communication as if they were on the moon.

As the German panzer divisions sliced deep into the Russian lines, first in the newly acquired Polish territories then into Ukraine and Russia proper, the speed and facility of which the Wehrmacht units manhandled the Red Army was astounding. However, on closer examination, the question could be asked 'were the Germans that good or were the Russian that bad?' The answer to both questions is, yes.

The rapid advance into the Russian positions was as follows in the first weeks of the invasion. Army Group North's IV Panzer Korps was approaching Rezekne in Latvia, almost 250 miles from its starting point on the East Prussian border. Close behind was Army Group Center's II and III Panzer Korps, both approaching Minsk, 185 miles in one week from its starting point near Brest-Litovsk. In Army Group South, VI Armee was at the Stalin Line 20 miles from Berdichev and I Panzer Korps was 100 miles past Ternopol, just to its south. These advances would have been admirable in any of the earlier German invasions, but that they had been made on the poor or nonexistent roads in Eastern Poland and Western Russia is all the more significant. The portents of an early and successful conclusion to the Russian campaign were good ones.

However certain shortcomings were making their first appearance in the invasion. For example, In Army Group North, as the 6th Panzer Division of Reinhardt's XLI Korps approached the village of Rossieny a Russian tank unit with over 300 tanks counterattacked. When the usual deployment of the standard German 37mm anti-tank guns failed to stop the attack, field artillery and air attacks were called in to provide support. 6th Panzer was forced to retreat almost 8 miles before the Russian attack dissolved into uncoordinated starts and stops and finally the surviving vehicles withdrew. Among the attacking tanks was a new big Russian tank, it was eventually identified as the KV-1B with thick armor and equipped with what was to become the nemesis for the Germans in Russia, the 76mm main gun. It was to be the first of many surprises in Russia.

The losses in the early months of the campaign also indicate something else. In addition to the unpreparedness of the Red Army in the early days of the invasion was that of resentment and unrest in the ranks of the Russian Army. The conscription of non-Russians into the Russian Army in the rapid period of expansion without the time to properly train, blend and inculcate Russian and communist dogma into these newly made soldiers gave rise to the early reports of mass surrenders, defections and led to the German belief of the success of the Blitzkrieg. It probably accounts for the 'hit and miss' quality of Soviet units mentioned in many German action reports. These truly were the darkest days for Russia, communism and the Russian Army.[198]

The impact of the German invasion on the still organizing and deploying Russian Army was considerable. For days, and in some cases weeks, at a time, Russian Army high command did not know where many of its divisions, and in some cases even larger field formations, were. A Russian general replying to a question of where a soldier could find his division said, even he did not know where is units were.

Inside the Soviet borders Stalin had created an ideological world that seemed to be self contained and answerable to his will; suddenly on 22 June 1941 the realities of the outside world crashed in.

Such was the OKH's expectation of impending collapse of the Russian Army that Hitler was already planning for a post-military Russia policy. On 8 July, two weeks into the invasion, he instructed von Braushitsch, army chief of staff to halt the dispatch of additional new panzers to Russia. With greatly misplaced optimism, the planned conclusion of mobile operations would permit the number of panzer division to be reduced and inactive panzer crews to be rotated to Germany for rest and refit and the forming of new panzer divisions.

The western Allies were also shaken by the inability of the Russian Army to contain, if not halt the German invasion. The British Military Mission dispatched to Moscow to offer support and encouragement awkwardly suggested that they might be able to hold out in Siberia and to please destroy the oil facilities in the Caucasus.

---

[198] A number of Red Army soldiers, attempting to avoid fighting shot themselves in the left hand in the mistaken belief they would be sent to the hospital and then home. Whatever the cause of the wound, a left hand wound was deemed to be self-inflicted (*samostrel*) and a soldier faced death at the hands of SMERSh.

In addition to the human losses were the immense equipment losses. The numbers in this category are staggering. Total personnel losses from all causes for the June to December 1941 period were 4,473,820.[199] The material losses for 1941: Tanks and self-propelled guns, 20,500; artillery of all kinds, 63,100; aircraft of all kinds, 17,900.[200] These numbers tell us many things in addition to the obvious military tragedy. One is the huge size of the Red Army prior to the German attack, the vast number of tanks, artillery and aircraft stockpiled prior to the invasion and the Red Army's ability to absorb these losses and still have enough resources to continue fighting; a truly impressive set of statistics. These numbers, both men and material could easily staff and equip any western army. No wonder the Germans were confident of an early victory, just like all the others. The amount of captured war material enabled the Germans to equip parts of their panzer units with captured weapons, especially the excellent 76.2mm anti-tank guns that appeared as the PzJag 36(t) and the PzJag 38(t) H tracked anti-tank vehicles. The Russian materiel losses in these early months were immense.[201]

The Turn South

So confident had Hitler become of an Russian collapse and an easy seizure of Moscow he decided on 19 July to halt the units of Army Group Center and divide their mechanized forces to assist the attack against Leningrad to the North and to the close up with Army Group South, whose northern flank was under heavy pressure from the Russian 5th Army. Also at this time the original flank support maneuver was expanded to become a major inter-army group double envelopment.

[199] *Soviet Casualties and Combat Losses In the Twentieth Century*, Edited by Colonel-General G. F. Krivosheev, Greenhill Books, 1997, p. 94.

[200] *When Titans Clashed, How the Red Army Stopped Hitler*, David M. Glantz and Jonathan M. House, University Press of Kansas, 1995, p. 306.

[201] In a desperate attempt to stem the seemingly unstoppable German armies, Stalin resorted his favorite method of insuring compliance: executing those who failed to follow his directives. On 22 July 1941 he had the four commanders of the Western Front shot. In fact so many requests flowed into the Kremlin to shoot traitors they clogged the telegraph wires, Mekhlis (Lev Mekhlis, Chief of the Red Army's Main Political Administration) then told the requesters to sentence and shoot their own traitors. Considering the Great Terror invoked by Stalin in 1935 and the hundreds of thousands (some say as many as a million) resulting executions, the starving of the Kulaks in the early 1930's, the war dead, caused by the Wehrmacht or Russian security services, the deportations of 'untrustworthy' or suspected populations, and the post-war arrests, expulsions and executions it is truly a wonder that the U.S.S.R. was able to function during and after the war. It's another reflection on the adage that when one has a surplus of something it is usually wasted until it is once again scarce.

The large open ended pocket around the Pripet Marshes, extending just east of Rovno to the Dnieper River, some 175 miles into the German front separated two Russian army groups, the aforementioned Russian 5th Army and the 21st Army operating to its north against the southern flank of Army Group Center. These two Russian armies were causing a certain amount of concern as more and more German units were being diverted South to fend off these incessant and strong attacks.

The final attack plan was for Germanys 2nd Panzer Group and 2nd Army to halt its eastern operations and to turn south and prepare for a fast offensive in that direction. To meet it, Army Group South, whose long left flank was deep along the central Dnieper River as far as Dnepropetrovsk and had taken a large bridge head over the river at Kremenchug. The stage was set for the operation.

Initially 2nd Panzergruppe commander Heinz Guderian was opposed to discontinuing the operation to take Moscow when the Russian units in front of him seemed to be in disarray and confused and in some cases altogether missing. The ring around the group of Russian Armies at Smolensk had closed and by 5 August was destroyed freeing his units for the continued advance east. He was partially mollified by the opportunity the operation afforded him to secure his right flank against Russian forces arriving from Roslavl.

By the end of August, Guderian was moving south, taking Gomel and Starodub a week later. During this same time Stalin, after Army Group South's penetration of the Stalin Line west of Zhitomir and aware of the growing threat to Kiev, began reinforcing his Southwestern Front under S. M. Budenny, and on 30 August launching a counterattack north of Gomel that the Germans fended off.

By this time Army Group South was prepared to perform its part of the double envelopment. On 12 September the 1st Panzergruppe attacked out of the Kremenchug bridgehead and with flank support from 6th Army to its east, headed north across the Psel River. Despite the onset of the autumn rasputitsy, on 15 September 1941 to two Panzergruppes met at Lokhvitsa. In the next week three Russian army's, the 5th, 21st and the 37th were surrounded, reduced and destroyed and the city of Kiev was now in German hands.

The successful double envelopment of three Russian armies (and parts of the 26th) of the Western and South-West Fronts represented the loss of some 450,000 men equaling 42 rifle divisions. In addition to the personnel losses, 3,900 guns and mortars was captured. Of this huge number of surrounded men, less than 15,000 managed to escape the clutches of the German panzer and mechanized forces.

The huge losses notwithstanding, the Red Army held on. On 30 September 1941, Army Group Center and Army Group South launched Operation Typhoon the assault to take Moscow. But prior to the onset of winter was that interval between the dry summer heat and dust and the frozen winter ice and snow, the period of rain and mud.

The delay in moving on Moscow before the fair weather campaign season ended caused by the Kiev operation was now upon the hapless German infantry. In one of the earliest and coldest winters on record, the first snows arrived in late September; it was a somber warning of what was to come.

The Return to Moscow

The German victory at Kiev (and the panzer support sent North to Leningrad) has taken on a controversy of its own, the giant capture of Russian men and equipment notwithstanding. The need to stop and rest and refit the panzer and mechanized units had been an original part of the Barbarossa plan and the conquest of Smolensk was the logical stopping place for this to occur. The 'land bridge' between the Dnieper and the Dvina Rivers was occupied and there was no significant physical barriers between that city and the Russian capitol. The diversion to the South, however much tactical opportunity and economic gain it promised preempted the planned panzer refitting. In addition, the additional 500 miles of use on the engines, transmissions and tracks only added to the already worn German machines, which would soon make its needs known very soon.

In addition to the additional wear on German equipment was the delay of a month in the offensive against Moscow. The delay was put to good use by Russian General I. S. Konev who was made commander of the Western Front consisting of six Armies (the Russian Army at this stage of the war had the strength equivalent of a German division). A series of three defensive positions was constructed during this period, one known as the Vyazma defense line stretched from east of Lake Seliger in the north to a point some 20 miles north-west of Bryansk, a second shorter one known as the Mozhaysk defense line from the Volga Reservoir in the north to a point 40 miles south of Kaluga. Finally there was a series of three defense belts in front of Moscow, starting about twenty miles outside of the city covering the northern, western and southern approaches. All of them consisted of a series of earth works, rifle trenches and anti-tank ditches, the deteriorating weather, lack of time and materials prevented any more substantial development.

As the Wehrmacht approached Moscow the Soviet Central Committee instructed the city defense authorities to camouflage the most conspicuous and well known landmarks. Known as the Camouflage Service or *Sluzhba maskirovka*, a committee organized and reporting to the Moscow City Council, it was responsible for concealing or deceiving the true purpose of important military, industrial, cultural and governmental buildings and facilities. The Great Palace was hidden behind a large net containing tree branches; the golden domes of the Kremlin were painted gray and the walls were painted a bizarre combination of yellow, black, cream and orange paint. In addition, the large public squares were painted to resemble rooftops from the air and even the canvas backdrops of the Bolshoi Theater were hung from the outsides of office buildings. How ballet theater backdrops would have assisted in concealing the city from the enemy is anyone's guess.

With a Russian winter looming over the *Ostheer* and with historical precedents of disaster notwithstanding, Hitler forged ahead with his winter offensive against Moscow, Operation Typhoon. If one seeks an answer to why proceed with such a risky venture, Hitler himself may be the answer. During the preparation for the French and Lowlands campaign in the West, the army generals advised him that winter and its difficulties could cause problems in cold weather operations to men and machine. Hitler responded that 'technology defeats winter'. With that mindset it is no wonder that the German army suffered as it did in that fierce winter of 1941.

Winterschlacht

The German attack, known as Operation Typhoon,[202] was to be solely conducted by Army Group Center. This was to be the capstone event of the campaign, the culmination of six months of hard fighting and dying and it was filled with risk.

---

[202] Also known colloquially as *die flucht nach vorn*, or the flight forward/to the front.

It was launched on 30 September and despite the adverse road and field conditions for the mechanized units made good progress and enjoyed two major double envelopments of Russian armies. The central envelopment at Vyazma surrounded four Russian armies and the one to the south near Bryansk captured two. The Russian losses from 30 September to 5 December were over 650,000 men and uncounted numbers of tanks, artillery and aircraft. Despite the deteriorating weather and growing exhaustion, German combat units continued to advance, but each day the number of miles and the number of men grew less and less. Hitler was certain that after losses from the summer and additional losses such as these, there could not be any more Russian combat units left in front or in back of Moscow. However, still more surprises awaited.

The German Wehrmacht was especially vulnerable to this spring and fall phenomenon, known as the *rasputitsy,* meaning "time of no roads". With their vehicles designed for use on paved roads or at least the firmer soils of western Europe, the lack of paved surfaces and the softer Russian soils, especially the rich, dark Chernozem soils, proved an obstacle worthy of military recognition. If it was not on rail rolling stock, one's vehicle, should it be panzer, half-track, tractor, heavy truck, staff car, motorcycles and even bicycles sank up to their axles and on some occasions deeper. Draft horses suffered similar difficulties.

One solution was to utilize the hundreds and in some cases thousands of destroyed, derelict and abandoned Soviet tanks and tracked vehicles. With little effort, in some cases all it took to put some of these vehicles into service was to fill the fuel tanks, a ready source of conveyance was available.

The reason Russian tanks worked in the mud when German ones did not was due to two superior design features all Russian tanks possessed; a higher ground clearance and wider tracks than the German vehicles. This allowed passage over soft soil and mud, as well as reducing the overall vehicle weight on the ground. The Christie tank suspension system used on the T-34 series tanks, used a large rubber coated road wheel system that was a combination road wheel and return roller. The other major suspension system, known as the vertical volute suspension system of coiled and leaf springs used separate and smaller road wheels and separate return rollers to guide the treads of the tanks track. One major advantage of the Christie system was the road wheels could also be used to power and drive the tank if the tracks came off, either during combat, rough terrain or poor driving skills.

The second risky element was the onset of the foul weather season in western Russia, which begins with the arrival of the autumn rains, the rasputitsy. In and of itself rain would have been a marginal nuisance (more so for the Luftwaffe) to the offensive had it been conducted in Western Europe, with its extensive hard surfaced road and rail network. However this essential ingredient in mechanized operations was sorely missing in western Russia in the early 1940s and never having been confronted with such poor operating conditions, the Wehrmacht was not only unprepared, but unsure what the impact would be on their now very narrow margin for success for concluding the operation before the snows and intense cold of a fearful Russian winter arrived.[203]

By October the rains turned the roads to mush but the still mild weather, mostly above freeing for October and November; then winter arrived; the weather became incredibly cold and snowy. Although the freezing temperatures restored mobility, men and horses froze without the protection of proper winter clothing, shelter and food; the vehicles broke down from overuse and lack of cold weather preventative measures. With one last lunge at the Soviet capital the Germans tried to seize the prize; it was not to be. On 15 November the offensive was stopped for good; the remaining momentum brought the spires of the Kremlin in sight on 5 December.[204]

The Moscow Counteroffensive

On the night of 5/6 December Stalin began what was to become over the next month a series of local attacks that became a massive attack against the Typhoon forces and drove them back, in some instances 125 miles, finally stopping in a confused mish-mash of extended positions, pockets and thinly held lines that snaked for hundreds of miles. Over a span of 650 miles of front the Russian Western and Kalinin Fronts (and a part of South-West Front) assembled over a million men for the offensive, a total of 105 divisions and 44 independent brigades, many of them new faces,

---

[203] The rapid conclusion that was planned and expected for "Barbarossa" was reflected in the pre-invasion planning for only 20% of the invasion force to remain in the U.S.S.R. for occupation duty, and that figure was the one used to calculate the amount of winter clothing needed for the 1941 campaign.

[204] The unit that approached closest to Moscow on 30 November 1941,was one of the reconnaissance battalions of the 2nd Panzer Division. It had penetrated to Khimki, Ozeretskoye and Lobnja suburbs north and east-northeast of Moscow within sight of the spires of the Kremlin but was there for only a few days when driven out by a few tanks and a handful of workers from the city's factories.

Asiatic faces, from the far east. Although the Germans still outnumbered them, the German units were exhausted and hungry, their panzers and aircraft frozen into immobility. Their stopping positions were exposed and no defensive accommodation could be made in the frozen ground which provided little protection.

The source of this miracle on the Moskva was information.[205] Stalin had received reliable reports indicating the Japanese would not attack on the mainland in Asia against the Russians, but against the possessions and colonies of the western nations in Southeast Asia and the South Pacific. This knowledge resulted in the release a number of high quality divisions from Siberia and the Pacific regions to be transported via the Trans-Siberian Railroad to the front door of Moscow all during November in time to reinforce the thin ranks of the Kalinin and West Fronts, and launch the counterattack.

After four months of almost constant fighting and horrendous losses to both sides because of the cold, malfunctioning weapons and equipment, (mostly to the Germans), the Russian counter offensive itself ran out of energy and came to a halt in late April, early May 1942 from the spring thaw, lack of fuel and exhaustion. The German losses, especially of mechanized transport was such that Germany commandeered civilian trucks from all of occupied Europe in Operations *Elefant* and *Christophorus*. Despite this European-wide truck and car dragnet approximately only a quarter of them arrived for various reasons in Russia, complicating an already difficult vehicle management and maintenance situation, but was still insufficient to provide the mobility Germany needed in the wide expanses of Russia.

The Russian Winter

The fighting in Russia in the winter was now a matter of desperately finding the men and equipment to seal a shattered front line from the many Soviet penetrations. The threat to supply and communications networks was the major concern of the German command in the late winter and early spring of 1941-1942. The forces in place were the best in the world, fully trained, experienced, and skilled in all the fighting arts; however there was a problem that was almost impossible for the Wehrmacht to solve: there were not enough of them to fight the enemy, and what there was, were sick, exhausted and demoralized.

---

[205] Stalin was to receive high quality, reliable and timely information on the intentions of his enemies all during the war from his well trained and highly developed secret intelligence organs.

The frozen conditions made many of the operations of the vehicles difficult and in some cases impossible. Gun sights became opaque, engines were left running or needed fires under them to defrost the oil with the consequent penalties of additional fuel consumption and engine wear. Cases of frostbite were rising alarmingly and the effect of the cold on the weapons, especially machine guns and artillery was causing many malfunctions.

Short term solutions to the lack of adequate manpower came in several forms: roving combat groups that moved across fronts to police areas that should have been covered with line infantry divisions; the now famous 'hedgehog' defensive positions established in critical locations such as road junctions, bridges, river crossings and other key topographical locations. In some areas there was simply no one there-empty. This last condition was one that would frighten any commander the most.

Empty, unmanned front line positions facing an active, aggressive enemy is, as the popular phrase goes, a disaster waiting to happen. Not only is there no organized resistance to prevent an enemy from penetrating a position, there is no defense to prevent an enemy wreaking havoc in undefended or lightly defended rear areas, such as administrative offices, mess facilities, command and control structures, hospital and medical units, rail sidings, bridges, supply and distribution buildings, training commands, and rest and recreation areas.

The German army defending its positions that winter in Russia can be very much compared to an egg. With its hard, impervious shell it is an excellent defense to almost everything. However, should something pierce that shell, there is very little defensive mass behind it to offer resistance to an invader. With the offensive stance taken by the Wehrmacht that winter, no defensive positions were prepared and now with the ground frozen, none could be adequately constructed. Eleven hundred draft horses perished every day.

The Wehrmacht, now in the unplanned winter of 1941-1942 found itself in just such a position in the frozen wastes of European Russia. With the attrition suffered in the eight months of combat and the weather, the offensive mass-the panzer and motorized divisions were now needed for the simple duties of maintaining the front. Panzer and mechanized divisions were now used for static defense due to their mobility and the loss of valuable infantry.

In place of being the charging, offensive component of any army, the motorized units were doing double duty. They now not only had to defend a front that was much too wide for them, but to detach themselves from this patrolling, observation and largely maintenance duties, and almost immediately go over to offensive action in counter attacks and other like missions. This means that these units now became the military equivalent of a 'fire brigade', rushing from one danger area to another 'putting out' fire after fire of enemy activity. This not only prevented these highly specialized units from performing the duties they were trained to do, but the constant action prevented them from regular rest for the unit personnel and performing the maintenance needed on such maintenance-intensive vehicles as fully tracked tanks, half-tracked vehicles, wheeled trucks and cars. Not only was the standard wear and tear maintenance not being performed but the winterization necessary for use in cold environments was not performed as well. Such treatments were additives to the coolant to keep from freezing, thinner oils in the engines and drive systems and tire and wheel traction attachments for snow operations, etc.

There is one anecdotal account of a captured Russian officer watching a Luftwaffe unit attempt to get aircraft machine guns and cannon to operate in such severe weather. He asked if they had sunflower oil.[206] When told no, he indicated that what they needed to do was to prepare a large barrel of boiling water and immerse the guns in this boiling water for a few minutes. The puzzled Germans observed what he was doing, and when the guns were removed from the hot water so was their lubrication. That was just the problem, the Russian indicated. In these low temperatures no lubricant was necessary and the guns worked perfectly without them.[207]

In addition to the need to rush from point to point assisting the remaining infantry units in maintaining the front, such as it was, these units also lost one very valuable asset; that of initiating action against the enemy and not, as they were now doing, reacting to enemy initiatives. Although quite capable of performing such alert and response duties as we have and will see in the future, the value of mechanized units was to carry the war to the enemy, and not vice a versa as was now the situation the Germans found themselves in.

---

[206] Sunflower oil was the only available lubricant that permitted the proper functioning of weapons in cold weather. However it was in short supply and usually only in the southern portion of the front where most of the sunflowers were grown.

[207] In addition to the frozen guns and engines, the artificial rubber the Germans used in making their tires became very stiff in very cold weather and cracked and split when in use.

The condition of the Wehrmacht after the winter fighting of 1941-1942 was so poor that the defense of the eastern positions was threatened and the army's survival was a concern. A status report issued in March 1942 indicates that of 162 infantry divisions in Russia only 3 were ready for offensive missions (2%), 8 were ready for general missions (5%), 47 were able to conduct limited offensive actions (29%), 73 were suitable for defensive missions (45%), 29 were capable for limited defensive missions (18%) and 2 were unavailable (1%). The mechanized divisions, both panzer and motorized were in even worse condition. In the 16 panzer divisions on the Eastern Front there were a total of only 140 operable 'panzers', which is fewer vehicles than would equip one full strength division! The motorized divisions were in similar shape.

One decision Hitler made in the first winter in Russia that saved his Wehrmacht in Russia was the 'no retreat' order of 20 December 1941. What has come to be one of the most controversial orders issued during World War II was, in hindsight, the order that saved the German army during its first great trial. Maintaining the positions the army held against the Russian 5 December counterattack provided some protection against the harsh winter weather. Had the army begun a retreat across the frozen ground it could have resulted in an out of control rout, especially when it was pursued by a newly reinforced and invigorated Russian army. Holding the line, as much as possible, was the correct order, however unpopular and, at the time, unreasonable it sounded. The real tragedy was that with this being the correct decision, it now became *modus operandi* for Hitler in time of defense, however misused as it later came to be.

Given the condition of the Wehrmacht in the east, it is a wonder that within four months they were ready to launch a second major offensive, albeit a regional one. Never again would all three Army Groups in Russia launch a coordinated attack as in June of 1941, the exhaustive fighting that was symptomatic of the combat in Russia was slowly reducing the combat abilities of the world's greatest and most modern army to that of, say, Poland in 1939, a stunning turn of events by any standards.

The first year of the campaign in Russia put Germany in a disadvantageous strategic position. Never again would the Wehrmacht get so close to the prize, get so close to seizing the capital of world Communism, to calling the Kremlin their own. The Russians held Moscow; with its warm housing, transportation links to north, east and south, its factories and plants turning out war material, some of it coming off the assembly lines straight into combat. The Germans huddled on the frozen open ground, blasted by wind and snow with little or no protection, as most of the villages and towns had been burned in the scorched-earth retreat by the Russians the previous September and October.

The suffering by the Army Groups that winter of was such that a medal was struck for those participating in the winter offensive against Moscow. On a blackened silver disk, bearing a *stahlhelm* (steel helmet) atop a *stielgranate* (hand grenade), eagle and swastika on the obverse; the reverse reads *Winterschlacht im Osten* 1941-1942. One of the criteria for awarding the medal was the loss of a limb due to frostbite. There were 3,000,000 awardees.[208]

With the onset of the rainy season in March and April 1942, the return of the 'rasputitsy', most fighting in Russia came to an end, with the exception of scouting parties and similar reconnaissance probing. Both sides welcomed the respite, to rest the troops, re-establish lines of communication, resupply, train new replacements, and prepare for future action.

To demonstrate the inability of German industry to properly maintain the combat units in the field, on 18 February 1942, OKW instructed the panzer and motorized units in the east which were to be rehabilitated were to receive 50 to 60 per cent of their authorized motor vehicle equipment and infantry divisions were to receive only 50 per cent. By the end of the winter of 1941 - 1942 Army Group Center was 227,000 men short of authorized strength. The same army group had lost over 4,000 anti-tank guns, almost 6,000 mortars and 3,400 large caliber field guns.[209]

As referred to above, the unit rehabilitation in all three army groups was not to be total, but only a limited number of divisions were to be 'rehabilitated'. The rehabilitation was prioritized based on division type; the order being: panzer, motorized, then infantry. Nine divisions, three panzer and six infantry from Army Group Center were to be transferred to France for a thorough overhaul, retraining and reinforcement. The remainder of the divisions in Army Groups North and Center were to be rehabilitated in the line as best as could be accomplished.

---

[208] The award was designed by SS *Unterscharfuhrer* Ernst Kraus and was instituted on 26 May 1942.

[209] *When Titans Clashed*, p. 103.

This 'rehabilitation in the line' turned out to be almost useless. The almost constant Russian, probing and scouting activity kept these units in a state of near constant readiness, which prevented any meaningful rehabilitation and the loss of their heavy equipment like artillery, motor vehicles and horses prevented many of these units from moving to their rehabilitation areas.

The End of the First Campaign

The opening months of the campaign were desperate ones for the Russians and wonderful ones for the Wehrmacht. Massive numbers of Russian troops were encircled, captured or killed by the fast moving panzer and mechanized units. At a number of locations the numbers of Red Army troops captured was immense: Defense of Belorussia, 417,790; Defense of Kiev, 700,544; Leningrad, 344,926; Battle of Smolensk, 344,926; Moscow, 658,279.[210] Just the losses in these more noteworthy battles came to 2,466,465 killed, wounded or missing, and there were many smaller engagements that could be added to the total. By western military standards these were astonishing numbers. No wonder Hitler felt confident that the campaign would end before winter; no other army in modern times had suffered such losses and continued fighting. As we shall see this war was to be unlike anything in memory.

When the Germans swept into Russia in June the numbers of aircraft, tanks and guns captured and destroyed was enormous. However, on closer inspection one would see that the equipment the Germans destroyed was mainly older, mostly obsolete, and much of it worn out, anticipating its replacement with the new T-34 and KV models. So the tally of captured and destroyed Russian equipment is a somewhat misleading indicator of success. It just may have really been a blessing in disguise for the Russians in that this old equipment now had to be replaced with modern and new machinery, and if this old equipment managed to inflict a few losses to the invader during its destruction, all the better.

By the end of February 1942 total personnel losses for Germany from all sources[211] in the fighting in Russia had passed the one million mark. With the campaign beginning with 3,050,000 officers and enlisted personnel, this represents fully one third of the invasion force eliminated. If this is

---

[210] *When Titans Clashed*, p. 293.

[211] Killed, wounded, missing, transfers.

examined in toto, it is the equivalent of the Wehrmacht having lost one entire Army Group by the beginning of the next campaigning season, which would start sometime in mid to late April.[212]

In addition to the magnitude of the losses is the rate of loss, another astounding aspect of the war in the east. In the first six months of the invasion the Red Army lost over 225 division-sized units. Even though these units were approximately at half the personnel strength of their German attackers, allowing for this strength disparity this still amounts to some 115 full strength division-sized units in some 180 days, a rate of loss no western armed force would or could physically or politically sustain, such was the abilities of totalitarian societies.[213]

With Germany's military commitments now stretched from northern Norway in the north to the Sea of Azov in the south, (not to mention Rommel's forces in north Africa) from the English Channel in the west to south of Moscow in the east, the Wehrmacht was confronted with a situation that was beyond its current manpower and economic abilities to manage properly and the future did not lend itself to a positive outlook.

---

[212] German losses during this same period from frostbite alone were 112,627: Shirer.

[213] The fate of Russian captured depended on a number of factors, among them: condition at point of capture (wounded, hunger, morale), length of time with Wehrmacht and time in civilian managed POW camps. There is ample evidence of the German captors attempting to improve the condition of their Russian captives, such as tending to wounds and feeding, even at the point of them going to short rations to provide for the Russians.

Close-up of T-34/76 with supporting infantry. Postwar: note AK-47 assault rifles of the riflemen.

Chapter Eight:
The Quest for Oil
The 1942 Campaign

"What men dare, I dare. Approach thou like the rugged Russian bear... Take any shape but that, and my firm nerves shall never tremble."

- William Shakespeare
Macbeth

Forced into an unplanned second campaign year in Russia with the failure the year before to attain any of the original objectives of Operation Barbarossa, Germany was in a serious political, economic and military position. This chapter will look each of these areas and examine what decisions Germany made to solve the problems they presented. In addition an overview of the 1942 offensive to the south-east will be conducted with an emphasis of the crucial battle of Stalingrad and its aftermath the second Russian winter offensive.

The key decision of the 1942 campaign - whether to continue the attack on Moscow or the attack south into the Caucasus to seize the needed oil - will be discussed as will the benefits and shortcomings of both strategies. The final decision taken by Hitler, to go for the oil may have taken the German war effort in Russia in the wrong direction, the perceived economic imperative of supplying the fuel needed to run the German war machine was, in the end, a questionable choice as we will see.

The immediate goal of the second campaigning season was economic. The raw materials that Hitler saw in the east and needed to power the Third Reich still eluded him and a second campaign year was necessary. This was not only to seize the resources necessary to carry on the war as a whole, but to also force Russia out of the war once and for all.

The military situation for Germany was serious. The *Ostheer*, as the German army in the East was now known was in a precarious tactical position. With an unbeaten Russian Army in front of it a growing Partisan movement behind it, its own army weaker then when it started the campaign, a solution was needed to bring the war to a successful conclusion. By late Spring of 1942, the front in Russia was some 1,300 miles[214] in length and the economic situation, especially fuel, was becoming a deciding factor in the conduct and planning of the war.

To the Caucasus

The decision, however, was not an easy one. Moscow still lay within reach of Army Group Center, approximately 175 miles to the east of Gzhatsk, the closest German held point. The great prize, missed by so close a margin a year ago, was still attainable. All that was needed was the political and military will to make it happen. However, more than political and military will was needed. The extended campaign was now desperately short of the energy to power it all, oil. And the need for oil overcame whatever desire still remained to try for Moscow again.

The major activity of the second year of Operation Barbarossa began in June 1942 with the commencement of *Fall Blau* or Case Blue the advance to the Volga and into the Caucasus. Unlike the previous year when the entire German army was on the offensive, this attack was planned for only one of the three Army Groups, Army Group South. The Eastern Armies were unable to initiate an all out offensive as they had in 1941. This was due

[214] By November 1942 the front was to extend some 3,100 miles.

to the losses and damage inflicted by the Russian winter campaign, several small Russian offensives in the Army Group South sector in March,[215] and the leftover exhaustion of the previous year's campaigning.

The Lure of Oil, Case Blue

Germany's fuel situation, especially its petroleum reserves, were growing smaller as the war progressed. The Kriegsmarine and Luftwaffe, two large consumers of oil fuels were voicing concerns of adequate supplies to maintain operations and the army's panzerwaffen, the biggest user of oil on land had been chronically short for most of the Eastern campaign already. The decision was to make this campaign one for fuel and there was plenty of that in the Caucasus.

With the focus of the campaigning season to be in the south, Army Group South received the lion's share of new equipment. In addition, for those units not permitted to leave the east, 'rehabilitation areas' were to be established for each Army Group. For Army Group South it was to be near Dnepropetrovsk; Army Group Center's was to be near Orsha, Minsk, Gomel and Bryansk; and for Army Group North, their units scheduled for rehabilitation would be transferred back into the zone of the interior, as they would have the fewest units permitted rehabilitation.

Had the army groups completed their reconditioning as planned and been able to fully reestablish their divisions, the overall position of the armies in the east might have been one of significant potential, at least of holding their present lines. However the OKW plan for the late spring of 1942 called for Case Blue or the attack by Army Group South to the lower Volga and into the Caucasus. As such, Army Groups North and Center were ordered to transfer most of their rehabilitated panzer and motorized divisions to Army Group South for the planned attack to be launched in May. It left these Army Groups without any offensive capability and with limited counteroffensive ability to repel enemy advances.

---

[215] In addition to the counter attack in front of Moscow in December 1941, the Russians also launched a smaller attack against Army Group South at Izyum in May 1942. After a penetration of some 60 miles, the Germans counterattacked, known as Operation Fridericus I, throwing the Russians back to their start line and advancing another 30 miles to the banks of the Oskol River by the end of May. Stalin's lesson in Soviet optimism was an expensive one. By 22 May the Germans had surrounded the attacking Red Army units and destroyed or captured the equivalent of three rifle (infantry) armies and an operational group. These forces were going to be sorely missed in repelling the German attacks in less than a month.

The targets for year two in Russia for the Wehrmacht were economic as well as military ones, as opposed to the political and military ones of the first year; e.g. the seizure of the principal cities of Moscow, Leningrad, Kiev and Rostov-on-Don. This change in the overall objectives was a significant change in Operation Barbarossa. Barbarossa was to knock Russia out of the war by capturing the above mentioned cities with their political and administrative organs, their productive capacity, and encircle and destroy the Red Army before the Dnepr River. None of these objectives were met, condemning Germany to conduct what was becoming an endless campaign.

In planning for the second campaign season, the choice of economic objectives indicates that Hitler had abandoned the need to destroy the Soviets. He never renewed the assault on Moscow and the main Red Army units that were assembled there for its defense. Army Group Center's lines were still only about 100 miles from the city, about 40 miles east of Vyazma, and would never get closer to it in the future than it was now. It really was a case of now or never. As it was, it became never.

Leaving Moscow to the Russians leaves the place of Russian leadership intact. The symbolism of the Russian hold on the capitol in Moscow was a strong physical and spiritual rallying point for this nation in its most desperate hours, and its influence was immeasurable. The Russian grasp on its own capital was also a strong signal to the western allies that Stalin and the Russian people intended to stay in the war and fight it out, and to not abandon the fight as did other victims of German aggression.

The signal Hitler was sending to Stalin by not renewing the assault on Moscow was one of granting his survival; to live on, to fight another day. This was a monumental admittance of a failed eastern strategy. The German Wehrmacht could not defeat the Russians and their Russian Army, plain and simple. And each day that undefeated Russian Army stood between Moscow and the Germans meant it grew larger, stronger, and more dangerous. If anything, rather than continuing the attack in the summer of 1942, the Wehrmacht would have been well advised to go over to a strategic defensive. However politically risky or personally unacceptable that may have been to Hitler, his foreign policy and the coalition of Axis nations supporting him, it would have been a wise move.

It has been argued that Germany, with the limited abilities indicated above, should have stayed on the defensive in 1942 -- permit the divisions to rebuild and retrain their new replacements and the panzer and mechanized divisions to absorb the newer models of the PzKw IV's coming off the assembly lines in Germany, ones that now had to the power to defeat the Russian T-34. Let the Russians bleed themselves against a bulwark of Krupp steel and German determination! Unfortunately for Germany, she found herself caught in an impossible position both economically and militarily. Economically, she needed the Caucasus oil to not only power her military but also her allies, her home front and domestic industries as well. Militarily, in the east she was in a precarious position, and could not remain in place for long against a rapidly growing and strengthening Russia. The war in Russia had to be concluded soon, and victoriously, or she needed to retreat from the current positions to much shorter, easily defended positions closer to Germany. She had to save her eastern armies from exposure from the elements and destruction by the enemy. Militarily, the choice was made for it by the economics of a nation at war and driven by its needs; seize the oil in the Caucasus. Hitler chose to attack and thereby cast Germany's fate to the winds.

Fending off the Germans from Moscow and with its security increasing daily, Stalin could now rest secure that although the Germans were still tactically superior, they were strategically beaten in the sense that they were no longer the masters of the entire battle front in the east. Hitler was soon to realize that he could no longer 'call the shots' along the entire front, and had to relinquish command of large sectors to Russian initiatives and the Wehrmacht to defensive efforts. From now on he would seek a more limited agenda in Russia.

Germany's shift to the south was to attempt to seize resources, which while conceptually valuable, the practical value of which was far from certain and would not immediately assist Germany in her fight against the Red Army. The targets for Army Group South were raw materials, not finished goods, land or destroyed Russian armies. If the Wehrmacht was fortunate and was able to seize these resources undestroyed, a considerable 'if', these bulk, unrefined materials were over a thousand miles from the closest industrial region controlled by Germany. They would have had to be shipped over already overstrained rail lines in increasingly scarce rail cars already in use transporting supplies to an already stretched German Army. It would be a significant amount of time before these materials became fuel, lubricants, artillery, panzers, ammunition, or food for the Wehrmacht.

Indeed, the practical value of the petroleum in the lower Caucasus seems to have never entered the planning levels of any German organization, military, economic, or political.

"It appears that during this period there was little discussion between Hitler and his military advisers over the important question of how Caucasus oil was to be transported to the Reich. The overworked Fuhrer may not even have realized the importance of this matter, considering it best simply to "cross that bridge when he came to it". Apparently he supposed Axis convoys would carry much of the oil across the Black Sea to Rumanian ports, while the remainder would be carried across and through the Bosporus and Dardanelles, and into the Aegean. From there it would travel to Italian and occupied Greek ports. He had almost certainly not read the March 1941 report by the War Economy and Armaments Office, appended to a letter sent by *Feldmarshall* Wilhelm von Keitel to the OKH. This report warned that, even if the Caucasus oil fields could be captured intact, very little oil (only 10,000 tons per month) could be carried shipping, there would be no ships available for the transport of the oil up the Danube because the river tankers there were already working to capacity transporting Rumanian oil. The only remaining route was across the Black Sea, through the Dardanelles, and on to Mediterranean ports. Accordingly, the report concluded, 'The opening of the sea routes and the security of the tankers in the Black Sea is the prerequisite for the use of Russian supply sources in sufficient quantity to support the continuation of the war.' Clearly, to attain this prerequisite was virtually impossible by early 1942; the Germans would have to wipe out the Soviet Black Sea Fleet (which still had, according to Admiral Raeder, 'naval supremacy... (allowing) great freedom of movement') and eliminate British air and sea power from the eastern Mediterranean.[216]

If we are to take this report in its fullest meaning, the entire premise for the second campaign season in the east was flawed. (this is not surprising, as most intelligence supplied to OKW and OKH from *Fremde Heere Ost* was of questionable value) it was a goal not completely thought through

---

[216] *Stopped at Stalingrad, The Luftwaffe and Hitler's Defeat in the East 1942-1943* by Joel S. A. Hayward, University Press of Kansas, 1998, pp. 20 – 21.

and in deeper examination impossible to meet. Even if the Germans had attained all the 'prerequisites' stipulated in the March 1941 report from the War Economy and Armaments Office, once the Allies, in their now fast growing strength, discovered the oil shipments moving along such lengthy and exposed routes, they would have come under increasingly accurate Allied attack and the Germans would, given their strained situation in the east, be unable to provide adequate security for the shipments. There would be numerous points where this slender, vulnerable floating pipeline could be severed; the Dardanelles, the Bosporus; the Mediterranean; the Aegean, and even further west into the Ionian Sea enemy aircraft, naval units, (both surface and submerged) would be waiting. All would be potentially armed with intelligence intercepts of shipping tables and schedules gleaned from Ultra decoded radio messages and other intelligence sources. Hitler, ever the gambler, working on the slimmest margins, was rapidly exhausting his quickly dwindling portion of luck.

The decision to shift the campaign emphasis to the south was not lost on the Russians. STAVKA was well informed as to what was planned in Berlin and Zossen,[217] and from other sources who knew of Germany's desperate need for energy, especially oil. Armed with this information, STAVKA was able to determine the new shift, despite Stalin's fear of a renewed attack on Moscow. With no signs of rebuilding or replenishment of Army Group Center and no similar activity in Army Group North and with plenty of activity and movement in Army Group South, the signs were plain to see. Soviet Marshall Timoshenko had this to say regarding Germany's economic needs:

> "If Germany succeeds in taking Moscow, that is obviously a grave disappointment for us, but it by no means disrupts our grand strategy... Germany would gain accommodation, but that alone would not win the war. The only thing that matters is oil. As we remember, Germany kept harping on her own urgent oil problems in her economic bargaining with us from 1939 to 1941. So we have to do all we can (a) to make Germany increase her oil consumption, and (b) to keep the German armies out of the Caucasus."[218]

---

[217] Zossen-Wunsdorf, located about 20 miles south of Berlin was the location of the Army high command (Abbreviated as ObdH) and was later joined by the Luftwaffe (ObdL) and Kriegsmarine (ObdK) and was also their main communications center.

[218] *Stopped at Stalingrad*, pp. 10 – 11.

The German army command, initially reluctant for any offensive operations for 1942, or until the losses from the winter 1941 operations made good, grudgingly admitted the fuel situation must be rectified. The seizure of the Caucasus fields promised the only solution at hand. For example, General Halder confided to his journal:

> "One thing is now clear: without Russian oil we simply cannot utilize fully the regions we now occupy. But above all, without Russian oil, the German war machine must from now on become increasingly more impotent."[219]

One additional aspect of the second portion of Operation Blue, the descent into the Caucasus should be addressed, that of space and time. The 'sideways funnel' land shape that European Russia presents to the western attacker, takes on new meaning in the discussion of space and time with regard to the Caucasus. The German movement into this region opens a new page, not only in German offensive audacity, but also in an entirely different form of mechanized warfare. This form was to take the shape of how OKW and OKH intended to provide the means to conduct the operations in such a remote (from Germany) operating theater. Not only did Hitler not consider how he was to bring the captured oil back to Germany or, closer, Rumania, but how he was to capture it intact in the first place.

The age when attacking armies lived off the land or moved at the pace of the slowest baggage wagon was long gone. If Hitler was to conduct his blitzkrieg in the steppes of central Asia, he made no provision, consulted no operational source or authority; he just extended his hand, as had the Caesars of old, and commanded his armies to comply with his wishes.

The ability for a mechanized army, even a partially mechanized one at that, to depend on supply lines that are so slender, so fragile that even on maps it appears hopelessly inadequate. To provide such meager sustenance to a major attacking force, much less one with tanks, trucks, tractors, heavy artillery, aircraft and supporting motor vehicles of all shapes and sizes is nothing less than profound military incompetence.

There was little forethought as to how this modern army was to travel, attack, pursue, and seize hostile forces and objectives. One wonders if any thought was given by the German high command on how they expected

---

[219] Ibid, p. 20.

this force, the newly (as of 7 July 1942) designated Army Group A, formerly part of Army Group South, was to live off the land and captured enemy supplies to attain its goals of seizing the oil producing regions known as *Unternehmen Edelweiss*. The planned offensive assumed a quixotic nature.

In light of the objective, consider the distances involved. When this new army group 'turned the corner' at Rostov-on-Don at the eastern edge of the Sea of Azov on 22 July and plunged south, Rostov was 208 miles from Maikop, the *nearest* of the oil objectives. Grozny was 416 miles, and the final oil objective, Baku, was 746 miles.[220] This was the same distance that the Germans had advanced since the invasion began 13 months earlier. Considering that half of the former Army Groups strength was directed to Hitler's new-found focus, Stalingrad, is it any wonder the now seriously under strength, and now almost out-of-supply armies slowed and stopped?

For example, of the 67 divisions involved in the attack only 22 were being fully rehabilitated behind the front; the remainder was to be rehabilitated in the front line. The newly rehabilitated spearhead combat divisions were to receive 1,000 replacements each, with no more than basic training of two months duration. In addition they were short of horses and the reconnaissance units were to use bicycles! The loss of vehicles in front of Moscow the previous winter was having its affect still, as even attacking divisions were to be provided with only 80 per cent of their motor vehicle requirement.

Indeed, OKH sent 1,100,000 replacements to the armies in the East, and still were 625,000 short of bringing the divisions back to the authorized strength. Considering this shortfall, and with no solution to solving it prior to the start of the 1942 offensive, the majority of these men went to restoring the strengths of the divisions in Army Group South. Even with this massive infusion of new manpower, the southern divisions were still short of full strength. On 1 May the OKW operations staff reported that infantry division strength was now at 50 per cent of its 1941 level while Army Groups Center and North were never to exceed 35 per cent! With a final effort to bring the divisions in Army Group South as close to maximum fighting strength for the coming offensive, they never exceeded 75 per cent of their 1941 strength.

---

[220] Baku was a justifiable military and economic goal, however distant it was from the jumping off point for Operation Blue, accounting for 80 per cent of all Soviet oil production.

This reinforcement effort for Case Blue demonstrates the lasting effects of the winter battles west of Moscow just six months before, and the impact of the failure to successfully conclude the summer 1941 campaign. Even with increased amounts of manpower being released from industry, new infusions of volunteer and slave labor from all over the Reich and occupied Europe, Germany could do no better to restore its armies to these pitiful levels. This was in the boom days of the Third Reich's military successes. Already, in mid-1942 Germany was feeling the strains of maintaining its offensive posture in the war and in its most crucial theater. The short war in the East Hitler had gambled on was exposing one of Germany's Achilles heels-that of adequate manpower to accomplish her military and economic objectives.

This straining, to not only restore the German forces in the east but to assemble an offensive mass, was almost beyond the capacity of Germany at the height of its newly conquered empire. The summer of 1942 was the zenith of German military and political achievement. However, its inability to marshal the industrial resources necessary to maintain its victorious armies in the field, and to finish the task were significant, and a warning signal to Berlin. It was now reduced to conducting offensives with only one of its Army Groups while the two others in Russia were 'cannibalized' for men and material.

Here we see the first subtle indication of the effect the war in the east was having on the fighting ability of the Wehrmacht; of what would become the height of German power. True, by September of 1942 more territory would be under German control, but the men, materials and resources to manage and maintain the conquered territory would be less and less; a military 'tipping point' was quickly being reached.

Although Hitler could be confident that the western Allies could not yet launch an invasion to restore their presence on the continent (demonstrated by the Allied invasion of French Africa). However he knew the clock was ticking in the Allies favor. His undivided attention to the Russian campaign was running out.

The Attack Plan

When preparing the intelligence estimate on the number of Russian divisions available in the spring of 1942 in preparation for the summer campaign, the German estimates were, as in the previous year, too low. The three Russian Fronts who were the targets of the German offensive, the South-Western, Southern and the Voronezh Fronts had some 74 rifle divisions, 6 tank corps and 37 independent brigades among them, totaling some 1,311,000 men.[221] Fremde Heere Ost's estimate of Russian strength was about two-thirds this number. German preparations in Army Group South for the offensive amounted to some 65 divisions; 45 infantry, 5 light divisions, 4 motorized divisions and 11 panzer. In addition there was some 25 Axis allied divisions brought the number to 90 divisions, but Germany's allies divisions were smaller in manpower, lighter armed, slower transported leaving aside any questions concerning their battlefield performance. This inability to properly judge the number of enemy combat units in the field as well as their force generation potential was to hinder German operational activities all during the campaign in the east with disastrous results

In preparing for the second campaign season, Hitler issued two orders, known as Fuehrer Directives, numbers 41 and 45. These were instructional orders from Hitler to OKW concerning the military objectives were to be attained. Fuehrer Directive 41 ordered the planning to commence for Operation Blue for execution in the summer of 1942, Fuehrer Directive 45 ordered the concurrent operations against Stalingrad as well as the operation to seize the Caucasus objectives.

With German resources provided and what was actually accomplished it is a wonder if the three components of planning, logistics and results were part of the same effort, so different and diverse were their conclusions.

Uncertainty became the hallmark of the southern operation. The attractions of the city of Stalin on the Volga was a strong magnet for Hitler, both the city and the fabled river, the southern end point for Barbarossa. The other draw was the need to obtain the fuel to run Germany's economy and military. Could he have both?

The certainty, or the lack of, with which the operations for the second campaign season were planned, is probably best demonstrated by the number and variety of operational code names assigned to the offensive, Fuehrer Directive Number 41. Initially it was known as Operation *Siegfried*. Soon to be renamed Operation Blau (Blue); then Operation Blau II, and still later Operation Blau III and finally Operation *Braunschweig*, subdivided into Operation *Heron* (the Stalingrad assault) and Operation *Edelweiss* (the assault on Maikop, Grozny and Baku). If the reasons were to ensure

---

[221] Krivosheev, pp. 123 - 4.

security for the planning, to mislead and confuse the enemy would be one thing; but we know that was not the intent. The multiple names, whether due to uncertainty, major or minor changes in plan, or as it would soon bear out, resulted from a lack of strategic objectivity and thus the subsequent catastrophe that resulted.

Hitler's Fuehrer Directive 41 code named *Unternehmen Blau* or Operation Blue was issued on 5 April 1942 and in it contained the broad strategic plan for the second summer campaign in Russia. What is significant in this directive was the objectives to be achieved and the great distances they were away from the campaign start lines.

From the front line of 28 June 1942 to Stalingrad on the Volga was 275 straight line miles. Practical combat miles for the same distance would add some additional 75 to 100 miles. The distance from Stalingrad to the final objective, Baku on the Caspian Sea was another 625 miles, also straight line distance, factoring in the additional back and forth of combat, as above, would add another 150 to 175 miles making the total distance to be covered in Operation Blue almost 1,200 miles. From the start of Barbarossa on 22 June 1941 the maximum advance into Russia to 28 June 1942 was some 925 straight line miles, measured from Lvov in South-Eastern Poland to Taganrog on the North coast of the Sea of Azov, 50 miles west of Rostov-on-Don. Add in the inevitable combat activity and a more probable practical distance is closer to 1,150 to 1,200 miles.

The new objectives for the second summer campaign season were to be the same distances as the first campaign season. However this was not the same German army that attacked Russia year earlier. The start point was not in Western Europe, but in Western Asia. The forces assembled were not the same number nor the same caliber as was available a year earlier. The operational reach was farther, the risks greater and the objectives cloudier.

Also alarming was the subdivision of one of the Germany's three major operational Army Groups, Army Group South into two subsections, Army Groups A and B. This splitting of the offensive force to obtain two objectives was in and of itself a flaw in conventional military doctrine, one never divides a given force in the face of an undefeated enemy. If this violation of time tested procedure were not enough, the objectives for each were located in diametrically opposite directions from each other, preventing one force from providing support and flank protection for the other. In the plan Army Group B was to punch through the Russian lines and seize Voronezh on the Don River and, providing flank coverage for the campaign, seal off the lower portions of the river down to Kachalinskaya, a short 40 mile jump to the Volga, near Stalingrad. South of Army Group B was Army Group A, its role was to follow through on its successful defeat of the Russian spring offensive at Izyum and, turning South, seize Rostov-on-Don and as many river crossings as possible for the advance into the Caucasus and the final advance to the south-east seizing the oil producing cities of Maikop, Grozny and the final prize, Baku on the western shore of the Caspian Sea.

If 1942 was not to be year of the invasion in the West by the Western Allies, Hitler also knew that his time conducting a one-front land war was not unlimited. Some resolution had to brought about in the east to free the forces that would be needed to fight off the amphibious landings anticipated somewhere on coast of France from 1943 on.

As Hitler admitted by his actions in the east with his decision to attack economic targets in the south and in the Caucasus, the western Allies did much the same by pursuing an African and Balkan strategy, ostensibly seeking entrée to Europe from the south. This was a much longer route for them to take and one that could be more easily defended with minimal forces. Although units would still be needed to man the eastern shores of the English Channel to observe Allied intentions developing in England, the need for a strategic force to repel an invasion in 1942 did not exist. Hitler still had a little more time.

The Attack

However, the early weeks of the campaign were a reprise of the previous summer; surprised Russian defenses, easy penetrations of the Russian battle positions, cut and slash panzer penetrations and retreating Russian units, some in great disarray. Despite Stalin's Order (Number 228) of 28 July, the "Not a Step Back" (Ne Shagu zapad!) the movements of the German 2nd, 2nd Hungarian Corps, 4th Panzer and 6th Armies were largely unopposed and concluded the first phase of Operation Blau with the capture of the almost undefended city of Voronezh on the east back of the Don River. After the bleak winter and its retreats before Moscow, it seemed like the German armies of old were back.

As satisfying as these developments were to Hitler and the OKW, there was a disturbing situation brewing in the combat units in the field. German intelligence organizations began to notice from field reports and captured

Russian officers that the Russian retreat was much more orderly than in previous offensives, and the catch of prisoners and equipment was much less too. The beginnings of the new Russian Army were appearing, a more disciplined, more organized army was in the making.

A month into the advance the panzer strength in the attacking forces had dropped significantly. By the end of July there were 435 tanks for all eight attacking panzer divisions, the best division having 176 panzers and one had as few as 52 vehicles.[222] In addition, the fuel situation had become such that the mechanized elements of the entire XLIV Infantry Corps were immobilized due to lack of gasoline. By 25 July the fuel situation had grown so critical that both panzer armies were halted for lack of fuel. What the snow and cold had done before Moscow the previous year, the length of the supply chain was doing now in the steppes of central Asia. At the very moment the Russian resistance was growing stronger, the Germans were running out of fuel and running out of tanks, men, and luck as well.

The successes enjoyed by the field armies in Operation Blau were beginning to be warped by the attraction that the thin city on the Volga was having on Hitler. Stalingrad was beginning to assume an importance out of all proportion to its location, and meaning to the Wehrmacht's effort in southeast Russia, the seizure of the Caucasus oil fields. Admittedly, the city occupied a semi-strategic location as gatekeeper to the southern Volga region east of the river as well as safeguarding passage of vital supplies of river traffic north to Moscow and points further north. It was the water lifeline of the southern transport system and the primary one from the Caspian Sea.

The City On The Volga

One cannot also help suspecting the political and emotional attraction the name of the city had on Hitler as well. Had Stalingrad any other name, one wonders if the outcome would have been the historical one. There is an old Russian saying that Russia will never be conquered as long as the enemy does not cross the Volga. Stalingrad and Volga, the two names that symbolized the Rubicon for Hitler were now at his doorstep and the Red Army seemed to be in headlong flight and they were his for the taking.

[222] It is important to remember that even at this late date in the war the panzerwaffen was still employing PzKw I's, armed with two 7.9mm machine guns and the PzKw II, armed with a 20mm cannon, when the smallest main gun of the Red Army tanks and some armored cars was 45mm.

Stalingrad contained all the magnetism necessary to attract anything German in 1942. For Hitler it was the namesake of his now greatest foe. For Albert Speer, the soon to be German Armaments Minister it was the chief source of T-34 tanks until "Tankograd" in Chelyabinsk assumed that title. For the military planners the Volga was not only a "stop line" for the originally planned invasion of Operation Barbarossa, it was also one of the few places that the Wehrmacht planned to pin the Russian Army against and prevent escape. For the economists it was the main transportation from the middle east to points north and west, especially important in view of the vast petroleum reserves and one of the main Lend-Lease pipelines. Is it no wonder that this city assumed such importance? It became the waterloo for Germany in Russia. Despite the need for Caucasus oil, Stalingrad developed into a major objective of the German effort in 1942. The original operational plans did not include a provision of forces for its seizure. It was Stalingrad, rather than the Caucasus oil that became the focal point of Operation Blue.

Closely connected to Stalingrad was not only its captivating name for Hitler, but the history of how it got its relatively new name. During the Russian Civil War Tsaritsyn, its original Tatar name, was the scene of heavy fighting. It was occupied briefly by Denikin's "White" pro-Czarist troops in 1919 but as the Red Army overcame the "White" units, they abandoned the city a year later. In April 1925 the city was renamed Stalingrad in honor of the defense commanded by Stalin.

Instead of completely rehabilitating the fighting units in Russia in the spring of 1942 and building new units to continue the fight, an incomplete German army attacked again in May 1942 near Voronezh and plunged south-east along the Don, establishing a thinly defended line along the river 300 miles in length, one which would be mostly manned by units of Germany's foreign Axis allies, mostly Romanian and Hungarian divisions. Not only was Germany opening a new phase of the war in the east, but also the utilization of foreign armies introduced a new and unpredictable element into German military planning, one that was to develop beyond the influence and ability of the Wehrmacht to control in adverse situations.

East or South?

The city of Stalingrad is a long rambling place stretching for about 15 miles on the western bank of the lower Volga river. To the Russians the Volga represents the emotional and spiritual border between the European and Asiatic portions of their nation. To the west stretched a thousand miles of the Kuban, Don and Ukraine regions; to the southeast, thousands of miles of desert and dust, little unchanged since the days of Tamerlane.

The fight for the city is now well known. Suffice to say it became the distorted focus of the entire offensive operation. The titanic battle in and around the city, the drawing of more and more German troops into the city battle from the southern command and the failure to seize the oil producing objectives in the Caucasus was having devastating effects on all operations.

The objective for the second campaign season at first took Stalin by surprise. The objective violated most military theory. With an enemy leader still commanding, his capital intact, and strong armies defending that capital, the objective should have been self-directing. Clausewitz, the brilliant military theorist, educator and Chief of Staff for von Gneisenau, and a German no less, clearly indicated what a commander should do faced with the same circumstances that Hitler was:

> "It is not by conquering one of the enemy's provinces, with little trouble and superior numbers, and this unimportant conquest to great results, but by seeking out constantly the heart of the hostile power and staking everything to gain all, that we can effectually strike the enemy to the ground."[223]

By mid-November 1942 the goals of the Caucasus campaign, the seizure of the oil producing fields around Baku, Grozny and Maikop ended in failure. Even the smaller fields to the north of these main areas that were captured by the Germans produced no usable oil.

Stalingrad

By August 1942 the XIV Panzer Korps of the German 6th Army was across the Don River and by the 23rd had reached the Volga north of the city. From that time until the middle of November the greatest battle of World War II in Europe was fought in and around the city that soon became a tomb for millions. As the German's inched nearer and near to the Volga and conquest of the city seemed so close, the Russian 62nd and 64th Armies were fed just enough troops and munitions to maintain the precarious foothold on the city. Hitler completely misread the Russians

---

[223] "On War" by Karl von Clausewitz, E. P. Dutton, New York, 1918.

strategy. As long as Stalin could hold Hitler's attention on the city, he just might overlook or ignore the growing threat to its northern and southern flanks. What was happening was the German 6th Army, the principal operational combat unit in the fight for the city was being reinforced as its losses mounted in the vicious street fighting, the reinforcements came from the flank army's, and from Army Group A units fighting a desperate battle in the rocky crags of the Caucasus. Replacing these units were those of the foreign allies, the Rumanians and Italians to the north and more Rumanians south of the city. The mesmerizing hold that Stalingrad had on Hitler and his determination to take the city was distorting the safety and security of the entire German position on the southern front. It was becoming a very big spear point attached to a very vulnerable shaft.

If the German units that launched Operation Blau were under strength to begin the campaign the Axis allied armies holding the flanks on the banks of the Don five months later were in even worse shape. The Rumanian and Italian units never had the fighting strength or their Wehrmacht counterparts. Their equipment was antiquated, adequate quantities of it was lacking, their units were almost entirely infantry with the exception of small battalion or brigade armored units of older or obsolete tanks and their leadership heavily dependent on German guidance. Their use up until this time has been to police quiet parts of the front and for rear area security.

Uranus

The Russian counteroffensive against the Axis units in and around Stalingrad, known as Operation Uranus launched on 19 November 1942 was a double envelopment of the city from attacking forces to the north and south, meeting at the Karpovka River on 23 November. The operation the Germans excelled at was now used with great effect and authority against them.

A rescue attempt to free the surrounded 6th Army in the city was made on 12 December by General Erich von Manstein from the south, made good progress at first but was eventually stopped at the Myshkov River after an advance of some 30 miles and then forced to retreat due to mounting Russian resistance and the deep snow hampering movement of the panzers in the relief force. The failed relief attempt sealed the fate of over 300,000 German and Rumanian troops and large amounts of hard-to-replace equipment.

The failure of von Manstein to achieve a rescue was the one and only attempt to rescue the trapped army, there would be no others. In place of rescue, the Germans in Stalingrad, forbidden by Hitler to break out and leave the city were now to be a human form of bait, a source of magnetism to attract and hold as many Soviet units as possible from advancing further into the void west of the city. The status reports from German General Friederich von Paulus, German 6th Army commander, on the conditions of the trapped army grew more and more somber and finally desperate. Among the last, in January 1943 was the following:

> "Troops without ammunition or food... effective command no longer possible... 18,000 wounded without any supplies or dressings or drugs... Further defense senseless. Collapse inevitable. Army requests immediate permission to surrender in order to save lives of remaining troops."

Hitler's reply was cold, heartless and adamant:

> "Surrender is forbidden. Sixth Army will hold their positions to the last man and the last round and by their heroic endurance will make an unforgettable contribution toward the establishment of a defensive front and the salvation of the Western world."[224]

Shortly thereafter, on 3 February 1943, the last German pocket in northern Stalingrad surrendered. Into Russian captivity went the cream of the eastern armies, the 6th Army. It would be resurrected again but as shadow of its former self; but the economic and military situation would continue to change for the worse for Germany, and the new, reconstituted 6th Army would never have the same combat effectiveness as the old. [225]

The Russians surrounded over 300,000 men in Stalingrad; however the exact total will never be known. The conflicting figures are caused by the initial surround, minus the 30,000 wounded flown out during the encirclement. Soviet sources give 147,000 German casualties killed and

---

[224] In December 1944 a conference between Hitler and his Chief of Staff General Kurt Zeitzler discussing the impending loss of the Crimea referred to the possibility of "another Stalingrad". The very name Stalingrad had become a part of speech, indicating the worst outcome in a military confrontation. It was used here in reference to the trapped German and Romanian units in the peninsula.

[225] The German 6th Army encircled and destroyed at Stalingrad in November 1942-February 1943 was to have the dubious distinction of being reconstituted and then surrounded and destroyed once again on the Prut southwest of Kishinev on the Rumanian border in August 1944.

wounded, 91,000 captured. In the captured number were some 24 generals and 2,500 officers of other ranks. Of the 91,000, fewer than 5,000 would make their way back to Germany in the 1950s and '60s.[226]

Consequences

The tragedy on the Volga is rather simple to summarize: with the opening weeks of the offensive comfortably similar to the opening days of Barbarossa a year previous, Hitler felt entitled to take liberties with his attack objectives. As the offensive ground on his desire for the invaluable oil, was replaced by an equally strong desire to own the city bearing his arch rival's name. With resources already strained to the limit, he began moving whole armies about the region huge distances to insure that he could claim the prize trophy of that year, Stalingrad. As it came to be, he wound up with neither.[227]

Stalingrad became the Verdun of the Second World War, with each side pouring vast quantities of men and material into this huge battle. With each leader determined to have his way, Hitler to conquer the city bearing the name of his nemesis, and Stalin just as determined to defend it. The city now had far less value than the men lost in defending it or attempting to take it.

The Russian winter offensive of 1942-1943 pushed the Wehrmacht back almost 200 miles in some places and inflicted major damage on Army Group Center and on the renamed Army Group South, Army Group A in the southern portion of the sector and Army Group B to the north. The Soviet offensive finally came to a halt with the panzer counter offensive by General von Manstein on 19 February 1943 with the II SS Panzer Corps and the First Panzer Army from the Krasnoarmeyskoye area in the south and Krasnograd in the west. The result was to halt the Russian offensive and retake the city of Kharkov.

[226] The attempt to keep the encircled 6th Army supplied via the Luftwaffe took a heavy toll on its tri motored transport aircraft, the Junkers Ju-52. When the airlift commenced in November 1942 it possessed 477 planes, which included three Heinkel He-11H groups and one Junkers Ju-88A group. On 31 January 1943, after the 6th Army surrendered to the Russians, only 146 of these machines was airworthy an astounding loss for the Luftwaffe and the Army they were called upon to supply. It was a loss that was never made good for the rest of the war. Stalingrad effectively destroyed the Luftwaffe's air transport ability.

[227] On 13 May 1943 the German forces in Tunisia surrendered to the Allies, it would be the second large defeat and surrender of German troops in the war to date. The term *Tunisgrad* began to be heard.

The loss of Stalingrad, the 6th Army and allied Rumanian soldiers was a great blow to German morale, military, national and international prestige. The loss of men and equipment also created a gaping hole in the southern front that was difficult to patch. The defeat at Stalingrad was the first major defeat for the German military in World War II. The chain of victories was broken, and more importantly, the mystique of the invincible Wehrmacht was shattered.

One wonders what if the German military leadership had used the time from the conclusion of the Russian winter offensive in front of Moscow (in March to the beginning of a new campaign season in June 1942) to allow the eastern armies to fully rehabilitate. That would have been four months to replace the lost equipment, train and establish new men and divisions with a full strength Army Group Center. What could the alternatives be? With support from Army Groups North and South, the centerpiece of the 1942 campaign season could have been the conquest of Moscow. Making this the sole objective for the entire year recognizes that the Russians would desperately fight for this target. The battle would be a terrific one, at the conclusion of which would be a very exhausted German army already at the end of its supply lines, but perhaps holding its prize, Moscow.

With the successful conclusion of the capture of Moscow, the winter of 1942-1943 could have been spent replenishing men, equipment, and securing the city and its sprawling suburbs, lines of communication and supply; and broadening the territorial approach to the city, and planning for the 1943 season. With the fall of the city to Germany, symbolically Stalin would be on the run, a fugitive in his own country, being pursued eastward, ever eastward.

This would have been a moment of decision for Russia: Also one for Stalin, Russian patriotism, and Communist discipline. Could the Red Army be reconstituted east of the capital? Would the Communist leadership fall apart? The Germans would have the upper hand in such a situation. With control of the communications and transportation centers in Moscow, the pursuit of the remnants of the Red Army would have been made easier, had Stalin survived the assault on his capital the pursuit of him could have been left to specialized units like the *Brandenburgers* and *Luftwaffe Fallschirmjager* units.

With the action soon to be centered in the south, the northern and center army groups went largely dormant. With the objectives in the east now definitely focused on economic goals, the original targets of Moscow and Leningrad were left 'on hold' for future consideration. The unspoken tasks of these two army groups were to maintain the positional status-quo and be prepared to take whatever action necessary to maintain their current lines.

With the failure of Operation Blue, the Wehrmacht would never again reach as far into the Soviet Union. The failure of the German summer campaign of 1942 was plagued with the same command failures as in the previous year: The failure to set a firm objective, changes in the direction of the campaign; inadequate forces committed to the operation, intelligence information on enemy movements and concentrations were ignored, or were faulty, and inadequate supplies were provided to attain the objective.

With the failure of the summer 1942 campaign in the Caucasus, Operation Blau, the quest for oil to fuel the Third Reich's vision of a German world order was ended. Never again would German armies be directed via economic and military objectives; from here on in, the emphasis in making the command decisions would be political.

The failure of the Caucasus campaign also had foreign diplomatic consequences. First among them was the decision of Turkey to stay out of the Axis camp. The German failure of the second campaign season clearly illustrated who would now be in the ascendant in the war and Turkey wanted no part of an alliance whose future looked bleaker by the month.

Perhaps this is a good moment to evaluate just how close the Wehrmacht came to realizing its goal in capturing the oil. The German attempt to seize the Caucasus oil fields was halted at the half way point, just south of the Terek River. Of the three major producing cities, Maikop, Grozny and Baku, only Maikop was taken. Grozny was still 50 miles from the closest German advance and Baku was a safe 300 miles away.

When elements of the First Panzer Army seized Maikop, their initial joy was tempered by the poor condition of the drilling fields. Soviet rear guard units had seriously crippled the ability to bring the wells back into production. Hundreds of wells had been destroyed, the oil storage facilities had been wrecked and refining equipment had been damaged or removed. Although the oil exploitation units had anticipated possible damage, the actual damage was far more extensive than Hitler had anticipated.

Two weeks after the city fell, the inspector for oil defenses reported that only two wells were capable of operating, one was still burning and many other wells were put out of use for long periods of time by having cement poured down their drilling pipes.[228]

The short term potential for extracting oil from the Maikop fields was almost nonexistent and the long-term prospects were dim as well. General Georg Thomas[229] of the War Economy and Armaments board reported "only insignificant amounts of mineral oil were found". The conditions of the fields, residual partisan fighting in the area and the final in-depth examination of the wells and supporting equipment were indicating dismal prospects of the productivity of the Maikop facilities.

A month later, fires were still burning at the wells and Dr. Schlicht of the *Mineralöl Brigade Caucasus* reported to General Thomas, the difficult terrain was slowing the importation of the heavy drilling equipment and the damage inflicted by the retreating Soviets included distribution pipelines as well. He forecast that it would require an additional six months to bring the wells back on line and to commence production. In the meantime only 4,000 cubic meters of oil have been uncovered.

Reichmarshall Göring's understanding of the conditions at Maikop and the processes needed to bring the fields back to production was clearly obvious, when he asked when the army units could be supplied with *fuel* (italics added) from the Maikop fields.

The failure to obtain the Caucasus oil did not doom German military operations that year or for the next two. The German oil situation turned out not to be nearly as grim as his economic advisors or as the heads of several military branches were telling Hitler. History has demonstrated that

---

[228] A key reason the Germans were unable to prevent the demolition of the Russian oil fields at Grozny was their intelligence agents dropped behind the Russian lines to kill the Russian demolition teams were all captured. Most were shot a few used for double-agent activities. The star agent was Russian Lieutenant Nikolai Rakhov who the Germans thought was working for them was in reality a Russian double-agent, who in July 1942 was captured by the Gestapo, identified for who he truly was and shot.

[229] Georg Thomas served under Beck in the Dresden military district in the early 1920's and in 1928 was assigned to the General Staff on the economic amt (office) and by November 1939 had become a Major-General. He was fired by General Keitel under Hitler's direction as the Fuehrer did not like being lectured on the risks of incomplete and improper planning for the war. From *Hitler's Decision to Invade Russia 1941* by Robert Cecil, David McKay Company, Inc., New York, 1975, pp. 142-143.

the true oil shortages were not as dire as had been suggested. In 1943, synthetic oil production peaked; when Italy defected to the Allies in September the shipments to Italy, amongst the largest drains on German supplies ceased, and when the Wehrmacht occupied Italy, large amounts of stored oil were found. In addition, the true amounts reported by the various branches of the armed forces were larger than the amounts they reported. Although scarce by comparative means, Germany had and would produce sufficient amounts of liquid energy to carry them to mid spring of 1945, even launching large-scale offensives along the way, before Allied forces occupied the nation.

By the spring of 1943, the front had stabilized. Both sides were again exhausted and in need of rest and rehabilitation. In the Army Group Center and South sectors, the front line had taken the shape of a large bulge to the West centering on the city of Kursk. The southern portion of the bulge was created by the panzer counter attacks by von Manstein the previous winter. OKW and Hitler had been examining this locale for a possible major action for the 1943 campaign season. By April of that year plans would be prepared to eliminate the Kursk bulge, code named Citadel or *Zitadelle*.

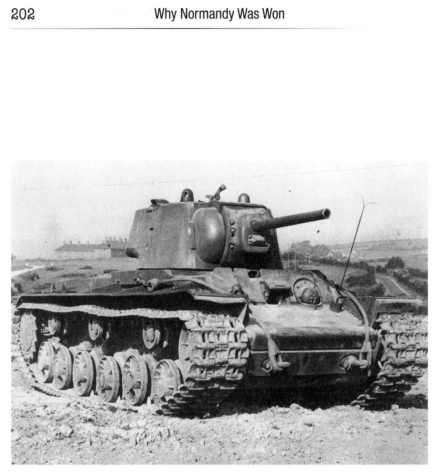

Russian heavy tank, KV-1, 1941.

Chapter Nine:
The Turning Point
Unternehmen Zitadelle
The War in 1943

"This attack is of decisive importance. It must
succeed, and it must do so rapidly and convincingly.
It must secure for us the initiative for this spring
and summer. The victory of Kursk must be a
blazing torch to the world."

Instructions from Hitler to OKH for the July 1943 attack

"How many people do you think even know where
Kursk is? It's a matter of profound indifference
to the world whether we hold Kursk or not.
I repeat my question: Why do you want to attack
in the east at all this year?"

*Communication between Gen. Heinz Guderian
and Adolf Hitler*

This chapter will discuss the largest armored vehicle battle of World War II, the German double envelopment attempt by Army Group Center near the Russian city of Kursk. The military options available to Germany for the turning point year 1943 will be examined as well as the choices that were made. The political and military situation for this year will be discussed and what were the options and the risks to Germany as its time fighting on one front was about to run out. Germany had a major decision to make in 1943, one that could radically change the course of the war in the east and the war in Europe: Does Germany continue to plan and execute offensive operations in Russia or does it transition to a strategic defensive posture?

1943 turned out to be the year of Russian military revival. This year they were able to meet the Wehrmacht in a summer engagement and meet them on almost equal terms. With logistical support from the west beginning to make itself felt in the trenches at the front, with the experiences and lessons learned from the 1941 Moscow winter counteroffensive and in 1942 at Stalingrad and follow-up advances and related operations, this was the dawn of a newly confident Russian Army. Unfortunately for the Germans they were slow to recognize it.

The Situation

The greatest opportunity of the invasion of Russia, the surprise and shock of the initial invasion was now a thing of the past, and with it the speedy Blitzkrieg that had brought such astounding successes in those early days. The partially mobilized, organized and poorly deployed Russian Army of 1941 had now demonstrated its ability to mount complex maneuver offenses in 1942 and now in 1943 was rapidly gaining in experience and capability and developing into a force soon rivaling that of their enemy. Not quite yet, but growing.

Western military and economic aid was now safely arriving into Russian ports, and was filling the rail cars, supply depots and factory yards. By the Spring of 1943 the vast industrial relocation program began in the face of the German invasion in 1941 was almost complete. The Ural and Siberian factories were built, the workers were housed and trained and mass production was coming on line. Whatever Germany did next in the war against the Russians had to be carefully and soberly considered. The decisions to be made by Germany in year three of the war in the east had to be made with the utmost care and prudence, using the best military and economic information available. The political and military leadership of the Third Reich had to lay out the available options for a Germany now threatened by more than just the unbeaten enemy from the east. The ideal choices were few and those were unpalatable to Germany's "greatest warlord of all time."

The first and most intriguing question for Germany's military dealt with Russia's productive capability. What precisely was Russia's current military strength? The finite infantry and tank divisions of the West had no bearing on what Stalin could demand from his people and industry. Even without Western aid, Soviet military capacity, was quickly outgrowing Germany's ability to match. Add Western aid via Lend-Lease shipments and the contest was predetermined. Hitler's Minister of Munitions, Fritz Todt, met with Hitler after a tour of the eastern front in November 1941, and told him, based on the current and rapidly building weapons production capacity of the Allies, Germany could not win the war. However, with the opportunity to destroy his nemesis at hand, Hitler was not about to listen to a counter alternative.

The Battle Site and German Plans

Kursk is a small mining town in western Russia, about 250 miles south of Moscow, little known but for a magnetic anomaly beneath the surface of its rolling steppe, one which renders magnetic compasses useless. The important battle fought here stunned some of the best divisions of the German *Panzerwaffe*, the result of a six-month accumulation program during which the strained German industry strived to provide the latest in weapons for its proudest service

Most importantly, the great improvement in weapons quality, quantity and the development of a vehicle-based logistical support network in place of a rail supported one would allow the advance to continue deep into the German rear areas. This caused much greater damage to the enemy and permitted the gains to be better defended against enemy counterattacks. This was exactly the type of counterattacks launched by the Germans that established the Kursk salient during the early spring of 1943.

The Kursk "bulge" was the aftermath of Field Marshal Manstein's *Unternehmen Stern* (Operation Star) in the early Spring of 1943. The Russian post-Stalingrad offensive continued on into the late winter months of 1942 and into 1943. The rapid collapse and disruption of the German Second Army and the Hungarian Second Army of German Army Group B under heavy pressure of the Russian Bryansk, Voronezh, South-Western and South Fronts pushed the front line by the beginning of March 1943 across the Donets River, capturing Kharkov, Belgorod and as far west as Sumy, Novomoskovsk and Krasnograd. By the beginning of March, Manstein noticed the pace of the Soviet advance was slowing, a sure sign that exhaustion was setting and fuel and ammunition was at a similar point.

With the Russian offensive appearing to be at the end of its logistical tether, Manstein cobbled together new units arriving from Germany and the West as well as local ad hoc formations and launched one of the most audacious attacks of the war, a stinging counteroffensive from Sumy in the north to Slavyansk in the south. The overextended Russians were quickly pushed back and in many cases surrounded by German panzer double envelopments, retaking Kharkov, Belgorod and reestablishing the front along the Donets. By the arrival of the Spring rasputitsy the front was once again on the Donets River, the Russian forces suffering significant equipment and personnel losses from the almost constant fighting.

Attack or Refit?

With the fierce post-Stalingrad defensive battles of the previous winter coming to a close, and the anticipated spring rasputitsy slowing mobile operations, it was time for German OKH to decide what the third campaign season should consist of. There were a number of opinions on the matter.

First of these was the defensive school of going over to the strategic defensive in the east. It proposed allowing the exhausted divisions to rest and refit, fortify defensive positions and let the Russians tire themselves attacking a well dug in Ostheer. This had a number of advantages and supporters, chiefly from Hitler's oldest ally, Italy. In April 1943 Mussolini suggested to Hitler that an "East Wall" be constructed to defeat any Russian offensives, and to allow the release of units to be gathered to defend the anticipated western Allied landings in Europe. This position interested Hitler himself, calling such a potential position along the Don "Lines Germanicus" and was supported by several high-ranking German military commanders, notably General Heinz Guderian and the economics minister Albert Speer, Germany's industrial organizing genius.

In the offensive school of thought, Hitler was examining the positions he anticipated the Germans and their allies would occupy by early or mid-spring. He was attempting to see where along the front he could strike to obtain a favorable outcome. The thought was to keep the Russians off balance by attacking in areas that would entail minimum risk of failure, minimum use of German forces and casualties, and maximize Russian casualties. The most promising operations he was examining generally consisted of a strengthening of the front line and an attempt to finally seize Leningrad. Other than Leningrad the three areas of attention were the conspicuous bulge around Kursk and two smaller protrusions into the German lines around Chuguyev and Izyum and a later expansion of this area to include the front between Volchansk in the north to a point on the Donets south of Svatovo. These prospective plans were assigned the code names: *Zitadelle*, the Kursk operation, *Habicht* the Chuguyev-Izyum operation and its expansion *Panther*, the Volchansk-Svatovo operation.

All of these proposed plans were predicated on a quick, preemptive strike, before the Soviets could offer strong resistance or before they launched an offensive of their own, or had an opportunity to recover from their winter operations. However, the Germans were also in a similar state and also needed time to organize, especially as they had a major operation already under way to the north. Army Group Center area had commenced the evacuation of the large bulge south of Rzhev, just west of Moscow, a remnant position from the Russian winter counteroffensive of 1941/1942. This delicate operation, if completed successfully, would not only straighten the line in that area, but would also provide badly needed divisions for other operations and form a strategic eastern reserve.

However, in addition to the military considerations, Hitler also had political and diplomatic ones on his mind as well. To the far north Finland was growing weary of a war that, for them, was turning in the wrong direction. The "Continuation War", as they called the effort with the Germans, was an attempt to regain the territory they lost during their Winter War of 1939-1940 with Russia. By early 1943 they had accomplished just that, and were now casting about for a means to extricate themselves intact from the conflict. In North Africa the war for the Axis was almost lost. The Fifth Panzer Army and the Italian First Army were trapped in north-eastern Tunisia, and in May would be forced to surrender. It would not be long before the U. S. and Britain would leap from there to the Italian mainland or the Balkans.

Germany's smaller and weaker allies were also eyeing the growing red menace getting closer to their countries with each passing month, and sought reassurance from Berlin. These already shaky governments obtained their strength from a successful and powerful Germany. As this declined in 1943, the task of seeking alternative alliances began. Perhaps most importantly, their fear of an omnipotent Wehrmacht began to wane. The new Russian Army of 1943 was closer to their countries and it was on wheels and tracks and its command and control of men, units and machines had vastly improved.

Hitler was also interested in adding new members to the Axis collation, chief amongst these was Germany's former World War I ally, Turkey. Winning over Turkey to the Axis cause would shore up the now exposed southern front of the German effort in the East as well as controlling the important access to the Black Sea and improved access to Russia's Black Sea naval ports in the Caucasus region. Turkey had just announced that it would follow a neutral position concerning the war raging all around it. However, Hitler, desperate for any alliance to assist the war effort, was convinced that one smashing success in Russia would move Turkey and perhaps other teetering or undecided potential allies to come over to the German side.

Considering Hitler's predisposition for the political, these considerations trumped the military ones and after consideration, *Zitadelle* was chosen for the operation for the 1943 summer campaigning season.

Plan Zitadelle

The original plan for the attack drafted in March was a sound one, namely to quickly gather a panzer force, attack and pinch off the Kursk bulge, destroy the Russian units holding the 250 miles of frontage, and take advantage of whatever tactical opportunities that might result from the operation. In the Spring of 1943 this was a viable operation and its limited scope and objectives wear clearly within the capabilities of the German field armies. However, time was of the essence. The key to a German victory was to strike suddenly, without warning or a lengthy preparation and with all the possible strength. Time was on Russia's side, her relocated factories had now settled in and the fruits of their production were filling the depleted Russian divisions from the winter counteroffensive and allowing the rapid creation of new ones.

Unfortunately for the *Ostheer* this sound plan was not to be. Hitler imposed a number of delays to the start date of the operation, to await the arrival of the new medium tank, "Panther" in significant numbers, as well as additional production to enhance the massing panzer divisions. The planned April start date was delayed to May, then into June and finally into July. The Russian intelligence services were aware of what OKH was planning and this information gave the Russians valuable time to prepare by establishing formidable defenses.

By the time of the final start date of 5 July, the rationale for the operation had long since passed. General Manstein was so concerned about the increased difficulty and time consuming effort in breaching the now deep and formidable Russian defenses, that in June he proposed shifting the point of effort from Kursk to Staraya Oskol, but the difficulty and additional delay of relocating the assault divisions, and the longer attack objective nullified the advantages.

Considering the now very difficult task facing the German assaulting armies, it is of interest that there was not more debate and discussion, if not outright resistance to the attack. Part of the reason was the generals on the eastern front were beginning to see their theater of operations come into competition with OB West and Army Group C in Italy for men and material. Should *Zitadelle* be cancelled they were concerned that a sizable number of their divisions would be moved from the eastern front and transferred elsewhere. The disappearing monopoly of the one front war was already manifesting itself before the Allies had placed one soldier on the ground.

The attack points for Operation *Zitadelle* were also rather obvious. The position consisted of a conspicuous bulge seventy miles wide, measured at its base, projecting from the Russian line into the German position; the shape of the line was the tactical equivalent of an invitation to attack, the double envelopment, approximately 65 miles deep into the bulge. It had all the hallmarks of the perfect attack start position advantages for the attacker, (in this case the Germans); and a dangerously exposed position for the defender. It contained advantageous attacking positions and terrain for mechanized units and a logical meeting place for the attacker to conclude the operation, east of the road and rail junction city of Kursk.

It is of interest that the double envelopment championed by Zeitzler was questioned by Hitler. On 15 April Hitler suggested a frontal thrust at the westernmost center of the bulge on either side of the Seim River, just west of Lgov and Korenevo, rather than the pincer attack as planned by OKH. However, Zeitzler replied that the redeployment of the forces assembling and the delay of the attack would be a detriment to the success of the operation. Indeed, Hitler was primarily concerned with *Zitadelle* disrupting any Soviet offensive preparations for the spring and summer of 1943 to allow the fuehrer to siphon off the necessary divisions to transfer them to Italy and the Balkans to defeat the anticipated Allied invasion. However, Hitler backed off as the depth of the Russian defenses became known he was losing considerable enthusiasm for the operation.

The planners made the case for *Zitadelle* with the following points: The operation would shorten the front and release badly needed units for operations elsewhere. The reduction of the bulge would attract large amounts of Russian armor and, with the planned use of the new Porsche tanks, (the Panther[230], Ferdinand and Tiger), soundly defeat the Russians, thereby eliminating a major threat and if the conditions permitted, possibly a follow-up advance north to Moscow.

With this information easily gleaned from a glance at a map of the front, the defense of the position was just as easy for the Soviets. Little more was needed than to develop a dense line, or lines, of defenses to absorb the attackers force, enough artillery, both field, anti-tank and mortar to stop and destroy the attackers units and an adequate mechanized force to repel the now weakened attacker. Indeed STAVKA had convinced Stalin to allow the Germans to attack first, wear them down in a massive defensive system and when the enemy's attack was absorbed, to launch a counterattack to take immediate advantage of the now weakened enemy and throw them back. It is to Stalin's credit that he had the necessary confidence to now trust the judgment of his generals and his revitalized army.

---

[230] Several sources quote the effectiveness of the PzKw Mk. V, "Panther" its initial technical shortcomings notwithstanding. The U.S. Army in an after action analysis after the war concluded that it required five M4 "Sherman" or nine T-34 tanks to destroy one Panther.

Preparations and New Weapons

Despite the extensive Russian defensive preparations, even with the place and time of the attack well known to the Russians, Hitler was convinced that the Germans could not lose due to the momentum and power of the planned massive panzer assault. Indeed, the 2,528 panzers[231] and assault guns planned for the attack also included a few new mechanized surprises for the Russians. As mentioned earlier, the new vehicles, in addition to the PzKw V "Panther" was the *Jagdpanzer* "Ferdinand" and the 150mm *Sturmpanzer 43 Brummbar* (Grizzly Bear) howitzer, *Nashorn* tracked anti-tank vehicle (Rhinoceros), mounting an 88mm gun, the mechanized heavy field howitzer *Hummel* mounting a 150mm gun and the mechanized 105mm howitzer *Wespe* (Wasp). That these artillery and anti-tank weapons were mounted on fully tracked vehicles gave the Panzerwaffe strong hitting power and the ability to move and maneuver to exploit any breakthroughs in the Russian battlefront.

In early July 1943 the Germans gathered 23 infantry divisions, over 2,500 tanks and assault guns, representing 16 *panzer* and *panzergrenadier* divisions or 63 per cent of all battle worthy *panzers* on the eastern front. It was at this battle that the now famous PzKw V "Panther", and the ill-fated PzJag "Tiger" (P) "Elephant"[232] tanks, this last weighing a massive 68 tons, were introduced, among others.[233] It was the above named 'Panther' which became the great hope for the coming offensive that was the cause of the three month delay in setting *Zitadelle's* attack date, due to new vehicle technical and unresolved development problems.

The Panther's (technically known as the *Panzerkamphwagen Pz. Kw. Mk. V Sd.Kfz.* or special vehicle 171 Panther) importance in and the cause of delay for the planning for *Zitadelle* cannot be overstated. This was Germanys first wartime designed armored fighting vehicle, all other panzers being pre-war designs. Its conception was a direct result of encounters with the Russian T-34 and KV-1 and 2 vehicles in the opening weeks of Operation Barbarossa. What made the Panther such a valuable and potent

---

[231] Despite the introduction of much new mechanized panzer machinery, as late as 1 July as much as half of the attacking panzer force consisted of obsolete PzKw Mk. III panzers with 50mm main guns. These obsolete machines were all but useless against the latest Soviet models.

[232] The original name given to this vehicle was "Ferdinand", after its designer Dr. Ferdinand Porsche.

[233] *Armored Vehicles, from the Conception to the Present Times*, George Bradford, The Miniature A.F.V. Collectors Association, undated.

weapon was its balance of firepower, protection and speed, just what the T-34 was to the Russian tank forces.

But Panther was to go it one better. Weighing in almost 48 tons, it was actually in the heavy tank class of WWII vehicles, even the KV-1, the current Russian heavy tank, weighed only 45 tons. Panther's thick frontal armor was thicker then the Russian KV tanks and would hold that advantage until the introduction of the Russian JS series main heavy battle tanks in early Spring of 1944. Its firepower came not from a bigger main gun but the old reliable 75mm gun found on the Pz. Kw IV, but improved. The new 75mm on the Panther had a far longer barrel and fired new high velocity ammunition, giving the Panther greater armor penetration at long distances and battlefield equality with the up gunned T-34/85 and JS tanks.

However, Panther was a new vehicle and as with any new vehicle, especially one as complex, heavy and expensive as the Panther, there were bugs to be discovered and worked out. The primary problem area was Panthers transmission. Part of the new design requirements in German armaments production instituted by Armaments Minister Speer was simplicity in design and conservation of material, all with a view of enhanced production, lower cost and fewer man hours invested. The new production methods and guidelines resulted in a transmission which was prone to failure, with difficulty in handling the weight of the new tank and would frequently fail under load. It was a problem that was not fully resolved by the July 1943 start date of *Zitadelle* and throughout Panther's short life, would continue to hinder the reliability of this elegant machine.

The second and most novel of these new machine was the *Panzerjager Tiger Elephant* or *Ferdinand*. These slow, heavy assault guns weighing some 65 tons with armor up to 200mm in thickness was to engage enemy bunkers, artillery and tanks, blasting a path through the Russian defenses. Armed with a powerful 88mm main gun some 90 of these vehicles were organized into two battalions for the attack. Almost impervious to enemy fire, there were nevertheless stopped by their problem prone electric drive system and faulty fuel systems resulting in engine fires. Its most serious tactical flaw was the lack of onboard machine guns to fend off infantry attacks. It was these attacks that destroyed most of the *Elephants*.

Other new armored vehicles making their first appearance in combat at Kursk was the open topped panzerjager *Nashorn* (Rhinoceros) equipped with the 88mm gun, the *Wespe* (Wasp) another open topped vehicle, this one on a Mk. IV panzer chassis with a 150mm cannon and the *Brummbar* (Grizzly Bear) another Mk IV mounted assault gun, this one fully enclosed mounting a 150mm howitzer, originally designed for street fighting.

Growing Allied Activity

By the early Spring of 1943 the Allies had completed their conquest of North Africa and were in the final stages of planning the next leap forward into Southern Europe. The most obvious was a short hop, staying under the umbrella of Allied fighter cover from Malta and that limited the choices to Sicily or Sardinia. As Allied experience with amphibious landings was still somewhat brief and new, the landings in North Africa under Operation Torch in November the previous year were uncontested and did not provide the real test of a landing under hostile fire, the choice of Sicily was made. Hitler knew that with Africa under Allied control there would soon be new offensive activity in that region, it was just a matter of where. How much time did Germany have before the Allies land somewhere in mainland Europe? How much time was there to conclude things in Russia? Could they be concluded? If not, what would be the cost in *panzers* and men to stave off Russian encroachment of the Reich? The hourglass of the undisturbed German conflict in Russia was about to run out.

True, a landing in Southern Italy or Sicily or Sardinia was still a long way from Berlin and there was a lot of ocean and mountains between them and the capitol to slow down even the fastest tank or soldier. However, it was not tanks and soldiers that Hitler was really concerned about, at least initially, his immediate concern was the long arm reach of Allied strategic airpower that worried him most, especially should bases be established in southern Italy, that would put the U.S. 15th Air Force with easy striking range of Ploesti, Rumania and its vital oil fields and industrial targets in Southern and Central Germany.

In addition to the activity in Southern Europe was the continuing Allied buildup of men and equipment in England and the very short hop from South-Eastern England to mainland Europe and its much closer and more direct path to Germany. German intelligence indicated that1943 would be the earliest the Allies would attempt an landing in North-West Europe. Would it come this year? The worry of the second front was growing and making itself felt in German planning and decision making.

The New Troika: Rokossovsky, Vatutin, Konev

Russian intelligence had learned early-on the details of Zitadelle's plan and prepared their defenses accordingly. On both 'shoulders' of the salient north and south of Kursk, defensive positions were prepared in great depth, in some places 110 miles deep! This included some 40,000 mines, 6,000 anti-tank guns, 920 *Katyusha* rocket batteries and some 300,000 civilians[234] digging 3,100 miles of trenches and strong points.[235] The fact that German intelligence failed to discover or failed to impart the degree of difficulty the depth and extensive nature of the defensive preparations would make on the attacking units in breaching them, and make this information known to OKH was a serious breach of responsibility, it was the direct cause of the failure of the operation. The question remains, had German intelligence known the extent of the depth and complexity of the Soviet defenses, would the attack have gone forward? The answer is yes. In a summer campaign, the German Wehrmacht had not yet been defeated and with the addition of the new weapons felt confident that as difficult as the task may be would eventually succeed.

The Russians had, as early as February, in addition to the intelligence reports from sources in Germany and Switzerland, established intelligence based on field reports. This information from captured Germans and air reconnaissance showed that the Germans were preparing an offensive in the Kursk region. This information, in conjunction with that supplied from spy sources was to do more to harm to the successful conclusion of the German operation than anything the Germans could forecast and in their preparations. To be forewarned is to be forearmed, and the Russians were.

However, Stalin despite having this knowledge of German attack plans wanted to attack first. He was adamant about not letting the experienced German panzers do again what had just happened to them a few months earlier. However, Zhukov persuaded Stalin to allow the German force to attack a fully developed Russian defense position. Allow them to spend their offensive power and strength against anti-tank guns, artillery, mine fields and attack aircraft. Allow it to entangle deep into the belt of defenses and then when the German force was exhausted and halted, strongly counterattack the now weakened enemy. Warily, Stalin decided

---

[234] Montefiore, in his *Stalin, the Court of the Red Tsar* states that Beria provided the 300,000 laborers and they were not civilians but slave laborers.

[235] The density of Russian artillery in the Kursk defensive zones was truly astonishing; in Central Front's 13th army there were 85 guns and mortars per kilometer of front!

to risk it and agreed to the strategy, a sign of how he was coming to trust his commanders.

The Battle

The German attack was launched in the first week of July and quickly bogged down in a maze of Russian trenches, anti-tank ditches, barbed wire, troops, tanks and mine fields. The northern attack barely advanced 8 miles against a ferocious Russian defense, the south did a little better advancing about 20 miles; however the Germans were bleeding themselves white against the Russian defenses, time after time hurling unit after unit into the Russian lines.

The battle was a great disappointment for the Ostheer as the other, smaller planned operations depended on its success, and a quick conclusion at that. After modest penetrations in the northern and southern bases of the Kursk bulge, the German panzer forces found the advance, especially in the north slow going and soon stopped. In the south, the battle went more in the Germans favor but was still not the cut and slash panzer penetrations of the past. However, just when the fighting in the southern sector seemed about to yield modest results, Hitler called a halt to the attack.

With news of the western Allies landing at Sicily and the modest progress to date, Hitler cancelled the attack and the Germans began a controlled retreat back to their start lines. In addition to the Allies' invasion on the Italian front, it was the Russian Army that, in addition to the Kursk fighting, launched several counterattacks, especially the one against the Mius River positions south of Kursk. Also, in the north, a Russian offensive south of Sukhinici was threatening the entire northern pincer of *Zitadelle*, which also hastened the decision to halt the attack.

The Russians, having so much advanced warning and information of the coming battle, prepared a strong counteroffensive. At the high tide mark of the battle, July 12, reached after the conclusion of the largest tank battle in the world in the southern attack area, at Prokhorovka, the Red Army launched a strong attack in both the northern and southern sectors, and by 23 July the Soviets had recovered all the territory lost in the German attack.

As the battle lines crept further and further west, Hitler ordered that there was to be no retreat without his permission; to enhance this order he began designating certain places, mostly cities to be 'Festung' cities, or fortress cities. Cities such as Vitebsk, Mogilev, Bobruysk became *Festung* cities; Hitler's attempt to build a stopping place against which the Russians would be held against further advances west. This was to have dire consequences for the Ostheer, as we shall see in the summer of 1944.[236]

With the Russian repulse of *Zitadelle* north and south of the city of Kursk in July 1943, a general and pre-planned Russian counteroffensive began, erasing the hard won German gains and continuing on to the west. From Nevel in the north to the Sea of Azov in the south the Germans were unable to stem the Russian offensive. Their momentum carried the Soviets to and past the Dnieper River to Kherson on the Black Sea in the south, to Korosten northwest of Kiev and Vitebsk northwest of Smolensk.[237] What made this massive offensive possible was, in part the impact of allied Lend-Lease aid that was now reaching the Russian Army. The damage inflicted on the retreating Germans could have been greater, especially on the panzer divisions if it were not for the intervention of Luftwaffe ground attack aircraft.[238]

The components of this aid that enabled these extended Russian offensives were the transportation and communication items, most notably railroad locomotives, heavy trucks and radio equipment. This assisted the Soviets' offensives in two important ways. The wheeled trucks[239] enabled the supporting components of Russian units, primarily the infantry, to keep up with the tank units, providing the support, punch and tactical staying power they were missing in the past. This was the combined arms tactics that were most successful as demonstrated by the Germans. Until this time during Soviet offensives, German units would permit the Russian tanks to

---

[236] During the war the Germans were to designate 95 towns and cities as *Festung* or fortresses, beginning in 1943. This figure does not include fortified areas (*Verteidigungbereiches*).

[237] The Luftwaffe was among the first air forces to field a machine specifically for attacking ground targets, the first was the Soviet Union with its unbeatable Il-2, introduced in May of 1941. The first purpose built ground attack machine for Germany was the Henschel Hs-129. This heavily armed and armored aircraft was to take a heavy toll of Russian tanks and other vehicles on the Eastern Front. One version of the machine, the Hs-129B-3/Wa carried 75mm automatic cannon in a ventral gondola, one of the largest guns carried on an aircraft during World War II.

[238] In addition to the Hs-129, the Junkers Ju-87G-1, which was armed with two 37mm automatic cannons, one under each wing, also operated far and wide on the Eastern Front.

[239] Mostly Studebaker trucks. During and after the war "Studebaker" became synonymous with truck in Russia.

pass through their front line, the few Russian infantry riding unprotected on the backs of their tanks, vulnerable to small arms and artillery fire, would be eliminated, then letting their anti-tank gun and mobile units deal with the tanks. Stopping the supporting infantry with machine gun, mortar and artillery fire was next. This separation of the attacking elements permitted the German units to deal with the Russian offensives piecemeal, permitting the defenders to maintain their lines, and limit the Soviet advances.

The railroad locomotives and vehicles supplied to the Russians provided the increased supply capacity needed in mobile operations and allowed the offensive to continue, deep into German rear areas. This made German countermeasures difficult due to unit disruption by the deep penetrations. Finally, the arrival of the radio and telephone equipment enabled the field commands to properly coordinate this now more mobile style of combat.

This newfound Russian mobility was bringing the Red Army's capabilities closer to that of the Wehrmacht's. In the last three years, the Russians had learned many important lessons from their attackers, as noted earlier, and the basics of *Blitzkrieg* were no longer a German monopoly. In addition to the new mobility and new equipment was increased radio and communications discipline, which were put into effect. In the past the Germans were able to exploit weak Russian discipline with their communications intelligence units, intercepting Russian radio messages that often provided early notice of Soviet intentions.

As will be mentioned elsewhere in this work, the nature of combat in Russia was one of intense savagery. The willingness of both sides to fight to lengths rarely found on the other fronts in Europe was frequently commonplace in the East. What is seldom found in the western press is the frequently suicidal methods the Russian Army utilized to achieve their battlefield objectives. For example:

> "General G. K. Zhukov, on his way to HQ, stopped at Prokhorovka (near Kursk) and for a few minutes was silently looking at the field covered with black ruins of burnt, blown and deformed tanks. Everywhere in sight were pieces of armor, tracks... near the General was a Panther (German PzKw Mk. V) with a T-70 (Russian) stuck in its side. In some twenty meters (further away) a Tiger and T-34 in the last dance, both blown. Zhukov said, as to himself, 'This is an encounter battle'"

Conclusions

Zitadelle also demonstrates the shrinking combat power of the *Ostheer* in the face of rapidly growing Soviet power. In the opening weeks of Barbarossa all three army groups were part of the offensive, as one would expect with the commencement of such a major operation. After the major losses of men and equipment in front of Moscow that first winter, the second campaign season was limited to Army Group South. By the third campaign season, the summer of 1943, again, suffering from disastrous losses of men and equipment from the Stalingrad battles the previous winter, the Germans were seeking only to straighten their lines (the Kursk bulge) and, should opportunities avail themselves destroy as much Russian men and material as possible.

What we see here again was the hand of Hitler's "gambler instinct", his *gefuhl*, his feeling, the insertion of political desire into the military calculus, always a deadly and risky proposition. The need to stake everything on the grand show, the constant need for a battlefield-like *Gotterdammerung*, was to again consign to an early grave, as at Stalingrad, tens of thousands of Germans at a time when such risks by a nation the size of Germany could no longer be afford.[240]

The unfortunate truth for the Germans was that their secret plans for *Zitadelle* were discovered by the Russians early on and they had prepared their defense lines accordingly. In addition to the defense, they prepared a large counter attack force that was launched against the stalled Germans and pushed them back to their start-lines in a few days. By the 15th of the month the Russians were in full attack mode, and the now weakened Germans fell back. The retreat continued all that autumn to the banks of the Dnieper, and Kiev, once again, became a front line city.

By the fall rains of 1943 the German line stood on most of the Dniepr River and the outlook for them was grim. The one bright hope of stopping the Russians at Kursk, or at least inflicting enough injury on the Russians to slow their progress was gone. The attack was foolishly permitted to proceed even with the suspicion of extensive Russian defensive preparations. Approximately 300 of the *panzers* collected for Kursk, the best and

---

[240] For additional study see: *Kursk 1943: A Statistical Analysis* by Niklas Zetterling and Anders Frankson, Frank Cass Publishers, 2000. *The Battle of Kursk* by David M. Glantz and Jonathan M. House, University Press of Kansas, 1999 as well as the aforementioned *Soviet Casualties and Combat Losses in the Twentieth Century* by G. F. Krivosheev.

brightest panzer men of both the Heer and the Waffen SS units were lost. Never again would such a mighty panzer force be assembled in Russia, nor would the Wehrmacht launch such an ambitious operation in Russia. From August 1943 until the war ended in May of 1945, the German experience in Russia was to be one long retrograde movement west.

The defeat at Kursk is considered by many historians to be the real turning point of the war in the east. Kursk would be the last strategic offensive launched against Russia, and its failure sealed the fate of the German campaign in the east. This collection of armored might, had it been launched in May, could have brought the victory badly needed by the Germans, the two month delay in the German attack caused it's doom. However, it could also have been used as a mobile defensive force as many German commanders advised, and could have stabilized the front in Russia, if not permanently, then perhaps until a political solution to the conflict been reached. The armored defeat at Kursk is frequently overlooked as just another battle in the east the Germans lost, and not the one with the potential to bring about a possible solution there. It was not the loss of another battle but the loss of a "solution" in the east that is tragic for the Germans. The cursory intelligence gathering, inadequate evaluation of Russian defenses and their skillful use of deception plans, and the follow-up or pursuit plans to exploit success turned the tide in the East.

The most conspicuous German error was the constant delaying of the start of the operation, almost four months. With obvious signs of the Russian defenses thickening by the day and all that would entail for the attacker, the 'confidence', (or was it wildly misplaced battlefield tactical and panzer technical superiority displayed by the Germans) was astonishing. The Soviets had a number of intelligence agents[241] placed within the German high command that had been sending timely, high quality information back to Moscow regarding the name of the operation, the probable start dates, attack sites, the operational order number, and a fairly good tally of the forces the Germans planned to use in the offensive.

The losses suffered and the opportunities lost by the Germans in *Zitadelle*, while disappointing, were not critical. The lost panzers were soon replaced by even better and newer machines; the most serious casualty was the lost infantry. The already weakened supporting infantry were further

---

[241] The Russian agent providing this invaluable information was code named "Lucy", based in Switzerland.

weakened, and even with the addition of the automatic weapons and organic artillery with the recent divisional reorganization, there were never enough of these valuable fighting men.

This would be the final opportunity to extract some positive outcome from the actions in the east before the arrival of the second Allied front, and it had been squandered. The growing and relentless Russian pressure all along the fronts was having a deleterious effect on the German ability to gather and maintain a panzer reserve for offensive operations. The panzer formations gathered for *Zitadelle* would never be seen again in the east in such size and quality, the opening of the Allied front in Italy and France would see to that. From July 1943 to the end of the war in the ruins of Berlin, the *Panzerwaffe* would only be able to gather units amounting to no more than a handful of divisions for offensive actions. From this hot summer on in the steppes of central Russia, the direction of the war would move west.

Zitadelle's failure would put into question the ability of Germany to successfully conclude the war in the east. *Zitadelle* is included here to demonstrate how important this battle was to the development of the German tactical and strategic situation in Russia in 1943; how this battle shaped the German field position for 1944; affected German unit combat strength and morale and how, through questionable planning and decision making at the highest levels, greatly minimized Germany's hopes of staving off defeat in the East. What must be kept in mind is that *Unternehmen Zitadelle* was just one of the battles, albeit the biggest, that was fought at several locations along the long front during the summer of 1943 in Russia.

Opportunities Lost

The relatively modest panzer losses suffered as a result of *Zitadelle* and the actions afterward to counter the Russian summer offensive seriously affected the ability of the Germans to contain the oncoming Soviet summer offensive. Additional losses were suffered in August attempting to stem the Russian counteroffensive, not only at Kursk, but both north and south of the operational area. With the loss of the battlefield itself, there wasn't even the promise of recovery and restoration of damaged or disabled vehicles. A number of vehicles on both sides were put out of action by simply running out of fuel. Unlike earlier battles where the *Wehrmacht* advanced or at least held the field of battle, what was lost at Kursk was to be lost forever.[242]

Kursk failed to achieve its objectives, which was to restore the German offensive momentum in the East by bringing the bulk of Russian armor to one place, fight it out using the newest machinery and best talents of the *Panzerwaffe*. It was to destroy the Russian tank forces, eliminate the large bulge in the front line, and tear open a large hole in the Russian line. Should conditions permit, it could conduct a follow-up offensive on Moscow from the South. It was not to be.

It was inaccurate enemy strength assessments, faulty and incomplete intelligence gathering and evaluation, political meddling, repeated and unrepentant German arrogance and underestimation of Soviet military capabilities, and flawed communications security (such as the *Enigma* coding system) that caused many of the military difficulties for the Germans; especially in the east, it lead to the biggest clash of mechanized armor in World War II to take place.

Had OKH a reliable informant, a spy, an agent, any ability to 'read' Russian military and political intentions, especially as they pertain to the defensive preparations to receive the German offensive around Kursk, the

---

[242] An example of how important it was to control the battlefield after conflict is aptly demonstrated by the vehicle recovery and maintenance operations of the Red Army SPAMS units. Christopher Duffy in his *Red Storm on the Reich, The Soviet March on Germany, 1945* (Da Capo Press, 1993) provides the following: "Out of all the Russian tanks and assault guns which were lost temporarily or permanently in the Great Patriotic War, about one-quarter bogged or broke down, and three-quarters were knocked out by enemy action. On 11 November 1944 STAVKA put all the facilities for mechanical repair under unified command, a measure that increased their productivity by 50 per cent. A significant role was played by the recovery tractors and workshops of the SPAMS damaged vehicle assembly points, which attended to running repairs. The more difficult cases were left for repair at the army corps or front level. The result was quite remarkable. In the first six days of the Vistula-Oder Operation, the Eighth Guards Army (1st Byelorussian Front) had a total of 159 tanks and assault guns disabled, but only 71 of them permanently inoperable. In January as a whole the 1st Byelorussian Front carried out 3,786 successful repairs of tanks and assault guns, and the 1st Ukrainian Front 4,267. This means that many of the vehicles were patched up more than once." p. 349.

Also from Duffy, we have a view from the German side on vehicle recovery and repair: "Mechanical repair workshops were unable to operate sufficiently long in a single place to do any useful work, even if there had been any way of rescuing damaged vehicles from the battlefield. In the 5th Panzer Division Major von Ramin reported how his 53rd Panzer Jager Detachment was virtually crippled in the course of the month, "The roads were completely jammed by the columns of refugees and the detachment did not have the means of retrieving all of the damaged Jagdpanzers in good time. Out of fourteen complete write-offs, only three were lost through enemy action – the other eleven had to be blown up, for we did not have the tractors to save them from the enemy" p. 384.

operation would have surely been cancelled; even Hitler would have had to see reality eventually. Perhaps then, just perhaps, OKH would have asked the question, why were the Soviets preparing such a defense in depth just where we planned to attack? Why indeed? What did they know of our attack preparations? How did they know of our planned offensive? From whom? Where? Questions that, if asked at all, were never answered, never answered all during the German experience in Russia. Remarkable.

Perhaps the most significant aspect of *unternehmen Zitadelle* was not in the Germans' preparation for the battle, as lengthy as it was, not the quality of German weapons and training, as the fact that this battle was the premier of several new and deadly tracked German weapons for which the Red Army was to "pay dearly" in the near future. The real mystery manifested at Kursk was the entire lack of imagination in the choice of location of the Kursk offensive. Unlike von Manstein's brilliant mechanized counteroffensive, *Unternehmen Stern* just a few short months before, the choice of battle for the July 1943 battle was so obvious so as to defy military judgment. One would expect such a choice of attack position to be made by a green, untested, novice army, hardly by the experienced Wehrmacht. What the Germans had brought to the world of modern battle was the innovative use of weapons, their combination, daring application, and a subtle, almost nuanced knowledge of calculated risk-taking and prudent battle management. If Kursk was the best their decision-making could do, political interference notwithstanding, the balance of power had truly changed.

One last word regarding *Unternehmen Zitadelle*: Perhaps the biggest loss to the Germans that hot summer of 1943 was one of opportunity; the opportunity to launch one last major offensive against the Soviets with no other major military power in Europe distracting the Wehrmacht. The loss of the precious panzers (the lost opportunity of the proper preparation and introduction of the "Panther"), their crews, and just as important, the dead infantry, *Zitadelle* would mark the end of Germany's chance to fight one enemy at a time. By the end of the month, the Allies would be landing in Sicily, and shortly thereafter on the Italian peninsula, and with it, entry to mainland Europe, or so it appeared. As it was, it was enough of a concern for Hitler to call off the offensive and begin juggling divisions to the threatened sector. The 300 or so lost panzers amounted to a month's production, but in the final evaluation the greater loss was another precious opportunity squandered.

Chapter Ten:
The Shadow War
The Russian Partisan Movement

"Our units are on the march night and day, without sleep or food. Our position is hard, but we shall get out of it. The enemy is making an extreme effort to annihilate us, but he will not succeed."

Tito

"The Russian has stood poverty, hunger and austerity for centuries. His stomach is flexible; hence no false pity!"

Herbert Backe
German State Secretary in the Ministry for Food And Agriculture

This chapter will discuss a unique aspect of the war in the East, the Russian Partisan Movement, the army behind the front. It will discuss what the Partisans were, how they were organized, commanded and supplied and how they contributed to the war effort and assisted the Russian Army in general and in Operation Bagration in particular in the summer of 1944.

The German Map Of Eastern Europe

If you place your finger on a map of central Europe, starting at the eastern edge of the city of Warsaw, Poland is the first nation conquered by Germany. If we move it east, one encounters the recently seized eastern Polish lands of the former Union of Soviet Socialist Republics occupied in 1939. As the Wehrmacht advanced eastward in the summer of 1941 through the former Polish state, into the Baltic and Soviet Republics one left German civilian administration and came under German military administration.

Germany divided up these eastern lands amongst themselves and their new allies; Hungary received parts of former Rumanian territory (Transylvania), Germany granted Rumania a collection of small lands (former Bukovina, southern Bessarabia, small parts of Ukraine, Odessa, Vinnystia and the western Mykolaiv oblasts) naming the new entity *Transnistria*. However, Stalin taking advantage of German preoccupation during the invasion of France, demanded and got from Rumania, with Hitler's encouragement, the provinces of Bessarabia and Bucovina. Eastern Galicia and all of German occupied eastern Poland came under an administrative entity called *General Gouvernement*.

As the Wehrmacht advanced into Russia the follow-on German civil administration created two huge territories known as *Reichskommissariat Ostland* and *Reichskommissariat Ukraine*, the larger of the two Germany's biggest colony. The former were made up of the Baltic nations of Lithuania, Latvia and Estonia and parts of Byelorussia. *Ostland* was not an over-inflated East Prussia this was rather the Bialystok region which was annexed directly to the Greater German Reich and organized into a *Gau*. Reichskommissariat Ukraine was originally planned to contain the entire former Ukrainian S.S.R. and was to extend all the way to the banks of the Volga, but due to the deteriorating military situation the actual border fell generally between the Dnieper and Donets Rivers. The remaining portions of the U.S.S.R. under German control were administered by the Wehrmacht under its administrative body known as Rear Army Area authorities.

Genesis

If a Russian Army in front of it wasn't enough, in the rear of Germany's Army Group Center was another army, the largest concentration of Russian partisans on the Eastern front. In the first five months of Barbarossa, now with vast tracts of land under its control Army Group Center captured and bypassed tens of thousands of Russian soldiers during its headlong rush towards Moscow. Despite the thousands were able to escape back to Russian lines and re-absorption into the Russian Army, many more thousands, for just as many reasons, did not, and stayed behind in the German occupied areas. Initially these men hid in the dense forests and swamps which occupied a large part of the rear area of the Army Group, and struggled to maintain themselves and avoid contact with the German occupiers. The potential of these thousands of ex-Russian Army soldiers and soon to be added civilians and their strategically beneficial position in the region did not go unnoticed by Moscow.

The large forests and woodlands of this area had concealed an active resistance movement, in its early days sporadic in nature, since the early days of the German invasion, and by mid-1944 organized and controlled from Moscow their numbers had grown to over 250,000. The affect of partisan activity on the German operations was to tie down 15 percent of German strength in Army Group Center in the form of six security divisions and other police unit personnel. In addition to inflicting significant damage and delay to German logistics, the partisan presence provided invaluable military intelligence via clandestine radio transmissions, as well as to deprive the rear area units of peace of mind. The partisan activity was to disrupt enemy operations and to, as Lenin phrased it during the civil war, deny the "stability of the rear" to the invader.

The Russian partisan movement is a unique element in the war in the east. The vast, forested and swamp areas of western Russia and Ukraine afforded ample opportunity for irregular or guerrilla operations against the German invader. The Soviet partisans stayed in place, unlike the conduct of western armies which, when bypassed, cut-off, or surrounded during the conduct of a battle, sought to return to their own units as soon as possible. This was done by seeking to penetrate the enemy's lines to achieve contact with friendly units and thereby arrive 'home' to rest, re-equip and eventually return to the fighting if the physical and psychological state of the soldier permitted.

The conduct of the Russian soldier was to be quite different in the war with Germany. The Communist Party's involvement in the command and control of the Russian Army via the Commissar positions did stiffen many Russian Army units and ensured they did not to surrender or break ranks and run away in the face of the devastating German attacks. The Party Commissar had responsibilities with units behind the enemy lines as well.

This unique 'army in the woods' was to complement the Russian Army. The term 'partisan' quickly identifies what theater of the war one is discussing, and the name is indelibly connected to the war in the east with Russian (and Tito's partisan forces in Yugoslavia) activity behind the front lines in German occupied areas. The origins of the partisan movement go back to the 1920s when the young Russian Army under the direction of Marshal Tukhachevsky was ensuring that if the bandits of the post-revolution period ever returned, there would be a prepared means to deal with them. He prepared hidden bases and buried weapons; however, Stalin quashed the preparations fearing that armed groups not under the control of the Russian Army could pose a threat to him.

However effective the partisan movement became in the 1943-1945 period, there was no pre-war planning for partisan operations in the event of an enemy attack. The Party apparatus attempted to exercise some control over the bypassed Red Army units and the general civilian population behind the German lines, lest they become influenced by the enemy propaganda and the style of the occupation, and be won over to the German side. The Communist Party was very concerned by reports of the local inhabitants welcoming the German invaders with open arms and gifts of food. The Communists, after the Revolution of 1917 spent many years suppressing political, cultural and religious dissent, and was not about to have their efforts overturned by the invasion.

One of the fears Stalin had regarding the partisans was based on the Communist experience during the Civil War period. A characteristic of the highly centralized Stalinist regime was to exercise as complete control and administration over all aspects of Soviet civilian and military life as possible. The fact that the partisans were cut off behind enemy lines, and not subject to the almost constant examination, supervision, order, obedience, discipline and the hierarchy of the Soviet military as well as political and civil control permitted a certain amount of independence and it was feared this independence could blossom into uncontrolled and unapproved thought, and possible fracture with Soviet authorities. The uncertainties of military and political unreliability, their lack of a political consciousness, lack of discipline and amateurism, all contributed to a deep mistrust in and of these units. This fear of lack of control of these dispersed and amorphous bands of armed men were to be a constant element and worry of STAVKA all during the war. However, with the deteriorating military situation, desperate for any distraction or diversion of the hard charging German Army, Stalin relented and sought to organize and formalize these bands to support the defense of the Motherland.

The Early Years

One type of the uniquely Russian units organized in the early days of the partisan movement was known as "Annihilation Battalions". These grimly named units were organized by NKVD members, and gathered into their units the most politically reliable members of bypassed Red Army units, factory workers and volunteers. Their primary mission was to maintain internal security in the enemy rear areas and the destruction of all usable equipment and machinery of use to the enemy. The maintenance of internal security in the enemy rear also included waging a campaign of terror against the local population to 'prevent political deviation'. For support partisans were expected to seek out others in similar circumstances and if his rank or experience provided, take command of others needing command and guidance. He and his unit were expected to live off the land or enemy assets to include food, shelter, weapons and ammunition.[243]

Another interestingly named organization within the partisan movement was the "Diversionary Unit". They were one of the smaller units, consisting of groups of three to ten men each, and their mission appeared to be no different than the other partisan units behind the German main line of resistance: that of destroying enemy assets and causing disruption wherever and whenever possible.[244]

Both the Annihilation Battalions and the Diversionary Units were early attempts at controlling the Russians in the German rear area. They were eventually absorbed into the mainline Partisan organization beginning in 1942. However impressive the names of these units, their effectiveness in the early months of the war was small. Training was spotty or non-existent, food and weapons were obtained on a 'catch-as-catch-can' basis and many 'volunteers' ran away at the first opportunity, especially when the leadership was killed or became separated from the unit. Although the Germans identified a number of these units, their ability to inflict harm or seriously hinder German operations was slight and hence the attention

---

[243] *The Soviet Partisan Movement, 1941-1945*, By Edgar M. Howell, Department of the Army Pamphlet No. 20-244, August 1956.

[244] Ibid.

paid to them by the enemy was equally slight. Their strength at this stage of the war was in their potential threat -- what they might do if not disrupted, displaced or destroyed.

If poor organization and guidance characterized the Russian partisan movement in the early part of the war, German response to them was an equally lackluster operation. Rear-area security was entrusted to nine security or *Sicherungs* divisions created from three standard sized but third-class infantry divisions, minus heavy weapons. The standard of training and equipment of these security divisions was far below that of a front line-division. The men used to staff them were in the 30 to 45 years old age group and the small arms were provided from captured French, Polish, Belgian and Czech stocks. The vehicles in the motorized units in most divisions were based on foreign makes, and no spares were provided. So haphazard was the equipping of these units one had no tires! The most reliable of the 'motorized' units were the bicycle-mounted units, which were considered suitable for 'local commitment only'. In addition to the use of third-line units, the German command also used their foreign allies whenever possible, and we frequently see Hungarian and Rumanian units, some up to division size. operating with these German units in certain anti-partisan 'actions'. Also, local Russian residents were recruited into security units as well as local labor gangs to supply much needed labor and later intelligence information to the regional and local German security administration.

The methods and enforcement of security were entirely up to the local commander, and implementation was lax. The locals and partisans soon learned ways around checkpoints, villages considered safe from German control and unobserved roads. One partisan commander found that the local German security unit did not check the passes of well-dressed Russians. The locals frequently traveled the roads in ones and twos and traveled at night to avoid curfew. The Germans imposed a travel curfew soon after occupying the area to avoid unauthorized communications and contact with other Russians, road congestion and possible attacks against German rear area installations. The Germans were guilty of carelessness too and failed to do some of the more obvious administrative items, such as issue of identification documents that contained expiration dates. There is anecdotal evidence of a few locals traveling in 1944 with passes issued in July of 1941.

The German Anti-Partisan Operations

Propaganda played an important part in the partisan war in the east. Most propaganda was in the form of single-sheet leaflets either printed on small manual presses or machines in the larger partisan camps, or it took the form of small newspapers printed in Red Army or Communist Party organ headquarters and airdropped over the occupied areas.

The attempt to change the allegiance of the occupied populace was almost completely ignored by the Germans. The policy for the eastern occupied areas, especially Russia, was clear and unambiguous. There was to be no attempt to co-opt the populace into assistance or even to chide them into neutrality. The orders were clear. Any resistance, any refusal to obey German orders, any lack of cooperation, any sign of supporting the local partisan operations was punishable by death.

The execution of those caught or even suspected of aiding and abetting the partisan enemy was to be carried out as conspicuously as possible as a warning. Shooting was quickly replaced by hanging, which afforded a more theatrical setting for the punishment. There was the building of the scaffolding, usually in a town or village central square or marketplace, main road intersection, any place that would ensure the maximum possible exposure of the victim and the visibility of the punishment of their 'crime'. Then came the preparation of the ropes; next a large sign was prepared for draping around the victim's neck indicating the 'crime' and, usually a warning to others that this was what awaited them if they should commit similar offenses against the German authorities. The victims were then executed by nothing more sophisticated than having the stool, plank or bench on which they stood kicked out from under them. Technically it was hanging, but in reality it was strangulation, a much slower form of death. The victim was left hanging for a number of days to drive home the point of the exercise and when removed, taken away by the Germans and dumped in an unmarked grave or buried with other victims of the German authorities.

The reprisals by the Germans began to mount near the end of 1941. In the Fourth Army Area two locals were shot for each German; in an attack on an important German installation three locals were shot for each German lost. Persons found wandering in the streets after dark or found near rail and highway bridges were to be shot on sight.

Beginning in March 1942, the Germans launched Operation *Bamberg*, their first coordinated anti-Partisan multi-division action. Known generally as the *partisanenbekampfung* or anti-partisan war, the area chosen was the triangle of Glusk-Paritschi-Oktjabrski, situated south of Bobruisk, in the eastern Polesje region. The units involved were the 707th infantry division, 203rd Security division, a Slovakian infantry regiment and the 315th German police battalion. The operation was less an anti-partisan operation than an extermination action against the locals in the "triangle" area. The official Russian dead were listed as 3,500, but actually was thought to be much higher. The partisans saw 5,000 as a more accurate figure. The Germans lost seven dead and captured 47 weapons of all types. Of the estimated 1,200 to 2,000 actual partisans in the action area, not one was captured.[245]

For example, a member of *Einsatzkommando VIII* testified as follows:

> "We members of *EK VIII* reacted thereto by destroying whole villages in this area, the inhabitants of which were shot. Our goal was to deprive the partisans in the wood(s) of any means to avail themselves of food, clothing, etc. from these localities. In one or two cases we members of *EK VIII* combed through woods in this area to track down the partisans in their hideouts. Such methods we quickly gave up, however. We considered them too dangerous for us, as we might ourselves be attacked and destroyed by the partisans."[246]

The analysis of Operation *Bamberg* indicated a reluctance to allocate the necessary number of troops and time to properly execute the task. A frequent mention in the after-action reports was the need to meet 'daily objectives' at certain dates and times, which led the units in the operation to utilize roads and well used trails to clear their areas, concentrating on occupied villages and towns which were considered to be occupied by the enemy. These 'captured' residents were summarily executed, frequently by very barbaric methods.

The German rear area security forces conducted these operations with no discernment as to age or gender or the method of execution. Few were questioned or interrogated, they were simple herded into any available open space or building for execution. They shot, burned and hanged all who were snared by their dragnet operations.

[245] Ibid.

[246] Ibid.

Consider the following testimony of Georg Weisig, commander of SS police regiment 26 regarding Operation "Otto" at the end of 1943 and the beginning of 1944 in the Osveja area:

> "About 250 inhabitants of the villages located outside the woods we transported to camps. The people we found in the villages inside the forest area, however, we all killed. In the whole area between Sebesh and Lake Osweskoje, where the operation was carried out, there was not a living human being left after our regiment had passed through."[247]

The reports, far from reading like a military after-action report, has all the hallmarks of an *Einsatzkommando* extermination report. Further investigation by the Wehrmacht command discovered that the operation was improperly carried out, missing many of the goals and objectives of the planned action, and instead chose 'targets of convenience' to attack; hence the high non-combatant death tolls. This was the first of seventeen identified anti-partisan operations in just 1942, and does not include local, smaller-scale actions undertaken by local commands with their own partisan problems.

Operation *Bamberg* was the first of fifty-six such anti-partisan operations conducted on the Eastern Front; 17 in 1942; 28 in 1943; and 11 in 1944 and as mentioned above were only the planned, larger anti-partisan sweeps. There were certainly other, smaller, localized actions. These operations grew in size and scale, especially in 1943 when the partisans received more and more support, and were better led and, especially when the local populace could see that Germany was losing the war and made the decision as to where they should place their allegiance much easier. The behavior of the units used in the anti-partisan actions continued to be more brutal, vindictive and increasingly directed to the most vulnerable, easily reached portion of the population, women, the young and the elderly. The men of military age had long since fled the sweeps, joined a partisan group, the Russian Army or were dead.

In addition to the German anti-partisan operations, one of the chief reasons the locals joined the partisans was because of the harsh labor recruitment methods used by *Gauleiter* Erich Koch, methods which were so harsh that even senior Nazis complained to Hitler about the effects it

---

[247] http://forum.axishistory.com/ and *Kalkulierte Morde* by Christian Gerlach, p. 884-895.

was having in their ability to manage the country. However, Hitler sided with Koch based on the warped Nazi racial theories. This method of casting a wide net that swept up everyone in its path was a major recruitment tool for the partisan movement. The anti-partisan operations behind Army Group Center follow the tenor of the larger conflict being fought in Russia; that of the no holds barred, vicious kill or be killed struggle.

For the Germans, the anti-partisan operations never did have the intended result due to the reasons mentioned above, and the partisans became bolder, more coordinated and more effective, culminating with the attacks against the German rail and road systems in preparation for Operation Bagration in June 1944.

Partisan Life

The life of a partisan was a harsh one as is seen from the following:

"Joining an existing partisan group was never easy. Males who wanted to do so were told to join the (German) auxiliary police, to obtain arms and ammunition there, and then to desert. Newly recruited Russian Partisans, as they often called themselves, pledged to serve "my motherland, the party, and my leader and comrade Stalin." They underwent a harsh probation period. Although partisans, Soviet or not, tended to consume a lot of alcohol, all were subject to severe disciplinary rules, which were enforced with beatings and other punishments by not only the commanders, but also political commissars or (in the large units) special sections (*Osobyi Otdel* or OO) of the NKVD. Unauthorized plunder and being drunk or asleep on duty often brought the death penalty. Partisans with a serious illness that endangered the group also could be killed."

"Female partisans worked as cooks and cleaners. As long as they did not accept a steady boyfriend, the males considered them common property. Pregnancies were usually aborted; babies born often were given away to peasants or killed. Very few partisans had medical knowledge. In all, the partisan life was restless and often brutal, marked by semidarkness, damp cold, dirty water, disease, lice, and shortages of food, tobacco, clothing and shoes".[248]

[248] *Harvest of Despair*, p. 278.

There was no neutral position in which the local populace found safety. The Germans expected them to work and support them with all their hearts, while the NKVD and partisan movement expected active resistance to the occupiers. The Russian people, especially the simple peasants in the small villages or on the collective farms were caught in a terrible dilemma. Some were so frightened that they left their farms and went to hide in the woods, forests and swamps, attempting to wait until the war was over then re-emerge and continue life. Others stayed true to their Russian-speaking authorities and either burned their farms or joined the partisans, others stayed on the farm and secretly ensured that their produce was delivered to the local partisan units. Others tried to satisfy both powers and offending both, paid the ultimate price. Many suffered horrible punishment, from one side or the other. There was no place to hide.

There was yet another tragic aspect of the war in the East and that had to do with escaped Jews. Byelorussian peasants were subjected to terrorism by two groups of partisans, 'unofficial partisans', those not organized by the Soviet government, and the "official" partisans, who were led by Russian Army officers parachuted into occupied areas to organize resistance.

The unofficial partisans in Belorussia, including the former eastern Polish territories, were to a large degree Jews who had escaped from the ghettoes and fled to the forests. These Jews lived by stealing food from the peasants, usually by violence and threats of violence. The actions of these "unofficial partisans" were not part of a war against the occupier but simply a means of procuring the means to live.

Naturally the Russian peasant objected to having food supplies stolen and they resisted. In some areas, the peasants attacked the hideouts of the 'unofficial partisans' themselves, in an effort to wipe them out thereby protecting their food supplies. More often, they reported the presence of these 'unofficial', Jewish partisans to the German authorities, which then mounted campaigns to flush them out if they had sufficient strength or time. German counterinsurgency actions resulted in the extermination of many of the groups of escaped Jews who had been robbing the peasants.

In order to preserve themselves, the Jewish partisans then undertook retaliatory actions against the peasants who had reported them to the German authorities. Sometimes, these retaliations took the form of the extermination of entire villages and the massacre of all their inhabitants.

They were intended to prevent the betrayal of the Jews in hiding to the Germans, both by killing off the peasants who could betray them and by terrorizing the rest.

The issue of obtaining adequate supplies of food was a daily and constant preoccupation for partisans. The ability of the center[249] to supply the partisans with food, weapons and other necessities was, especially in 1941 and 1942 very limited. Indeed, it became official policy in August 1942 that the partisans should obtain their own supplies. P. K. Ponomarenko, chief of staff for the Central Staff for the Partisan Movement in Moscow made it official policy that "Only inactive detachments will experience needs, but it is hardly expedient that the center should supply such detachments. It is forbidden to accustom detachments to demand and receive supplies only from the center, and to encourage this carelessness."

Thus, it was expected that if a partisan wanted to eat, he had to obtain his food from the enemy or the land. This had the intended effect of keeping the partisans active and aggressive against the enemy. In times of high anti-partisan operations by the Germans, when the partisans had to flee their normal bases of operations or in winter conditions, food became scarce. It was not unknown for some desperate partisan commands, such as in the Crimea in the winter of 1942-1943, resorting to cannibalism. Occasionally in extreme cases, some starved.

The anti-partisan operations conducted by the Germans and their allies were not all one-way affairs when it came to who died. One example that Hitler used again and again when the issue of forming Russian combat divisions was raised was the November 1942 Russian volunteer revolt. A Wehrmacht organized secret anti-partisan unit of some 2,500 men revolted, killing their German commanders and even handed their Russian commander over to the partisans. Such was the wide range of reactions within the Russian volunteer units and one that was always in the backs of the minds of any German operating with a Russian counterpart.

The Partisan Anti-Rail Campaign

As the fighting front moved east, the German lines of supply and communication became longer and more vulnerable. As the length of these lines grew, the use of wheeled vehicles became more and more difficult

---

[249] Soviet publications, instructions and orders frequently referred to Moscow or high commands as "the center" or "the mainland".

with the few surfaced roads and the severe changes in climate in the area of operations. Because of the massive quantities of all types of supplies needed by a modern army, the reliance on rail for supply quickly became necessary. With the large forested and swamp areas 'channeling' the rail lines into a few corridors, the vulnerability of these rail lines was great.

It quickly became apparent to the Russian command that the most effective manner in which the partisan movement could help and support the fighting fronts was to attack these exposed rail lines. That became the chief occupation of the movement from 1943 to the end of the war.

By 1944 the Soviet partisan movement had reached sufficient field effectiveness and STAVKA was counting on their support in preparation for Operation Bagration. By this time there were approximately 144,000 partisans in over 200 identified and independent units, the strengths of which varied considerably. Their most important contributions to Bagration were in reconnaissance and rail demolitions, a main effort in that the Wehrmacht depended so heavily on rail connections for communications and supply.

The high point of partisan activity in the East was in support of Operation Bagration in the summer of 1944. Beginning on the night of 19/20 June the partisans struck against the German communication and supply lines in the rear of Army Group Center. Over a period of three days and nights the partisans set off 9,600 demolitions out of 14,000 attempts. The rail lines connecting Minsk-Orsha and Mogilev-Vitebsk were disrupted for several days. In addition to the rail lines, attacks were also made against German security posts as well.

One significant factor that hindered partisan operations in support of Bagration was the three German anti-partisan operations begun in April. Code-named Operations *Regenschauer*, *Fruehlingsfest* and *Kormoron* these operations were conducted in the area Polotsk, Vitebsk, Orsha, Borisov, Minsk and Molodechino, immediately behind the planned Russian attacking sectors. As a result, by the time of the Russian attack, the partisans and their supply bases and redoubts had been significantly disrupted; this was demonstrated by the haphazard level of activity by the partisans.   The Germans had compromised the Russian radio net and had learned of the dates of the partisan operations and this is why they were able to interrupt many of the 14,000 demolition attempts.

The support given Operation Bagration by the Partisan movement was the swan song of the movement. By the time the offensive halted in mid-August of 1944 the front line was no longer in Russia but deep inside Poland and on the border of East Prussia. The partisan units then either joined the Russian Army, faded away to their home regions, or in a few cases they took up arms against the Russian Army, especially in Ukraine.

The partisan movement in the East during World War II, despite a successful propaganda campaign, was more effective in some areas than others. It certainly hurt the German war effort, especially in the 1943/44 time period; every damaged or destroyed locomotive, freight car and bridge caused the delay of vital war material to the front or diverted crucial front line units to deal with them. As effective as the partisans became in 1944, some units having their own airstrips and armored vehicles, they were never the equal of Russian front-line units, nor were they expected to be. Their value lay in their potential; to strike at vulnerabilities in the German rear, to deny the enemy the relative security of rest and rehabilitation in the occupied areas. When confronted with a superior force, they were instructed to fade away to live and fight another day. An attempt to confront even third class German security divisions would most likely end in their destruction and put an end to their usefulness and value.

However limited its effectiveness in influencing German strategy in the east, the damage the partisans inflicted was on a more individual basis. In the Ukraine alone, from April 1943 to January 1944 partisans killed almost 60,000 German military and support personnel. The real effect of the partisans was to reduce the comfort level of the Germans and their supporters. It made them feel that no place was safe and no one could be trusted; it gnawed away at the peace of mind and personal security in all areas of the front, military and civil areas, adding to the stress and discomfort of serving in Russia.[250]

---

[250] Taking a cue from Russian partisan operations, Germany attempted to form its own 'partisan' units to be used behind the Russian front lines. Known as Operation *Zeppelin*, Himmler ordered Walter Schellenberg, chief of SD/Ausland of the RSHA to establish an organization to ferment unrest and sabotage behind the Russian front. The operation failed to meet its objectives because of the same problems the Abwehr had in its intelligence gathering operations: intensive Russian counterintelligence efforts to seal off the zone behind the front lines, native suspicion of all strangers, declining interest in serving German intelligence organizations and operational problems such as insufficient aircraft to parachute the agents behind Russian lines.

This lack of security, perceived or factual extended to all units in the German rear areas. Units rotating out of the front lines for rest and recuperation were subject to serve in anti-partisan duties as needed. The reluctance of the additional task of anti-partisan operations is aptly described below:

> "Many a division brought to the rear for rehabilitation and there, as a sideline so to speak, employed in anti-partisan operations, requested after a short time to be relieved of such duties and permitted to return to the front. This reaction alone should well support the contention that the front-behind-the-front is a theater of operations in its own right. No longer is it appropriate to treat this zone as a stepchild or to regard it merely as a zone of communications in the traditional sense."[251]

For most Russian civilians living in the German occupied portion of the country, the anti-partisan 'actions' came to resemble the anti-Jewish 'actions' of the *Einsatzkommando*, the results were frequently the same: roundup, interrogation, separation of suspected partisan supporters, who were then shot or hanged for all to see, the village was burned down, the transportable food was removed to leave the young and old (usually the most innocent) to starve. This response to the partisans was also sharply driven with the overall Nazi racial policies in effect for the eastern populace; the feeling went, either we kill them now as they are assisting our enemy or we wait till we are successful on the battlefield and we starve them to death anyway. With such a choice, what would anyone do? This is the key reason the Partisans fought so fiercely and bravely against the Germans; there was little alternative left to them.

The partisan participation and effectiveness in the war in the East is in stark contrast to those of the conquered nations the German occupation forces encountered in the west. At no time during the war did the Wehrmacht or Waffen SS require the maintenance of organized units to combat subversive military activity; certainly not of division size in any of the western occupied countries. The peace was maintained such as it was, by the Gestapo, French police units, French militia (in France) and local police units. (When the guerilla activities in France reached their stride, especially in 1943, such as the Free French of the Interior (FFI) they were

---

[251] *Historical Study, Rear Area Security In Russia, The Soviet Second Front Behind the German Lines*, Department of the Army Pamphlet No. 20-240, July 1951, Washington, D.C.

organized and managed not by their respective absent governments, mostly in London, but by a foreign power, the British.) This is not to devalue the supreme sacrifice made by thousands of French men and women, as well as Belgians and citizens of Holland and Norway during the occupation. The fate of these intrepid soldiers without uniforms history was to prove, more frequently than not, would end in tragedy, usually after the captive was subject to terrible hours and days of torture and interrogation. The partisans never forgot that one lost battle could be their very last. After 1942, Russian Army soldiers rarely faced encirclement; for the partisans, it defined their existence.

A German "Partisan" Movement?

One aspect of the Partisan movement, and behind the lines guerrilla movements in general, which has been seldom discussed was the possibility of a similar German effort behind Russian lines. The *Ostheer*, especially after 1943, was by now fully aware of the effectiveness of the Partisan movement behind their lines and the burden it was causing to combat them. Why not duplicate the effort behind the Don and the Volga? Why not indeed.

The most obvious answer is that all such successful and effective resistance movements are based on belief of their eventual liberation by friendly forces. This was plainly demonstrated in the first year of the war when the Partisan movement was ineffective and frequently inactive when German victory seemed at hand. It was not until after the Russian winter offensive of December 1941 that large swaths of formerly German occupied territory were reclaimed and, especially after 1942, the implied promise of friendly recovery became more certain.

By late 1942, especially after Stalingrad, with the *Ostheer* in the retreat in most of Army Group Center and Army Group South areas, it became obvious and unlikely that the possibility of a German reclamation of their recently lost gains would occur. As such, a liberation or partisan movement behind Russian lines would be doomed from the start.

Even in the halcyon days of German advances in 1941 and 1942, a program of a behind the lines sabotage and political warfare operation been considered, possibly directed and managed by the *Brandenburgers*, held potential. However, by 1943, with the requirements for conventional warfare taxing the Wehrmacht to the limit, an unconventional operation requiring air support for agent insertion, supply, command and control, specialized language and local knowledge training would have stretched the capabilities of the effort to make it a long odds chance of success at best. With the anticipation of a quick victory in Russia, German planning for Barbarossa never saw the need for the creation of such a program.

In summary, the question must be asked: Was the participation of the partisans and their activities behind the German front line in the East of benefit to the Russian Army? Unlike their sister organizations in the west, the answer is yes. The primary impact of the partisan movement was the diversion from combat of security units to seek them out, destroy them or at least render them impotent; during 1942 and 1943, these units were up to division size. This diversion materially affected the war at a key stage. Even during inactive phases it still affected the German military and political command by, at minimum, robbing them of peace of mind due the conquering occupier. In the active stages of their involvement in the war, they were an integral part of the Russian Army, especially in our focus of operations in the summer of 1944 against Army Group Center. The Russians utilized the partisans as a front of their own, uniquely positioned to inflict acute damage to the German war effort that Red Army via conventional means could not. The attacks against rail lines, bridges, supply stores and command centers was just as important as the advance of the Red Army's tanks, planes and riflemen.

So, why was the Russian partisan movement so successful, relative to those in the west? Geography certainly had much to do with it, the vast forests and swamps of central European Russia provided the cover and concealment essential to such movements. However, one can find such areas, albeit certainly not as large, in south-eastern France and southern Norway, so what made the Russian movement the most effective? It's effectiveness, such as it was, had to do with the nature of the war in the East. Stalin made it clear that the only defeated Russian soldier or citizen was a dead one. As long as one was alive, he or she was expected to attack the enemy whenever and wherever they were found, surrender was not an option. This injected a sense of terror and desperation into the movement, while harsh and cruel, was effective in generating the environment behind the German lines that made it so dangerous for the German occupier.

Part 3:

Overlord and Bagration
The Inter Front Connection

Russian T-34/85, Berlin 1945.

Chapter Eleven:
The Situation
June 1944

"I declare today, and I declare it without any reservation that the enemy in the East has been struck down and will never rise again. . . Behind our troops there already lies a territory twice the size of the German Reich when I came to power in 1933."

- Hitler, 3 October 1941

"HGM (Army Group Center) is responsible for the security of 137,000 square miles of country, an area slightly smaller than the US states of Texas and Pennsylvania, for which they are given 3 under strength security divisions, 2 second rate infantry divisions and an SS brigade."

- Report of HGM to OKH

This chapter will begin by describing the efforts of the Western Allies to assist their Eastern Russian ally with war material via what became known as the Lend-Lease program, it will also discuss the North Atlantic convoy lifeline that delivered the goods to Russia. However, the bulk of the chapter will examine the growing labor shortage for Germany in that fateful year 1944. With the two-front war now a reality for her, it will also examine how Germany, under increasing pressure, coped with the crisis. It also will describe what the affect the manpower shortage had on the Heer and domestic industries and the solutions she sought, especially the dependence of ever increasing amounts of foreign troops from her Axis allies. We will also examine Hitler's growing dissatisfaction with the performance of his field army and his increasing reliance on his Nazi forces, the Waffen SS and Volksstrum to stem the approaching Allied forces. Finally we will see the death throes of the German war effort in the use of the Hitler Youth organization and training and support units to form the final defense of the crumbling Third Reich.

East and West and The Second Front

The relationship between Russia and the Western Allies, principally the United States and Great Britain, was a flawed marriage from the start. Russia was an essential but difficult ally in the war to defeat Nazi Germany. These nations represented the two polar opposites of the world economic order; the centrally planned economy of Russian communism and the liberal independent capitalism of the Western democratic nations. If the Second World War demonstrated anything about opportunistic alliances it was this one, simply reduced to: the enemy of my enemy is my friend.

However different the two systems, however antagonistic they may be in times of peace all recognized the threat of German National Socialism to the future of European civilization, culture and economics. Roosevelt, Churchill and Stalin soon realized that they all had to lay aside their differences and defeat a powerful and aggressive Germany under Adolf Hitler.

With the powerful French army defeated and France occupied and the British Expeditionary Force pushed off the continent at Dunkirk in the Summer of 1940, there was only one enemy of Germany left, Soviet Russia. After the failure of the Luftwaffe to defeat the R.A.F. in the Battle of Britain, Hitler turned his attentions east and a year later attacked Russia, a nation with which he had recently concluded a non-aggression pact.

As that fateful summer of 1941 unfolded the world watched with trepidation as German panzers rolled within a few dozen miles of the Kremlin in Moscow, the Soviet capitol saved by a combination of weather and German exhaustion. With the Russian armies reeling Stalin, appealed to the West for immediate support for his war effort to push back the Nazi's and to defend the newest ally Soviet Russia. Churchill was the first to respond and with great risk and generosity assembled badly needed war material that would have gone to rebuilding a badly depleted post-Dunkirk British Army and sent them to Russia instead. Great Britain, with its major partner the United States, organized this effort, which came to be known as the Lend-Lease program, contributed significantly to the Russian war effort and in the early months of the war keeping alive the hopes of stopping Hitler.

Stalin, who had been almost alone in fighting the Germans initially requesting, then pleading, finally demanding a second front be launched by the Allies to relieve the German pressure on his armies. By late July 1944 the Western Allies were securely ashore in Northwest Europe and Finally Germany was confronted with the second front she had sought to avoid in all her military engagements.

The appearance of the Allies in Northwestern France now forced Germany to split her land armies in two directions, East and West. The one front 'honeymoon' for Hitler and his Wehrmacht was over and a new reality was about to impose itself onto his increasingly slim resources. The most important of these resources was the troop strength of his combat divisions, a task he was finding difficult to solve, for it is easier to build a tank then a man.

Manpower

It is an interesting juxtaposition of fact that as Germany's manpower situation reached troubling levels, its production of war material, especially aircraft, reached the highest levels of the war. In spite of night and day Allied bombing and the dispersal and concealment of their manufacturing facilities, now heavily manned with foreign labor, emergency German efforts enabled their arms industry to maximize output of items such as small weapons, armored fighting vehicles of all types, the aforementioned aircraft, and U-Boats. The 'down side' of this productive equation is that as Germany's major manufacturing giants, such as Krupp, Henschel, Daimler-Benz, BMW, Messerschmitt, Focke-Wulf, Rheinmetal, Dornier, Heinkel,

Mauser, MAN, Borsig and a plethora of others, were reaching new highs of production, the trained manpower to manufacture or operate their products and the fuel and lubricants to power then was in sharp decline. Despite these remarkable manufacturing achievements the final stage of Germany's war manufacturing phase began: The increasing reliance on foreign and slave labor to produce the weapons of war, because of the diversion of manpower to the military and the forced reorganization of the land forces into new divisional structures to make do with fewer troops.

In September 1944 there were 13,528,100 German men working in German industry, not including those in the Wehrmacht. Of this number, 6,905,000 were exempt from military draft because of their manufacturing occupation. In 1944 the largest occupational employer was manufacturing industries, utilizing some 32 per cent of all available labor. Undoubtedly the majority, if not all, of this manufacturing was employed in the war industries. However, no matter how severe Germany's labor situation was, the statistics for this same period shows that the largest draft deferral was to those who worked in government jobs, 4,324,200 or almost 32 per cent of all German men. In addition, incredible as it may seem to us now, in 1944, 143,600 men were deferred who worked in the tourism industry![252] This disparity of need and employment assignment indicates the complex and contradictory nature of German wartime management all during the Third Reich and the ability of workers to find a protective niche, no matter how small that would afford legal exemption from war service.

Organized Labor

As the western democracies did,[253] Germany created a home-grown labor organization in the early 1930's known as the *Reicharbeitdienst* (RAD) or National Labor Service headed by Konstantin Hierl. Immediately recognizable by their distinctively stylish caps, the *Tuchmütez*[254], and their cleaver-styled hewer (*Haumesser*) sidearm, this was a six month compulsory uniformed labor service for all males from 19 to 25.

---

[252] Although this author has no data to support these suspicions, the number employed in the tourism industry almost certainly catered to internal tourists, e.g. German tourists. The number of non-Germans touring the Third Reich during this period (September 1944) must have been small indeed.

[253] In the United States this organization was known as the Civilian Conservation Corps, or more popularly, by its initials, CCC. A similar organization, but with military training as its purpose, was the CMTC or Citizens Military Training Camps, operated for one month each summer by the U.S. federal government from 1921 to 1940.

[254] The German's called it the *Kaffeebohne-Mütze* or the coffee bean cap.

The RAD was put to work on a variety of public works projects. Among them was swamp reclamation, road grading and construction, deforestation and re-forestation and similar type projects. In the late 1930's the RAD was assisting other labor organizations in the construction of military defense works, the most notable was the *Westwall* along the western German border as well as the *Ostwall* along the German-Polish border.

With mobilization declared in August 1939, the RAD construction units were transferred whole into the Wehrmacht, specifically into the Heer or Army forming the *Bautruppen* or construction troops, however the RAD was kept in service providing training in construction and agricultural work in preparation for the military by providing national service through productive labor. As the war turned against Germany, especially in the East, a large number of RAD units there were pressed into combat during threatening moments and provided much needed manpower to these combat units as their numbers declined.

RAD units found themselves performing many para-military tasks including prisoner guarding, laying minefields, building and manning defensive positions, transferring supplies, repairing buildings and even as Luftwaffe *flakhelfer* in manning anti-aircraft guns at the front and in Germany. The RAD's final act was being formed into Germany's last army the *Volkssturm* battalions in 1945.

The search for manpower in the Reich was as thorough as one would expect in a totalitarian society. When 6 million workers were 'discovered' to be employed in the consumer industries, Goebbels attempted to shut these industries down to utilize the workers in the war effort. Small businesses and handicraft shops were closed and their workers transferred. It was also found that there were firms still manufacturing fountain pens, cosmetics, toys and cameras, and these employees too joined the ranks of the newly disenfranchised and found their way into the business of war production.[255]

One promise for Germany in the developing picture in the East was that the Germans were not the only ones finding it difficult obtaining the infantry manpower to fill out their units. The Soviets, now in the fourth

---

[255] Such was the lack of manpower that much of the bumper potato crop of 1941 had to be left in the ground as there were insufficient farm workers to harvest it, causing strains on an already dwindling food supply in the Reich. The potato is especially symbolic as it is the primary staple in the German diet.

year of war with Germany, were also finding it difficult to maintain their rifle divisions at authorized strength. They too began using older and younger age men that they would never have considered just a year ago. They were similarly under- trained and equipped and when the Germans discovered this, it gave them new encouragement that the Russian Army could be stopped, and stopped soon.

No matter how hopeful the desperate Germans were in discovering now that their enemy had manpower problem just like they did, the Red Army was nowhere near as desperate as the Germans were. In addition to having more resources to draw on, it began to equip the populations of the recovered and newly conquered countries to fight against the Germans.

At the same time U. S. production in all weapon areas; aircraft, tanks, artillery, small arms, vehicles and ships of all kinds was reaching its zenith undisturbed. The greatest advantage the Allies had was the United States. The United States truly became the Arsenal of Democracy and had numerous advantages over the other Allied nations. For example it was not being bombed day and night as were Germany and Japan. The U. S. also had the great advantage of an almost unlimited and intact resource base from which to draw both personnel and raw materials for the production effort. In addition, the U. S. still had the great advantage of the protection of two vast oceans on its eastern and western borders, a friendly member- of the-family neighbor to the north and a close but impoverished one to the south.

For Germany the picture was far less optimistic. Germany, Italy, Rumania and Finland, the chief participants of the Axis in Europe, mobilized a total of 32.6 million males of military age. Despite the generous sounding number, consider the following manpower levels of Germany's major enemies:

> Russia: 35+ million
> United Kingdom: 5.9 million
> USA: 16 million
> TOTAL: 56.9 million

Keep in mind the above are three of the largest of the Allied combatants. It does not include the balance of the British Empire forces as well as a dozen of other smaller, but just as vital, Allied nations manpower contributions. As can be seen, Russia alone mobilized more men then all the Axis European nations combined.

What Germany failed to realize when attacking Russia was the vast population residing within the U.S.S.R. Despite the language and cultural differences of the many nations that made up the nation when the atrocities committed by the occupying German forces were revealed these disparate peoples joined together into a cohesive body and forged a fighting army that no nation on Earth could resist.

Finally, German manpower losses by this time had become a major concern to OKW. In the month of June 1944 alone over 142,000 were lost on the eastern front for a total of 1,233,000 to date. This was a hemorrhaging the Wehrmacht could not sustain for long. Their manpower supply was not unlimited, as their Russian opponents seemed to be. This manpower shortage brought about unit organizational changes as well. One of the sought after benefits of the Kursk offensive in central Russian in July 1943 was not only the planned destruction of 15 Russian Armies in and around the salient, but also captured Russians would help add to the pool of potential volunteer (or slave) laborers for German industry.

The Divisional Shell Game

In late 1943, the Germans responded to this growing manpower shortage by restructuring their infantry divisions, from a strength of about 18,000 men in 1939 to 13,000 by 1944. This was accomplished by reducing each regiment from three to two battalions. Overall manpower was reduced by 27 percent and fighting infantry was reduced by 31 percent. At the same time, however, additional automatic weapons and heavy mortars increased divisional firepower by about 10 percent. In 1944 as the manpower situation continued to deteriorate, additional reductions in personnel strength were made resulting in several infantry division types; the *1945 division* with about 12,000 men, the *Luftwaffefelddivision* with approximately 10,000 men, mostly from deactivated bomber squadrons, and the last such organized division, the *Volksgrenadier division* with about 9,000 men. The numbers given above are all authorized or 'paper' strength, by the middle of 1943, rarely were any German infantry division at full strength.

However, the additional firepower gained by the infusion of more automatic weapons and larger mortars was somewhat of a chimera. The combat regiments were still formed by men; reduce the number of men from deaths, wounds, illness or desertion and all those new additional weapons are useless. The reorganization maintained unit presence in the field at the expense of unit depth. The smaller units, especially in the last months of the war, were unable to perform with the efficiency of the earlier unit organization due to the loss of the critical infantry units, despite the additional or promised weaponry. This caused a level of 'brittleness' in German combat strength and decreased their combat effectiveness. In the past, when a division was under severe pressure from enemy attack, the presence of multiple division components enabled the division commander to choose from several defensive options, with retreat a last resort. However, by 1944 the brittleness referred to above removed many of these tactical options (not to mention meddling from above) from the commanders 'tool bag' and frequently retreats or destruction became the only option.

Even with the new divisional force structure at 13,000 men, to some members of the armed forces this was no improvement in the divisions' fighting ability, for rarely were any Wehrmacht infantry divisions near authorized strength. In the aftermath of the Stalingrad disaster, *Generalfeldmarschall* Wolfram Freiherr von Richthofen, (fourth cousin of the famous Red Baron of World War I fame), mentioned to *Generalfeldmarschall* Erich von Manstein that "It was pointless having divisions of 12,000 or so men if only 600 do the actual fighting in the front line. He (Richthofen) had been impressed by the new Soviet command system, involving tight command, small rear area organizations and a strong (combat) front. We must finally go over to that type of thing ourselves." This was a clear reference that the highly specialized German army structure was now a luxury that it could no longer afford; not after the losses experienced in North Africa and in Russia. Shortly, the German command was to exercise just such a reduction in rear area troops, however not as a formal structural reorganization, but selective culling out of inflated or superfluous support units.

Within a year the Luftwaffe was forced to recognize this with the loss of its bomber fleets, and thousands of ground crew and supply troops who now had nothing to do were used to form Luftwaffe ground combat units, several division-sized units in fact. Sadly, rather than making these men available to the army, Goering insisted in keeping them under his control and formed his own Luftwaffe combat divisions. Without the experienced command and control the army could have provided they suffered higher than normal casualties under their inexperienced Luftwaffe commanders. Another example of Nazi waste and bureaucratic infighting.

As there were now fewer fighting men per division, during heavy fighting, when the combat units were exhausted and losses mounted; the command cadre, technical and specialist units were pressed into the line to fill the gap. The use of these highly trained and valuable men caused additional decline of the divisions' fighting ability; these were the support elements that the infantry relied on to provide critical assistance in the form of artillery, flak (anti-aircraft artillery) command, control, supply, engineering, communications and logistical support that made the German fighting division the envy of the military world. As any military commander knows, retreat is a last choice, and an orderly retreat in the face of an engaged enemy is a most difficult maneuver to execute even in the best of circumstances. In the last months of the war, Germany rarely was in anything like good circumstances.

In September 1941, just three months after the start of the campaign in Russia, Germany welcomed into its ranks what they came to call the *Osttruppen*. These were captured Russian soldiers and civilians that volunteered to work for the Wehrmacht, initially in service capacities such as hauling supplies, building roads and bridges and other general building and maintenance tasks; these were known as *Hilfswillige* or the more popular abbreviated form, *Hiwis*. However, a month before, unknown to Hitler, the Wehrmacht began to organize these people into actual combat units, initially in Army Group North and later in Army Group Center, primarily for use in guarding German facilities such as railroad depots, marshaling yards and bridges and on anti-partisan duties. These *Osttruppen* proved their value time and again and even were used, in certain instances, as unit reinforcements. In all, by 1943 some 250,000 were in use in all capacities in the east. Many continued to volunteer their services to the Germans to the very end of the war, in May of 1945.

However, the *Osttruppen* were not to stay in the East for long. An incident on 17 August 1943 where a security battalion armed with German provided weapons revolted and seized a railway station and handed it to the Partisans. It was this incident that Himmler used to charge the army with inappropriate use of the *Osttruppen* without OKW authorization. With the growing speed of the Russian advance in the East, Hitler was concerned that uprisings like this were about to become widespread and had plans drawn up to transfer the Osttruppen West to the Atlantic coast to man the defenses there. His feeling was in this far from home location, there would be no Russian or Partisan units to surrender to. As many as 800,000 men were involved in the transfer, weather this entire number ever made it to France and the Netherlands is debatable, but the Allies claimed 30,000 were captured on and after the D-Day invasion.

Finally the difficulty of raising of new recruits for the Wehrmacht is demonstrated by Hitler's Directive Number 51 in November 1943. The aim of this Directive was to raise an additional 1 million fighting men from all portions of the population and support units of the armed services themselves.

"...The plan reduced the service elements in the table of organization of divisions by 25 per cent and abolished some independent service and headquarters organizations. The goal was to save 560,000 men: 120,000 from 150 divisions, 20,000 from panzer and panzer grenadier divisions, 120,000 from service units, 260,000 through substituting Russian "volunteers" for German troops in service units, 20,000 from headquarters, and an additional 20,000 from miscellaneous sources. Special control commissions were organized to visit units to ensure that the cuts were made."

"Under the order, many men previously considered unfit for duty were reclassified as fit for limited service. These limited-service men replaced combat-fit men in service, communications, and headquarters units. Those with stomach disorders were formed into battalions and even into a combat division that received special food-stationed in Denmark, where dairy products were readily available. Deaf men were formed into "ear battalions" and assigned to defensive positions. In addition to transferring men from the rear echelon, Navy and Air Force men were sent to the army. The result was a great increase in available men to build new divisions. Fortunately, most of them remained in the Replacement Army until after July 1944, and few new divisions were created before June 1944."

"To supplement German manpower, the army recruited an additional 300,000 *hiwis* and men previously exempt because of doubtful loyalty to Germany..."

"The number of *hiwis* increased steadily. The new type of division of late 1943 increased the authorized strength of *hiwis* from 700 to 2,005, although not all divisions had full allotments. The Germans also initiated aggressive recruiting among Soviets in the prisoner of war camps, and by June 1944, 200 Ost battalions had been formed. Given the option of dying of starvation and ill treatment, many Soviet prisoners volunteered, especially members of dissident minorities. The Ost battalions were not used in Russia; they were sent to Italy and France in exchange for German battalions sent to reinforce divisions in Russia, two Ost battalions for one German.   Sending the Ost battalions to Italy and France also made desertion difficult. Specific instructions were given regarding the use of these troops; they were to be employed only when supported by German units, even though that plan prevented the release of larger numbers of German battalions. Discipline was to be maintained by the severest methods."[256]

One of the most feared methods of maintaining fighting strength which was used by both Germany and Russia was the use of penal units and other like convicts. However, for Germany this took the form of soldiers, including officers, who were arrested for the slightest sign of wavering faith in the national leadership, such as making unguarded anti-Nazi or anti-Hitler comments. These men were sent to the front, especially to infantry line units, the ostensible intention was to expose these men to almost certain death. One can imagine the effect on the morale of the *Landsers* in these units, desperately attempting to stay alive and save their nation from the encroaching communist- Bolshevist hoard. If serving in the infantry was tantamount to 'almost certain death' what did that hold for him and his comrades? Turning infantry combat units into penal punishment detachments is self-destructive.

Another seldom recognized aspect of this divisional reorganization was Hitler's preference of creating new divisions rather than resting and restoring existing divisions. The advantages in unit restoration are numerous; the existing command structure is maintained, regional identity adds to unit morale and cohesiveness, an existing training cadre for new unit members, and the existing infrastructure of an established organization is enhanced

[256] *Heroes or Traitors*, by Walter S. Dunn, Copyright © Praeger, 2003, p. 56 - 57. Reproduced by permission of ABC-CLIO, LLc.

(clerks, quartermaster staff, medical, transport, commissary, etc.). When a new unit is created the entire 'back office' has to be created as well. In the newer divisions this was not always possible, with the fighting component getting short shrift in necessary support. But with Hitler's preference in seeing as many divisional pins on his map boards as possible, this wasn't about to change.

Another, more difficult problem with all this movement of men from branch to branch and unit to unit is that it caused a lot of resentment and lower morale. The German army creation and reinforcement system was based on a regional *Wehrkreis* or *Gau* organization, thus the men in a certain *Heer* unit, for example, all came from the same villages, town, city or region. They were friends, perhaps even relatives or at least their regional proximity speeded the formation and trust of the fighting unit, and was a great source of strength, reassurance and cohesion during combat.

With the breaking up of the regional identity of the combat units, the faith and confidence of having to depend on strangers or even former enemies absorbed into the unit began the decline at the very time Germany needed its best fighting efforts. During the final year of combat there was little time for these groups of strangers to form the essential relationships of trust and reliance on one another, and as they went forward into combat, tended to trust no one.

The Eastern Allies

The combat personnel losses to date brought about significant changes in troop disposition in the east for the Germans. The Wehrmacht was forced to rely more and more on their weaker and more ethnically diverse eastern allies, most notably Rumania, Hungary, Slovakia and Italy to contribute combat units. In addition to the Eastern Allies, the Germans reached far afield to embrace anyone and any nation sympathetic to the cause of National Socialism and the anti-Communist crusade. For example there is photographic evidence of Field Marshal Rommel greeting Indian volunteer troops on the French coast, part of the Atlantic Wall fortification troops. There were 123,000 *Osttruppen* in France at this time, and even Cossacks defended Omaha beach. There even were volunteers from Thailand and reports of a thousand Tibetan bodies in German uniform were found in the ruins of Berlin.[257] Far afield indeed! Is it difficult to fathom Nazism having

---

[257] *Origins of the Swastika*, http://www.crystalinks.com/hitler.html.

this much appeal in this many cultures. Part of the appeal may have been racial indeed, and part was probably, in the early years of the war, to simply be on the winning side.

In May and June 1944 approximately 15% to 20% of the men in German units in France were not born in Germany, in fact, there were soldiers from 28 different nations in these units.[258]   The languages, diet, religious practices and clothing requirements of these foreigners all added to the complexity of commanding, organizing and supplying this disparate group into an efficient fighting machine to repel the strongest armies in the world, it was an impossible challenge and as one would expect, the results were poor.

In June of 1941 the German army was entirely German and prided itself on its 'pure' racial make-up.   However, with the bottomless needs of manpower generated by the campaign in Russia, Germany not only reached farther and farther afield in search of sources of new manpower, they were also to relax the standards that constituted 'pure' Germans. One example of this was the recruitment of the so-called "racial Germans", or *Volksdeutsch*.[259]   The recognition of these one-time Germans now living outside of Germany, some as far away as the Volga river valley and Finland, aptly demonstrates the creeping desperation of Germany and her war with Russia. The extension of a ten-year conditional German citizenship made these people eligible to be drafted into the Wehrmacht.   However, these recruits were forbidden to rise above the rank of private first class, a questionable 'privilege and honor' to be sure.

Not only had the racial makeup of the German army changed but the method of obtaining her soldiers had changed as well. By the end of 1943 some 75% to 80% of all the men in the east were conscripts. The men that had made up the professional armies that went to war in 1941 were all volunteers, in spite of national conscription. These new men were mostly older, perhaps married with families, and even had they been the young, single soldiers of two years earlier; they were all becoming alarmed by

---

[258] The nationalities of these "volunteers" were as follows: French, Italians, Croatians, Hungarians, Romanians, Poles, Finns, Estonians, Letts, Lithuanians, North Africans, Russians, Ukrainians, Ruthenians, Kazaks, North-Caucasians, Georgians, Azerbaijani, Armenians, Turkomans, Volga-Tartars, Volga-Finns, Kalmucks, Crimean-Tartars, Indians and even Thais.

[259] The *Volksdeutsch* differ from the *Reichsdeutsch*, those Germans living in the Germany proper.

the news from home especially about the Allied day and night bombing campaign. The Allied bombing offensive was to have severe effects on German morale on all the fronts, but especially in the east as that is where the bulk of the Wehrmacht was and would be until the end of the war.[260]

In December 1943 there were 173 German divisions in the east; of these, 10 panzer and 50 infantry divisions were *abgekaempft* or exhausted, unfit for further fighting. Eleven of the divisions were really *kampfgruppen*, greatly reduced combined versions of their former selves. These *kampfgruppen* were usually battalion or regiment-sized units, remnants of former divisions combined together to form the strength of full divisions. At this same time there were 12 full divisions in Italy and 46 divisions in OB West, and another 7 that were forming in the Reich homeland. The number of divisions in the east needing replacement and reconstitution was greater than the total number of divisions in the two western theaters combined![261]

At the beginning of the campaign in Russia, Germany's two eastern allies were Finland, manning their long border with Russia from Leningrad to the Rybachiy Peninsula on the Arctic Ocean in the north; and Rumania, on their border from near Chernovsty on the Polish border down to the Black Sea in the south. The Finns were clearly the most reliable Axis co-belligerent (as opposed to Axis ally) and performed well all along their frontier against the Soviets; however when they had reclaimed all the territory lost during the Winter War of 1939-1940 with Russia, they halted and were of no further assistance to the Germans further south, leaving the vital city of Leningrad largely unthreatened from the north. No matter how much the Germans pleaded and cajoled them to continue their advance south to Leningrad, they refused. To them it was clearly a war of reclaiming lost land (known in Finland as The Continuation War) at an opportune time; however it cost this small nation of 4,000,000 (1939) 86,400 casualties to do it.

On the opposite end of the front, the Rumanians with the largest of the satellite forces, attacked along with the Germans with their Third and Fourth Armies, largely infantry affairs, with a small-mechanized brigade and the remainder of their mobile troops' mounted cavalry.

---

[260] *Under the Bombs*, p. 151.

[261] *Cross Channel Attack*, by Gordon A. Harrison, Office of the Chief of Military History, United States Army, Washington, D.C. 1951, p. 143.

However, there was less than perfect harmony between the armed services of Rumania and Germany. In an attempt to better utilize the modest resources of the Rumanian navy and air force in December 1941 Germany instituted an inter service training program to maximize the benefits of combining the resources of both nations in the Army Group South command area; especially in the western Black Sea region to combat the superior Russian Black Sea Fleet. The animosity was such that the Rumanian units that had been through the German training program quickly re-converted to doing things their own way, thereby wasting the time and effort expended by their German allies, not a favorable omen for future cooperation.

All told, the Rumanians provided 31 divisions in the war in the east and suffered 350,000[262] casualties against the Russians and a further 170,000 against the Germans and Hungarians when the Rumanian government switched sides in August 1944. It is to Rumania's dubious credit that they were Germany's longest-serving ally in the east in the war, outlasting all the others.

Hungary was another Axis partner in the war in the east that contributed significant numbers of troops to fighting the Russians, all together 800,000 men joined the Hungarian armed forces during the war and 147,000 became casualties, a significant percentage considering a pre-war population of 8,000,000 (1937).

Italy was another large contributor of manpower to assist the Germans in Russia during the war, initially sending three divisions totaling 60,000 men. An additional 227,000 were sent in March 1942 for the second German summer offensive, by wars' end 45,000 were prisoners and 48,900 were killed. The German relationship with Italy was long one, especially between Hitler and Mussolini, as he had been a 'role model' for Hitler in the early years of the Nazi party; but as the war continued the closeness the two men enjoyed during the prewar period deteriorated greatly. Mussolini, without consultation with the other Axis partners went off on his own and launched attacks against Albania and Greece that the Italian army could not win and as partner of the Axis, Germany felt obligated to come to her rescue and thereby became involved. In the last two years of the war Italy became dependent on Germany, especially for oil and advanced weapons.

---

[262] Such was the optimism in the opening months of the war, especially after the occupation of Odessa; the Rumanians began demobilizing their forces in October 1941.

By late 1942 Italy had realized that joining the war with Germany had been a big mistake and by 1943 she was a liability.

That Hitler failed to see this growing Italian dependency and reliability on Germany is unusual for a man that prided himself in being a good observer of personalities and strategy. In the waning days of the Axis involvement in North Africa, Hitler almost tepidly asked the Italians to do more in protecting the sea lanes across the Mediterranean ensuring that supplies for his *Panzer Army Afrika* arrived unscathed. Given Italian performance in the field in the last year in Africa, it is startling that Hitler would entrust the care and supply of his prized and most popular army with such a shaky ally.

Germany's use of its Axis allies was reaching significant numbers by the end of 1942. At the time of the Russian counterattack at Stalingrad, the Axis allies made up 28.5 per cent of total strength in the East. This increasing reliance on non-German forces was adding to the weakening position of the Third Reich. Germany's Axis allies were only as good as the German performance in the field. With the exception of Hungary who kept 11 divisions in the field with Germany until nearly the end of the war, despite political conflicts at home, the others dropped out, as did Spain, recalling its 'Blue' division home in December 1943, or switched sides when the Red Army arrived on their borders.

However, unlike the harmony with which the western Allies cooperated with each other, such was not the case with Germany's allies. For example the Rumanians and Hungarians had to be kept separated or they would resume age-old disputes to the determent of Axis goals and objectives in Russia.

The use of Germany's eastern allies and those volunteers from the western nations fighting in Russia became the litmus test of loyalty to the Germans and also changed the nature of the involvement in the East. By early 1944 the German command was to use a new standard of loyalty for their eastern Axis allies. German propaganda now presented the war in Russia to the world as a 'European Crusade' against the "red menace" from the east. In its early stages, when the battle lines were still in Russia proper or even in eastern Poland, this line of propaganda failed to carry much weight; but with the inability of the Wehrmacht to halt the westward movement of the Russian Army, the message of a united crusade against Bolshevism reached a new pitch; even hysteria would not be inaccurate.

The ulterior motives of Germany's allies were not altogether altruistic in sending their young men to fight in Russia. They were seeking to enlarge their eastern borders at Russian expense, or to assist in eliminating a potentially aggressive neighbor. The example of Finland and eastern Poland in 1939 was not lost on them. Any combatant nation utilizing a collation organization in warfare must always be alert to the common interests of the relationship. Allies are not the same as friends. When those interests diverge or are strained combat reliability is put at risk.

Such was Germany's strained manpower needs that her reliance on her foreign allies was turning a blind eye to their actual combat potential. This was to prove fatal in November of 1942 when the Russian Army opened its Operation Uranus, the winter offensive against Stalingrad. The Soviets carefully selected their points of attack, all of them occupied by Germany's Axis allies.

Overall, Germany's allies fought well in the early part of the campaign, usually under German direction, and sometimes, command. However the industrial capacity of these counties was limited and as such unable to properly supply their troops with the required equipment, especially heavy equipment such as tanks, artillery and motor vehicles. As the war went on, the Germans were forced to provide these armaments to their allies. These weapons usually came from captured French, Russian and Polish stocks. As the German manpower situation became acute, OKW and agreements with their governments used these units to guard long stretches of front, frequently unsupported by German units. Their lack of proper equipment, leadership and low morale were amply demonstrated in November 1942 when the Soviets began their Operation Uranus the offensive against the German 6th Army at Stalingrad. In the opening days of the battle whole Axis divisions, especially Rumanian divisions, were destroyed so quickly they seemed to disappear, or surrendered or fled west ahead of the speeding Soviet double envelopment, opening large holes in the Axis line.[263]

The issue of combat reliability of Germany's foreign allies has been and will be commented upon in this narrative again, and the issue deserves

---

[263] After a three hour tirade from Hitler to Antonescue on 10 January 1943 about the Rumanian failure at Stalingrad, Antonescue hastened to remind der Fuhrer that eighteen Rumanian divisions were destroyed on the Don and Volga Rivers, numbering some 200,000 men, and the fact that four Rumanian Generals were killed, meeting their deaths in hand to hand combat; something to consider when evaluating Rumanian combat performance in Russia.

additional scrutiny here again as well. The increasing German reliance on these allies should have been a loud warning bell in any OKH planning document. The abilities of these armies, their political and command declarations notwithstanding, were limited. Even with German liaison officers to ensure proper communication with Wehrmacht units providing planning, advice and guidance, their desire to fight the Allies was far lower than that of the German *landser*. Like Finland, Romania and Hungary, whose border regions the Russians had seized in 1940, once these lands had been regained, their zeal and ardor cooled and so also their ability to withstand Russian pressure: especially deep inside Russia, far from their home countries their resistance became an issue to with which almost all regional German commanders had to be concerned. This is not to say that these foreign allies were of lower quality across the board. There are many examples of small combat units of these armies fighting with great élan and reliability in difficult circumstances. However, these fine fighting examples were the exception, as in the Spanish 'Blue' Division, and not the rule and the Russian command was more than eager to search out where in the German front line the non-German Axis allies were located, and make their plans accordingly.

Although announced as the united effort of Europe to crush Godless Communism, the inclusion of the eastern Axis allies introduced an element of liability into the German eastern force structure, one on which the OKH became more and more dependent as the war ground on. Perhaps it was a case of self-deception, whereas a division pin on a command map at supreme headquarters is a division pin, even if the color is different denoting a foreign or non-German unit. The German political command saw this unit as its German equivalent and tended to use and place them accordingly. It was not until the disaster at Stalingrad that this fallacy was exposed, and by then the Soviets were pouring through the German front line.

In defense of the non-German Axis Allies, these nations were not the equivalent of German or French or British troops. They were Europe's 'third world' countries, recently emerged from an agricultural and monarchial past, and were in the beginning throes of industrialization. Their armies were largely infantry and artillery, not much changed from World War I. Their baggage, like that of the German, was hauled by horse, and their mechanization was limited to small tank brigades with obsolete vehicles, at most division-sized units. These armies had very little motorization and their infantry, when transported; either marched or was moved by rail.

The most significant aspect of these armies and their reliability was in their command organization. The officers in these armies were usually members of a privileged class or group that had ties to either royalty or hereditary families that reached back into these nations' distant pasts. They had been commanders or admirals in their nation's armed forces. However well connected they might be, they tended to treat their enlisted ranks with the distain of a stratified society that one would expect. Examples of officers abandoning their men in moments of crisis, consuming scarce rations rather than insuring their men were fed, and securing safe billets far behind the front did little to bond these leaders with their soldiers.

The Waffen SS

Another method Germany used to fill out its combat units was that used by the *Waffen SS*. This private army headed by *Reichsfuhrer-SS* Himmler was to be the Praetorian Guard of Germany, selecting, recruiting and training only the most fit, intelligent and racially pure members of the German nation. Originally formed into regiment-sized units, these units quickly proved themselves in the early battles in Poland and France, and were enlarged into divisions; however commanded tactically when attached to and directed by the *Heer* (Army) in the field. Originally, Himmler only had approval from the *Wehrmacht* to recruit 100,000 so-called "police reinforcements" in the event of war.

The first four SS Divisions, and later a few others, were also called the "classic" divisions as they were largely formed before the war and contained 'pure' Germans. They were, using their full nomenclature: 1st SS Panzer Division *Leibstandart Schutzstaffel Adolf Hitler* (Armed Bodyguard), 2nd SS Panzer Division *Das Reich* (The Empire), 3rd SS Panzer Division *Totenkopf* (Deaths head), the 4th SS *Polizei* Panzer Grenadier Division and the 12th SS Panzer Division *Hitler Jugend* (Hitler Youth).

As the need for additional field units increased the Western nations were tapped for volunteers to fight global communism. To the above list is added seven more divisions of what has become known as "the Western Legions", the 5th SS Panzer Division *Wiking* (Viking), 6th SS Mountain Division *Nord* (North), 9th SS Panzer Division *Hohenstaufen*, 10th SS Panzer Division *Frundsberg*, 11th SS Volunteer Panzer Grenadier Division *Nordland* (Northland), 27th SS Volunteer Grenadier Division *Langemarck* and the 28th SS Volunteer Grenadier Division *Wallonien*. These SS divisions were the first to formed from non-Germans. However, Himmler saw the nations providing the manpower for these division as close members of German racial stock and therefore acceptable for service.

Beginning roughly in mid 1943, the now desperate need for additional combat formations grew, especially in the East, and led to the SS to further loosen their racial and ethnic standards; they recruited men from central and Eastern Europe. By and large these divisions fought acceptably well; however if involved in severe combat and if enough casualties were inflicted, they tended to rapidly lose their combat effectiveness. Examples of the "eastern" divisions are the 14th *Waffen Grenadier Division von der SS Ukrainian No. 1*, 15th *Waffen Grenadier Division von der SS Latvian No. 1* and the 20th *Waffen Grenadier Division von der SS Estonian No. 1*. One clearly distinguishable characteristic of these divisions were their infantry composition, no panzer divisions coming from this "eastern" group.

It is, however, the higher numbered and last formed divisions of the *Waffen SS* from which it derives its most sinister reputation. For example, take the 29th SS Division, formerly the *Kaminski Brigade* made up of Soviet citizens that fought partisans behind the lines of Army Group Center. This division committed so many atrocities in Warsaw that the commander, Kaminski, was executed and the remaining members were sent to form the still organizing "Vlazov's Russian Liberation Army" and the most notorious SS unit, 36th *Waffen Grenadier Division Dirlewanger*. This division was originally manned with convicted poachers and expanded its manpower strength through the induction of criminals, military convicts and local police units. Its notorority was attained while fighting the Polish Home Army in Warsaw in October 1944; noted for committing numerous atrocities and for the remainder of the war used in behind the lines security work fighting partisans and quashing uprisings in occupied cities in the East. Its final operation was on the Oder River front in April 1945 against the Russians, where it disintegrated, the survivors moving with the front south of Berlin were it was trapped in the "Halbe Pocket". A handful of men and the division commander reached American lines to surrender in early May 1945.

The rise of the *Waffen SS* had a significant negative effect on the Wehrmacht's ability to recruit and retain quality manpower. With the Germanic romantic military cachet the SS had established early on, it accepted only the best and the brightest in Germany and they joined the

SS only after extensive tests and family research indicated no traces of 'questionable' ancestry, which meant Jewish blood. As the SS was Hitler's 'favored son', it has been suggested that the Waffen SS's abilities were frequently derived from their ability to make first claim to equipment and in quantity.

The preference in arms, equipment, transport and action usually went to the SS, with the Wehrmacht often taking what was left. This two-tier army usually left the Wehrmacht serving as the poor stepsister in any requests, needs and support when in competition with the SS. This had serious affects in combat effectiveness, unit morale and maintaining unit strength. The only redeeming aspect of this relationship was that when in combat, the Waffen SS units were still commanded by the Army.[264]

One of the largest Russian ethnic peoples to assist the Germans was the Cossacks. These nomadic peoples were excellent horsemen, were encountered during Operation Blue, the German summer offensive in June 1942. As Army Group South approached the mouths of the Don and Volga rivers, these people greeted the advancing Wehrmacht with open arms, and offered to fight against the Russian Army, requesting in return, German recognition of Cossack independence after the war was over. Initially joining the *Heer*, the *Waffen SS* assumed command and control of the Cossack cavalry, and the *XVth SS Cossack Cavalry Korps* was created in the autumn of 1943. Additional Cossack units were formed. Initially two brigades and later smaller units were added to the rolls. In all, about 250,000 of these hardy horsemen fought alongside the German's in the East.[265]

The Germans used the Cossacks primarily for anti-partisan duties behind the front in Army Group Center, and from time to time, they were used to fill in holes in the front line as the fighting situation required. Later,

---

[264] The numbers of foreign volunteers to the Waffen SS is truly astonishing and represents almost every nation and ethnic group across Europe: Walloons (15,000), Flemings (23,000), Danes (11,300), Norwegians (6,000), Dutch (50,000), French (8,000), Italians (20,000), Spaniards (1,000), Cossacks (50,000), Byelorussians (12,000), Ukrainians (26,000), Latvians (39,000), Estonians (20,000), Croatians (20,000), Serbians (15,000), Albanians (3,000), Romanians (5,000), Finns (1,000), Bulgarians (1,000), Eastern Turks (8,000), Czechoslovakians (45,000), Poles (5,000), England (10) and also from such distant regions as Japan (2), Sumatra (2), Southwest Africa (3), China (3), Brazil (4), Palestine (2), India (1) and Australia (1). From *Forgotten Legions, Obscure Combat Formations of the Waffen SS* by Antonio J. Munoz, Paladin Press, 1991, p. 369.

[265] *Russian Volunteers in the German Wehrmacht in WWII*, Lt. Gen. Wladyslaw Anders and Antonio Munoz, **http://www.feldgrau.com**, 2002.

they were sent to Yugoslavia, again for anti-partisan duties and even as far as France to fight the Allies, although in violation of the condition of Cossack leadership that they were to fight the Soviets only.[266]

The Squandered 'Russian' Army

One opportunity to improve the manpower situation on the Eastern Front that fortunately went nowhere was the fate of the Russian Army of Liberation, also known by the Russian abbreviations ROA and RONA.[267] The Wehrmacht, eying the vast numbers of Russian POW's and front crossing volunteers wasting away in the open prison corrals, decided to ascertain the level of anti-Communist sentiment in these captured soldiers, and was surprised to find a high number that had very strong feelings against their national government; and furthermore they also indicated they were willing to fight against their former comrades in the Red Army. The Germans had a natural leader for these men in the form of ex-Soviet-now-German ally General Andrey Vlasov, former commander of the 37th and 20th Soviet Armies and later deputy commander of the Volkhov Front south of Leningrad. Captured in June of 1942 he became disenchanted with Communism and offered to form an army to fight the Soviets.

The story of what could have been a natural and effective fighting force became bogged down in political and ideological clashes and for more than three years. The fate of the ROA/RONA lingered in administrative indifference. The force was finally permitted to form three divisions, the 1st, 2nd and 3rd RONA Divisions in November 1944. However the Germans would only allow remnants of burned-out SS Divisions of Russian soldiers

---

[266] Ibid.

[267] ROA *Russkaia Osvoboditelnaia Armiia* or Russian Liberation Army. This was Lt. General Andrey Andreyevich Vlasov's army; his collection of units may have contained as many as 750,000 men. There was also RONA *Russkaya Osvoboditelnaya Narodnaya Armiya*, or Russian Liberation Peoples' Army. This was the savage and infamous anti-partisan unit led by Bronislav Kaminski, which numbered some 15,000 men. Formed in late 1943 of mostly Ukrainian criminals and officially known as the *Waffen Grenadier Division der SS Russisch Nr. 1*, it never reached division-size strength; the unit was formed from a brigade and most likely it stayed at that strength. It performed security duties (mostly anti-partisan actions) behind Army Group Center. They committed such widespread atrocities that other SS commanders demanded their withdrawal! Kaminski was shot by the SS in late 1944, under somewhat disputed circumstances. Kaminski's flair for killing was such that in one day, 5 August 1944 during the uprising of the Polish Home Army, his men killed 10,000 Polish civilians. With Kaminski gone, the unit was broken-up, half sent to the Vlasov Army and the other to the 30th *Waffen Grenadier Division der SS 'Russische Nr. 2'*.

and the most notorious SS formation of all: the infamous Kaminski SS Division to join. It was really not a military formation; but they joined the divisions of ROA and RONA. The 2nd and 3rd RONA Divisions completed the formation; the 3rd in Austria in 1945, never reaching more than 2,700 men. Due to command difficulties the "Russian" units finally reached the front line in April 1945. They were assigned to attack the Russian bridgehead on the Oder River at Frankfurt-on-Oder and failed with heavy losses. At the end of the war, a number were captured by the Russians, and those that surrendered to the U. S. and British forces were turned over to the Russians. These traitors to the Soviet Union were harshly treated by the Soviets, a large number being shot outright soon after their transfer.

Germany, her hands tied by her twisted ideological outlook, missed opportunity after opportunity to alleviate her manpower shortage, especially in the East. In the opening days of the Russian campaign, the advancing units were greeted as liberators by the Belarus and Ukrainians, and especially by the peoples of the Baltic States. Tanks and trucks bearing a black cross were pushing away the godless red-star Communists; relief and joy! Gifts of bread and salt were offered as the traditional Russian presents to the newcomers. The Germans could have organized and equipped scores of divisions from these people and captured Russian Army prisoners, and with a friendly populace in the rear areas, could have alleviated much of the anti-partisan and security duties. But, these same enthusiastic, friendly people, who could have been most helpful to the Germans achieving their aims in Russia, were foolishly sidelined, ignored, separated, starved, brutally interrogated, hanged and shot with ruthless, sadistic, efficient Germanic enthusiasm.

The Germans in Russia seemed to go out of their way to make the local populations hate them. Master race or no master race, the pacification of conquered peoples by fair and humane treatment has been shown throughout history to be the best route by a conquering army to maintain a tranquil occupation. With all the intelligence and ingenuity the German people are known for, why was this matter such a blind area for them? Could it all be chalked up to Nazi racial theories; did the Germans really 'buy' the Aryan superiority theories of the SS and Party organs? Was there, under all the civilization and *kulture* a Teutonic animal, lurking, with a terrific "inferiority complex" waiting for the opportunity to 'get even' with what they perceived as the perpetrator of their oppression? Did they not realize what the expense and effort would be to maintain a large security force inside Russia to suppress a restless and abused populace? Did they not realize how much more productive a carrot would be rather than a stick? With such shortsightedness for an otherwise organized and efficient nation, this inability to recognize an effective and inexpensive method for managing a captured populace is simply astounding.

The average Soviet Russian citizen wanted only a few things in life: breakup of the collective farms, religious tolerance, education, enough to eat and the promise of a better future. The issue of the collective farms was a flashpoint since their institution approximately ten years earlier. The parceling out of the land to the Russian farmer, allowing him to keep all he produced would, given the profit motive, surely have generated sufficient production to not only feed himself but to provide a surplus that could have been used to support the German army in Russia and the surplus shipped back to Germany or elsewhere in Europe.

The typical Russian, especially the peasant, is very religious; icons appear in almost every Russian farm and home, and the churches are not only well attended, but well supported.[268] Allowing them to worship as they pleased would have cost the German occupation administration little, but the barring of importation of foreign priests and closure of their only seminary caused unnecessary friction.

One founding member of the Axis I have so far omitted mention of is Japan. Throughout the war Japan rarely, if ever, consulted with Germany on the overall war strategy. The Japanese Imperial Empire never reciprocated with Germany or Italy in any technical exchange, usually being the recipient of a large number of technical information and weapons deliveries from Germany, frequently at great risk to Germany's surface merchant marine and later in the war, her U-Boat fleet. Although it would have been of little advantage to Japan, her active participation in Barbarossa could have made the difference between success and failure for Germany, especially in the first year of the campaign. However, with a self interest much like Finland, she pursued her own military-economic agenda without any notification or warning of impending action. If Italy ultimately

---

268 When it ruled Russia, the Communist Party would have had just as difficult time displacing the Eastern Orthodox Christianity of its people with atheistic Communism as did Germany's SS attempting to install a new Nazi religion. Russian Marshall Mikhail Tukhachevsky once said that "Vladimir the Holy wasted his time when he brought Christianity to Russia. Our people have a tremendous primitive energy-they should have been allowed to keep it!"

became a liability to Germany, Japan likewise went her own way with all the appearances of never being a member of the Axis at all. All during the war, Hitler attempted to extract whatever positive affects her actions might hold for Germany on the other side of the continent, to no avail.

Germany seems to have a bad habit of entering into alliances in wartime without ascertaining their allies' military, social and economic abilities. Perhaps it is the fact that nations led by dictators make poor choices, as their first priority is political similarities; all else appears to be secondary. I have been confounded by the military alliances made by Germany in both world wars, and all have been less than beneficial to her. With such political blindness, perhaps one cannot see the difference between economic and military capabilities. One just has to count the frequency with which the words 'zeal' and 'ardor' appear in speeches and orders from Hitler and Mussolini, especially in the latter part of the war. These are idealistic, philosophic mutterings of a desperate leadership. Perhaps with an open political system, with an open, democratic discourse, a more prudent war management would have been pursued. A clearer understanding of what the assets these nations brought to Germany could have been examined, and incorporated into Germany's military planning.

One might say that due to German racial, social and political strictures they handicapped themselves in the prosecution of the war. The self proclaimed 'purity' of their calling was unable to garner the needed support from the rest of Europe in cleansing the continent of what Germany identified as "sub-human" elements. Their obstinate, stubborn belief in racial theories prevented them from utilizing the benefits of co-opting native populations into the German war effort, especially in the opening weeks of the attack into the Soviet Union.

Instead of the German racial blindness that was becoming a recruiting tool of the Partisans, a more practical and altruistic outlook might have starved the manpower for the Partisans and, turning the issue around, formed a formidable fighting force allied with or part of the German army. This is another example of the racial blindness that was to destroy Germanys *weltanschauung* and its army.

Desperate Measures: Leuthen and the Volkssturm

As the Allies approached the borders of the Reich in late 1944, and the military situation for Germany reached desperate levels, as a result the OKW put into effect the *Leuthen* Project. This plan to increase the manpower strength of front line units, was to work as follows: At the broadcast of a coded signal, men in training units, or specifically the Replacement Army, would be immediately transferred to line combat units or sent as a unit to the front. With Germany almost completely surrounded by her enemies, the plan was sound enough; the problem with the plan was that it was instituted too late. If it had been put into action sooner, say, in September 1944, there would have been regular line units in sufficiently combat capable condition to welcome these new replacement units and give them the guidance, direction and support they so sorely needed. As it actually happened, these units, when they were available, were sent to almost certain death or capture. They were frequently ordered straight into full-blown combat to fill holes in the line in a crisis. They were found to be badly equipped, poorly led, and almost unsupplied. They were quickly annihilated by the Allies, especially the Russians.

It was in August 1944 that a turning point in the way the Germans were to find additional manpower arrived. With the severe mauling of Army Group Center in Russia the month before, the western Allies beginning their rush toward the Rhine River on Germany's western border, and with the loss of faith in the Wehrmacht to defend The Reich against her enemies, the idea of civil militias took hold.

Hitler had long since lost trust in his "Prussian Generals", and the attempt on his life by these same men in July 1944 confirmed his belief in their lack of faith and their determination to replacing him, at any cost, even assassination. The long string of defeats, especially in the East, the constant retreats, frequently against his express orders, now all came to culmination in the formation of an army he himself would create and control: the Volkssturm.

The issue of militias had never been popular with Hitler, as he blamed them for the loss of national morale in 1918, and the collapse of German fighting will that same year. He was also now afraid that an armed force outside his or the Nazi party's control could be turned against him. But, a Nazi managed and led militia would be an excellent defense against a general uprising of the Wehrmacht against him and the party.

All OKW resistance to a militia was abandoned with the disastrous events in Russia that summer as a result the Soviet's Operation Bagration. There was no possibility of Germany making good the loss of 350,000 men (of which 150,000 were captured) and the rebuilding of the 25 to

30 mauled divisions, of which 17 were completely destroyed. In addition to the catastrophic loss of men and materiel was the presence of the Russian Army at Warsaw, an almost 200 mile advance in five weeks.

What the Nazi party thought it could instill in the fighting units was a sense of ardor, fanaticism, excitement and determination that Hitler, Bormann and Himmler were convinced was missing from *Wehrmacht* leadership, especially in the East. With the party in control of this new civilian militia it would provide the fiber and backbone it felt was missing from the armed forces.

Volkssturm

The final attempt to create a force to stop the advance of the Allies was the formation of the *Volkssturm*. This order covered all men not currently in the armed forces or in critical industries, and reached from the lowest to the very highest age levels, from 16 to 60, the average age of the first levy was 52. This 'army' was not the creation of the *Wehrmacht*; this army was organized, commanded and equipped by the Nazi party. The *Gauleiters* were responsible for raising and equipping the units in their districts. Only when committed to combat would these units come under the command of the Army. These units were almost useless in the intense combat of the Eastern Front in the closing days of the war, and many of them readily surrendered at the earliest opportunity, especially on the Western front. Seldom were there weapons available to them; heavy equipment was almost unheard of; and their uniforms covered the spectrum from the latest Wehrmacht issue to First World War, Reichswehr and captured British battle dress or none at all was the rule, a sad commentary in a nation that honored the uniform above almost everything. The iconic and most useful weapons issued to the *Volkssturm* was the *panzerfaust*, but their most common light weapon were captured rifles and pistols, coming from training schools and obsolete stocks. These men, some dressed in business suits, shirt and tie, dress shoes, overcoat and fedora wore just an armband that read *Deutscher Volkssturm Wehrmacht*,'in the service of the German armed forces'. Ironically, the same date the *Volkssturm* was taking its oath of service in Berlin, 12 November, the first Allied home army, the British Home Guard, held its farewell parade and disbanded.

Born on 25 September 1944, this new army in Germany, its fourth[269] since the 1920's, was given the inspiring name of *Volkssturm*, roughly

<hr />

[269] The Nazi party's SA, the Wehrmacht, The Waffen SS, and the Volkssturm.

translated into English as Peoples Storm or as it was colloquially known at
the time 'the People's Army'. In time its name became synonymous with
any desperate, last ditch, poorly equipped citizens' armed force. Germany,
along with its archenemy, the Soviet Union had become the showplace of
new army creation.[270]

Once again the *Wehrmacht* had to contend with another diversion of its
rightful, potential source of replacements for its badly decimated fighting
divisions; that of the German civilian population. Not only was this
new army in competition with the supply of human raw material for the
Wehrmacht; it was also given the task of providing arms and ammunition
for this new army.

No matter how enthusiastic the Nazi party was with the creation of
its new army, it would never reach its desired combat potential. It was
short of all the essential elements an army requires to perform its duty. For
example, the following description for the search for equipment:

> "...the NSDAP launched valiant efforts to provide each
> *Volksstrum* man with some type of uniform. Officials procured
> surplus garments from the *Wehrmacht*, police, *Reichsbahn*,
> border guards, *Reichpost*, SA, NSKK, RAD, SS, HJ, DAF, and
> any other conceivable source-even zookeepers and streetcar
> conductors! Captured foreign or obsolete German uniforms were
> also utilized... "*Volkssturm* men disliked brown Party uniforms
> because they feared anyone wearing them would be taken for
> a Soviet and shot by Germans or taken for a Nazi and shot by
> the Soviets... To raise both clothing and a sense of community
> the Party launched a national "People's Sacrifice" (*Volksopfer*)
> collection drive in January 1945... to encourage donations from
> the families of men killed in action. However the results of the
> collection were encouraging, *Gau* Bayreuth netted over 38,000
> complete uniforms... Success was reduced by repair, cleaning and
> distribution problems, and the *Volksopfer* ultimately fell short of
> *Volkssturm* clothing needs. Despite numerous improvisations,
> many *Volkssturm* men served in civilian attire, in some instances
> even without armbands, pay books, or identification tags... Many
> *Volkssturm* units lacked full field kitchens and had to resort to
> scavenging cookware and utensils from bomb-damaged buildings

---

[270] The Russian's called them 'the stew', as they were a mixture of young green recruits
and old tough meat.

or procuring military or civilian supplies that could not be evacuated... Overall the *Volkssturm* experienced shortages of virtually every necessity because of the strained war economy, transportation problems, and inadequate preparation."[271]

With such an army we see the final gasp of German military effort; the *Volkssturm* was going to stave off the Allied advance in the West and the Russian Army from the East. However, the Wehrmacht was actually able to make use of this new force, which, in a long and in a roundabout way, answered its needs for new infusions of manpower to rebuild its depleted infantry formations.

The NSDAP was never able to properly equip and train this new army, but when it found itself in the front lines, as it soon did in the east, it was seriously lacking in all manner of military items; training, weapons, supply, administration and transport. In short, it was an armed mob, which was quickly destroyed, routed or pushed aside when confronted with Russian Army units.

In contrast to fighting the enemy alone, when coupled with regular *Wehrmacht* units, the *Volkssturm* performed better. In the waning days of the Third Reich, the *Heer* still had the best, in most cases, the only supply, training and administrative capacity to properly lead and fight an army, including the *Volkssturm*. There are numerous examples of *Volkssturm* units, under *Wehrmacht* command and control, performing as well as front line infantry units. Although never intended to play the lead in the front line, the *Volkssturm* was, in a practical matter, used to administer areas behind the front line They were used in such roles as escorting refuges, removing economically valuable goods, police auxiliaries, rounding up downed enemy aviators, tracking infiltrators and spies, and fighting partisans.

In some of the final battles in the East, especially for Berlin and other cities on the Oder River, the *Volkssturm* made up approximately half of the city's defense forces. However, no matter how much zeal, dedication and, eventually fear, the *Volkssturm* was never able to provide the desired performance for its Nazi leaders nor could or would it ever. An example could readily be found in the Berlin defense mentioned above. One *Volkssturm* commander reported that his defense zone unit had fifteen different rifle and ten different machine gun types to equip his men.

[271] *Hitler's Volkssturm, The Nazi Militia and the Fall of Germany, 1944 - 1945,* by David K. Yelton, University Press of Kansas, 2002, p. 112.

Although many *Volkssturm* units fought relatively well, the age of the men and lack of all manner of military necessities soon manifested itself. Its casualty rates were very high compared to the Heer, in some cases as high as 70 to 80 per cent. When they weren't properly led and directed, many *Volkssturm* units fled in disorder. When the *Volkssturm* units found themselves near their own homes, shops and villages they frequently abandoned their positions to look after their personal interests.

Part of the problem the organizers of the *Volkssturm* were facing was in the nature of raising the units. The plan was to recruit these units in, and to fight for, their home regions. This local effort was intended to give the poorly equipped units a stake in their own and their family's survival, and to give the *Volkssturm* a reason to fight harder. One problem that was encountered was that some areas that needed to be defended were made up of what is known as 'Germanized' peoples, especially border area Poles and ethnic Germans resettled from evacuated areas. They had very little intention of dying for an area they could little identify with or a nation that was clearly on the verge of destruction.

Desperation

In the seemingly never-ending search for manpower, whether it be workers or soldiers, one interesting if desperate solution to the problem was decided early on, that of "growing" the needed manpower as quickly as possible. As mentioned in an earlier chapter during the 1930's the German government undertook a program of awarding mother's medals for having large families in three medal classes (gold: eight or more children; silver: six or seven, and bronze: four children). Based on the number of children, it was a form of Olympic motherhood. In addition to medals, there were a number of support and assistance programs provided by various arms of the government to aid these "model" families, provided they met the stiff standards of acceptable family hood to receive the medals in the first place.[272] On registration of the new arrival a gift of 100 marks was issued. In addition to the attempt to generate larger numbers of children by government inducement, there were various plans to create them without families, via the *Lebensborn* program. The government was so adamant about increasing the number of births it penalized those without children

---

[272] Known officially as the *Ehrenzeichen der Deutschen Mutter* or Cross of Honor of the German Mother. In some circles it was called "the rabbit cross".

via taxation. The childless couples received invoices from the government taxing their lack of children, which went to support the child subsidies, an interesting slant on total social control if there ever was.

The separate *Leuthen* Project and the *Volkssturm* efforts highlight, for the last time, the lack of an effective central defense coordinating body in Germany during World War II. The fact that these two armed forces were organized, called up, and sent into combat separately clearly and tragically illustrates the failure of the dictatorship that ruled Germany from 1933 to 1945. True, these two armies contained mostly old men and young boys armed with rifles, pistols, light machine guns, captured weapons and single-shot rocket propelled anti-tank weapons (*Panzerfaust* and *Panzerschrek*)[273] which would have been of marginal use in any army, the fact that the German government saw them as the last hope also illustrates that extreme desperation of their military position. What has been overlooked in the multifaceted approach to the defense of the Reich is that had there been a coordinating body to manage the desperate defense of the nation, especially in the east, these two armies might have been combined, pooling what assets each had, magnifying their strengths and given sufficient time to equip, train, and organize and prepare defenses, could have proved of some value to the *Wehrmacht* and *Waffen SS* forces in the field.

The real failing was that in calling up of what was the most marginal of usable manpower that remained in the nation; Germany was eating its seed corn. The elderly men were most probably taken from positions in the factories and farms that they had been filling for the last two years when the manpower problem first became severe. The loss of this knowledgeable and skilled mass of men also represented the last of the males of most families. These were the grandfathers that were left to hold the families together; with their removal, the look of acute desperation was on everyone's face.

The other end of the age spectrum was the young men and boys, some even too young to qualify for the Hitler Youth, ages 14 to 18. What experience, knowledge and skill possessed by the old men of these armies, was 'replaced' by strength, ardor and the single minded determination of

[273] These two weapons, especially the *Panzerfaust* was to be the forerunner of a long line of single shot unguided rocket propelled anti-tank weapons in all modern armies giving the infantryman something of equal status fighting against tanks. The affect of the *Panzerfaust* and the *Panzerschrek* were to account for 22.8% of all tank losses in the Russian *2nd Guards Tank Army*, part of Zhukov's *1st Byelorussian Front* during the fighting for Berlin in April/May 1945 (From **http://orbat.com/site/sturmvogel/sovtankl.html**).

youth. As was demonstrated by the *12th SS Panzer Division Hitlerjugend* in the fighting in Normandy in the previous summer, the fanaticism of youth is an awesome force to witness. The British forces opposite the *12th SS* frequently had to destroy every last one of the young German fighters as they were told not to surrender and they followed this order to the tragic end. Their devotion to the *Fuehrer* was clearly shown by these youngsters, what they lacked in experience they made up for in zeal.

When weapons were issued to the *Volkssturm* the weapon most available that would do something useful was the *Panzerfaust*. This rocket propelled anti-tank weapon, if properly used could destroy the heaviest Russian tank. However it took much nerve and stamina to wait until the tank closed to firing range to make a sure kill. As this weapon was a one-shot affair, the life span of an unaccompanied panzerfaust armed solder was usually a short one. Such was the sacrifice these hapless units were frequently called upon to make. It was the German version of the Japanese *banzai* suicide attack.

A history of the *Volkssturm* complied by A. M. Quesada adds the following information on the organization and effectiveness of the concept of the use of a civilian armed force:

> "The mission of the *Volksturm* was to surround and contain large sea borne and airborne landings; to eliminate agents and small sabotage groups; to guard bridges, streets and key buildings; to reinforce depleted Army units; to plug gaps in the front after enemy breakthroughs and to man quiet sectors; to crush feared uprisings by the estimated 10 million prisoner-of-war and foreign workers in Germany."

> "The fighting ability of these *Volksstrum* units was practically nil. Lack of adequate weapons, ammunition and time for proper training, with units receiving only a few days and with some only a few hours instruction had its effect on morale. The desertion rate was high, both to the Allies and with many of the members drifting home when the opportunity presented itself. Fanatics did exist within the ranks and these tended to be members of the Hitler Youth. Enthusiasm for the *Volkssturm* was almost non-existent even among the *Volkssturm* themselves and especially from the regular troops and the civilian population. Opinion was that if the professional German Army could not stop the Allied advance into Germany what hope did the civilian *Volkssturm* have.

There was no remuneration for service in the *Volksstrum*, except when a member was taking part in actual combat. This together with the lack of a uniform caused a great deal of disgruntlement throughout the militia. Many of its members felt that they were assuming the duties but with none of the privileges."

"Hitler deceived himself into believing that a huge civilian army, led by militarily inexperienced Nazi officials could have staved off Germany's defeat. The *Volkssturm's* ultimate failure, however, should not blind us to the bravery of many of its members who, though unfit, untrained and under equipped, fought not to preserve the Nazi state but to save fellow Germans from a Russian Army eager to exact vengeance for the brutal German occupation of the Soviet Union. It should be stated that due to fierce bravery, many *Volkssturmer* earned aircraft and tank destruction awards, War Merit Crosses, wound badges, the 1st and 2nd Class Iron Crosses, and the highest decoration of the all: The Knights Cross."[274]

Defense of the Reich

In addition to these desperate searches for manpower, the weapons the Germans used were also being converted for last ditch use. One example is the so-called "Buzz Bomb", the winged guided bomb, the Fieseler Fi-103 known to the Germans as the A-1, also as the V-1 (*Vergeltungswaffe Eins*, Revenge Weapon One). This weapon, which had wreaked such havoc over southern England, Belgium and the Netherlands was now being modified to a piloted version to be known as the Fi-103 *Reichenberg IV*. Although a unit had been designated to command the aircraft, the 5/KG 200 and 103 missiles had been converted to the piloted configuration, the unit was suppressed in October 1944 and no operations took place.[275]

Other aircraft were designed or considered for modification for these desperate attempts to defend the Fatherland, such as the Bachem Ba-349 *Natter*, a rocket powered site interceptor in which the pilot, after being launched from a vertical rail flew his stubby winged glider and fired his

---

[274] *History of the German W.W. II Volkssturm, Der Deutscher Volkssturm: Organization and Military History of the German People's Militia*, Compiled by A.M. de Quesada, August 2000, http://www.adeq.net/volkshist.htm.

[275] In another example of the promised amenities offered by the Nazi party disappearing due to the needs of the war, the KdF cars Fallersleben plant (now known as the Volkswagen) began producing V-1's.

cluster of 24 73mm rockets at Allied bombers. He would then bail out and parachute to earth. The now empty machine would deploy its own parachute. On the first trials of the machine, it killed the test pilot and no further use of the aircraft was made.

Perhaps the most famous of these 'desperation' aircraft was the tiny liquid fueled rocket powered Messerschmitt ME-163B *Komet*. This former glider flying wing was converted into a powered interceptor by the installation of a rocket motor in the rear fuselage, which after takeoff, powered the machine almost vertically at the astonishing maximum climb rate of 37,000 feet per minute and attained speeds of 620 mph, the fastest operational aircraft of the war. Several units were formed and went into combat with promising results as the machine was almost impossible to see in flight, and equally difficult to shoot down. Armed with two 30mm MK 108 cannon firing exploding shells, it required only one or two of these shells to destroy an American B-17 or B-24 bomber. The major liability of the design was the fuels used to generate the rocket thrust: hydrogen peroxide and hydrazine hydrate. These very volatile liquids when mixed caused the contained explosion that developed the rocket thrust. The problem with the arrangement was that these fuels were very corrosive and if they were to come into contact, as they occasionally did in the bottom of the fuselage due to leaks from piping connections, they violently exploded, usually destroying the aircraft and killing the pilot. So corrosive were these liquids that the pilot had to wear a special rubberized suit when piloting the *Komet*. However, there was never a shortage of volunteers for these units. Their operational life ended when the Allies over-ran their bases or the units ran out of their exotic fuels.

Gotterdammerung

In the last days of the Reich, especially in the cities in the East, a *Wehrmacht* report noted that the mood of the citizens had become so bleak that many were exhibiting signs of depression and many openly debated the best method of committing suicide. One young *Luftwaffehelfn* (Luftwaffe woman auxiliary) working at the thousands of anti-aircraft gun sites asked her company commander to shoot her. After long and tortured hesitation, he acceded to her request and directly afterward killed himself. In February 1945 a "suicide epidemic" began, especially as the Soviets began to approach the capital. Several thousand each month took their own lives and that of their families. In May the number was over 700.

In October 1944 the first German towns were occupied by the Russian Army. One of the first was Nemmersdorf. Here Russian soldiers committed a number of atrocities against the civilian inhabitants, some very ghastly. Goebbels was not slow to capitalize on this event to demonstrate what lay in store for the rest of Germany should the Russian Army advance further into the Reich. Germany was about to reap the whirlwind. Inflammatory writings by Russian Ilia Ehrenberg which urged the most dreadful revenge against the Germans and their allies contributed to the mass hysteria.[276]

German women were not the only victims of Russian soldiers' lust: A Russian newspaper reporter stated:

> "Two hundred fifty of our (Russian) girls were working at the Focke-Wulf plant (near Warsaw). German's had brought them from Voroshilovgrad, Kharkov and Kiev. And according to a man from the army newspaper said, these girls have no clothes, are lice-infested and are swollen from hunger. They had been clean and well dressed, until our soldiers came and robbed them blind and took their watches. Liberated Soviet girls often complained about being raped by our soldiers. One girl said to me, crying: 'He was an old man, older than my father.'"

It is illustrative to include the following example of the rage and aggressive behavior demanded by the Russian Army commanders of their soldiers. When crossing the border into Germany for the first time, a Red Army officer stopped his small convoy of trucks and ordered all his men out, indicating they were now in Germany and to urinate on the ground.

The excesses committed by the Russian Army now that it was on enemy soil were also noticed by the Russian Army high command. General Chuikov, commanding the 8th Guards Army in February 1944 admitted that his men were no longer being fed; they were living off the land and eating better than they ever had. The excesses also led to unfortunate results to their own side. The Red Army soldier's propensity to get drunk

---

[276] Zhukov not only contributed to the prevailing state of mind, but lent it a semblance of legitimacy in one of his Orders of the Day in which he stated: "Death to the Germans! We'll take revenge for all those burned to death in the Devil's furnaces, poisoned in the gas chambers, shot and martyred. We'll take cruel revenge for them all. Woe betide the land of murderers, Hitler's cannibals; this time we will destroy the German breed once and for all." This was followed soon after by Stalin's Order Number 5 which read, in part "The German people is to be destroyed. All German factories and property are to be laid waste. The German animal must be battered to death in its hovels."

at almost any opportunity was the cause of death of one of their finest tank commanders, Hero of the Soviet Union Colonel Gorelov. While attempting to sort out a traffic jam he was killed by drunken Russian Army soldiers. The issue of drunkenness increased measurably when the Red Army entered Germany. The stress of combat and the harshness of life in the Red Army itself was undoubtedly a contributor to drunkenness; however there are numerous anecdotal stories of Russian soldiers drinking anything they found, including several men who died horrible deaths after opening 55 gallon drums and drinking the contents: industrial solvent.

In another example, a Russian officer entered a German wine cellar, found several corpses of his men drowned among the smashed wine barrels and the one meter deep wine flowing out of them. The men had shot up the large wine barrels, and drowned in the resulting flood.

The issue of drunkenness was not restricted to the Russian soldier's behavior in battle. The nature of life in the Soviet Union fostered a determination to sooth the harsh reality in alcohol. Recruits arriving at the collection points deep inside Russia often arrived drunk or hung over, and this state of affairs was tolerated by the military and political authorities, as it made the terrified soldiers less stressed and simplified managing them.

The End

Soon after the end of the war in May 1945, a group of Hitler Youth that was captured in Munich was given a detailed tour of a place up until then which was only spoken of in whispers: Dachau. After seeing the railway cars filled with corpses, the survivors and the crematoriums, the boys' world collapsed. One boy said of the experience: "that night was a sleepless one. The impact of what we had seen was too great to be immediately digested. I could not help but cry."

The war being over, the members of the Hitler Youth were back to being regular civilians. It was a hard adjustment for many to go from high ranking officers in the Hitler Youth to schoolboys. When Alfons Heck heard that his school might reopen soon he thought that "the idea of going back to school seemed preposterous. What could we learn after this?" While the adult leaders of the Hitler Youth were on trial in Nuremberg, some Hitler Youth members were on trial as well. Heck was captured in the French sector and was tried for prolonging the war. He was sentenced to 2 years restriction in his hometown, 6 months expulsion from a college (it was not open anyway), and a month of hard labor. One job that he was required to do was to exhume the mass grave of French prisoners. He and other Nazis were required to be de-Nazified. The French showed them films from the death camps. Heck and many others could not believe that the films were real, which enraged the French. It took Heck 30 years to accept a sense of guilt for the Holocaust.

Germany's manpower problems were of her own making. The battles of Moscow, Stalingrad, Tunisia, Kursk, the destruction of Army Group Center and many others, all exceed Germany's ability to replace these losses. This level of combat 'wastage' was far beyond what the German armed forces were prepared to cope with in terms of obtaining replacements, training and re-equipping them.

> "During the post-war years, Alfons Heck realized that he was an especially tainted citizen of the most despised nation on the face of the Earth. I developed a harsh resentment toward our elders, especially our educators, they had delivered us, their children, into the cruel power of a new God. That god had nearly destroyed an entire generation of German children"[277]

---

[277] *The Backbone of the Der Deutscher Volkssturm: The Hitler Youth in WWII*, Compiled by A. M. de Quesada, **http://www.adeq.net/HJ.htm**.

Russian JS-2 (IS)-2. Russia's answer to the German "Tiger".

Chapter Twelve:
Planning

"How should one treat them, Comrade Captain?
Just think of it. They are well off, well fed,
and had livestock, vegetable gardens and apple trees.
And they invade us. They went as far as my oblast
of Voronezh. For this, Comrade Captain,
we should strangle them."[278]

- A sapper (combat engineer) in the Russian 3rd Shock Army
Belorussia, June 1944

This chapter will look at how the two combatants prepared for the third summer campaign season in Russia, the summer of 1944. It will look first at what the German high command anticipated the Russians would do and the preparations they made to defend their positions. It will examine the defensive preparations and the dwindling number of Germany's weapons and how and why they were placed and where. Finally we will look at Russian preparations and their vast accumulation of arms and manpower. It will also look at the growing sophistication of Russian battlefield intelligence and camouflage preparations for the giant battle about to commence.

[278] *Dresden, Tuesday, February 13, 1945*, p. 411.

German Planning

The fourth summer of the German war in the East marks a significant turning point for them. For the first summer since the invasion in 1941 there were no plans to initiate an offensive against their Russian foes. As the size and scope of Germany's summer offensives grew smaller each summer, the summer of 1944 marks a true turning point for the Ostheer; no offensive was planned. Although a clear recognition of how the fortunes of war had changed, psychologically it was a major milestone in the German military condition.

The errors, mistakes and missed opportunities had all taken their toll on the German Army and now that the war in Russia was no longer the sole claimant on her finite military resources, Germany was now faced with a grand guessing game regarding her foes intentions. The might of Russian military production was reaching its zenith and coupled with the steady stream of Allied Lend-Lease material, it was obvious to all in Berlin and Zossen the year of controlling the battlefield and the course of the campaign was over. Germany would now be forced into playing the losers game of delay, disrupt and confuse its enemy and to attempt to pry the Allied coalition apart and hope for its collapse. As events would shortly show, the Allied collation was stronger than Hitler thought, the intentions and its motives purer and its mission and purpose more noble.

German *nachrichten* or intelligence and *gegenspionage* counterespionage organizations, particularly *Fremde Heere Ost* in addition to losing its edge at this stage of the war had also been badly compromised by infiltrations of Russian intelligence agents that adversely influenced German command decisions and judgment. Postwar assessments of German agent success behind Russian lines indicate as many as 90% had been captured, killed or imprisoned. Part of the German intelligence problem was systemic and organizational. As German intelligence gathering was divided into two components, one operated by the *Reichssicherheitshauptamt* or Reich Security Main Office abbreviated RSHA and the Army's *Abwehr* or military intelligence. The fact that these organizations were at loggerheads with each other severely limited their operational effectiveness. Adding to these difficulties was the general state of Russian domestic and civic paranoia instilled by the state security organs which made planting foreign or even 'turned' Russian POW agents vulnerable to detection. It was this lack of quality high level military intelligence that, in part, caused the surprise of the discovery of the T-34, KV-1 tanks and Katyusha rocket artillery in the opening months of the invasion.

The Summer of Disaster

Because of the realities of geography, most of the operational movement in the East took place in the area of the German's Army Group Center and Army Group South, primarily due to the vast expanses of the Russian steppe region. This area of the western Soviet Union is more open, less crossed by rivers and more level than the forested and marsh covered north. Furthermore, this area contained most of the Soviet Union's industrial and agricultural productive capacity. This region favored mechanized movement and allowed greater mobility of the opposing forces and this is where the Germans expected it.

By June 1944 a line had been reached that extended from Narva on the Gulf of Finland in the north, south to Ostrov, curved to the east of Vitebsk, south again to the east of Mogilev, southwest to Rogachev and almost due west for 175 miles into Poland just north of Kovel where the line veered south again to the east of Tarnopol and into Rumania, a linear front of some 1,400 miles

Prior to June of 1944 OKW had the relative luxury of transferring combat units from front to front or sector to sector in reaction to actual or perceived dangers. However, with the build-up of undeniable evidence that this summer would be the year of the cross-channel attack from England, a steady transfer of combat units, especially mechanized divisions began from the East to the Western Front. By the end of June seven of the valuable panzer divisions were sent to France as well as additional units held in Germany for quick transfer to either front, which because of Allied air interdiction of road and rail denied both fronts their use.

To demonstrate the threat of Allied invasion of Western Europe on German unit disposition, in July 1943 approximately 80 percent of German mechanized strength was located in the East; however, by June 1944 little more than half was on the Russian Front. The Western Front, in preparation for the invasion had been given priority of reinforcement since November of 1943.

By the summer of 1944 Army Group Center was able to call on 46 combat divisions, however only three of them mechanized. Included in this total were seven security divisions, which depended largely on foot for transport, had no heavy weapons and were half the strength of an ordinary infantry division. In addition, these units were not in the front line but behind it, in some cases many miles behind it fighting the partisans and securing the rail lines, bridges and supply points for the Army Group. There were scant Army Group reserves to counter any breakthrough. The positioning of the German line units could be called an 'egg shell' defense; a tough but thin front line; once an enemy broke through, there was nothing behind it except geographical features to deter the attacker. Army Group Center in Russia was rapidly becoming the equivalent of the *bodenstandige* divisions along the Channel coast in France, stripped of its most useful and potent divisions, which were sent to other sectors perceived as more threatened, primarily Army Group North Ukraine, to the South of Army Group Center.

In June 1944 there were a total of 4,740 panzers and assault guns in the East, of which Army Group Center had 553, just 11 percent.[279] Of these 553 vehicles, 480 were assault guns assigned to the infantry divisions, making the assault guns 87 percent of all mechanized strength prior to the Soviet attack, Operation Bagration. Keep in mind that this disparity of panzer to assault guns (*sturmgeschutz*, StuG III, IV) was caused by the German expectation of the Soviet attack coming in the south, against Army Groups North Ukraine and South Ukraine. Army Group Center was expected to be a secondary attack area and was expected to fight a defensive battle, hence the large number of assault guns, with only a few units having the excellent panzerjager (tank destroyer) *Hornisse* and 29 of the powerful PzKw VI Tigers, the largest battle tank in the German inventory.

The emphasis on the number of *sturmgeschutz* compared to *panzers* is an important one. The turret-less *sturmgeschutz* is primarily a defensive vehicle, assigned to likely avenues of enemy approach and located in ambush positions. The early vehicles were originally fitted with low velocity howitzers and were intended for infantry support against enemy strong points when no *panzers* were available. Later, as the war turned against

[279] For specific German armored fighting vehicle production, see Chamberlin and Doyle, *Encyclopedia of German Tanks of World War Two*, Revised Edition, 1993. Kliment and Francev, *Czechoslovak Armored Fighting Vehicles, 1918 - 1948*, Shiffer, 1997.

Germany the *sturmgeschutz* found themselves engaging enemy tanks and a more powerful main gun was needed. By early 1943 the main gun of the *sturmgeschutz* was the same type and size of weapon that the turreted *panzers* had but mounted in a fixed, forward firing position with limited left and right traverse. While adequate for defensive fighting, in a fast moving, 360 degree battle, the ability to fire the main gun in all directions is crucial.

German Strategic Uncertainty

In May as the lull of the Spring rasputitsy ended and the roads and trails dried and vehicular movement became possible again, OKH, aware of Russian activity behind the front, began assembling a tactical reserve of panzers, artillery and sturmgeschutz in its LVI Panzer Korps on Army Group Centers' right flank to counter any Russian action. German Field Marshal Model, saw an opportunity to strike first, using his *schild und schwert* (shield and sword) theory of active defense and offered to attack the Russians in an offensive solution, forestalling any Russian action. Over the next few weeks the intelligence picture changed; new information on Russian forces were detected causing second thoughts on German unit deployment, as well as OKH political and personal intrigue (some German generals were afraid of another *Zitadelle* disaster) in Berlin and the force, assigned first to Army Group Center, where it started, was finally assigned to Army Group North Ukraine where the Germans anticipated the main Russian attack to come. The Russian *maskirovka* (masking or deception) activity was working.

The situation in the 36 infantry divisions in Army Group Center is of more concern. None were at authorized strength, around 16,000 men, most were around half strength and most of these units now included a large number of non-ethnic or *Volksdeutsch* Germans mostly from eastern Europe; in some replacement battalions as many as a third were from outside Germany. As noted elsewhere, the inclusion of these foreign soldiers into what was otherwise very homogenous German units reduced the combat effectiveness of the units. The loss of the regional identity of the divisions affected the 'bonding' that is vital in combat units. As OKH drafted more and more 'marginal' Germans, who had less enthusiasm for defending and dying for Hitler and a German homeland most had never seen, their fighting performance declined, just as the manpower quality of the Soviet units was reaching its zenith.[280]

Even though the German command was certain the Russian attacks were to be directed against Army Group North Ukraine, defensive activity continued all along the front in Army Group Center. The materials and manpower once directed for construction of the Atlantic wall were now available for use in building defensive positions in the East.

With the looming Russian offensive expected to occur at any time haste to overcome the neglect of fortifying and reinforcing the eastern armies resulted in a plethora of handsomely named but minimally constructed defense positions: The *Rollbahn* Line, The *Panther* Line, The *Wotan* Line, The *Tiger* Line, The *Oder* Line, The *Gouverment-General* Line, The *Bear* Line, The *Prince Eugene* Switch Line, The *Trajan* Position and the *Pomeranian* Line. Unlike the Atlantic Wall and the West Wall, few of these positions contained concrete and steel defenses, most were constructed of earth, logs and sand bags. With the serious lack of infantry to man them they would do little to stop, or even delay, the Russian advance.

The major rivers in the region, the Dneper, Berezina and Drut were surveyed and developed into defense lines and the forward cities and towns were declared *festung* locations. The defense lines included such lavish, by Eastern Front standards, features as steel turreted machine gun and cannon positions, extensive anti-tank ditches were dug, mine fields laid and miles of barbed wire strung, as well as mortar positions and log and earth bunkers. Also, the first of the larger *Panzerfaust* anti-tank rocket weapons were delivered. Finally, a series of five trench lines were excavated, a mile apart creating a five mile deep defensive zone.

---

[280] The June 1944 distribution of panzer and panzergrenadier divisions in the east are as follows:

Army Group North: 12th Panzer Div., 11th SS Panzergrenadier Div.

Army Group Center: 20th Panzer Div, 5th SS Panzer Div., 25th Panzergrenadier Div.

Army Group North Ukraine: 1st Panzer Div., 4th Panzer Div., 5th Panzer Div., 7th Panzer Div., 8th Panzer Div., 16th Panzer Div., 17th Panzer Div., 9th SS Panzer Div., 10th SS Panzer Div., 20th Panzergrenadier Div.

Army Group South Ukraine: 13th Panzer Div., 14th Panzer Div., 23rd Panzer Div., 24th Panzer Div., 3rd SS Panzer Div., Grossdeutschland Div., 10th Panzergrenadier Div.

In Greece: 4th SS Panzergrenadier Div.

In Yugoslavia: 18th SS Panzergrenadier Div.

However extensive the earthworks and defense positions were, the fact remained that there simply was insufficient infantry to man the positions. The replacements arriving, although most of them were ethnic Germans, came from the occupied regions and did not have the determination, training and tenacity of the *soldaten* of years past. These men were expected to defend a front extending over 300 miles with little or no immediate reserves to call on should a breakthrough occur.

This development of fortified lines and the designation of *Festung* cities reflects Hitler's conqueror mentality. A mind-set that refuses to yield a meter of territory unless forced to. This strait-jacket thinking confines the commander on the ground to almost predictable responses to enemy advances. By the summer of 1944 the Soviets were beginning to have a feel for German military reactions to their offensives, especially when it came to yielding sizable parcels of territory.

In the opening months of the war it was the Wehrmacht that brought the war to the Russians, seeking routes around forests, swamps and bridges across the many rivers. In this third summer of the war the Russians were now bringing the war to the Germans and doing it with now equal aplomb and with far superior manpower and equipment. Also, the knowledge gained by Russia was allowing it, along with its superior intelligence and reconnaissance abilities to know what lie on the far side of the hill, all hindrances that handicapped Russia early on.

With defense sectors now as wide as thirty miles per division no longer exceptional, the rivers that should have been defensible barriers were no longer. The very geographical lines that could have been such an asset to a defender, because of Germanys deficient manpower, they were now presented more of a minor obstacle.

Just as revealing as the development of fixed line of defense was also the death of the German way of war; the *Bewegungskrieg*, the war of movement at the operational level, that the *Wehrmacht* favored, was trained and had become expert and was a German tradition in all its military campaigns. The need to fight behind defensive positions demonstrated the transfer of the initiative of battle to the Russian opponent and fixed the German military to positions so that it could now be battered to destruction by superior Russian might risking, if not inviting, casualties it could not afford.

The success of the Russian's ability to mislead the Germans was complemented by the growing inefficiency of German intelligence units and services. The *Wehrmacht*, possessing at one time the premier radio intelligence intercept skills depended heavily on radio intercepts to determine the intentions of Russian activity. As more and more Russian Army units were equipped with radio from Western Lend-Lease sources, this should have meant a better opportunity for the Germans to 'read' the Russians intentions. However, and less skilled German radio intelligence intercept units and specialists, the use of less skilled radio operators as replacements and the growing Russian sophistication via their *maskirovka* efforts the result was a serious loss of intelligence for the now badly strained German Army, and just when it needed it most.

Fatal Miscalculations

A milestone event was about to happen, like the one which took place the previous summer at Kursk, but this time with devastating results. The *Wehrmacht* was about to join its deadliest foe in a life or death combat that could decide the outcome of the war in the east without almost any meaningful information, intentions, or intelligence of the plans and preparations of the attacking Russians. Hitler was risking all on what his intuitive 'voice' told him would happen. Although he was correct in guessing the general area of the Russian attack he failed to identify its focal point and ensure that there was sufficient force there to repel it. No doubt the evaluation of enemy intentions was a shrewd and a well thought out possibility, but it was just that, a possibility, a giant guess. None of the preparations of Army Group Center in June of 1944 were based on sound, real, current information gleaned from the most reliable sources: the enemy.[281]

The Germans had an organization that could have tapped into the minds of those in the highest circles of Russian military or political leadership, and read what was about to unfold, but it had no one in place to report the enemy's plans, a major intelligence failure. In the field, the Luftwaffe, all but nonexistent, should have been providing real-time photographic evidence of what the Soviets were up to, but with the miss-allocation of these air assets and the growing fuel and aircraft shortage, this

---

[281] In September 1944 Himmler, using the cover excuse of investigating the 20 July bomb plot to kill Hitler, discovered incriminating documents in the former *Abwehr* chief Admiral Canaris' safe in a Berlin suburb. This was to result in his arrest and internment, and eventual execution by hanging on 9 April 1945.

precious information was missing. Even a captured Red Army intelligence officer disclosed that a major attack was planned for the Smolensk area, and information of a massive movement of Russian air assets was ignored and, once again, *Fremde Heere Ost's* Colonel Gehlen wrongly forecast an offensive against the Army Group North-Ukraine, just as the Soviets had hoped he would.[282]

The Russian NKVD security units, especially the counterintelligence Special Departments *OO/NKVD* and *SMERSh* closely guarded and observed all movement on, behind and within the front lines and insured that nothing went unreported. As mentioned elsewhere, the German field radio intelligence units were active but with the quantum leap in the number of Russian radios in use, compared to the same time three years earlier, the Russian army had improved its access, use, organization, security and deception procedures of their communications systems. Even the most rudimentary form of field information, the night raiding parties, failed to produce the information to warn what was afoot. The Germans were left with Hitler's intuition for guidance.

H. P. Willmott in his *June 1944* sums up the German rationale for holding the current position against the Russians:

> "As the Soviet winter and spring offensives died away, Hitler determined to hold the Minsk salient where Army Group Center had the 3rd Panzer, Fourth, Ninth and Second Armies under command. The reasoning for this decision was obvious and could hardly be faulted. The German retention of a position that overshadowed the Soviet re-entrance into the south served to check any Soviet inclination to move against Lvov and into Galicia. With Army Group North Ukraine in position between the Carpathians and the Pripet Marshes, Army Group Center was well placed to move against the flank and rear of any Soviet attempt to take the direct route via Lvov and Lublin into Germany, and it could even menace any Soviet move against Army Group South Ukraine and Romania. Thus in the spring of 1944 Hitler

---

[282] Fremde Heere Ost intelligence forecasts were significantly influenced by Russian counterintelligence activities and accounts for many of their inaccurate assessments. Colonel (*Oberst*) and later General (*Generalmajor*) Reinhard Gehlen was the staff officer charged with determining the boundaries of the German Army Groups during the planning phases of Barbarossa and resolved many logistical problems leading up to the invasion.

considered the Minsk salient and Army Group Center as the corner stone of the defense in the east, and accordingly he took two steps to guard against the possibility of a Soviet breakthrough in this general area."[283]

On the maps of OKH the German inclination for the grand tactical option would have been for the Russians to strike in the Army Group North Ukraine sector, at Kovel and then advance north-west to the Baltic by way of Warsaw, ending up at a point near the mouth of the Vistula River, a similar *Sichelschnitt* or sickle cut style operation made by Germany in the West against France four summers ago. However STAVKA preferred a more operational approach to the offensive; having learned that slim, lengthy single envelopment offensives can easily become liabilities, as they discovered in 1942 and 1943.

H.P. Willmott in his *June 1944* aptly described the preferred Russian method of developing a grand offensive; the broad, artillery and infantry intensive assault:

> "Its inclination was towards a series of small offensives that would be built up into a general offensive that would rip not just Army Group Center but Army Group North Ukraine to pieces. At the operational level the Soviets planned to overwhelm Army Group Center with a series of massive frontal attacks and then, with the enemy forced to commit everything he could to closing this breach, to switch the point of attack with an offensive designed to shatter Army Group North Ukraine. In the spring of 1944 the German high command failed to grasp the nature and scale of the offensive the Soviets planned for the summer. It could not appreciate that the enemy intended to attack frontally and run its efforts against the two most powerful German army groups in the east at more or less the same time."[284]

In the north the situation was similar. Offensives against Army Group North had been going on since January and by early March the Leningrad, Volkov and Second Baltic Fronts and had arrived at a line Narva-Lake Peipus-Ostrov-Novorzhev-Pustoshya, and ground to a halt as they were exhausted.

[283] *June 1944*, by H. P. Wilmott, Grub Street, 1999., p 123.

[284] *June 1944*, p. 124.

[285] *The Road to Berlin*, p. 199.

Soviet Planning

There has been much debate and discussion regarding whether or not the Soviets had been in collaboration with the western Allies regarding their timing, planning and launching Operation Bagration. As was mentioned earlier, the Western Allies considered it essential that the *Wehrmacht* be as fully engaged as possible, particularly in the East, to provide as large a margin as possible to ensure the success to Operation Overlord.

There is evidence that STAVKA received notification of the cross channel attack from the joint American and British Military Missions to Moscow on 8 April 1944. The date they gave for the commencement of Overlord was 31 May, with a few days either way as a margin. The Western Allies were concerned that the Russians, so extended by their successes during their winter campaign against the German Army Group South Ukraine, would not be ready to launch their summer offensive to coordinate with Overlord; as such they wanted to provide STAVKA with as much advance notice for the invasion as possible. To ensure that there were no misunderstandings, Churchill and Roosevelt sent their own messages to Stalin in mid-April, indicating that the invasion would take place 'around "R" date', reinforcing the message sent earlier by the military missions.[285] Although Stalin could have launched Bagration to coincide with Overlord, the coincidence of him delaying it to begin on the 22nd of June, the third anniversary of the German invasion of Russia, a much more significant date for the Soviets, is of interest. A more likely reason was the difficulty in bringing up men and supplies due to the extensive German destruction of rail lines and bridges as part of the "scorched Earth" activities during the retreat.

The date of 22 June, both for the year 1941 and 1944 has a large meaning for the war in Russia. That date, the German invasion of the U.S.S.R. in 1941 was a defining moment for all Russians and the date rings with meaning and moment. The latter year, 1944, Operation Bagration will have similar meaning in Russia in the launching of the first Russian summer offensive, a time that heretofore the Germans had established as their premier campaigning season. The playing field of combat was leveling. The connection here, if one can be made is, did STAVKA delay launching Bagration, as they posit, due to the delay of assembling the materials and manpower, or was it a more practical and calculating propaganda decision, one based on the success or failure of the Western Allies in Normandy? It is a question that bears consideration and further research.

The Russian Schwerpunkt

The Russians had been eying the conspicuous bulge of German Army Group Center for some time, the so-called Byelorussian "balcony" for its overhanging shape on maps. It was a tempting target as it contained most of the German units on the Eastern Front. In light of the significant advances made against Army Group South, later Army Group North Ukraine, which was now holding a thin line just inside the old 1939 border from 50 miles north of Kovel south to Kolomiya and along the Dniester to the Black Sea near Odessa, Army Group Center's position was conspicuous indeed. To continue the advance against Army Group South would require extensive regrouping and re-supply, and additional time, as the First Byelorussian and First and Forth Ukrainian Fronts had been on the offensive since early March and were exhausted. Army Group Center guarded the direct route to Warsaw and then on to Berlin, making this Army Group the target for the main summer offensive a logical and typically Russian choice.

The description of the battlefield for the attacker did not inspire much hope for easy passage. The gently rolling sunflower and wheat filled fields of Kursk they were not. The operational area of the offensive was swampy, criss-crossed by streams and pools and locally built canals. It would not be a first choice for an offensive by any commander, especially one to be spear headed by masses of armor. Stalin too was concerned about the ability of the fronts to assemble a tank force larger than a corps in size due to the soft ground and wooded areas. The decision of how big a tank force was one of the earliest planning problems to be addressed by the Soviet general staff. The poor road network and soft ground decreased the likelihood of a mechanized offensive in this area and the Germans planned accordingly.

That the Russians were able to so clearly read the German intentions as to the defense of their forces in the Byelorussian 'balcony' was due to the maintenance and control of their superb spy and intelligence network that was now firmly in place throughout the German military command and government for at least the last two years.[286]

Another new development was in the command and control of the Russian attacking forces. This was the new STAVKA instructions that informed the front commanders to issue the broadest directional orders to

---

[286] Considering the ruthless efficiency with which the Gestapo, SS and SD were to demonstrate the following month in rooting out the conspirators of the 'July bomb plot', it is fascinating as well as bewildering that the Soviet spy network continued to function for the duration of the war almost untouched and undisrupted.

the combat units, and allow the field commanders to make the necessary modifications or allowable changes to ensure success. This was no small achievement for the Russian Army, and was an acknowledgement of trust and faith in it that started at the top, with Stalin. It was Zhukov that persuaded Stalin to accept the defensive posture as the strategic method in the Kursk battle a year earlier. With that overwhelming success behind them, the demonstrated ability of the Russian army to manage its own details without the seemingly constant, interfering and meddlesome instructions from a remote STAVKA headquarters hundreds of miles away was certainly a significant achievement, especially for Zhukov. For a military raised on the doctrine of unquestioning obedience from the political organs, where the word 'initiative' was almost non-existent, this was truly a leap forward.

Razvedka

Over the last year the Soviets had become quite good in their ability at concealing preparations from their enemy. Learning largely from experience they had developed systems and procedures, termed *Maskirovka*.[287] They developed two approaches to this maskirovka; a positive and negative system. Loosely described, the positive use involved physical concealment of troops, tanks, artillery, vehicles, aircraft and airfields, supply points and obvious signs of impending action. The negative aspects to maskirovka utilized mis-information, decoy radiolocation units broadcasting false or misleading information (known as "radio games" or *radio igry* to the Russians, *funkspiel* in German), positioning forces in other than the prime attack points to mislead the defenders and other like activities. The balance of both positive and negative approaches to deceiving an enemy is important in that one without the other focuses attention on the missing element. Stalin called the *maskirovka* system 'military cunning'.

Also by 1944 the Russian intelligence and counterintelligence organs had reached a level of sophistication and effectiveness that all but nullified German attempts to learn of Russian operational intentions. Russian *razvedka* or intelligence operatives had approximately 140,000 trained

---

[287] The Soviet process of denying intelligence information to the enemy. Usually referred to the cover and concealment of men, materials and the preparations for future operations. One of the tactical intelligence terms Red Army officers used seeking local information on German or German-allied forces was to get a 'tongue'. This referred to the capture of an enemy soldier that would divulge the needed information, hence the 'tongue' reference.

agents operation all across the front and behind the front and engaged in a number of mutually interconnected activities, which included apprehending enemy agents, generating and issuing 'controlled' information broadcast to German receivers, collecting information on all enemy activities, managing security of military operations and recruiting captured enemy soldiers to be used or 'turned' against their former units.

Soviet Might

The Russians brought an amazing amount of military might to bear against the Germans. Four Fronts were involved in the planning totaling 251 divisions of all types (the Russian rifle division strength is generally equivalent of two infantry regiments in the German TO&E, in a three regiment organization), eight mechanized corps of 4,000 tanks and assault guns, six cavalry divisions and 13 artillery divisions with 24,400 guns and mortars, a new Russian invention with terrifying destructive power, soon to be copied by the Germans and 5,300 aircraft. These units combined had 2,500,000 men including STAVKA reserves with 1,200,000 in front of Army Group Center, more than double the Germans in the same sectors. The addition of six cavalry divisions might seem archaic at this stage of the war, but they found ready employment in the poor terrain that makes up some of western Russia. They were to prove their value again in this operation. All together over 75,000 rail carloads were required to bring this force to the Fronts.[288]

The mechanized 'punch' for the offensive was to come from the 2,715 tanks and 1,355 assault guns, more than six times as many tanks as the Germans had in Army Group Center. In addition, almost a third of the Russian tanks would be of the T-34/85 variety, mounting the larger 85mm gun and this offensive would introduce the new JS-2 'Stalin' tank, with its 122mm main gun, comparable to the German PzKw VI 'Tiger', but lighter, faster, more reliable mechanically, and with a larger main gun, the Tiger's being 88mm.

Air power on the Soviet side was a large factor too. Of the 5,300 aircraft against both army groups, 2,000 of them were the feared IL-2 ground attack fighters[289] and over 1,000 bombers of all types. Russian air power was to be

---

[288] Army Historical Series *Stalingrad To Berlin: The German Defeat In The East* by Earl F. Ziemke, Office of the Chief of Military History, United States Army, Washington, D.C. 1968, pp. 314-315.

even more effective than usual as there was almost a total lack of Luftwaffe presence in the attack sector, allowing the Russians to roam at will over the battlefield undisturbed. An additional advantage the Russians enjoyed was that this entire air fleet was under Front control, allowing much faster assignment and direction of air assets to where it was most needed.

The final big hammer in the Soviet arsenal was artillery. There were 6,900 guns of 76mm caliber and larger, and over 2,300 rocket launchers assigned to the four fronts. In addition there were 4,230 45mm and 57mm anti-tank guns. Finally, there were over 11,000 mortars issued to the attacking units. This armament was organized into two artillery corps, one to each front and ten artillery divisions and three rocket divisions. For the first time, the Russian Fronts attacking would be provided a rolling barrage to facilitate their gaining their objectives, two Fronts, the 1st and 2nd Byelorussian were to be provided two rolling barrages, a sure sign that infantry-artillery coordination had improved markedly. With the massive armament output of Soviet industry and Allied Lend-Lease support Stalin was heard to remark after the battle of Kursk, "Quantity has a quality all its own," this comment certainly applied to the preparations for Bagration.

Even by the most optimistic assessments, the German forces awaiting the Russian attack had little or no chance of stopping this massive assault. The German focus was south of the Pripyat Marshes and should help be needed north of it, there was little that could be done to provide assistance.

When one completes the calculations of opposing forces, the stark reality of the matter was that the Germans were being simply being out-produced and now, in the summer of 1944, out guessed as well. The Russians now had the raw materials, industrial plant and productivity at their disposal to fight the battle the Germans could not; the head-on frontal attacks the Russians so favored were all based on the massive production of weapons and an equally large supply of manpower. The key difference in the summer of 1944 was that the Russian Army no longer had to rely on the masses of infantry to mow down the defending Germans. Added to this mass of men were now some of the most effective field weapons to be used in

[289] The Ilyushin IL-2 *Shturmovik* of the Russian Air Force with its 23mm cannon and air to ground rockets was the equivalent of the Junkers Ju-87G or the Henschel Hs-129 in the Luftwaffe, although not as heavily armed as the German aircraft with their 37mm cannon, it was heavily armored and produced in very large numbers, over 30,000 according to one source.

World War II: the largest and most reliable tanks, rocket artillery, large caliber field artillery, mortars and ground attack aircraft, all in seemingly endless supply.

When one thinks of the German-developed *Blitzkrieg*, one expects to see masses of tanks and panzers springing out of camouflaged shelters, ditches and ravines to lunge at the enemy, accompanied by motorized infantry and artillery and lavishly supported by close air attacks. One of the less known doctrines of this type of warfare was the initial need for an infantry opening to be made in the enemy defenses to allow the attacker's mechanized forces to pour through into the enemy rear and exploit the advance. The initial phase of the *Blitzkrieg* attack is for the infantry to pry open 'lanes' through which the mechanized units can proceed unimpeded. This requires the use of combat engineers and supporting infantry to remove physical obstacles; remove land mines, repair key roadbeds and bridges first. This initial phase has been frequently overlooked, intentionally or inadvertently, as it is one of the less appealing portions of the more stylish panzer powered *Blitzkrieg*.[290] By 1944 the Russian Army had become as proficient at these penetration attacks as were the Germans. The Russian tactics, if not as complex and flexible, was at least as competent and effective.

A final comment on the Russian preparations for Operation Bagration: one of the more taxing aspects of commanding the troops under his command was the language barrier. Initially a Russian problem and later to be experienced by the Germans as well, the many and varied nationalities and peoples in the Union of Soviet Socialist Republics presented a command and control problem from the earliest days of the invasion. This restricted the ability of a higher echelon commander to properly direct the battle. This was simplified by the forming of national divisions that had Russian speaking liaison personnel to connect it with a higher level command. In a nation as vast as the U.S.S.R. it was just one more hurdle to be overcome.

---

[290] For example, in the final assault on Berlin by the 1st Byelorussian Front on 14 January 1945 Soviet combat engineers removed 90,000 anti-tank and personnel mines to clear over 800 lanes for the attacking mechanized forces.

Operations In the North: Knocking Out the Finns

In addition to the preparations for the giant battle against Army Groups Center and North Ukraine, there were major preparations in the far north against the Finns and the German ally units between Petsamo and Murmansk, and a little farther south around Salla. The Russian Army was determined to eliminate the tenacious Finns once and for all prior to their main battle against the German Army Group Center. In addition, they were not about to repeat the mistakes of 1940, and brought overwhelming numbers of men, artillery, tanks and aircraft to bear on the tiny nation. This operation began on 9 June 1944 and by 25 August after some of the most vicious and brutal, but largely unknown, fighting of the war the Finnish government contacted Moscow to arrange a cessation of hostilities. The Second World War was over for Finland and after acceding to Russian demands for recovery of all lands lost in the German invasion of June 1941, the Soviets added important parcels to their demands such as the naval base at Hanko, at the mouth of the Gulf of Finland.

Desperate to regain her conquered lands from the Winter War, Finland had allied herself with Germany with the ulterior motive of using German economic and military assistance to regain her lost territory. With Germany and the other members of the Axis unable to force a decision in Russia, Finland was unwilling and unable to commit more effort after regaining the lost lands, to what was now a doomed adventure. Sparsely populated Finland paid heavily for her geographic location next to her aggressive neighbor. Of a pre-war population of 4,000,000 she lost 84,000 during the war, two and a half times that of Britain's war losses percentage-wise.

Germany's northern experience in the war did not repay the effort expended. In April 1940 she lost most of her destroyer fleet in the capture and occupation of Norway. Her investment in Finland, both in men, material, and politics resulted only in partially achieving one of the objectives she set out for herself, the interdiction of the Murmansk rail connection of Medvezhegorsk, Petrozavodsk and Lodeynoye Pole north and south of Lake Onega.

Finally, her biggest waste in the north was the tying down of some 400,000 valuable troops in Norway until the end of the war, a result, no doubt of the successful Allied misinformation program based in England.[291] The confinement of the equivalent of an entire army in isolated Norway, long after her strategic importance had disappeared with the destruction of the Kriegsmarine, was another unsung victory almost unknown in the West. These troops would have greatly assisted in making up the losses of Zitadelle and Bagration.

---

[291] For the groundbreaking story of the Ultra decryption story see *The Ultra Secret* by F. W. Winterbottom.

Chapter Thirteen:
Normandy

"The Fuhrer is sleeping and cannot be disturbed"

- Response by Jodl to von Rundstedt's request
for release of the panzer divisions

This chapter will examine the preparations Germany made to its occupied Western coastal areas in defense for the expected Allied invasion sometime in the summer of 1944. It will look at the cover and deception plans of the Allies to protect and guard their preparations and their effectiveness. It will also look at how Germany's command of the west, *Oberbefehlshaber West* (OBWest), was planning the defenses of the French coastal areas and the labor and material problems encountered and the solutions they sought to them. German unit composition, condition and mobility will be looked at in detail and the impact these factors had on their ability to repel the invasion. Finally, a we will make a general assessment of the impact the war in Russia was having on the ability of Germany successfully manage and conduct war on two fronts, its defensive preparations in Normandy and its success in doing so.

"Fortitude"

One aspect of the war the Allies did superbly was to keep the Germans fooled as to where and when the invasion of Europe would come. From the earliest moments of the Allied planning efforts to return to Europe, an insurance mechanism had to be developed to give the highest possible chances of success to the coming invasion. Known as "Operation Fortitude" this was the masterful cover and deception scheme that greatly assisted the chances of Allied success on the shores of France. In preparation for the Allied landings at Normandy, code named "Neptune", a vast and complicated two part deception plan was created called "Fortitude", subdivided into "Fortitude North" and "Fortitude South". "Fortitude North" was created to deceive Hitler that the Allies had a plan to invade Scandinavia, either Norway or Denmark from Scotland, and "South" was the attack force that would invade at the obvious location, Pas-de-Calais, using the fictitious First United States Army Group (FUSAG).

The "Fortitude" effort was a deception that simulated not only the incorrect intentions of the Allied planners as to where the landings would take place, but also 'invented' a fictitious allied force known as the First US Army Group, (FUSAG) 'commanded' by none other than America's most aggressive general, George S. Patton.

The details of Operation Fortitude read like a page out of Hollywood's central casting for props, smoke and mirrors. To give a convincing presence of the non-existent FUSAG[292] extensive communications and radio nets were established and a script of names and places were compiled and used in generating radio chatter that would simulate the assembly, training and movements of FUSAG. For example, supply orders were transmitted, personnel transfers, medical status and even the status of soldiers arrested while on liberty in nearby towns. As would be normal operating procedure, this radio communication was transmitted in a code that was known to be compromised by German radio intelligence organizations listening in across the English Channel in Germany and the occupied countries.

In addition to the radio and communications disguises were the physical efforts put forth to fool the Germans. General Patton and Field Marshal Bernard Montgomery[293] or convincing look-alikes were conspicuously driven around the assembly areas of FUSAG and Patton's presence made

---

[292] FUSAG was the brainchild of British Lieutenant Colonel Dudley Clark, RA, who ran the British strategic deception operations during World War II.

known in theaters, hospitals and even pubs and inns of the area, to ensure that word got back to Germany to complete the charade.

Another aspect to the Fortitude effort was the more visible and quite fascinating portion of the cover and deception operation. In the FUSAG assembly areas the Allies had designed and built in the U.S. hundreds of rubber inflatable Sherman tanks, White heavy trucks, 155mm artillery pieces and other remarkably lifelike rubber weapons. This was also augmented with huts, tents, camouflage netting, street lighting, parking lots and the thousand and one other elements of a military occupation site, all of it fake.

In addition, Fortitude was able to convince the Germans to overestimate the invasion force by 40 percent, believing that there were as many as 85 or 90 divisions prepared to invade Northern France.

When Allied radar picked up Luftwaffe photographic reconnaissance aircraft heading to England, Allied fighter command was alerted and the intruder was intercepted before any photography could be done. However, if the German aircraft was seen to be heading to the FUSAG area, Allied fighters were scrambled, and a pursuit, as before, was conducted, but not before the German was permitted to snap a few images and permitted to 'escape' with poorly directed gunfire.

All this misleading activity resulted in confirming in the German command that the Allies were indeed coming in the very area they had thought the most likely, the Pas-de-Calais area of the French coast. The FUSAG activity helped confirm this as its bogus military activity was conducted in Dover/Felixstowe area east of London. If the FUSAG activity was not enough to convince the Germans, real Allied units were also quartered in the same area, but not the D-Day first wave assault units, but follow-up units, such as the British XXX and I Corps.

Fortitude was an essential ingredient in the overall Allied strategy to land on the beaches of Normandy without the mass of German strength based in western Europe waiting for it. So thoroughly were the German's fooled as to the real landings in Normandy and not the fake ones in the Pas-de-Calais there was only one first line infantry division in the Normandy landing beach areas, the 352[nd.] Probably in no other area of effort in the Allied preparations for the invasion, have so few ensured the success of so many.

[293] See the film *I was Monty's Double* in which M. E. Clifton James plays a very convincing Montgomery.

German Defense Strategy

There was almost constant debate at OKW on the positioning, command and control of the combat units in the Normandy region. The Rommel school of thought had the combat units positioned along the invasion beaches to repel the Allies as they landed based on the belief that Allied air cover would prevent rapid, large scale movement of the panzer and panzergrenadier counterattack units to the threatened sectors. The von Runstedt school was to keep the reserve forces in a centrally located position that, once the main landing zones had been positively identified, the reserve force would then counterattack. Both strategies had much to commend them, and von Rundstedt's would have been acceptable had this been 1940 or 1941. The argument against this plan was, once again, Allied air support. However, the Luftwaffe's loss of air supremacy rendered Rundstedt's plan impractical. The reasoning was that this force would be attacked mercilessly on route to the landing beaches; when the survivors arrived, they would be exhausted, wounded, missing vital parts of their equipment or division; they could be cut off and isolated, starved of supply and reinforcement. The debate of which strategy was superior was still raging on 6 June.

As it was, the Western strategic panzer reserve consisting, of 2nd Panzer, 116th Panzer, 12th SS Panzer and Panzer Lehr divisions, were located in positions that were too far from the invasion beaches to be of effective use and too far away under control of OKW in Berlin, to fully understand the gravity of the situation. When the decision to allow OBWest freedom to deploy these divisions, it was too late, the beachhead had been well developed and defended by that time and Allied air power was having its effect on the daylight movement of these precious German units.

The Axis forces the Western Allies clashed withon the shores of Normandy were a shadow of their former selves. France, with her mild climate, lush agriculture, excellent transportation, communications, and proximity to Germany, had become a center for rest and refitting of units from Russia that had been 'burned out' or destroyed and were transferred there to be rebuilt. Out of the 50+ divisions in France and the Low Countries in June 1944, fully 12 were in a recovery or fitting-out status. In addition, 33 were static, or unmovable[294] or in reserve. Add to this a modest panzer reserve near Paris that could not be committed to combat

---

[294] What is meant by 'static' or 'unmovable' is to be used in its military context, meaning without motorized or mechanized transport. These units, known as *bodenstandige* or

without the express permission of Hitler, uncertainty of exactly where and when the Allies would land, and you have a thin margin for error in repulsing an invasion.

But life in France for the typical German soldier was not all touring the sights of Paris, eating fine food, drinking rare wines and admiring the pretty girls.[295] The units that were resting and refitting were also expected to assist in hunting down French partisan units; this additional duty delayed their recovery and impaired their effectiveness when they returned to combat. By the summer of 1944 it has been estimated that 200,000 French resistance fighters, organized and armed by Allied agents were at large in the countryside.[296] Finally, by this stage of the war, the Wehrmacht had to resort to its Axis partners and forced conscripts of the conquered nations to fill out its manpower needs, both military and industrial. These moves caused a serious loss of German fighting ability, degradation of unit quality, and reliability.

In addition to France being the rest and recuperation region for the Wehrmacht, it was also the chief training ground outside the Reich itself.[297] After initial training and unit formation in Germany, new units were sent to France for their advanced and specialized training. In addition to training, France was the medical recuperating area for the Wehrmacht. OKW decided if the soldier would recover sufficiently to fight again and was far enough along in his convalescence, and no longer needed hospital care, could walk or march he was sent to a *bodenstandige* or fortress unit along the Atlantic coast or English Channel. This released either younger or fit men for duty in Russia. As many as 45,000 men per month were assigned to divisions in the west, freeing up critical hospital/recovery space in Germany for the more seriously wounded.

In June of 1944 the German Wehrmacht had a total of 295 combat divisions of which 34 were panzer and 17 were *panzergrenadier* (motorized infantry), 244 or 83 % of them were located in the East, totaling 3,130,000

"bo" for short, could indeed move as all infantry units did, by marching. However marching in combat in the mechanized age is much too slow to be of use in reacting to enemy movements.

[295] Hitler voiced this same opinion in late June 1944 that it was the "women, good food and liquor" that softened his armies in France.

[296] *Cross Channel Attack* , p. 198.

[297] For more information see *The Kersten Memoirs, 1940- 1945* for Himmler's plans to form the State of Burgundy in France after the successful conclusion of the war in Europe.

men.[298] It was this imbalance of strength devoted to the Eastern Front that was the primary reason for the western Allies successful landing in France. For had the Soviets collapsed soon after the start of Operation Barbarossa,[299] or in the second summer offensive in June 1942, freeing units to be directed elsewhere, a successful Allied invasion in western Europe would have been highly doubtful.

The successful Allied landings in Normandy would confront Germany with the dreaded 'second front'; this was an event they had been striving to prevent. Now, because of foolish actions by Hitler; flawed *ostfront* strategy, conflicting economic policy, no long-term war plan; an already overstretched *Wehrmacht* had to engage not only two but multiple fronts. Some have offered to call the French front the third front in the war. With Germany already engaged with the Allies in Italy and Russia, this would chronologically make these the first and second fronts. Some have even offered to state that the Allies in France were the fourth front, making the massive Allied air campaign of the U. S. Eighth Army Air forces and the RAF Bomber Command a front in itself. However history cares to label and consider these major threats to the Axis, especially Germany, the war was entering a critical phase.

In addition to the extensive preparations made for Overlord, there was the 'miracle of the weather' that allowed to landings to proceed as scheduled. One recalls Napoleon's comments having to do with luck. As any general or field marshal will admit, the best planning and training can be undone without that elusive element of good fortune. The French leader once commented to his staff that he had enough good generals, what he really wanted were lucky ones.

One can argue that the German forces possessed better field commanders during the war, however the frequent political meddling imposed by both Stalin and Hitler on their field commanders, frequently undid whatever advantage that provided. On the other hand, the Allied command enjoyed

---

[298] *Strategy & Tactics Staff Study Nr. 1, War in the East: The Russo-German Conflict 1941-45* by the Staff of Strategy & Tactics Magazine, Simulations Publications, Incorporated, New York, 1977, p. 28.

[299] For information on the development and assignment of operational code names see, *The Art of Naming Operations* by Gregory C. Sieminski, *Parameters*, Autumn 1995. It will be noticed that Stavka preferred heroic and celestial names for their major operations, e.g. Uranus, Saturn (Stalingrad), Mars, Jupiter (1942 Moscow counteroffensive). As Operation Mars was a failure there was no follow-up operation, Jupiter.

a largely free hand in the exercise of the conduct of the war in the field. The Allies had their lucky general in the form of Dwight D. Eisenhower. The military pundits can say and write what they will regarding his overall field strategy, but Eisenhower's first and most important task was to hold the Allied coalition together, and that he did.[300] All success would flow from there, as Allied manpower and material superiority at this point in the war would prevail, even should mistakes or setbacks on the battlefield occur.

If one considers 1942 the turning point of the war with the battles of Stalingrad in Russia, El Alamein in North Africa, and the Battle of Midway in the Pacific, 1944 would be the year the war was "won" . The concept of 'won' in this context means a point in the conflict in which Germany could no longer win the war. With the impending Allied victory there were three critical military advantages the Germans no longer possessed: The *Blitzkrieg* attack; weapons quality and quantity; and superior training, coordination and leadership.

By the summer of 1944 the Allies had watched, suffered and learned how to conduct their own form of *Blitzkrieg*, or at least adapt the key operational aspects of it for their own use. The first three years of the war are filled with examples of Allied political and military incompetence and unpreparedness: The invasion of Poland in 1939; France, Norway, Denmark and the Low Countries in 1940; North Africa and Crete in 1940/41 and Russia in 1941, to name the most well known. This new, fast-paced form of warfare stunned the Allies and they soon realized that they had better develop defenses to it. Eventually they adopted much of it themselves, making modifications to suit their logistical and organizational capabilities.

In addition to the rest and recuperation center that France had become for the *Wehrmacht*, it also served another purpose, especially for the Eastern army. With the commencement of the Russian campaign, it was that of a recruitment and manpower replacement pool. In April of 1943 OB West Field Marshal von Rundstedt undertook a comprehensive examination of the defensive situation of the western armies. In his report to Hitler he indicated, among other things that sector frontages in France were among the largest of all German occupied countries. For example, the defensive front for the Fifteenth Army was 50 miles, in Seventh Army they were 120 miles in width and 217 miles in length along the Atlantic coast.

---

[300] British Prime Minister Winston Churchill was once heard to say in 1940 'There is only one thing worse than fighting with allies and that is fighting without them'.

The 15 divisions in 7th Army were responsible for a linear frontage of some 375 miles. Of the 15 divisions, 7 were *bodenstandige,* one was stuck out in the Channel Islands and two, 275th Infantry and 5th *Fallschrimjager,* were missing component units and all were under strength and, in addition, these divisions were responsible for rear area security and the defense of two major port cities, Brest and Cherbourg. The average frontage per division was some 20 miles. In the German Seventh Army, 25% of the battalions on D-Day consisted of Russian troops of questionable reliability.

At the end of the first Soviet winter offensive in April 1942, stock was taken of the exhausted German divisions in Army Group Center. A month later the 6th Infantry Regiment of the 7th Panzer Division was sent to France to recuperate and rebuild. A year earlier 12 trains were required to bring this unit East to the pre-invasion staging areas in central Poland; now, a year later, only one was needed to take it West to France.

In addition to the extensive defense sectors of the German divisions was the condition of the divisions themselves. Most had only two regiments instead of the standard three to four; they were lacking anti-tank guns and artillery and the most significant problem was their lack of mobility. In addition, the units stationed in the west lost the best men to the eastern fighting, being left with invalids, foreign recruits and older men. These could not stand up to the hard fighting in Russia. OB West complained that the best fighting troops were being siphoned off at an alarming rate, but to no avail; the desperate combat conditions and great expanses to be covered in the east demanded their transfer, and they went.[301]

In 1942 a system of unit exchange between Army Group Center and OBWest was established, but soon broke down under the terrific demands from the East. From October 1942 to September 1943 22 infantry and six panzer or mechanized divisions left for the East, in addition to the individual weeding out of the best personnel and equipment and sent east as well. The biggest losses in OBWest were quality troops, Luftwaffe units and motor vehicles.

The 1944 infantry division was set up as the basic type for new divisions as well as for the reorganization of certain old formations, as for instance, the Luftwaffe field divisions. The division which included the bulk of von

---

[301] Churchill captured the essence of the manpower needs of the two fronts when he is quoted to have said, "The armies in the west are too large for the front, while in the east the front is too large for the armies there".

Rundstedt's infantry, however, the *bodenstaendige* division was exempted from reorganization unless specifically so ordered. The static divisions were formed at the request of von Rundstedt in 1942 in order to exempt these units from being transferred to the east. Although they had the nine infantry battalions, they were weaker than the normal divisions in that they had no reconnaissance battalion and only three battalions of artillery. The standard infantry division of the 1944 organization would have had the reconnaissance battalion of 700 men and a full artillery regiment of 33 105mm howitzers and 9 150mm howitzers.

Another important but frequently overlooked point is that by the late spring of 1944 Germany really only had one competent field army, the one in the East. After the Allied landings at Anzio, Italy in January 1944, the German army there was tasked with defense only and was given only the forces required. The army in France, with the exception of the SS units in the Pas de Calais area was a rest and recuperation camp as well as a personnel depot for the eastern armies. Although desperate attempts were made, beginning in November of 1943 to bring the western armies up to their TOE strengths, the task was beyond that of German industry and the military. The Russian Army would continue to perform the one critical task the western Allies needed of it, that of bleeding the *Wehrmacht* at a rate that exceeded its ability to stem such losses or replace them. Germany in mid-1944 could fight one war at a time, not three or four, as it was being forced to. The result was to degrade all the fronts to a common denominator of performance that the Allies, both eastern and western could exceed.

Overlord

For the Allies to successfully launch their invasion of Europe via France, the defending Germans would have to be induced to perform two vital acts. The first would be to have the enemy to voluntarily remove as much of their defending forces as possible from the planned invasion site; the second was for the remaining defending forces to be set to defend any other locale than the actual invasion site. Both of these conditions had been met by the summer of 1944.

The Wehrmacht satisfied the first condition themselves, with the relocation of most of the ground forces transferred to Russia and neighboring countries, eventually including the best of the German military forces. The second was the cover and deception operations conducted by the Allies, code named Operation Bodyguard. This was the successful coalition of intrigues to persuade Germany to disperse its forces of OBWest throughout Western Europe and that the Allied landing was going to be at the Pas de Calais portion of the French coast on the English Channel and not at Normandy. The ability to induce the German high command to believe or at the very least question where the Allies would be coming at the most logical, and also the most obvious landing site for over two years during and even after the invasion, was nothing short of divine intervention.

Normandy was selected after extensive study of the conditions and geography best suited to a successful amphibious landing. Initially the Allied planners chose, under Plan Roundup, to use a widely dispersed series of landing sites, the theory being to prevent the enemy from concentrating against any one location and giving the remainder a fair chance at development into a permanent and defensible lodgment. In November of 1942 additional study examined other options. One of them was the opposite of the Roundup, the concentration of the landing force and this plan was eventually adopted.

The advantage of the new plan was the naval artillery and air support could be better concentrated and controlled at a single large beach head. In addition the landing units themselves could provide collateral support for each other. Another vital component of this plan was that it had to be within range of Allied fighter air cover based in England. The selected landing site had to contain airfields or have sufficient locations to develop airfields quickly. In addition, enemy beach defenses had to be as weak as possible and those that existed to be readily defeated by naval or air attack. This requirement eliminated small beaches, and easily defended coastal areas such as in the Netherlands that could be flooded by the enemy. Finally, the selected landing area must permit the Allied build up as least as rapidly as the enemy could defend against it. This meant a major port was required to be included in the landing area or have beaches that would allow continuous force maintenance operations.

With these conditions established, the planners began searching for a site that met as many as possible. The one that met most of them was the area around Caen. All the others were ruled out either due to limitations of Allied air cover, adequate exits off the landing beaches, geographic and manmade obstacles, proximity to known enemy combat units and obvious landing areas, such as the Pas-de-Calais.

Ostbattalion

In 1942 the staff of the disbanded German 162nd Infantry Division was assigned the task of raising and training *Ostbattalions*. The German system of *Ostbattalions* were combat units recruited from non-ethnic German populations from Russia and Eastern European nations. Stationed in Poland, the staff raised and trained 98 battalions until late in 1944 when itself was disbanded by the approaching Russian Army. The *Ostbattalions* varied in quality and strength depending on the source of recruits, the unit commanders and the portion of the front the unit was assigned to. Most of the time the *Ostbattalions* were integrated into German infantry divisions, releasing ethnic Germans for combat duty and the *Ostbattalions* taking over such tasks as construction troops, rear area security and occasionally as independent front line combat units.

In October 1943 OBWest reported a lowering of morale in the *Volksdeutsch*[302] men of the units in France. This had much to do with the recent reverses in fortune in the campaign in Russia. In the early months of the campaign the *Volksdeutsch* drafted into the Wehrmacht were, for the most part, able and willing recruits. However as the war in the east deteriorated for the Germans, the capability and reliability of the *Volksdeutsch* declined as well. By late 1943 Germany, in almost constant retreat in the East, decided to transfer them to the West in exchange for German troops. This exchange system was an attempt to constantly keep the most reliable troops at the most dangerous front. In September 1943 an exchange ratio of two for one was established, that is, two Eastern battalions (*Ostbattalions*) for one German battalion, but even this favorable rate of exchange was to change, in favor of the Russian front. In May 1944 the unit exchange rate of 32 *Ostbattalions* for 26 German battalions was ordered (about 1.28 to 1).

A number of the "static" divisions in France and the Low Countries were made up of foreign conscripts from conquered nations and Axis allies; a significant number of them were not at all thrilled with fighting and dying so far from home for a losing Germany. It gives one pause to wonder just how OKW planned to deal with the Allied invasion; it also gives one an idea of the reliability and effectiveness of the combat units awaiting the Allies.

---

[302] The Germans used a system known as the *Volksliste*, which categorized the ethnicity, of their 'pure' German descent. Level I was German descent, Level II was mixed descent and Level III was knowledge of the German language.

In addition to the foreign members of these divisions in the west, was the caliber of the units. A number of these combat divisions were made up from what the Germans called "stomach" soldiers, men that were suffering any of a number of ailments and/or recovering from wounds. The low fighting ability of these units was plainly evident and more than once sent shivers down the spines of many OBWest commanders. For example, there was one division, the 70[th,] that was composed of men suffering from dyspepsia for which a special ration had to be provided to avoid deadly cases of dysentery.[303]

Hardware

With the majority of the newest and best equipment going to arm the combat units in the East, OB West had been equipping its Western units, out of desperation, with mostly captured equipment; the few cars and trucks were mostly French and Czech, and the artillery and small arms came from all over the Reich and conquered territories. In some cases, this was a bountiful source of material, especially from France. However the advantages were more than outnumbered by the disadvantages. Most important among them was the supply of spares and replacement parts for the many makes and manufactures of these vehicles and weapons. When the vehicles broke down, for example, if the scarce replacement part was no longer in supply, which was usually the case, another vehicle of identical make had to be put aside and cannibalized for its parts. This had the disadvantage of taking not one but two or more vehicles out of service, exacerbating the transport problem.

In addition to the shortage of trained combat troops to man the Atlantic defenses was the weapons they were to use in defending it.

The miscellaneous armament of the panzer divisions was typical of the assortment of weapons in nearly all the units in the west and reflected the long drain on the German war economy from the Russian war and the increasing production difficulties imposed by the accelerating Allied

---

[303] Also known as "The White Bread" division due to the special diet required by these stomach or gastrically afflicted men. In 1944 the Germans decided to collect all these cases into one division. Years of nervous tension, bad diet and rough living had produced a number of these cases and with manpower levels reaching the danger level, they decided these men could be of some use. This division, the 70[th,] was assigned a static defense position guarding the entrance to the Scheldt estuary leading to the port of Rotterdam. The area was well chosen as it was able to provide the special diet of milk, white bread, eggs and vegetables they needed to maintain their fragile health.

air offensive. As long as the Russian front was the main theater of war and the west was not immediately threatened, it was natural to ship the bulk of the best material to the east and arm the west as best one could with what was left. The policy of equipping western divisions primarily with captured material was laid down in December 1941 when ten divisions were ordered so equipped. The east continued to enjoy priority on new equipment until the end of 1943, and although German-made tanks and assault guns were shipped to OBWest during that time, the deliveries were often more than outweighed by the transfer of armored units to the east. First-class armored equipment remained a comparative rarity in divisions assigned to OBWest until 1944. At the end of October 1943, for instance, there were in the west 703 tanks, assault guns and self propelled 88mm anti-tank *Hornisse* units. At the end of December the number had risen only to 823, the increase being largely in the lighter PzKw. Mk. IV medium tank. All the *Hornisse* and Tiger (PzKw VI) tanks had been shipped out to the Russian front and the stock of assault guns was considerably decreased. The total of 823, moreover, was less than the planned build-up of 1,226. The new year brought a change. January showed only a slight increase, but thereafter the deliveries to the west were speeded up. Although most new Tiger tanks continued to go to the east, deliveries to OBWest of the powerful PzKw. Mk. V Panther tank were notably increased.[304] The attempt to redress long status of the 'second class front' was underway.

The following is the selection of weapons with which the Cherbourg defense positions were equipped:

> "Actually the so-called main line of resistance consisted of strong points, which were called islands of resistance if they were weakly occupied and bases if they were more strongly defended. Generally the main weapons in the strong points were two light machine guns, one heavy machine gun, one medium mortar, and one 75mm field gun or 47mm anti-tank gun. The stationary

---

[304] As strapped as Germany's panzer divisions were in acquiring new armored fighting vehicles, the manufacturing system itself was causing unnecessary delays in deliveries of these now precious panzers. For example, in 1943 German panzers had an anti-magnetic paste called *zimmeritt* applied to all exterior surfaces. This gave a rippled appearance to the vehicle and was designed to prevent magnetic anti-tank mines from adhering to the steel surface of the vehicle. While generally successful in practice, the application of the paste was time consuming, and the drying of it added a week to the construction time.

weapons in the islands of resistance and bases were of varied models. They consisted of French, Dutch, Czech, Polish and Russian guns that made training difficult because the men had to know all these types besides their own German models. The distance between the islands of resistance and bases varied from 1,000 to 1,400 meters. Parts of them were secured by barbed wire and mines."

At the end of April the types of weapons in the combat units in OB West were just as bewildering as the transport vehicle mix. Again, the use of captured weapons was the most available source of equipping the fighting units. The problem here is similar to the transport problem. Equipped with German, French, Polish, Czech, Dutch, Belgian and Russian weapons, the supply of replacement parts and more importantly, ammunition, was not unlimited. The supply organization had to track what units had what vehicles and weapons, and attempt to either produce the ammunition locally in Germany, use captured stocks, or alter the weapons to use German ammunition. It was a system that would quickly break down in battle under the best of conditions, and the *Wehrmacht* was going to utilize such to defeat the most powerful attacking force in the world!

By the summer of 1944 two important events were creating havoc for Germany. As the Russian forces advanced West, they were destroying and capturing German panzers while the Allied day and night bombardment of German industry was making it increasingly difficult to make new ones. An emergency measure that was unsatisfactory in the long term was to increase production at the expense of curtailing the manufacture of spare parts and armored recovery vehicles. As the Wehrmacht was in many cases no longer to hold the battlefield, the panzers that ran out of fuel and those disabled but repairable had to be left behind and were lost permanently. In the last quarter of 1943 almost 1,500 *panzer* and *sturmgeschutz* were lost in this manner and an even larger number of artillery pieces as well.

Atlantikwall

The German disaster at Stalingrad confirmed to the German high command the growing fear that the war in the East was going to last far longer than planned and a successful outcome was in doubt. The impact was reflected in activity in France. In just eleven months, from May 1942 to April 1943 the amount of concrete consumed in *Atlantikwall* fortifications increased from 110,000 cubic meters to 780,000, drastically diverting this increasingly precious commodity from industrial and infrastructure projects due to the fear of Allied invasion on a long and conspicuously exposed coastline. Once again, the events in the east were having their impact on the future of German activity in Western Europe.

Much has been written of the extensive and impressive fortifications in the Pas de Calais region with its giant guns and concrete emplacements but defensive construction was also going on all along the Calvados coastal areas, especially at the actual invasion beaches.

A newly formed bodenstandige division in late 1943, the 709th, was assigned to the U.S. Utah beach area. When the division arrived some effort had been made to prepare the beach defenses, but the commander of its 919th infantry regiment considered them inadequate and began building additional defensive positions. The *Organization Todt* had created a system of pre-designed defensive structures made out of concrete reinforced with steel. They formed a catalog of fixtures that could be ordered as the location and terrain dictated. They were identified, for example, as *Type 667 bunker*. This defense construction was a bunker for a 50mm anti-tank gun. Other defense positions included *Type 134* (ammunition bunker), *Type 702* (squad bunker), *Type 206* (radar bunker) and so on. The types and sizes were designed to meet every possible defensive need. The problem the defenders of the *Atlantik Wall* faced was the shortage of time, labor and materials to build them.

The search for labor to fuel the Reich's war industries was not the only need for this increasingly precious commodity, the vast constructions projects along the Atlantic and Channel coasts were another. With work already progressing on simultaneous projects such as the V-Weapons sites, major port fortifications and railroad, bridge and road construction and maintenance the addition of the *Atlantikwall* project caused a severe shortage. When local labor pools were exhausted, such as the French Labor Service (FLS), the search went farther afield, frequently as far as Paris.

The one most obvious solution to the labor shortage was to utilize the large number of German combat units already on location into making up the labor shortage by adding construction work to their already overextended requirements. Important responsibilities such as training, field maneuvers with larger organizational units and rest were curtailed and the amount of labor hours increased. While this might not sound that injurious to the needs of the defense of the West, it must be kept in mind that most of the non-static divisions were created in 1944 and the need to form these new units in cohesive fighting organizations was paramount and extensive training was the method all armies use. For example, in the 7th Army sector all but one of the non-static divisions was organized in 1944 and all were assigned to construction tasks.

The increasing use of combat units for *atlantik wall* construction work was to adverse effects on combat ability when the fighting started. For example, the static 709th Infantry Division located in the Cotentin Peninsula near Carentan was required to spend up to three days a week on construction tasks and additional tasks were added in the form of transport and guard duties. What little time was left for combat training and rest was insufficient to deal with a unit whose personnel was almost constantly shifting because of inter-unit transfers from West to East and vice-versa.

In the 711th Infantry division sector to the extreme right of the invasion area south of Deauville to the Dives, the following is reported:

> The general training is now almost completely neglected. The whole Division, including the supply units and the rear services, became construction troops. In a few months, at a working speed increased tenfold, a continuous, strong system of obstacles in several rows came into being close to the beach in front of the whole coastal sector for protection against an enemy landing at high tide. Shortly before the beginning of the invasion, at single places (sic), there was under construction yet a second obstacle line- (with) so called "nutcracker" mines, which were sunk into the water by boat in front of the dry ebb-sector, for protection against an enemy landing at low ebb.[305]

What is less known is the difficulties the local commanders; *Organization Todt* managers and combat engineers were having in constructing the defenses in the Carentan, Bayeux and Caen areas. The 352nd Infantry Division in their area was hard pressed to obtain the necessary materials to construct the obstacles. The engineers and men of the Division even had to get permission to cut trees in the Foret de Cerisy for the wood! Even when the wood was obtained, it had to be carried at least 30 kilometers in horse drawn carts, (no fuel) had to be trimmed to size by circular saw

---

[305] *Fighting the Invasion, The German Army at D-Day*, by David C. Isby, Greenhill Books, 2000, p. 147. Reproduced by kind permission of the publisher.

(limited supply) and rammed by hand into the rocky sea bottom, which took a long time. Considering the difficulties with which they worked, the results were quite good.

What is less known was that the installation of these defensive positions, some of them begun in 1942, were beginning to show their age and wear just when they were to be most needed. In the sector of the 243rd Infantry Division the installations had been camouflaged when built but after two years the camouflage had worn away.

Back in the 352nd Division sector the beach obstacles filled up with tidal sand and had to be dug out repeatedly. During storms in April, the mass of these obstacles was torn out, the mines capping the poles and cages exploded and it was necessary to begin again. In addition, of the bunkers and dugouts built, only 15% were considered bomb-resistant and 45% were considered bomb splinter-proof. Almost half the installations were outmoded and improvised.[306]

The distribution of building materials was also a problem. In the Division (352nd) sector, for instance, the Luftwaffe built a personnel shelter with concrete, while the Heer, with their heavy machine guns and ammunition dug their fighting positions out of sand and earth. When the invasion came, the Heer ground holes were flooded with seawater and no longer occupied and the Luftwaffe command bunker with no provision for weapons was useless in the defense.

In other areas the lack of proper defensive measures was showing and improvisation was the order of the day. In the steep coastal area around Longues and St. Pierre du Mont old 240mm shells were embedded by the engineers in the cliffs and by striking a trip wire would come rolling down to explode. These were placed every 100 meters. In addition, small, motorized remote controlled "Goliath" tanks were sent but they arrived the day before the invasion and only a few were launched against the Allies.

The areas behind the beaches were required to be prepared for defense as well. The large open areas were to be made proof against glider and airborne landings. This was done by placing 2-meter poles in the ground and wire strung between them. This was left mostly uncompleted, as the wire never arrived in time. In other districts flooding was considered by

---

[306] In addition to the delayed construction schedule, there was fear that the French laborers were tainting the concrete mix with salt water to weaken it.

damming up streams. This was done but their effectiveness was lost in the warm and dry weather in May. The 709[307] infantry division is a good example for closer examination of German preparedness for the Allied invasion. After the war, its commander in France, *Generalleutnant* Karl Wilhelm von Schlieben was captured and set to work writing his impressions and observations of his unit during the war.

> After two and a half years of uninterrupted assignment as commander of a *Panzergrenadier*, a rifle brigade and a *Panzer* division in Russia, I took over the 709th Infantry Division on the Cotentin peninsula (in France) in December 1943, just before Christmas. My wide experience in all sorts of mobile warfare was not much use to me in my new mission, which was coastal defense.

> The 709th was a division of the 15th Wave.[307] *It did not even have horses* (italics added) and was classified as a static division. The quality of its personnel had decreased through being drained by repeated transfers of men to the Russian front. Apart from steady individual detachments, the entire 1st Battalion of the 739th Grenadier Regiment for instance, had been sent to the Russian front.

> The age of the soldiers and the high percentage of men inexperienced in warfare and belonging to *Volksliste III* were striking. The latter were not Germans but had originated from countries occupied during the war. Their reliability was doubtful. In addition, two Eastern and two Georgian battalions were assigned to the division; I doubted they would fight hard in cases of emergency.[308] The following statement in the London *Daily Telegraph and Morning Post* of Friday, 1 September 1944 makes the point, "In the first days of the invasion one was struck by the unexpectedly high proportion of non-German troops among the units opposed to us. [309]

[307] The Wehrmacht recruited its manpower in "waves", the higher number the Wave, the newer and by general understanding, the poorer the quality of recruits.

[308] An example of the use of eastern manpower to fill out the units guarding the Atlantic coast is shown by one unit in the Netherlands. 88th Armee Korps had 862 men from the north Caucasus, 938 Turks, 823 from the Volga region, 852 from Armenia and 732 from Georgia.

[309] *Fighting The Invasion.*

The recollections of the commanding officer of the 709th in France just before the Allied landings is instructive on a number of points, chief among them assignments of personnel. With the situation in the East in the winter of 1943-44 verging on crisis, the transfer from Russia to France of a skilled officer, experienced in mobile operations is noteworthy indeed. One of the most frequently mentioned subjects in Schlieben recollections was the steady transfer of the best officers and men from the units in France to the Russian Front. In his situation we have the reverse taking place that of his transfer to the Western front, at a time when every trained, experienced and skilled person, especially those in mechanized operations was highly valued in Russia. What can be made of this improbable transfer? Speculation can be made on a number of issues but the one that stands the best test is that of the severe shortage of trained and experienced field commanders. With the slow build up of mechanized units in the West the need for these men in France had to be recognized and included, despite the impact it had on the loss of his services in Russia. It is just one a numerous examples of the impact the war in Russia was having on both fronts. The transfer of Russian volunteers or recruits to France continued unabated, especially in early summer of 1943 and into 1944.

Coastal Artillery

One of the first images that come to mind when discussing the German defenses in northwest France is the giant gun batteries installed there. Without exception these were some of the largest land-based guns in Europe. Indeed, the guns in the largest of these locations at Pas de Calais were made by Krupp based on *Kriegsmarine* specifications. Goebbels' Ministry was quite aware of the propaganda value of these captivating images and the strength they conveyed.[310] However, the Pas de Calais area was not the only coastal area to receive such elaborate and expensive defensive attention. On a slightly smaller scale were the coast artillery emplacements on the Cotentin peninsula.

However impressive these coastal artillery emplacements appear to the casual observer, the men that worked the guns in these concrete fortresses found them to be death traps. They were almost impossible to camouflage properly and Allied intelligence knew their location, design and number from information supplied by French resistance, slave laborers working on

---

[310] One of the most famous of these images is that of the super heavy 406mm casemate and Wehrmacht soldier standing guard in front of one of these giant 16" armored gun casemates at battery "Lindeman" located at Pas de Calais.

the sites and aerial photographic reconnaissance. The concrete, when it wasn't sabotaged, proved to be too thin for the large Allied bombs dropped on them and when the concrete did provide enough protection, the blast effects disabled the fragile gun mounts and sighting optics, and stunned and killed the gun crews servicing the weapons.[311]

A more effective artillery deployment would have been to emplace smaller but more numerous guns in the 155mm to 175mm size range in emplacements spread over a much larger area, with empty alternate sites to deceive Allied naval and air attacks. The German determination to fight it out against Allied naval guns with equally sized weapons was doomed to failure. The Allied control of the air alone would have reduced these large, conspicuous and expensive targets to dusty rubble without interruption by the now enfeebled and distracted Luftwaffe. Ships are mobile and can perform a number of evasive and defensive movements for protection. The fixed, large and conspicuous concrete emplacements, once detected and ranged, became the death traps mentioned above.

Military barrier systems are subject to two conditions that history has shown to render them ineffective, decay and obsolescence. Technological progress of weapons and tactics have had profound impacts on these defensive systems. Unlike more mobile weapons systems such as tanks and aircraft, neither decay nor obsolescence of a fixed barrier may become visible. The forts and emplacements guarded by passive shielding of concrete, of permanently mounted artillery which is rarely tested prior to an outbreak of hostilities, minefields with explosives buried underground and untested (and virtually untestable) for years and the other odds and ends of defensive positions that go untested and are of unknown effectiveness until the heat of combat. Given the shortage of building supplies and of construction personnel it is no wonder that when the invasion came, the defensive promise of this barrier was less than expected.

---

[311] Kaufmann and Kaufmann in their *Fortress Third Reich, German Fortifications and Defense Systems in World War II* by J.E. and H.W. Kaufmann, (Da Capo Press, 2003) mentions in their Appendix 4 a post invasion study undertaken by a U.S. General Rudolf Schmetzer of the heavier defense positions in the invasion area. Entitled *The Effect of Bombs and Heavy Naval Guns on Fortified Defense System of the Atlantic-Wall*. One of the more interesting findings was of the blast and concussive effects of large bombs and shells on and near these works. He describes bent and unusable armored doors and a bunker with "its 11-man crew... were dead-burst lungs. One man... was thrown upward and was hanging under the roof by his uniform". In this same work, in Appendix 2 "Concrete Specifications" details of the type, amounts and methods of reinforcement of concrete for the many different types of defense works is discussed.

In his post-war report made under Allied supervision, *Generalmajor* Gerhard Triepel records the efforts made with regard to artillery preparation on the Cotentin. In his brief, but detailed report he is quite specific regarding not only the calibers of the guns and their units, but also the source of the weapons. In his listing of the bombed sites all but a few are equipped with French and Russian guns. Here is another example of the OKW fixation on the Pas de Calais as the Allied landing area. In addition to the *Waffen SS* panzer units assigned there the best and largest of the German gun batteries were located there as well. The Allied disinformation campaign on where they wanted the Germans to believe would be the real landing areas was alive and well.

However, this emphasis on artillery, its emplacement and use was a major issue for both sides. For the Allies, initially it consisted of naval gunfire until their land artillery batteries could be brought ashore and the battle moved away from the coast. For the Germans, as mentioned above, it was arming the coast with all kinds of large caliber weapons. To demonstrate the effectiveness of Allied artillery, the following is from the Canadian experience in France:

> "*Feldwebel* Hans-Georg Kessler of the 3rd Battalion described the frightening results of the bombardment on an element of the *Panzer-Lehr* Division: We were offered a glimpse of the most horrific face of war. The enemy had systematically hacked an element of the *Panzer-Lehr* Division to pieces with heavy artillery. Beside the obliterated vehicles and weapons lay the pieces of our comrades. Others hung from the trees. It commanded a dreadful silence." In fact, the reconnaissance detachment could only watch as Audrieu and a nearby chateau were reduced to rubble by naval artillery. The troops were forced back about a kilometer to Cristot to construct a new defensive position. Artillery alone had forced the outcome."[312]

In addition to the command of the air over the invasion beaches was the allied naval support in the form of the guns on the destroyers, cruisers and battleships lying just offshore. With their maximum effective range of twenty miles for the largest guns on the battleships, their ability to interdict any target within that range with impunity would have been very difficult for the Germans to overcome. This asset has been frequently

[312] *The Defeat of the 12th SS, 7-10 June 1944*, Oliver Haller, Canadian Military History, Spring 1996.

overlooked in the discussion of the Allies' strength in the preparation and execution of the invasion. Furthermore, the range of Allied naval artillery was grossly underestimated by the Germans. The German planning staffs estimated a maximum range of 10 kilometers where the coast was steep and a range of 20 kilometers where it was flatter. The actual maximum range was 30 kilometers overall. On more than one occasion, close inshore bombardment by the smaller gunships, the destroyers, made the difference in many engagements ashore, and ensured Allied success. A *panzer* force concentrating for a counter attack would have made a prime target for this naval artillery and one that would have been a priority in target selection and the results for the *panzers* would have been almost certain death and destruction.

This accurate gunfire came from six battleships, two monitors, twenty-three cruisers and seventy-three destroyers which supported the landings, not to mention the numerous smaller vessels, such as rocket firing landing craft and minesweepers lying close to shore, ready and able to provide fire support within just a few minutes of being alerted.

The Panzer Threat

The only serious threat to the success of the Allied landings was the 21st *Panzer Division*, located just south of Caen on D-Day. The label of '*Panzer*' division is somewhat misleading as this Division has a unique TOE composition. Originally sent to Africa with Rommel, it had been stationed in France since its re-construction on its return to Europe. Made up of motorized artillery batteries from captured British and French armored tractors in 1940, the Division strived mightily to maintain a mechanized status, in most cases creating and building its own armored vehicles with materials obtained from every source. The unit had no PzKw V "Panther" vehicles.

This creativity notwithstanding, the Division was badly mishandled by OKW on a number of occasions. For example, in the eleven months from July 1943 until the invasion it was stationed in seven different locations, most in France but one as far away as Austria. Finally, in March 1944 it was transferred to Hungary and was halfway there when the transfer order was rescinded. These transfers and their resulting impact on unit readiness and combat effectiveness can be imagined.

The *21ˢᵗ Panzer Division* was the only so-called 'full strength' mechanized combat unit closest to the Allied landing areas. The *12ᵗʰ SS Panzer Division* was a little farther away, but was missing some of its component units. Even with the 21ˢᵗ much closer to the landing beaches, its actual combat capabilities were much less than a standard panzer division. Its lack of combat experience due to a long posting in an inactive area, its unique organizational make-up, its collection of mix-and-match equipment exposed to the elements for years, having the affects one would expect, made this most important German unit much less than it could have been. The 21ˢᵗ was in the right place at the right time. Had it the proper staffing, manpower, training, fuel and equipment it could have been a major impediment to a successful landing for the British.

German Mobility

The Germans planned to add mobility to the units in Normandy but it depended on whether the units could be made mobile, and if the Army Group could provide the weapons to defend their assigned sectors. (The attempt was made by von Rundstedt by taking one regiment from the coastal division's mobile reserve and making them into *Kampfgruppen* by adding motorized transport.) To demonstrate the paucity of resources in OB West, the 243ʳᵈ Infantry Division was converted from a static defense unit into a mobile attack infantry division, following the new 1944 structure of six battalions. The mobility came from four of the six battalions which were to be made 'mobile' by the use of bicycles! This was the 1944 *Wehrmacht* concept of a mobile infantry unit; mobility was to be gained by the addition of bicycles and horses. The new definition of mobility was if a division that could maintain itself in the field rather than having an ability to move from one locale to another! It was an amazing and tragic change from the nation that showed the world what a motorized army could do; now reduced to its new concept of 'mobile' (as opposed to motorized/mechanized) warfare.[313]

The mobility issue applied to more than just the infantry divisions; it also affected the cream of the land infantry fighting units, the Luftwaffe's *Fallschrimjager* (parachute) divisions. The 6ᵗʰ *Fallschrimjager Regiment*,

---

[313] As has become common knowledge, the extent of German military mechanization was more myth than reality. Even in 1943 a German infantry division used 5,375 horses compared to 942 motor vehicles. Combat unit motorization never exceeded 20% during the war. This heavy reliance on real live horse power, in its most literal sense, in the harsh environments of battle and climate cost the lives of over 1.5 million of these faithful animals in the German Army alone during the war.

for instance, had only seventy trucks and these comprised fifty different models. It is no wonder that when these units met the Allies on 6 June their effectiveness was short lived.

The German development of *bodenstandige* division is a testament to the effects the war in Russia was having on the Wehrmacht's ability to field a competent army to fight and win the war. Along the 1,200 miles of the *Atlantik Wall* there were 23 of these divisions; they were missing all the essential items that they would need in the coming battle; weapons, transport, training and manpower.

Even the so-called mobile division, the *panzergrenadier* and *fallschrimjager* divisions felt the effects of the war in the east. The use of horses and bicycles, foreign and patchwork vehicles and equipment to make them mobile was an inadequate response to the serious and threatening challenge ahead.

Allied Success

Here again is another example of what effects the war in the east was having on the preparations in the west to repel the Allied invasion. With the eastern armies consuming almost the entire output of German weapons production, the armies under OBWest had to make do with cast-off, repaired, captured and second rate equipment. The list of needs is a long one: The lack of motorized transport of all kinds, a Luftwaffe that could command the skies over the invasion beaches; German led and equipped combat units; a single language in the units, mechanized counter attack units to launch the important counter stroke to defeat the invasion; artillery, automatic weapons, mines, construction equipment and labor to construct the beach defenses, fuel to run it all, and training to know how to operate it all.

The one bright spot in this picture of gloom was the units north of the Normandy invasion site, Seventh Army, those at the Pas-de-Calais. From Le Touquet in the south to Dunkerque to the north, in the Fifteenth Army area was deployed, not only the strongest units in OBWest, but in many cases, of whole the German Army. Located west of the Dives River, the dividing line between Seventh and Fifteenth Armies, was, from south to north: the *Panzer Lehr* division, the 12th SS Panzer Division *Hitlerjugend*, 116th Panzer Division and the 2nd Panzer Division. Within a one or two day road march of Normandy was the 1st SS Panzer Division *Liebstandarte Adolf Hitler* in Belgium, 17th SS Panzer Grenadier Division *Gotz von Berlichingen* southwest of Tours. Further away was the 9th Panzer Division on the Rhone River in Aix-in- Provence, the 2nd SS Panzer Division *Das Reich* north of Toulouse and the 11th Panzer north of Bordeaux on the Atlantic coast. They may have been the best but they were in the wrong place.

In the British sector, with the exception of the 21st Panzer Division located in Seventh Army, the sector to bear the brunt of the Allied attack, at Caen, no other panzer or panzer grenadier division was located in the attack sector. Although making a valiant effort in a counterattack on D-Day, driving to within a mile or so of the beaches, the unit took a terrific pounding from Allied shipboard guns and air support and was quickly forced to retreat. With that attack went the Germans first and only serious threat to the Allied efforts in establishing a beachhead and staying ashore.

In the U.S. landing sector, especially at Omaha beach, the one serious threat to a successful landing came from the only full strength German infantry division in the entire Allied landing area, the 352nd. The rough handling the U.S. Vth Corps received from the 352nd could have been repeated all along the invasion beaches had OB West not been used as the *Wehrmacht's* replacement depot for Russia for the last three years. It was not for want of trying, poor management or stupidity that OBWest was not properly prepared for Overlord on 6 June 1944. Allied air, sea and land strength was overwhelming, the weather cooperated, luck was there when needed and added to the scales. The extensive and very successful invasion deception scheme, Operation Fortitude, had OKW fooled not only as to where the landing would take place, but continued to befuddle OBWest and OKW for some weeks after the landing. This was so convincing that the plotters at Fortitude persuaded the Germans that the landings at Normandy were just a decoy for the even larger landings that would take place in the Pas-de-Calais, the landing that never came.

The German determination to defeat the Allies at or near the landing beaches was a sound concept, as long as they could react to Allied weapons in kind. The complete lack of German air support of any kind may well have been the determining factor in the Allied success. The lack of resources to provide protection for the shore defenders, disrupt the landing process, and defeat the naval guns on the battleships and cruisers was key. The Axis defense was hampered by very effective ground attack fighters, medium and heavy bombers and naval gunnery of all kinds. If only one of these weapon systems, air or naval, could have been eliminated or suppressed, the German ground defenders could have made the Allied landings much more costly and even defeated the Allies at one or more of the landing sites. Germany and the new Western front was a fortress without a roof.

Allied air support for the invasion was so crucial that the decision to launch the invasion on the 6th of June was based on the weather permitting Allied air activity over the invasion beaches. On 4 June, at the 0415 daily briefing meeting, Eisenhower said that if the air cannot operate we must postpone the invasion. Such was the Allied reliance on effective and uninterrupted air support.[314]

The German failure in the air deserves closer examination. The once preeminent air force in the world was almost non-existent over the landing beaches of France. Where was it? What happened to it?

The lack of adequate Luftwaffe support to the defense of the *Atlantik Wall* was not entirely because of the war in the East. With the onset of the Allied strategic bombing campaign against German industry, the Luftwaffe was now tasked with defending the air above the Reich as well as providing support to the field armies. With Germany fighting in Russia, Italy and now France and Northwest Europe, the capabilities of the Luftwaffe, already stretched to the limit was now beyond its abilities to be effective in any one of these commitments.

This is not to say that nothing could have been done in support of the forces in France. The subject of defensive mining along the Channel coast in suspected invasion areas could have been conducted or increased. Mining of British ports and harbors, not only by aircraft, but also using the surface vessels of the Kriegsmarine and the mine laying U-Boats of the *U-Bootwaffe*. In and of itself a mining operation would have not stopped or assisted materially in the defense of France, however it would have injected an element of caution and avoidance of suspected mined areas and the need to clear lanes for shipping and assault craft. As there was almost no German naval activity in the English Channel, even free-floating mines (mines not tethered to the sea bed) would have had added a cautionary effect to the invasion plans and operations.

---

[314] For an inside view into the decision making process of the Allied high command in launching the invasion, see *The Storm Before The Storm*, by Carlo D'Este, May/June 2010, *World War II*, Vol. 25, No. 1.

The conspicuous failure of the Luftwaffe to contribute to the defense against the Allied landings, its mismanagement by Göring was brought to Hitler's attention for a decision by none other than *Reichpropaganda Minister* Goebbels. As early as February 1943, after the German defeat at Stalingrad, Goebbels confronted Hitler with the need to replace Göring. As much as the evidence demonstrated it, Hitler could not bring himself to part with one of his *alte kampfer* one of his old fighters. Göring stayed on.

This represents a significant failure within the German military command and is noteworthy in that it demonstrates that even with limited capabilities there was more that could have been done to repel the Allied landings. This represents a lack of foresight and creativity in the highest levels of the Luftwaffe[315] and the OKW, and demonstrates the growing weakening and overall impotence of the Wehrmacht.

Finally, the Allied deception operations in the form of Operation Bodyguard and Operation Fortitude were so successful and influential that the most dangerous and effective German combat divisions were kept in and around the Pas-de-Calais during and after the invasion. So convincing was this masterful plan that even with the U.S. breakout into the heartland of France at St. Lo on 25 July and the more devastating rupture of the German defense at Avranches on 31 July, OKW still resisted in recognizing the Normandy landings for what they were, the main landing site, the real thing.[316]

"The German Command missed its opportunities. It was weighed down by the nightmarish fear that further large-scale landing operations might, indeed were bound to take place at other points of the coast. The dummy fleet in British ports and the cardboard-and-plywood army encampments in Kent, mistaken for the real things by German reconnaissance crews, served to confirm the High Command in its idée fixe. Moreover, the rules governing amphibious operations were unknown to the generals of the German High Command. Divisions were allowed to stand to on the west coast of France for fear of further landings,

---

[315] In August 1944, after repeated disappointments with the Luftwaffe and its head, Goering, the Germans began to consider completely dismantling it and replacing it with anti-aircraft guns!

[316] For an excellent discussion of the cover and deception planning and operations see *Bodyguard of Lies* by Anthony Cave Brown.

although such landings were in fact impossible in those areas because of weather and beach conditions. Thus, the paradoxical situation arose that by the end of June, the Americans alone had landed on their sector of the front four corps with fourteen divisions, which were opposed on the German side by only three intact divisions and the remnants of three shattered divisions and five regiments-a fighting force roughly equivalent, allowing for its equipment, to five divisions. Yet entire armies were helplessly watching the German tragedy from their quarters on the southern and western coasts of France and the seaside resorts of Belgium and Holland: pinned down by orders based on a total misreading of the situation."[317]

Eastern Influence

The disposition of German division strength throughout Europe was bewildering in its scope and breath. In June 1944 the *Wehrmacht* had the following numbers of divisions assigned to the following countries, from east to west, a total of 295:

> Russia, Army Group South Ukraine 35;
>
> Russia, Army Group North Ukraine 41;
>
> Russia, Army Group Center 41;
>
> Russia, Army Group North 40;
>
> Finland 6;
>
> Yugoslavia 21,
>
> Italy 26;
>
> Germany 9;
>
> Denmark 6;
>
> Norway 12;
>
> France 58.

Once again we see the imbalance of German force disposition with regard to the impending threat in France. The 184 divisions in Russia, Finland and Yugoslavia represent 62% of the total. It also represents the importance of the eastern front to the Allied war effort in draining away

---

[317] *Invasion, They're Coming*, pp. 222 - 223.

the bulk of German military field strength from the fragile amphibious invasion soon to be attempted in France. Consider if these percentages had been reversed, the success of the invasion at Normandy would have been questionable.

Given the extreme state of Germany's eastern armies, was there a need for 12 divisions in Norway or 6 in Denmark? The assignment of these units to these peripheral areas of the war can only be credited to the successful Allied efforts of the cover and deception plans for the invasion of Western Europe. Consider what the addition of 18 division-sized units to any of the German combat fronts in mid 1944 would have meant to the commander in that theater, it would be considered a gift indeed. It illustrates that the Germans really had no true knowledge of where the landings would take place and the troop assignments to Norway and Denmark are evidence of it. It was a German intelligence failure of the highest order.

Carell sums up the feelings of the German *Landser*, of the incomprehensible blunder made in western France that summer of 1944:

> "And yet it proves that modern war, for all its technical complexity, is decided as much by miscalculations as by weapons. There is a lesson in that for those who think of power only in terms of technical superiority."[318]

What is now evident is the desperation of an occupying nation the size and capability of Germany attempting to do what was patently impossible: fortify a significant portion of the Western European coastal land mass. It quickly became clear that Germany and its reluctant allies would never have enough fingers to plug the holes in its fortification dyke. Its only hope of a successful defense of Western Europe was to know where and when the Allied invasion was coming, and as we have seen in this they were terribly wrong. Their intelligence services had failed the military command and they were left to guessing.

Despite Germany's best attempts, it simply could not fight a multiple front war; it could not tolerate the damage to its fighting forces, and the cavalcade of strategic errors by its supreme command. It was also quickly running out of space and time to recover from them, not to mention the Allied day and night air raids on the Reich and occupied territories.

---

[318] *Invasion, They're Coming*, p. 221.

Germany had neither the manpower, the industrial capacity, nor the reliable allies to fight off what amounted to the rest of the free world.

From one of the most flexible, fluid and able armies in the world, the war in Russia was destroying the very essence of the *Wehrmacht*. The army that invented the *Blitzkrieg* now in Northwest France had no more ability to conduct the slashing, dashing, lightning offensive warfare than their opponents had four years previously.

With the impending Allied invasion of Western Europe, and especially France as the most likely location for the landings, Western Europe could no longer be the relatively quiet rest and refit areas for a tired *Wehrmacht*. Within weeks, France itself was to become a battleground, with the same destructive intensity of men and material that Russia was. By the spring of 1944 Germany and her allies were in desperate straits in the east, and soon was to have another front to cope with. The outlook was bleak indeed.

Chapter Fourteen:
Byelorussia
June 1944

"This was a perfect battle of annihilation. In the summer of 1944 the Roman battle of Cannae in Italy was replayed on the Berezina in Russia."

Paul Carell, "Scorched Earth"

"Time is Blood."

Vasily Chuikov commenting on the classic Russian strategy of trading lives for time

When discussing the invasion of Normandy, one tends to think of it as a major turning point in the Second World War. Indeed it was. The successful landings in Normandy announced the arrival of the Allies' return to the mainland of Western Europe, never to leave, their presence continually growing. What is less known in the West is that there was another turning point in Europe, in the same month and year, that was just as important and vital to the successful Allied accomplishment at Normandy. That was the Soviet June 1944 attack against the German forces in Eastern Ukraine and Western Russia in Operation Bagration.

This chapter will describe the events that spelled the end of any chance the German campaign in Russia during World War II would end in victory; Operation Bagration, the massive Russian attack against Germany's Army Group Center in Byelorussia in June 1944. The chapter will look at the present situation of the German Army Group, its defensive preparations and the warning signs of a coming attack. It will also look at the newest Russian weapons and their impact on the battle. Finally, it will examine the impact of the battle had on Germany's overall military situation and the impact it had on the war in France.

Before Stalin launched Operation Bagration the German forces enjoyed the ability to trade space and time, to outmaneuver and retreat in the face of superior forces and stave off disaster time after time. It also spelled the end of the one front war for Germany, the Wehrmacht in Italy notwithstanding. The fateful month of June 1944 brought the long awaited second front to the Allied war effort and Germany would now have to contend with the prospect of being caught in a vise-like position between East and West. Short of the Allied coalition falling apart, the sands of time were running out for Hitler. Russia was about to end the German dream of *Lebensraum* in the East.

By the third week of June the initial stages of the Allied invasion of North-western France was complete and the follow-on forces were growing and a secure beachhead was all but completed. By D+17 (D-Day plus seventeen days later) the Normandy invasion forces had pushed as far inland as Grenville in the west, Vire to the south and Cabourg in the east, a maximum advance of some 40 miles. Despite the best efforts of the German defenders in containing the Allies who were bringing in substantial amounts of men and equipment, the entire Cotentin peninsula and the Caen area of Normandy was firmly under Allied control.

With the battle in France about to slip out of control for Germany, the launching of Operation Bagration in Russia further constrained the actions of what the defending German forces could do to prevent catastrophe. The Allied buildup and advance inland in France had to be stopped and the Russian army's in Belorussia had to be, if not stopped, at least slowed and worn down in combat action. Failure of either meant a second world war loss for Germany in the 20th century.

Foreboding

With the end of the Spring rasputitsy in early May the Russian buildup of men and materials opposite Germany's Army Group Center did not go unnoticed. Despite the extensive efforts to keep the reinforcements from being detected, the weary veterans of four years of fighting the Russians had, like most experienced field soldiers, learned to "read" the enemy lines. Radio intelligence listening stations reported new radio nets originating from Russian units not detected previously, indicating the presence of new units in the area.

On the ground there was a real sense that something big was going to happen, it was the "gut feeling" of many of the German sentries and infantry in the line. By mid-June the summer weather had turned hot and dry and the ground, despite the generally marshy terrain became hard and dusty. The morning routine was unchanged, as it had been for months, there is the usual 4 or 5 plumes of wood smoke from the Russian side, probably from the field kitchens. But recently, as May turned to June, more are noticed, soon it is a dozen, several days later it is too many to count as they begin to mix and blend together. Even the birds, so plentiful in this damp region have disappeared.

At night there is the usual sounds of life at the front; the regular firing of flares to light the no-man's-land between the opposing positions, the occasional rip of machine gun fire, or crack of a bursting hand grenade checking some perceived patrolling movement in the dark. Occasionally one might hear the sound of an engine, but it's usually the battalion chow wagon or a staff car from HQ. But in the last week or so, the usual motor sounds have become deeper, different and muffled, the sounds of engines, many engines. These engine sounds are not from the Russian made trucks and cars, these sounds are new. The new engine sounds come from American trucks and Jeeps and generate worried comment in the dark among the sentries, the sound they make is different from Russian engines. But what worries the tired Germans most is the big engines, the deeper sounds they hear. What they are hearing is the newer up-gunned T-34, the T-34/85 tanks, and their new 'big brother' the JS-1 and JS-2 heavy tanks. As the days grow closer to the attack date, the sounds of the engines become more numerous, louder and closer, some men back from patrols report that they heard the actual clanking of tank tracks. There were many of them, far too many, many more then the Germans had.

In the air the usual Russian reconnaissance aircraft was present, jinking to and fro when they got too low and the German flak gunners took a few shots at them. But the usual daily airplane, its appearance as reliable as the *landsers* units 'goulash cannon', the field kitchen, was joined by several others and they came more frequently and when they arrived, stayed longer and flew lower, flak gun fire or not. They seemed to spend a lot of time over the front lines lately.

Other signs of significance were changing; sentry routines, soldiers wearing helmets instead of soft cloth caps, a sure sign of an impending attack, movement of soldiers across areas covered by German fire, another sign of new or arriving units unfamiliar with their positions and finally, from captured and Russian deserters was learned the politruks were issuing vodka, typical behavior prior to an attack. The signs were mounting.

Additional signs of the changing routine at the front of the Army Group was Russian artillery fire. The men occupying the front lines had learned to identify the source of the shells by the sounds they made as they passed high overhead and guessed where they would land. For months the counter battery fire and interdiction and disruption firing of the Russian guns meant these shells landed far to the rear of the front and they had learned to ignore them. But lately, the shells had a different sound, a shorter, quicker and more deadly sound. These shells were now landing in the front line positions, and not just occasionally and randomly, but in groups, more frequently and pointedly at the trench and communications lines. The veterans in the units knew what this change in artillery fire was for, the Russians were registering their guns range for an attack. New guns, many guns.

In response to these reports OKH responded that it's nothing more than a diversion. If it is, it seemed to be the biggest diversion these experienced men have ever heard. So confident were OKH in their assessment of enemy intentions the senior field command and Army Group Center commander left for home leave on the 19th.

Finally, the most disturbing of all, when the German sentries are relieved in the morning they report that sections of the defensive barbed wire that had been carefully and painstakingly laid in the last several months were missing and not just randomly, but in straight paths, paths that pointed to the German front lines. These reports were not limited to a few areas, but all along the army group front. It had been discovered that at night the Russians had been clearing the extensive German mine belts and are preparing the area by removing the barbed wire. That can only mean one thing, they are coming!

The Partisans

When the Russian artillery fire announcing Operation Bagration began on 23 June 1944, it was not the first actions of the attack, the first shots fired were far behind the front line, from the Russian Partisan units a day earlier.

The three years prior to Operation Bagration was one long period of recruitment for them, facilitated by the harsh German occupation and racial policies. By the summer of 1944 the strength of the Russian Partisan movement had grown to some 250,000 men and women, now firmly controlled from Moscow through STAVKA by a dedicated staff devoted just to Partisan operations. Many of the by-passed Russian Army soldiers from the early days of the great German encirclements and the terrified local population who fled to the dense forests to avoid German labor recruitment and anti-Jewish operations from the *Einsatzkommando* were now organized into a formidable force behind the German front lines. In the areas behind Army Group Center there was an estimated 150,000 Partisans organized into some 150 brigade sized units and 49 other smaller detachments.

Although Partisan operations were directed against many German installations, as time went by the most important of these, such as bridges, supply depots, rail yard complexes and communication centers had become too well protected and attacks against these objectives were not worth the higher casualties that usually resulted.

What the Partisans came to excel in was attacks against the most vulnerable of all German installations in Russia, the German rail network. The many thousands of miles of unprotected track in dense forests and remote locations were prime targets of the Partisans. Although the *Deutsch Reichbahn*, the German rail system, devised many defensive measures to defend this vulnerable and vital network, only a small portion of it could be protected at any one time.

In preparation for Operation Bagration, on 8 June the Partisan units were activated by a coded signal to begin their anti-rail campaign on 19 June. During the night of 21-22 June 1944 the partisans, despite an ongoing German anti-partisan operation, Operation *Kormoran*, in the Army Group rear areas, planted explosives at some 10,500 points along the German rail system. Although a third of them were detected and removed, the remaining charges severed thousands of track sections and was sufficient to stop all German rail movement for almost two days, two crucial days during the opening of the attack.

Russian Mobility

The Russian Army of 1944 was now largely a mechanized and motorized force. The incorporation of thousands of U.S. trucks and Jeeps, part of the Lend-Lease delivery's gave the ground forces a mobility and tactical "reach" that seriously disrupted German defense plans, causing what turned out to be a continuous fallback operation advancing the Russian forces much farther than they had in previous Russian attacks.

There are numerous photographs of Russian commanders and troops riding in and standing near U.S. made Jeeps and trucks of various kinds. These robust and rugged vehicles with their reputation for mechanical dependability would serve them well all during the war and for decades afterwards.

Russian mobility no longer was dependant on their old system of rail and marching to move their men and material by 1944. During the three years of German occupation, German railroad construction troops had changed the width of the Russian rails from the broad Russian gage to the narrower European gage Germany and the rest of Europe used.

In addition to the rail gage conversion was the state of the rail system itself. During the German retreat, their pioneer troops developed a track and rail roadbed destruction device known as a "wolfs tooth". This was a hook-like device mounted on a small flat rail wagon that was dragged behind the car and digging under the wooden roadbed sleepers, ripped them up and broke them in half, rendering the tracks unusable. In the past, this had been sufficient to slow and in some cases stop the Russian advance when the supplies of fuel, ammunition and food the combat units carried with them ran out. With the introduction of new Lend-Lease trucks this was no longer a tactic Germany could depend on.

Russian Artillery

Organizationally no army during World War II used as much artillery as did the Russian Army and in no battle was it used in such variety, quantity and effectiveness as in Operation Bagration. Separated into its two main classifications of cannon and un-guided rockets, Russian field artillery would come to dominate enemy artillery from 1942 until the end of the war.

The Russian artillery division as organized for Operation Bagration consisted of 76mm, 122mm (both guns and howitzers) and 152mm guns and howitzers as well as 120mm heavy mortars. The most widely used was the 76mm USV M-1939 divisional gun. It was also produced for the T-34/76A tank as well as in the ZIS-1 truck-towed anti-tank version. The 76mm gun became the best known of all the Russian guns as it was in production before the war and was widely available and it outclassed all the dedicated German tank and anti-tank guns. It was reliable, easy to manufacture and its high velocity and flat trajectory made it a potent weapon. Captured in large numbers in the first year of the war, and impressed with its performance, Germany turned it against its former owners under the designation *PaK 36 (r)*, the *PaK* was the abbreviation for the German *Panzer Abwehr Kanone* or anti-tank cannon, the small 'r' indicated Russian origin. It was also mounted on the German *Marder* II and *Marder* III tracked anti-tank vehicles.

In preparation for major attacks heavier artillery was usually needed to break open enemy defensive positions and that was the role of the heavy field guns. Included in the Russian heavy artillery inventory were the 210mm BR-17 and 305mm BR-18 siege guns. Although possessed of great range (the 203mm B-4 howitzer had a range of 28,650 meters/16.3 miles) the rate of firing the howitzer was less than one shell per minute. Technically classified as howitzers, these heavy, slow firing guns were organized and maintained by higher command units and used almost exclusively major operations, primarily against large fixed targets such as forts, cities, etc.

Finally, the most uniquely Russian artillery piece was the rocket mortar. Popularly known as the *Katyusha* or 'Stalins Organs' as the Germans called them the truck mounted multiple rocket launcher systems by the start of Operation Bagration had projectiles as large as 300mm (M-31uk) weighing over 63 pounds with a range of over two miles. There were two dedicated Guards Mortar (Multiple Rocket) Divisions at the start of the operation, one assigned to the 1st Byelorussian Front and another included with the 3rd Byelorussian Front, however there was additional rocket mortar units assigned throughout the attacking forces as needed. Stalin called artillery The God of War (*Bog Voyny*) and throughout the war no army has understood this better than the Russian Army.[319]

Shturmovik!

By 1944 the Russian air force had its own version of the famous German Junkers Ju-87 dive and attack bomber. The Ilyushin Il-2 ground attack aircraft, popularly known as the *Shturmovik,* this fully armored single-engined aircraft armed with a 23mm or and 37mm cannon was unique aircraft design in that it did not have armor protected areas such as for the engine, pilot, fuel tanks, etc. as other nations ground attack aircraft were, the *Shturmovik* was constructed out of armor plate, so it was really a flying tank and it is this unique construction method that made the Shturmovik very rugged and difficult to shoot down. For Operation Bagration over 1,744 *Shturmovik's* were included in the 5,300 aircraft assigned to the operation in several Guards Strike Aviation Divisions.

So vital was this aircraft to the successes of Russian ground operations that over 36,000 *Shturmovik's* were built during the war. When Stalin found a factory that was behind in its deliveries, he sent the manager a notice telling him to catch up as "they were as important to the Army as the air it breathes and bread it eats."[320] If this appeal to the manager's patriotism wasn't sufficient motivation, the rest of the message ends on a more sinister note, "I ask you not to try the government's patience. This is my final warning."

The *Shturmovik* was especially effective over the Bagration battlefront due to the sparse *Luftwaffe* presence. The 2,318 Russian fighters of the latest design were able to maintain complete control of the air all throughout the days and weeks of the fighting, the Luftwaffe was only able to muster 40 operational fighters. Although there were 106 German ground attack aircraft, mostly Junkers Ju-87D and G *Stuka* dive bomber and ground attack and Focke-Wulf A, F and G fighter-bomber machines, against the overwhelming Russian numbers, they had little impact on Russian progress.

---

[319] The development of the multiple rocket mortar system was a carefully kept secret in the Russian Army. The initial deployments in July 1941were entrusted to the NKVD units only. It wasn't until late 1944 that Western Allied forces were permitted to see the units in action.

[320] Hardesty, p. 70, 1982.

A Tank Named Stalin

One final weapon needs inclusion and discussion before we begin examining the battle of Operation Bagration, and that is the JS-2 or, in Russian, IS-2, heavy Russian main battle tank, the tank named for Stalin.

The battle of Kursk a year earlier revealed the need for a more powerful tank then the existing T-34 series. Even with the replacement of the 76.2mm gun with an 85mm gun, the T-34 did not have sufficient armor protection to confront the latest German tanks. The German Panther[321] with its high velocity 75mm gun and both versions of the Tiger with its 88mm gun easily penetrated the frontal armor of the most recent models of the T-34 at long ranges. The standard Russian heavy tank, the KV-1 by 1944 was no longer proof against even the German 75mm guns on the most recent models of the *Sturmgeschutz* IIIG. A new tank was needed.

Although Kursk demonstrated the need for a new more powerful tank, development and design for a replacement for the KV-1 had begun as far back as late 1942. Many combinations of hull and turret shapes were tested and main guns were considered. Early versions of the JS-2 were fitted with the 85mm gun (known as the IS-85) but to keep ahead of the 88mm German gun performance a new larger 122mm gun was to be the standard main gun armament to insure battlefield superiority. One interesting feature the JS-2 included was the ball mounted rear firing turret mounted machine gun. In addition to the more powerful main armament, the tank was powered by the V-2-10 series of diesel engine providing adequate operating power (520 hp) with the characteristic low fire risk diesel engines are known as well as excellent low temperature operation.

The new tank proved to be a success during the last year of the war, providing the Russian tanks forces with a weapon of equal lethality of the Tiger. Deployment of the JS-2 began in the March of 1944 with the first vehicles issued to the 11th, 71st and 72nd Guards Heavy Tank Regiment in the 1st Ukrainian Front and to the 6th and 14th Guards Heavy Tank Regiments in the 2nd Ukrainian Front.

The JS-2 met its opposite number, the Tiger II, in August 1944 for the first time in the vicinity of Sandomir in the closing days of Operation Bagration and acquitted itself well, the result was a draw. Field reports

---

[321] The German *PzKw V Panther* is considered, at 47 tons weight, a medium tank. Both models of the German *PzKw VI Tiger* were considered heavy tanks, Tiger I at 56 tons and Tiger II at 68 tons. The Russian JS-2 weighed 46 tons and was considered a heavy tank.

noted the slow rate of loading (3 rounds per minute) and the smoke from the main gun obscuring the gun sight were problems, but the tanks overall mechanical reliability permitted operations up to 40 to over 60 miles per day, road speeds of 16 miles per hour, half that going cross country and an engine life of 270 hours between service overhauls.

Almost a thousand of the JS-2's were made by the end of the war and went on to serve for another 30 years in foreign armies. The JS-2 provided the Russian Army with an answer to the latest German tanks and supplied the 'punch' for the breakthrough attacks in Operation Bagration and later in city fighting in Konigsberg and Berlin.

The Opening Movements

The first few days of the offensive were spent probing the German position looking for weak spots in the German lines after which the *frontoviki* supported by massive artillery bombardments shattered the German defensive units. The Red Air Force, now having complete air superiority, although hampered by an early morning round fog, supported the ground attack and caused such disruption in and among the German units that communications became all but impossible. Field telephone and telegraph lines were broken at numerous points, forcing division and corps to reply on human messengers on foot, bicycle and motor vehicle. These were much more exposed and vulnerable to Russian fire, and many were lost, went to the wrong units or were never heard from again. With total command of the air and ground communications now seriously disrupted, Army Group command had no picture of enemy intentions or points of effort and resulted in directing the few reserves to the wrong sector or failed to dispatch them at all. Frequently this delay was fatal to both units, the one to be reinforced and the reserve. As the Soviet advance was so swift, the German reserve reinforcing units soon found they were now the front line unit and they had barely moved!

The attacks were made by four Russian Fronts, from north to south; First Baltic, Third Byelorussian, Second Byelorussian and First Byelorussian. They began a series of concentric attacks to surround the German front line units, to prevent them from retreating and thus opening gaps in the line for the tank and mechanized follow-on units, such as the 5th Tank Army under Marshal P. A. Rotmistrov. In addition were 5 tank corps and two artillery corps, the newest and largest organizational size of field artillery in the Russian Army.

The first week of Operation Bagration the Russian attack was relentless and aggressive and the Germans were stunned by its location, direction, ferocity and scale. The operation was to last 68 days and the attack frontage spanned a length of some 620 miles. The Germans had badly miscalculated the focus of the Russian summer offensive, and with the panzer divisions in Army Group North and South Ukraine, and the restrictions of their maneuver brought on by the *Festung* cities, the German front collapsed quickly and completely. Whole German divisions disappeared in the curtain of Russian fire and steel, causing a headlong retreat to the west in spite of Hitler's stand-fast order. With the improved Russian transport and supply system, the offensive surprised the OKH with the newfound Russian tactical flexibility and movement. German strong points were bypassed and Russian tank units kept moving west.

The German *festung* cities of Vitebsk, Orsha and Mogilev and Bobruysk, intended to form outposts against which the Germans hoped the Russian attacks would be stalled, were bypassed, surrounded and later captured. Vitebsk and Rogachev on the 25th, Mogilev on the 27th of June. The valuable German infantry surrounded in them were lost; killed or captured. Attempts to break out and retreat west, in some cases in units as large as regiments, mostly failed as there was no close German positions to retreat to, so fast was the Russian Westward movement, surrounding, destroying, dispersing and pushing aside German units. The size of the attack, the Russian superiority in men, tanks, artillery and aircraft made any German attempt to form a blocking position, much less a front line, all but impossible.

By the end of June Bobruisk was encircled and Borisov was retaken. The progress was steady and constant, the pressure on the German units was relentless allowing no time to form up and prepare defensive positions to halt the attack. In early July the Berezina River was crossed along almost all its length in the Army Group area, a significant development as the Berezina was suggested at one time by the German command to be the front defense line for the Army Group back in the early Spring.

The content of radio communications flowing into Division, Army and Army Group headquarters demonstrate the shock, disruption and chaos in the German units from the Russian attack. From both infantry and panzer units the reports were stunning; phrases such as "completely encircled", "4th Luftwaffe Field Division no longer exists", "the commander of

134th Division has shot himself" and "Division command no longer has control over the division" and "confusion reigns" describe the magnitude of the unfolding disaster along the German front.

Reports of failed breakout attempts of lost, wounded, and missing commanders and men filled the airwaves. This was no diversion for an operation in another portion of the front, this was the feared Russian main attack and the German forces were not ready for it.

The Destruction of Army Group Center

It is important that the reader understand the gravity in the content of the sampled messages above. The German armed forces prided themselves on their Prussian discipline, their ability to withstand any enemy, any weather, any discomfort, and persevere. The wholesale destruction of almost an entire army group from a nation the size of Germany staggers the imagination; it certainly did the German one. Whole Army Corps disappearing, generals shooting themselves, *divisions* out of control? These things happened to other, more primitive armies; the Russian Army perhaps, certainly not the German Army. Losses on this scale were unsurpassed; even the terrible winter before Moscow in December 1941 (110,000 casualties)[322] and the white hell of Stalingrad of 1942-1943 (231,000 casualties)[323] pale in comparison.

This breakdown in discipline in the combat units was profoundly disturbing, not only to OKW, but to the soldier as well. There had been discipline problems prior to the Russian attack, but it had been confined to individuals or small units. But for the first time we see confusion, disarray, despair and outright disobedience on a major unit level; and large units at that, in some cases divisions. It was another sign that the combat units on the Eastern Front, especially the Army, had reached a new depth of ineffectiveness due to exhaustion, fear and defeatism, all of which required increasing amounts of threats and brute force to overcome.

Hitler's establishment of *festung* cities on the Eastern Front almost ensured the units entrusted with garrisoning and defending them would become surrounded by enemy forces.[324] The Russian double envelopment maneuver north and south of Stalingrad, another *festung* city, caused Hitler

---

[322] *Moscow 1941* by Robert Forczyk, p. 89.

[323] *Stalingrad to Berlin: The German Defeat In the East*, p.79.

[324] The Germans named the Army Group Center's defense line, which include the fortified cities, "The Fatherland Line".

to justify their remaining in place ostensibly to tie down Russian units and prevent them from advancing West. By 1944 there was always going to be more Russian units then German units, using entrapped German units to tie down equal or larger numbers of enemy troops was an absurd justification from any perspective.

When Hitler issued his 'stand fast' order to the *festung* cities of Vitebsk, Orsha, Mogilev and Bobruisk, he removed all tactical freedom of movement by the local commanders. In his orders of 8 March 1944, (Order Number 11) he defined the term "fortified locality":

> "The fortified localities are intended to discharge the same function as fortresses of the past; they must prevent the enemy from taking possession of strategically vital localities, they must allow themselves to become encircled, and in this way tie down the largest possible number of enemy forces. In this way they will also play a part in creating the prerequisite for successful counter-operations"

The order reads like one from the dark ages, the age of castles when a noble would close himself and his army in a castle awaiting eventual relief, staving off the attacker. Such was the mindset of the Fuehrer of the Third Reich; however there would be no savior rushing to relieve an encircled Germany.

Such a tactical doctrine has a serious negative effect on the encircled troops' morale. A doctrine that knowingly permits ones units to be surrounded by superior enemy forces with questionable hope of relief deep in a foreign land, cannot but help to undermine the fighting spirit of even strongest combat units. Secondly, a glance at the manpower balance sheet would clearly demonstrate that the Russian forces could easily devote the troops to surround and contain the fortress cities, while their mobile units pressed on ahead, pushing the potential relief forces further and further away from the beleaguered city or position. The net effect of this tactic was to demoralize the contained units and write-off the men and equipment in the surrounded city. It entailed the loss of, and the protection afforded by the city itself, (no small consideration in Russia in the winter months) and, if favorable conditions permitted, the use of scarce and irreplaceable mechanized units (and their equally scarce fuel and oil) to attempt a relief operation to rescue the trapped men. It was the tactic of a foolhardy and strategically bankrupt political and military command.

The tactic has been discussed and explained in detail in a U.S. Army post-war training publication:

> "The maneuver of deliberately allowing ones forces to be encircled by the enemy so as to tie up his troops in sufficient numbers to even the odds, rarely achieves the desired result. Should the total opposing forces be approximately equal, such a maneuver can be of value, but only if the number of enemy troops engaged maintaining the encirclement is large enough to affect the outcome of other operations. Even in this case, however, the deliberate creation of a pocket is a costly enterprise which will hardly justify the probable loss of the entire encircled force."[325]

Because of the savage nature of combat in the East, surrounded units, intentional or not seldom occurred, and if it did the German soldier could always take comfort in the fact that if his unit was cut off and surrounded, his parent unit or organization would do its utmost to quickly launch a counterattack to recover him. The concept of the unit or group being sustained at all costs was inculcated into the Landser since their Hitler Youth days.[326] Two successful such relief missions in Russia laid the groundwork for this practice, one at Demyansk and the other at Kholm, both locations in Army Group North in 1941. It was also to become the precursor for another relief attempt on the banks of the Volga a year later.

Of the 'pocketed' German units in Operation Bagration fewer than 900 men would successfully escape back to German lines, so thorough was Russian rear area policing and security and the extraordinary distance of the advance. The soldier on the run the longest was *Unteroffizier* Anzhofer of the 246th Infantry Division. He walked, marched, ran and hid for more than 465 miles, 69 days after beginning his journey, arriving in Schaulen in Lithuania on 2 September.[327]

---

[325] Department of the Army Pamphlet No. 20-234 Historical Study, *Operations of Encircled Forces*, German Experiences in Russia. Department of the Army, January 1952.

[326] Most Hitler Youth exercises consisted of physical strength development and memorizing Party propaganda, not intellectual improvement. The organization was primed to develop a strong unit or team approach to solving all problems; hence the comfort that was initially expressed by the surrounded units in the early entrapment battles of 1941-1942. It was this reassurance in any and all efforts to rescue trapped or lost men and units that permitted such astounding advances in the opening days of Barbarossa.

[327] The German term for a survivor returning to the lines or home is *Ruckkampfer*.

The Russian Advance

The long hoped for Russian exhaustion phase, that had been the hallmark of earlier Russian attacks, did not happen. By the 10th Vilna was retaken and the major German communications and supply city of Minsk was captured. By August Army Group Center had lost all of the territory that it had won and occupied for the last three years. In six weeks, it had lost approximately 200,000 dead, including 10 generals, and 85,000 prisoners, which included 23 generals.[328]

With the disaster unfolding in Byelorussia Hitler turned to his trusted and favored general. *Feldmarshall* Walter Model, nicknamed "Hitler's fireman" for his ability to stop enemy advances, looked every inch the typical Hollywood German general with monocle and Prussian hauteur. A hard driving panzer general in the early stages of the war, by 1944 he had developed into a competent and skilled defensive field commander.

---

[328] GL Rudolf Bamler – 12th Infantry Div.
GL Werner von Bercken – 102nd Infantry Div.
GM Alexander Conrady – 36th Infantry Div.
GM Joachim Engel – 45th Infantry Div.
GM Gustav Gihr – 707th Infantry Div.
Gen.d.Inf. Friedrich Gollwitzer – LIII Army Corps
GL Adolf Hamann – Commandant of Bobruisk
GL Walter Heyne – 6th Infantry Div.
GL Alfons Hitter – 206th Infantry Div.
GL Edmund Hoffmeister – XXXXI Pz. Corps
GM Günther Klammt – 260th Infantry Div.
GL Eberhard von Kurowski – 110th Infantry Div.
GL Kurt-Jürgen Freiherr von Lützow – XXXV Army Corps
GM Herbert Michaelis – 95th Infantry Div.
GL Vincenz Müller – XII Army Corps
GM Claus Mueller-Bülow – 246th Infantry Div.
GL Wilhelm Oschsner – 31st Infantry Div.
GL Johann-Georg Richert – 35th Infantry Div.
GM Friedrich-Carl von Steinkeller – Pz.Gr.Div "Feldherrnhalle"
GL Hans Traut – 78th Sturm Div.
GM Adolf Trowitz – 57th Infantry Div.
Gen.d.Inf. Paul Völckers – XXVII Army Corps
Gen.d.Art. Rolf Wuthmann – IX Army Corps

As an additional point of interest, of the seventeen Army field marshals to serve during the Second World War, ten (59%) were relieved of command by Hitler, three (17%) were executed for complicity in the July 1944 assassination attempt, two (11%) fell in action and one, Paulus 6%, was taken prisoner. Only one, Keitel served to the bitter end. Of the 36 Army generals of the highest rank *Generaloberst*, 24 were relieved of command (66%), two (5%) were dishonorably discharged, seven (19%) fell in action and only three (8%) served to the end of the war.

Although competent and reliable he frequently was known to task his subordinates with difficult and occasionally impossible orders and would accept no objections or excuses for failure. In March of 1944 he was assigned to command Army Group North Ukraine, replacing another defensive expert *General* von Manstein who had run afoul of Hitler, violating his no retreat order. In mid-June with Army Group Center disintegrating under Russian assault, he was assigned there to replace the ineffective *Feldmarshall* Busch. Hitler's fireman was going to face his biggest challenge of the war.

The extensive loss of men and equipment in front of Minsk led *Feldmarshall* Marshal Walter Model to order an immediate withdrawal of troops to the Polish border, the giving up of all the fortresses and strong points, all without consulting OKH; an unthinkable move at this period of the war, such was Model's reputation and relationship with Hitler. Few other generals would have considered such action on their own.

Finally, the question of strategy arises. The conspicuous 'bulge' in the front line in Belarus from Vitebsk in the north curving south, then west to a point south-east of Breast-Litovsk on the Dnepr-Bug Canal, was far too obvious a target for German consideration for a Russian offensive, which usually preferred the indirect approach to planning military operations. The Russian masking and operational plan was successful, demonstrating a keen understanding of the German military mentality. The traditional Soviet approach to military planning, tending to opt for the less complex, not to say less effective direct approach to target acquisition resulting in the massive assault in 23 June 1944 should not have come as a complete surprise to the German command as it did.

With the launch of Bagration and over the ensuing days and weeks as the attack grew in strength, the OKH fell back on the former method of dealing with Russian Army offensives: Get out of the way initially; counter attack their flanks and what can't be attacked will soon stop because of their weak logistical support.

The Results

By 23 August the Russians finally stopped deep inside Poland, just west of the capitol Warsaw, an advance of some 400 miles since the start of Operation Bagration. They were halted by a lack of supplies, exhaustion, and by German reinforcements rushed east and north to the battle area. The Germans lost 30 combat divisions in this battle and were never able to replace them. More than 450,000 men were lost in two months of fighting and the strength of the Army Group fell to 445,000 men. German strength went from 2,460,000 at the beginning of Bagration to 1,996,000 on 1 August. These figures include significant numbers of Axis allies. Although Albert Speer, the German Armaments Minister, was eventually able to make up most of the equipment loss, what the Germans needed most they would no longer get: trained, experienced and ready military manpower.

The huge losses of men and material by Army Group Center and the need to rebuild the Army Group and to halt the Russian Army as quickly as possible, the immediate task for Germany was to stabilize the eastern front. The loss of some 30 divisions was going to consume the final reserves of men and material the Wehrmacht possessed. With this emergency operation at hand, the transfer of any combat units from the *Ostfront* to anywhere the Allies threatened, to the South or to the West was almost certainly out of the question.[329]

Compared to other battles, this was by far the greatest Soviet victory in numerical terms. The Russian Army liberated a vast amount of occupied land, the population of which had suffered greatly under German occupation. The advancing Russian units found cities and towns destroyed, villages depopulated, many of them killed or missing, or conscripted for labor in Germany or German occupied areas.

Materially the *Ostfront* never recovered from the attack, both in equipment and personnel. The losses suffered by Army Group Center cost the German army in the East about a quarter of its manpower. Many veterans, both officer and enlisted were lost and could not be replaced.

Operationally the new front line was now in Poland, just east of Warsaw on the Vistula River. The Russian Fronts occupying this area now separated Army Group Center from its two neighboring army groups, Army Group North and Army Group North Ukraine who were now no longer able to support each other by troop and equipment transfers. They were also weakened as resources that would have been sent to their areas had to be used in reconstructing a new Army Group Center.

---

[329] The losses to Army Group Center as a result of Operation Bagration was a prime motivator in the 20 July 1944 plot to kill Hitler. In Count Klaus von Stauffenberg's briefcase that contained the bomb was also a detailed report on new recruiting methods involving the *Osttruppen* to replace the personnel losses in Army Group Center. See *The House Built On Sand*, p. 359.

Although by this period of the war the Russian Army had become more adept in minimizing combat casualties in the offensive and Operation Bagration was a good example of this new concern for the *frontoviki*. However, an offensive operation, any offensive, will incur larger casualties than the defender who has the advantage of concealment and defensive positions. The casualty costs of Operation Bagration to the Russian Fronts involved suffered losses of some 178,000 total casualties. The First Byelorussian Front alone suffering some 66,000.

H. P. Willmott indicates the importance of this month and year in the war:

> "June 1944 was significant not merely because of the changing nature of the Soviet army and its increasing effectiveness in mobile operations. This time was probably the peak of Soviet achievement in the war before Soviet stoicism; endeavor and patriotism gave way to the desperate tiredness and exhaustion in the last months of the war. In the second half of 1944 the Soviet Union drew upon its last physical, moral and manpower reserves for a final effort that left it totally exhausted; and it must always be remembered that the Soviets lost more men in the drive to the Oder and the taking of Berlin than either Britain or the United States lost in the whole of the war"[330]

Impact In the West

By contrast, Allied performance in Normandy was far more modest. The excellent defensive advantages offered to the German defenders by the bocage (dense hedge rows bordering pasture and crop fields) country behind the invasion beaches was now having adverse affects in the Allied push inland. By D+48 (24 July), the Allied armies had advanced approximately 20 miles inland and had occupied the Cotentin Peninsula, liberating the first major port of the invasion, Cherbourg. Despite the valuable achievement the port required many weeks of clearing before shipping operations could begin because of extensive German demolitions. Actual Allied progress was far behind Twelfth Army Group forecasts made back in February. Then, Allied advances were expected to reach Brest by D+50 and Paris by D+90.

The summer battles of 1944 in Russia significantly contributed to the successful conclusion of the invasion of Normandy; perhaps not in

[330] *June 1944*, p. 119.

the initial landing phase, but certainly in the battle of the build up and subsequent breakout phases. Still, the Allies were blocked at every avenue in the expansion of the bridgehead by growing German strength brought to the area from the north and Pas de Calais, east from Paris, and up from southern France. It was not until mid-August 1944, a full two months after the June landings (and weeks behind the original progress schedule) that the 'Battle of the Buildup' was won. The Allies with their successful attacks at Avranches, Mortain, Vire and Caen, and the eventual destruction of a sizable portion of the German Army in Normandy at Falaise, laid the potential groundwork for victory in the west.

The successes in France are all too often taken for granted. What would have happened if the Russians had not launched Operation Bagration in late June? And an even more far reaching question, what if had they not survived their earlier battles with the Wehrmacht? The result would have permitted significant transfers of German combat units from central Russia to northwestern France to meet the Allied invasion, even if only for a few short months. The transfer of these units, most probably mechanized units (due to their ability to transport themselves quickly and strike with great effect), could have provided the Wehrmacht the means to certainly contain the bridgehead. It might possibly have inflicted enough damage on the Allies to force them to voluntarily withdraw as the Germans, no matter how significantly reinforced on the ground, still would not have had control of the air over the combat area nor the impact of the long reach of Allied naval artillery support. The necessity of Soviet offensive activity in central Russia was imperative for Allied success in France. The one question no one can ever answer is just how successful the Germans would have been with additional strength in France. On the other hand, with the case presented above, rigid containment would have been the most probable outcome; barring an unforeseen Allied disaster, allowing the Germans to force them back into the English Channel.

The strategic effect of the fighting in the east in the summer of 1944 was to greatly hinder the ability of the Germans to transfer of units from front to front. The loss of 30 divisions and the wearing down of a dozen or so more meant that each front had to make do what it had in its own theater of the war, new units had to be raised from scratch at an accelerated pace, with all the disadvantages that entails, something the Wehrmacht was now finding very difficult. Inter frontal transfers now were made only as a last resort and had to be approved at the highest levels. At the same time, the Russian Baltic and Leningrad fronts were deep into the Baltic States and on the borders of the Reich at East Prussia and on the Rumanian border in the Carpathian Mountains in the south.

To Hitler the battlefield defeats by 1944 had a dimension over and above the military one; a political one. The loss of so much real-estate was having a profoundly unsettling affect on Germany's eastern allies, most noticeably Finland, Rumania and Hungary. Just before Bagration commenced, Finland requested a truce with Russia, isolating the German 20th *Gebirgsarmee* around Petsamo in the far north and became an enemy of Germany. Both Rumania and Hungary were becoming politically and domestically unstable, and before long would either defect to the Russians, claim neutrality or require German intervention, as in Hungary, to keep them in the war on Germany's side, albeit with great reluctance.

James Lucas in his excellent study of the German soldier in Russia has the following to say about the conflict between Russia and Germany:

> "One should at this juncture, state that the war on the eastern front was fought with a particular savagery. Neither side saw it as a mere struggle between nations, nor did they view it as a contest between ideologies: National Socialist Germany against Communist Russia. It was to many Germans and Russians a resumption of that conflict for domination between east and west, between Slav and Teuton, which had marked the progress of European history for over a millennium. It is well to remember this for only then do the sacrifice and effort, the atrocities and the brutalities of the forty-six months of war become comprehensible."[331]

The arrival of the second front came in June 1944 in Northwestern France. The Italian campaign, while hotly contested and a potential danger should the Allies breakout north into southern Austria and southern Germany, never amounted to the real threat it could have been. So, the argument of the feared second front for Germany until June 1944 was somewhat of a red herring. The planned short campaign in Russia of eight to twelve weeks would allow plenty of time for interior mop-up operations

---

[331] *War on the Eastern Front: The German Soldier in Russia, 1941- 1943.*

and to continue a limited invasion of Iran from the north and re-direction of the mass of fighting units back to central Europe for rest and refit. Such was the plan; the reality as we have seen was something altogether quite different.

1944 proved to be Germany's most disastrous year of the war in the East. One hundred and six divisions had been destroyed that year, three more than the total number mobilized to attack Poland in 1939. German intelligence estimated that in the assault on the Reich, the Russian Army would possess a superiority of eleven to one in infantry, seven to one in tanks and twenty to one in guns. Hitler dismissed such estimates as "bluff".

Damaged German Panzerkamphwagen (PzKw) IIL "Luchs" or "Lynx".

Chapter Fifteen:
Conclusion

"God forbid that the land should ever relapse into its former state, that the Slavs should ever drive out the German settlers and again undertake its cultivation"

-Prince Wizlaw of Rugen, 1221

"The work of a thousand years is nothing but rubble."

-Dr. Carl Goerdeler (Anti-Nazi resistance leader)

The final chapter will review all the elements that made the war in the East the important military, political, social and economic disaster it was for Germany. The war in Russia will be looked at in a retrospective sense; the impact it had on the German war in the West, in Normandy and to Germany's position in Europe as a whole. An examination of Hitler and his world outlook and actions will be examined and the consequences of his actions had on the war will be addressed. Finally, the question of how will the history of the war be written, by who and how factual will it be is examined and mankind's hope that such a world war never occurs again.

Retrospective

Much has been made of the German attack on the Soviet Union, prior to the completion of the war in the West: the defeat of Great Britain. One must also consider that in June 1941 there was no other front in Europe engaging the Wehrmacht. The German army was on occupation duty in the six western nations conquered in 1940. After the stand down of Operation Sealion, the planned invasion of Great Britain, the German army, with the exception of two or three divisions under Rommel in Libya and Tunisia was largely idle. The areas of activity in the West were primarily air and naval in character which had very little impact on the land invasion planned for Russia. The last enemy was Russia.

So much took place in the East in those ferocious four years. In that short period of time the "thousand year" Third Reich was destroyed. The catastrophic losses before Moscow, Stalingrad and North Africa were made good at great cost and effort in men, money and materials. However, the disaster of the destruction of Army Group Center could not be overcome; there the heart and soul was torn out of the German Army. Germany had frittered away all her precious advantages: Field technique, weapons technology, superb training and coordination, organization, dedication and the most precious of all, time. Germany was in the sixth year of World War II. Her reliance on short, sharp conflicts died with the invasion of Russia. The attack on Russia, with her massive manpower, larger industrial base, quantitative approach to warfare, the grinding down of her enemies (although Russian battlefield doctrine improved as the war went on) as opposed to the German method of surgically slicing up an adversary, was death by military tsunami. The extensive military hemorrhaging of tactical and strategic mistakes of a relatively small nation like Germany was one they could not long endure.

Germany, so sure of itself in the 1938 - 1941 period, stunned by its reverses in 1941 - 1943 and reeling from 1944 to the end of the war in 1945 originally saw itself as a unifier of Europe, very much like Napoleon but without the ethnic genocide component. It was certain in its belief that if the nations of Europe could be cleansed of poor and tainted blood and heredity, the base evils of capitalism abolished, a new and vital Europe would emerge under efficient German management.

The necessity of Russian participation in the East to insure an Allied success at Normandy should by now be quite evident. The struggle in the dusty steppes of central Asia, in the sunflower filled fields of Ukraine, and along the numberless streams and rivers of Byelorussia, was the deciding factor in Germany's destruction. Simply put, she could not win a war against a nation so much larger then herself in almost every respect. In addition to the titanic military struggle, was the economic one of production, and Germany lost both.

In addition, Germany was not only fighting Russia and the Russians; Germany was also fighting the collective military and economic wealth of the Allied coalition. Germany would have been hard pressed to continue the fight against just Russia without Allied material support, although it would have demanded a larger sacrifice by the Soviets to absorb the impact of the German assault, especially in the dark days of 1941-42; it would have taken longer, killed more men, destroyed more mines, factories, cities and towns, but under Stalin's leadership, with the communist party still in control and an intact patriotism, the Russians would have never given up. There is the strong possibility that Stalin would have retreated, a la Mao Zedong, to the far reaches of Siberia if necessary to rest, refit, and recruit to fight again the hated Germans.[332]

This part of World War II, the war in eastern and central Europe, which was almost a war unto itself, seemed to exist in its own self-made universe, to have its own rules, tactics, barbarity, weather, methodology, economics and even its own concept of time. It is no wonder that the dreaded phrase "Russian Front" took on a meaning to German soldiers unlike any other.

In the three and a half years following 22 June 1941, early estimates claim at least 18 million Russians (military and civilian) had died at the hands of the Nazi invaders; and more recent estimates have put the death toll around 24 million to 28 million. Not since the Mongol heirs of Genghis Khan conquered China in the 13th century had so much loss of life been visited upon a single nation. Even a limited nuclear strike upon Russia or the United States today would not produce comparable casualties and human suffering.[333]

---

[332] For a contemporary perspective on the western Allied contribution to victory in the war in Europe see "*Who Really Won the War? Soviet Sacrifice and Criminality are the Unspoken truths of World War II*" by Norman Davies, *World War II*, pp. 36 - 41, October 2007.

[333] *When Russia Won Big in WWII* by Martin Sieff, Johnson's Russia List, http://www.cdi.org/Russia/Johnson/6320-2.cfm.

There is little doubt in June 1941 that the Wehrmacht was operationally ready to attack the Soviet Union. What they were not ready for was the economic requirements such a campaign would impose on a much smaller economy than the Soviet Union's; hence the imperative for the shortest war possible. Superior tactical doctrine, superior leadership, morale, surprise and concentration of force all combined to give the Germans the best possible chances for a good start at the victory they sought. Should they begin to fritter these precious advantages away for whatever reasons, the victory they sought would grow more and more elusive. Despite these strong advantages, the fact remains that overwhelming force will win out in the end and Germany did not have the force for a long war, a war that Russia would always win.

The noted military historian John Keegan states in his *Intelligence in War*, "There are no examples in military history of a state weaker in force than its enemy achieving victory in a protracted conflict. Force tells."[334] Although Keegan was referring to the Japanese attempt to knock the U.S. out of the war by the decisive strike at Midway in 1942 the statement is also applicable to the war in Eastern Europe.

Germany and Russia could never co-exist politically, economically and militarily in the close proximity and confines of Europe. Their contrary politics and outlooks almost ensured conflict, a preordained development. Consider the alternative, a European *Teutoslavia*[335] governed and managed by Germany and supplied by Russia would be militarily unbeatable and would have terrible unforeseen consequences. How long such an awkward and unstable union could have lasted is anyone's guess and the world was fortunate that it never had to find out.

With all historical evidence to the contrary, Hitler was seemingly intent on repeating the results of the Great War, that is; attack a weakened enemy as was the case in 1941, one in the midst of a military reorganization and economic development, knock them out of the war quickly and turn all of one's force to the remaining opponent(s). The recent successful operations against the Western European nations blinded the German leadership to the perils of a Russian invasion, the historical Swedish invasion of

---

[334] *Intelligence in War, Knowledge of the Enemy from Napoleon to Al-Qaeda* by John Keegan, Alfred A. Knopf, New York, 2003.

[335] A term coined by French Premier Daladier describing the relationship between Germany and Russia brought about by the August 1939 pact.

Charles XII and French dictator Napoleon's experiences notwithstanding. The chances of success were so slim as to almost appear to the historian that any attack on Russia to be a self inflicted wound, with no one else to blame but the attacker. In other words, suicide.

Reading the accounts of Napoleon's campaign in Russia, the experiences in the summer and autumn of 1812 is strikingly similar to those of Hitler's. To name the most applicable to our study here: A two front war (The English in Spain and Portugal and Napoleon in Russia), a recent Russian conquest of Finland (the territorial conquests of the 1939 Winter War); violation of an existing peace treaty, initial rapid advances, lost equipment and exhausted troops due to accelerated pursuit of the enemy; delay or absence of timely supplies from the rear, failure to rest and resupply the army, retreat of the Russians deeper into central Russia (similar to the Russian Army tactics in the opening weeks of Operation Blue); the desire and failure to bring the enemy to a climactic battle to decide the war, the frequent reference to the Russians as barbarians by Napoleon; attacks behind the lines by Cossacks against supply trains (Partisans), the frustration of operations failing to comply to his plans. Napoleon assumed command of all activities of his corps (Hitler assuming command of all operational control of the *Ostheer*). Napoleons staff fear his wrath should perceived mistakes occur, and fail to exercise due diligence in their duties, etc. The blueprint for what mistakes to avoid in an invasion of Russia was written in 1812, and this was only in the advance of the Grand Army to Moscow. The other cautionary tale, the disastrous retreat was still to be enacted.

If any nation or army was in the best position to successfully invade Russia, it was Germany's *Wehrmacht* in the summer of 1941. All the lessons of history were there for the taking; all Germany had to do was follow them. To wit: the poor state of the Red Army undergoing reorganization; its poor performance in the 1939-40 Finnish campaign; the extended positioning of their western military districts in newly occupied Poland, and the ongoing purge of the Red Army officers to name the most significant. The absurd racial theories that shaped not only political policy, but also influenced German military tactics was nothing short of insanity.

Even Stalin cooperated in the effort; his army was not ready, and he had eliminated the bulk of his trained and experienced military leadership and by ignoring the obvious signs of impending invasion and complying with the terms and conditions of the quickly disappearing 1939 treaty between the two nations.

An Aggressive Russia

Speculation of what the war in Europe would have been like if the Germans did not attack the Soviet Union makes an interesting topic. Considering the economic benefits of the 1939 treaty, and the ample flow of goods crossing the Russo-German border into Germany, there is much to say for delaying, if not canceling the attack. Let's move the discussion to the opposite position, of a Russian attack on Germany. In this scenario the defender would have the immediate benefit of the moral high ground, that of Germany as victim. Even the actual unfolding of such an attack would be less damaging to Germany as the new eastern border of Germany now lies in the center of the former nation of Poland. With such a starting position, it is quite likely the Russian Army would have advanced approximately 100 to 150 miles before running out of fuel, food and all other military sustenance needed to maintain the advance. With the Russians now occupying so advanced a position with no defense works, the moment would be ripe for a massive and decisive German counterattack. The outcome of this scenario would be interesting indeed. However, Stalin knew the state of his army and it highly doubtful such a scenario would have happened.

At no time did the principle architects of the invasion, Paulus, Halder, Wagner and others give any consideration to the thought that the Soviet Union was too big a target, that Germany did not have the supplies or transportation assets to carry out the campaign as they envisioned it. In fact, it is ironic that the more the planning staff found out about the difficulties of the campaign, the less time they estimated they would need to complete it. What was initially estimated to be a five month campaign, Marcks predicted would now take as little as eight weeks, plus a mechanized reconditioning period. By December 1940, the planners believed they could do it in eight weeks or ten weeks including the reconditioning time. However, by April 1941 Braushitsch was talking of a tough battle at the border regions that would last up to a month after which enemy resistance would be broken. So, the *Heer's* projection of the required logistical support was beginning to merge with their belief in a quick Russian collapse. Only with difficulty can one escape the conclusion that they were engaged in a

---

[336] From 1938 to 1945 Germany occupied twenty-six European capitals: Vienna, Prague, Warsaw, Copenhagen, Oslo, Luxemburg, Amsterdam, Brussels, Paris, Bucharest, Sofia, Ljubljana, Skopje, Zagreb, Belgrade, Sarajevo, Athens, Vilnius, Riga, Minsk, Tallinn, Kiev, Rome, Tirana, Budapest, Bratislava and two African capitals, Tripoli and Tunis. However, it was the two capitals that were not occupied that mattered most: London and Moscow.

gigantic effort at self-delusion. The failure of *Fremde Heere Ost* to evaluate the force generation and recuperative abilities of the Russian Army was a signal failure and set the stage for the German disaster in Russia.

After the earlier nations he conquered, whether politically or militarily,[336] Hitler finally attacked a nation whose leader had a similar outlook to Germany's: A nation led by a totalitarian government, headed by a messianic leader who saw himself as infallible; in which his system, culture, ideology and will was far superior than the other, and therefore deserved to succeed.

There has been much discussion of 'turning points' in the war in the east; what they were and when they occurred. The most popular of these is the battle of Stalingrad. A long time favorite for almost the last half century, this view has been challenged in more recent decades by historians looking at the totality of the war in the East and its connections with the Western front. The newest opinions on this subject see the battle of Stalingrad as the eastern-most point reached by Germany; the loss of many men and much materiel, but not the turning point. A recent article in *World War II* magazine asked seventeen noted military historians and scholars the question of what was the turning point in World War II and of the thirteen, six mentioned Stalingrad, less than half of the responses.[337]

A recent view, one supported by this author, is the true turning point must be measured by the inability of the invader to mount a major offensive, albeit a regional one as opposed to an general, front-wide offensive, which would bring the new turning point marker to the battle of Kursk in the summer of 1943, four months after the conclusion of the battle of Stalingrad. One source opined that there could be three events that would qualify as a 'turning point'; the Soviet counteroffensive at Moscow in December 1941 should be considered the tactical turning point; the Russian victory at Stalingrad to be seen as the psychological turning point and the failure of the German summer offensive at Kursk in 1943 should be considered the strategic turning point. Indeed, this author suggests adding an additional dimension to the discussion by examining the Russian summer offensive in June 1944-Operation Bagration, as a yet unrecognized major turning point, if the definition of turning point be given its broadest usage in the discussion.

---

[337] See *World War II* magazine, "What Was the Turning Point of World War II" by Laurence Rees, pp. 28 - 36, July/August 2010.

War In The East

The savage nature of the war in Russia was due to its uncompromising 'winner-take-all' victory conditions based on contrasting political and economic value systems. Both Russia and Germany had been nursing enmity against each other for a long time. One could not live with the other; ultimately one would have to go, according to Hitler's master plan in his writings and speeches. Given this setting and the astonishing 1939 non-aggression treaty between them, Germany was in a much better position, economically and militarily to continue this tense treaty, provisions of which enabled it received vital grains and other raw materials from Russia for the exchange of selected military hardware, some of which was already obsolete. With the attack in June of 1941, Germany was now required to fight for these same commodities that she was getting delivered to her on time, and at a much cheaper rate in men and materials than war could produce. So much for the blindness of mixing dubious Nazi philosophy and earlier military successes, which was to cause a sense of confidence for the Germans out of all proportion to reality.

After the disaster at Stalingrad, Germany, especially the SS, began to emphasize a new approach to the war in Russia; that of a crusade. Goebbels' propaganda ministry attempted to show that the Germans were willing to take upon themselves the great burden of exterminating the Bolshevik menace and threat to European life and culture and called upon the peoples and nations of, first Europe and then the world to join with Germany in this most important mission. Although the lure for many young, desperate, hungry young men, especially in the occupied nations was overpowering, the sham argument was seen for what it was.

In his introduction to "The Russian Front" John Erickson describes the nightmare nature of the war in the east:

"The Soviet-German War of 1941-1945 which raged for 1,418 days without lull or respite, all restraint abandoned, is generally accounted a war like none other, a struggle to the death well-nigh traumatically unique in human annals. Half a century later the scars remain livid, wounds still gape, the nightmares yet to be suppressed. Neither conquest nor bestiality are new to history, but what took place on the Eastern Front was a pestilential visitation, far surpassing even the most baleful predictions of what might be. As early as 1887 Friedrich Engels had prophesied a war of unprecedented scale, engulfing eight to ten million soldiers and bringing about three to four years of ruination and impoverishment, the like of which Europe had not witnessed since the Thirty Years War. The inevitable consequence would be the 'universal enslavement of both troops and masses'. What materialized on the Eastern Front during the months and years after June 22, 1941 was unspeakable barbarization, a demonic exaggeration of Engels' worst predictions. It eliminated pity, abandoned any constraint, mocked even a semblance of legality".[338]

Lessons of History

Carl von Clausewitz had much to say, and warn military planners in the early 18th century about the risks and dangers of invading Russia, among them, "it (Russia) was a country which could be subdued only by its own weakness and by the effects of internal dissention. In order to strike these vulnerable spots of its body politic, Russia would have to be agitated at the very center."[339]

Von Clausewitz's quote is one that speaks to the heart of the question 'can anyone successfully invade Russia'? This was completely ignored by 20th century Germany. Here we have one of Germany's foremost military theorists on tactics and strategy, one of Germany's own, and the expensive lessons he quotes frequently in his famous work *On War* of the French campaign in 1812-14; the very nation that would be the beneficiary of the guidance and advice of its famous military son, unheeded. Many authors writing about the German invasion in World War II have very little sympathy for Germany, not only for the outcome of the campaign or the great losses it suffered there, but that it ignored all the lessons of invading Russia, lessons learned at great cost and sacrifice, from not one invader, but two: the Swedes and the French. Of the conclusions, the lessons learned, perhaps the Swedes and the French historians and generals can write all they want about how to go about invading Russia, but the real lesson is the one nobody has yet offered: Don't. After all due considerations, Russia's best protection may just be her great size.

---

[338] *The Russian Front 1941 – 1945.*

[339] *The German Campaign in Russia-Planning and Operations (1941-1942)*, Department of the Army, Historical Study, No. 21-261a, March 1955.

However, 20-20 hindsight notwithstanding, there was an element of hope that this time it would be different. To wit: the aftereffects of the Russian civil war, the just completed military and political purges and the disastrous Russian Army performance in the 1939 invasion of Finland, all these fed the German dream of a successful invasion.

The war in the east turned into a military 'black hole' for Germany, just as it had for previous invaders. These earlier invaders pointed the way for the German invasion; indeed studies of these invasions were made to purposely avoid the fatal mistakes made by them. Arrogance, reliance on new technologies, underestimating the potential of the enemy, and a confining racial stupidity blinded this most recent invader. When Field Marshal Bernard Montgomery, Britain's greatest general of the 20th century was asked to compile a list of military blunders and elementary disasters to avoid, he put at the very top of the list, "Invading Russia. It is always a bad idea."

Despite the economic advantages a conquered Russia would provide, Germany, guided by her fear and hatred of Bolshevism and her so-called 'need' for *lebensraum*, was compelled to complete her self-imposed mission of the destruction of communist Russia. It demonstrates the 'all or nothing' gamble in the Russian campaign. Russia was the vital key to sustaining the German conquest of Europe. In short, Russia and its contiguous appendages; Ukraine, Belarus, the Baltic States, were to become Germany's larder and storehouse, to make her what she had always yearned to be, completely self-sufficient and materially independent. It was this economic independence that would provide the sustenance for the Nazi European utopia. This would also provide the necessary space to grow and develop the German concept of the new Nazi racial theories as well as maintain and solidify the alliances with its Axis partners. The enlarged greater Germany, including her military conquests, would provide the industrial and agricultural resources that would make her truly a nation dependent on no one. Germany would be able to prosecute the war needing nothing. Her new challenge now was not insufficiency, but proper management.

Indeed, with such extensive historical examples of failed invasion attempts, no matter how well prepared and motivated the invader, the multiple failures seemed to have had no affect on Hitler's decision to invade. Surely, he recognized the distinct difference an invasion of the Soviet Union would require, compared to any country he had fought so far. Surely, he knew that Stalin, like him, would fight to the death to defend himself, the Russian way of life, and Russian Communism. Surely, he knew the vast economic resources and manufacturing capacity available to the Russian Army? Finally, he surely knew the grave risks of engaging another, completely different enemy without concluding the military situation in the West, the dreaded second front. Then why, indeed?

In the years following the war against Germany, the memory of the war and the great sacrifices it required attained almost sacred status in Russia. Each June 22 there is a great and solemn remembrance of the occasion in their major cities, especially Moscow. A minute of silence is observed around the country and museums and war memorials are crowded with visitors and tourists, and even newlyweds visit a memorial on their wedding day to pay respects.[340]

However great and spectacular the victory celebrations, nothing could erase the somber and heavy mood the beginning of each May for the next half century; such was the size of the loss in the national Russian psyche.

The Red Menace

The postwar appearance of Europe worried one very important man in particular, Winston Churchill. In a memorandum written to the new President of the United States Harry S Truman in the second week of May 1945, he gave voice to his concerns of the new power on the European landmass, the U.S.S.R. Now that the fighting was over and the political lines agreed to in the various Allied conferences he knew the main power brokers, the United States in particular, would soon be departing Europe, especially after the last remaining Axis enemy, Japan still had to be defeated. With the new superpowers attention turned to the Pacific and to long deferred domestic issues, what would happen in Europe? Who would be the bulwark against a powerful and potentially aggressive Soviet Union? Events happening in Poland were enough to make him very concerned that what little harmony that existed between the eastern and western Allies would soon be gone; agreements that seemed so sound and strong on paper were becoming worthless. England was a economic weakling after the long struggle to defend herself, France, the larder of western Europe

---

[340] As in all the combatant nations during the war, motion picture film was an important source of information, entertainment and morale building, none more important than in Soviet Russia. Two films are shown every year on the anniversary of the victory, *The Swinemaiden and the Shepherd* and *Six o'Clock in the Evening After the War* both starring the lovely Marina Ladynina.

was disorganized and experiencing the same political disruptions as was Italy. Germany, the traditional economic motor of Europe was a smoking pile of rubble- prostrate, divided, and full of displaced refugees. Who would begin the rebuilding of Europe in the face of a the new threat posed by the resurgent and victorious Soviet Union?

As was mentioned earlier, "the east" features prominently in the Third Reich. In Hitler's book *Mein Kampf* there is the frequent reference to the arch-enemy Communism, and the need to acquire *lebensraum* in the east. "The east" was referred to as the natural area of Germanic expansion and would be the focus of a Greater Germany, a Pan Germanic Europe with power concentrated in Berlin.[341] It is ironic then that the Second World War began with an attack to the east and would end with an attack from the east. This same newly risen eastern power would come to dominate a third of Europe for half a century until it collapsed upon itself, a failure of the theories of collectivism, socialism, central planning and the inability to build the workers' paradise.

One must not forget that the Germans fought the Soviets for almost the entire length of the war in Europe. The German war against Russia lasted 47 months. For the western Allies, the war on the ground with Germany, especially for the U. S. lasted a mere 11 months. The great fear and hatred the Germans had for the 'Bolsheviks' is amply demonstrated at the site of the war crimes trial in Nuremberg. The four major powers (U. S., Great Britain, France and the U.S.S.R.) shared the guard and trial preparation duty, each power taking an even portion of the year. When the Soviets had their turn at security duty at the Palace of Justice, where the trials were held, locals rumored to be former SS, emerged from the catacombs beneath the city at night and shot at the Russian soldiers. This continued far into 1947, two years after the war ended.

Emotionally and psychologically the Germans hoped for another Great War in the East, a great battle of decision that would knock Russia out of the war; one which would allow the Wehrmacht to turn west and await the Allied invasion. The Tannenberg battle of World War I never happened in 1941. Try as they might, the Germans were never able to bring to bear the

---

[341] See *The Kersten Memoirs, 1940-1945* by Dr. Felix Kersten. In his book he details the plans the Third Reich had for the restructuring of Europe after a successful German conclusion of the war, which included suppressing any language other than German. Ostensibly to eliminate misunderstandings due to linguistic confusion, the true reason rested firmly on belief in German racial superiority and arrogance.

main mass of the Russian Army and fight it out. Perhaps by 1941 the armies had grown too big to have a single war deciding battle. If a battle such as the giant Kiev encirclement did not destroy the Russian Army, what would? Instead for Germany there were the military disasters: Moscow, 1941; Stalingrad, 1942; Kursk, 1943 and Bagration, 1944. This is not to say the German armed forces failed to inflict serious damage on the Russian Army; not at all. There were the great battles of the border regions at Bialystok and Minsk in 1941, then deeper inland, at Kiev, 1941; Moscow 1941; Sevastopol, 1942; Kharkov, 1942 and 1943 and the approaches to Stalingrad 1942.[342] But the elusive, all determining, war-winning battle was not to be. The endless reaches of Russia proved too big and too far, physically and psychologically for Germany. Not a Greater Germany, not a mobilized anti-communist Greater Europe had the resources, physical and emotional to defeat a Russia. As Keegan said earlier, force matters, when it comes to Russia, so does size.

John Ellis, in his *World War II, The Encyclopedia of Facts and Figures* comments on the disproportionate balance of German fighting strength:

> "This book does not usually attempt to draw conclusions from the data presented and even less to be didactic about any of it. Nevertheless, it does seem to be logical to follow the table above with some information on the distribution of German ground troops during the war, and in so doing one cannot forbear to make at least passing comment on the clear proof these figures give of the enormous burden borne by the Russians throughout the last four years of the war." To illustrate, he cites the number of months spent by various types of divisions in different combat theaters. German infantry spent 5,127 months on the eastern front compared with 637 in North-West Europe, 193 in Italy and 6 in Northern Africa.

The Frustrated Artist

When Hitler attacked Russia, he grabbed a gigantic tiger by the tail, and when the expected results of a quick victory did not materialize, he could not let go of this very enraged animal; it was a fight to the death, and this fight, destroyed the Third Reich.

---

[342] The losses in Red Army tanks alone will give some idea as to the magnitude of the loss inflicted on the Soviets: In 1942, 15,100; in 1943, 23,500 (8,000 at Kursk alone); in 1944 23,700 and 13,700 in 1945. From *The Oxford Companion to World War II*, p. 1235.

This tenacious fight to the death is explained in many of the tenets of National Socialistic thought. The fight to make Germany and later Europe "a better place to live" was to eliminate the "impurities" they found. When the world rebuffed such a radical and brutal plan for the future and world war became a reality, Germany was faced with, especially in and after 1944, a struggle for survival or existence or *existenzkamp*, which was a war between two peoples in which one must destroy the other. In a confrontation between totalitarian states surrender is doom, a calamity, certain death or at least enslavement. The outcome offered is life or death, the usual stark black or white choices the Nazis presented to the Germans and the world since 1933. The party leadership was determined to have the former.

One aspect of Hitler's personality and its impact on his conduct of the war was his view of himself as an artist. As a failed artist in his youth, Hitler would spend the rest of his life proving to the world that he was indeed an artist of the highest caliber, talent, and taste. This lack of artistic recognition was to drive him, haunt him in every area of his personal and professional life. All things in his world were judged through the lens of its artistic value, an aesthetic that colored his decision-making, his choices both personal and professional, the suitability of various designs and the selection of people for various positions of great responsibility.[343]

The need for artistic ability, or at least appreciation, was to drive him to near distraction in the choice of his successor. All the closest people around him were evaluated and rejected as not having the artistic sensibility that he required in a successor. Although many of his inner circle realized that the path to Hitler's favor was through the arts, he was shrewd enough to see through some of the attempts of artistic pretense, and dismiss them as worthy candidates.

The Hitler-as-artist is not as frivolous as it may seem. With his self imposed, lonely existence, with only 'Germany as his bride' the frustrated artist perceived his relationship with the Germans as a form of extended marriage and when this marriage was harmonious, as in the early years of his Reich, the 'relationship' was beneficial to him.[344] However, when fate and

---

[343] The artistic side of Hitler was also demonstrated by his concern for the beauty of the major cities he conquered. He was quite proud that he was able to defeat the western Allies without harming their architectural gifts, for example; Brussels, Paris and Rome, Rotterdam being a glaring exception. For example the lovely bridges over the Tiber were spared destruction and even Wehrmacht troops were forbidden to enter Rome without a special pass. This is in stark contrast to the Allied offensives in 1944 and 1945 with widespread destruction, not only in Germany but in the occupied countries as well.

the world turned against him from 1942 on, he subconsciously saw this as a betrayal of his love for his Germany and began a series of psychological and physical 'punishments' to chastise his recalcitrant people, each escalating in intensity and severity until, in the closing days of the Reich he instructed his favored architect Albert Speer to destroy anything of value in Germany, as they (the German people) were undeserving of living. If it did not work, if his Germany was unworthy, it was doomed to extinction along with him. It was German victory or death. There were no other alternatives. One can almost hear Wagner playing in the background.

This artist-Fuehrer-bride-marriage dynamic was to color almost all is interactions with the German *volk*. Consider a few of his comments regarding the struggle of National Socialism and if the war should be lost to Germany:

> "My motto is, 'Destroy by all and any means. National Socialism will reshape the world."

> "Those who want to live, let them fight, and those who do not want to fight in the world of eternal struggle do not deserve to live"

> "If the war is lost, the nation will perish. This fate is inevitable. There is no necessity to take into consideration the basis, which the people will need to continue a most primitive existence. On the contrary, it will be the weaker one and the future will belong solely to the stronger eastern nation. Besides, those who will remain after the battle are only the inferior ones, for the good ones have been killed."

Michael Burleigh in his "The Third Reich, A New History"[345] captures this Nazi fatalism:

> "Although it paradoxically claimed to speak the language of applied reason, and was capable of sophisticated calculation,

---

[344] Hitler felt marriage, especially children, would be a burden and perhaps even a danger for and to him. In 1932 he mentioned to Otto Wagener, staff officer and SA chief of staff that if he should be made leader of the German people then the *volk* should not be burdened with his children as a son would never be what his father was and could even be a danger. See *With Hitler To the End*, by Heinz Linge, Skyhorse Publishing, 2009, for an in-depth look at Hitler's private life.

[345] *The Third Reich, A New History*, by Michael Burleigh, Copyright 2000, p. 12. Reprinted by permission of Hill and Wang, a division of Farrar, Straus and Giroux.

Nazism had one foot in the dark irrationalist world of Teutonic myth, where heroic doom was regarded positively, and where the stakes were all or nothing – national and racial redemption or perdition."

In every one of these utterances, there is a clear choice, a black and white decision to be made for and by Germans. Hitler offered his nation and its people one or the other, no equivocation, no gray or shaded areas. Gone forever, banished to the dustbin of history was the whimpering, servile government of the Versailles-directed treaty. Germany had to choose: greatness through constant struggle and victory or servile weakness through appeasement, compromise and defeat. In its choice lay its fate and destiny.

If Hitler's relationship with Germany was an emotional one, so was his political one was with England. This love-hate relationship with his undefeated enemy in the west arises frequently in many of his speeches and table-talk discussions during the war. Hitler frequently bases his future plans for Germany, especially those of the conquered lands in Poland and Russia as "our India". This modeling of the future Germany with her contiguous colonies in the East was based on the British model and it irritated him that he was unable to politically "seduce" Britain just as he had all his other two peaceful conquests, Austria and Czechoslovakia.

Death and Destruction

For the second time in the same century the Germans brought a destructive war to the heart of western civilization. Unlike the Great War of 1914-1918 the Second World War brought massive destruction to a much wider portion of Europe. From London on the English Channel to Stalingrad on the Volga the destruction and waste is beyond calculation. Russia alone had some 6 million houses destroyed, leaving 25 million homeless.

The combatant nations spent four years attempting to destroy each other and with the possible exceptions of Poland and western Russia, it is in Germany we see the most extensive destruction.[346] German industrial production had declined by 66%, in Russia 3,000 oil wells and over 1,000 coal mines were destroyed and the Germans stole 70 million head of cattle.

---

[346] By May 1945 the RAF had dropped 955,044 tons of bombs on Germany and the German occupied nations. The U.S.A.A.F. was close behind with 621,877 tons, for a combined total of 1,576,921 tons.

Poland and France had lost half of their industrial plants, 50% of the British commercial fleet was rusting on the bottom of the world's oceans.

The amount of damage and destruction inflicted on the Axis nations was due to their determined and tenacious defense of every village, town and city. All during the decline of the war for Germany there was not one attempt at internal civil insurrection to overturn the Nazi government, the exception was the failed military 20 July 1944 bomb plot to kill Hitler. The German Wehrmacht fought more or less willingly to the bitter end and the occupation of almost the entire nation was required to subdue the resistance. However, the end of this war was going to be different than the last, as Ken Macksey points out:

> "Thus the last rites of the Third Reich, which had collapsed into chaos, were in the hands of the military, as they had been in 1918. However, this time there would be no mercy, no attempt to retain German unity and no mention of stabs in the back by people at home. ...This time there were no German civilian signatories upon whom to foist the blame in the years to come."[347]

With the final occupation of Germany the victorious Allied nations discovered the extent of the collapse of the Nazi government and the necessity of providing essential services. The retreating Wehrmacht and Waffen-SS units destroyed most communications and transportation systems. The Allies, to prevent wholesale starvation and disease had to bring into Germany food, water, medical services as well as to begin organizing the construction of housing for not only the millions of bombed out and evacuated Germans but the other millions of displaced Germans and German allies that were forced out of occupied nations or historically German living areas.[348] The country was quite destitute.

A newspaper correspondent tells of his visit to Berlin in the days and weeks after the German surrender in May 1945, "[T]errified and starving housewives of Berlin plundering the shops and (he) described Berlin as a city of desolation and shattered dreams, inhabited by a half mad, half starving population, clawing its frenzied way into battered food shops, slinking for shelter into dark cellars and currying favor with the conquerors as they

---

[347] *Why the Germans Lose at War, the Myth of German Military Superiority* by Kenneth Macksey, Greenhill Books/Lionel Leventhal Limited, London, 1996, pp. 220 – 221.

[348] The postwar death toll of expelled Germans ranges from 2,111,000 (Glaser & Possony) to 3,100,000 (Keegan).

emerged from the catacombs, raising their clenched fists and shouting Rote Front".[349] A desperate attempt at forging a bond with their new Russian masters.

Alan Clark in his landmark work *Barbarossa: The German-Russian Conflict 1941-1945* captures the essence of life in Berlin at the end of the fighting:

> "For over a year the embers of the Ostfront smoldered in Berlin and in Germany. A hot summer followed the surrender, and plagues of flies multiplied in the stricken cities of the Oder, breeding in the corpses of man and beast. Rats and lice spread disease; food no longer came in from the countryside; the casual brutality of the occupying army showed no abatement. The autumn came, and those same portents of lengthening darkness and falling temperature which had for four years, chilled the hearts of the Wehrmacht closed in upon the whole population. How many died in that first winter of the peace will never be known. Children ate cats, raw, for sustenance, and burrowing in mountains of rubble at whose center there glowed, like that of the earth itself, the warmth of interminable fires, were suffocated there."[350]

When President Harry Truman and the new American military governor General Lucius Clay visited Berlin a few days prior to the Potsdam Conference in July 1945, they noted the stench hanging over the city, the countless thousands of dead buried under the rubble was suffocating. Many took to living in caves carved out of the piles of bricks and mortar. It was an astounding change from one of Europe's most developed societies to one of the stone age.

The German expansion to the east, the *Drang nach Osten*, begun by the Teutonic Knights in 1231 and continued by Hitler in 1941 had come to an emphatic end in 1945.

The New Russian Master

In their attacks in the west the Germans had faced enemies who were reluctant to incur heavy casualties; the Russians had no second thoughts

---

[349] *Defeat, Chaos and Rebirth* by Gerhard Rempel, Western New England College.

[350] *Barbarossa The German-Russian Conflict 1941-45* by Alan Clark, Quill, New York, 1965, p. 463.

about the ruthless - some would characterize it as careless - use of their manpower. The casualties in prisoners, dead, wounded and missing suffered in the opening months of the war would have crippled any western nation, but the Russians were prepared to trade not only space for time, but men as well.

To measure the impact of the war on the nations of Europe one need only glance at a map of Europe of 1946. With almost no changes in the borders of the western nations, with their capitals and major cities more or less intact, however the comparison with those in the east is impressive. In the east whole nations disappeared, borders were greatly redrawn, capitals moved or demoted and major cities almost ceased to exist. This alone should offer mute testimony to the nature of the struggle that took place here. In another comparison with the fighting in the west, that of the east was based on extermination, subjugation, enslavement, that of the west was of one defeating an enemy army with something resembling formal or honorable terms.

Finally, one may ask why it has taken so long to 'discover' the war in the east, and its effects on the Normandy invasion. One quick answer is the Cold War that followed on the heels of the war in Europe. The descending of the Iron Curtain and the animosity between the Eastern and Western powers had much to do in limiting anything positive the Russians or more specifically, the Soviets contributed to the history of the war. The silence of Soviet contributions for almost four decades because of cold war barriers coupled with a long anti-western propaganda campaign generated a vacuum or at least a thirst for objective, untainted and accurate information contained in the Soviet civil and military archives. For example, it took until 1964 for the first definitive Soviet account of the battle of Moscow in 1941 to be published, Marshal Sokolovsky's *Razgrom nemetsko-fashistskikh voisk pod Moskvoi.*

The Germans have been our allies since 1945, and our former allies the Russians have been our adversaries for almost as long, a difficult situation for any historian attempting to obtain evidence or information on matters that occurred prior to 1989, when the Communist government fell and a more democratic government replaced it. The passage of time, as well as political changes, has offered the promise of opening troves of long-hidden or long ignored documents and records in both Russia and her subjugated nations.

A New Russian History

Another answer to the delay in recognizing and understanding the Russian contributions in World War II is undoubtedly due to the language barrier that required translations from the Russian to the western languages, especially English. One advantage for German authored histories is that there are many more people in the west who speak German and far fewer who speak Russian. In American secondary schools in the post war era Russian language classes were seldom offered and German was a standard . In addition, the period immediately after the war was when the first, trend-setting histories were written. During this period the source material for those histories was the documentation and material captured by the western powers in the closing months of the war and aided by voluntary cooperation of surviving German military personnel. The researcher, in the interests of objectivity and accuracy must carefully evaluate the material from these sources to eliminate any self serving or exculpating histories.[351] Writers such as Paul Carrel (real name Paul Schmidt, former *Obersturmbannfuhrer* in the SS and press spokesman for foreign minister von Ribbentrop) through whose engagingly written and popular series books (*Hitler Moves East, Invasion! They're Coming and Scorched Earth*) introduced many to the war in the east and its impact on the war in the West.

A significant part of the problem of getting Russia's 'side' of the story is the Russians themselves. Consider the comments of Vladimir Petrov in his Prologue to A. M. Nekrich's "June 22, 1941":

> "[H]istory, traditionally the most political branch of knowledge in the communist world. History has always occupied a special place in the Soviet cultural life. Unlike arts and even literature, where manifestations of unorthodoxy were on occasion tolerated even during the darkest years of the Stalin era, history has at all times been chained to politics. The party has been extremely reluctant to permit diversity in the interpretation of politically sensitive historical events, and there have been precious few historical events in the recent past, which have not been considered sensitive."

---

[351] This is especially so as many of the German military generals were quick to produce their versions of the fighting in Russia and color, slant or embellish their participation in it. In addition, certain German generals have developed somewhat of a cult following based on their performance in a particular battle and their larger behavior goes unscrutinized. See **http://www.einsatzgruppenarchives.com/documents/wehr2.html** for examples.

As Merle Fainsod said a few years ago:

> "All Soviet historians to some degree, and historians of the recent past in particular, are expected to operate within the framework of Marxism-Leninism, as its requirements are currently interpreted by the party leadership. ...These requirements shift with changes in the party line, heroes maybecome tomorrow's villains, and books which meet every canon of orthodoxy when they are written may become politically unacceptable shortly after they appear. This means, among other things, that scholars... must develop a keen sense of the direction of impending change and be able to gauge its limits as well as the potentialities which it unfolds. Periods of transition... are periods of crisis for historians. When an uncertain trumpet blows, there will inevitability be some historians who fail to catch the tune."[352]

If we compare the repression of the free flow of thoughts and ideas in Russian society, especially its military, both before and after the war, one has been comforted by the gradual postwar government softening of the Khrushchev-era. The above certainly describes the problems and difficulties of obtaining unencumbered Russian historical versions of the war in the East. However with the strictures imposed by the communist party, one can understand the burden under which Russian historians wrote and researched.

The archival material from Russia that would have explained the war in the East to Western eyes, until recently was limited to the official Soviet histories on the subject, especially the government produced *History of the Great Patriotic War*. This is a heavily censored document that toes the Communist Party line, glorifies the Russian Army and its leaders, especially Stalin and Beria, is suspect in its lack of mention of Russian failures and shortcomings and is of value only in its supporting information. Eliminating the Russian side of the story is both unfortunate and dooms the accurate reporting of the war from the Russian perspective and makes the historical record unbalanced and incomplete.

With the 'opening' of Russia since 1989, and until a real 'perestroika' exists, it is hoped that the discussion of the events in the east during the Second World War will at last be openly and publicly discussed and treated

---

[352] *Soviet Historians and the German Invasion, June 22, 1941* by Vladimir Petrov, University of South Carolina Press, Columbia, South Carolina, 1968, p. 2.

to the critical evaluation it needs and deserves and will then become a valuable part of the historical record. However, recent good news of progress has been made. Authors such as David Glantz, Antony Beevor, Ronald Smelzer and Edward Davies, Catherine Merridale, Robert Edwards and Dmitriy Loza have done much with their writing to balance the historical picture of the war in the East and in Germany.

However, the promising beginning to a real opening and sharing of knowledge and information by East and West has stumbled in the last two decades. A newly democratic Russia is feeling the birth pangs of a system of openness it is not familiar or comfortable with. Despite the efforts of the historians mentioned earlier, doors, vaults and files so briefly opened and shared with an world eager to learn more of this period are once again closing. After a period of internal confusion and introspection, a resurgent and strengthened Russian government appears to be asserting who will determine who sees its checkered past and who will write its history.

Retribution

Much has been written by post war writers of the terrible atrocities inflicted on the retreating Germans in the last winter of the war. The acts of Russian barbarity against defenseless civilians, the Russian government urging the Red Army to 'kill, kill and kill more Germans' is hardly excusable. However, whatever excuses the actions of the Russian Army and the Soviets in general use, and just barely so, is what the Germans had in store for Russia had they won the war.

The Germans were the invaders, after all. The aggressor, regardless of what pre-invasion intelligence was presented by the Germans of the Soviet intentions in June 1941, is still the aggressor. There was sufficient evidence of their final plans for a conquered Russia in the German occupied areas to find a certain level of understanding for Russian actions in a conquered Germany. The actions of the *Einsatzkommando*, forced resettlements, confiscations of land and property, enslavement for forced labor in Germany, suppression of religion and the rejection of aid by locals to assist the Germans and the ultimate plan for the conquered territories, if played out in its entirety would yield a Russia (much less a Soviet Union) that would cease to exist in any recognizable form. If Russian behavior in occupied Germany was not excusable it is at least understandable.

What the Germans were doing to the Jews in the 'Final Solution' was to be perpetrated against Russia in gigantic form. A small nation can only increase its size and power by including the conquered countries into a unified empire where all share the same ideals, vision and values. The bogus Nazi racial theories of German superiority eliminated the only method Germany could have built a pan European empire with any hope of success. The actions of both combatants were despicable at various times in the war. However, the victors write history and aggressors, especially ones who lose wars, suffer accordingly.

The seeds of retribution the Germans unwittingly planted the previous five plus years were beginning to blossom. In addition to the barbarities inflicted by the advancing Russian Army at the close of the war, the end of the war in May 1945 was to provide little relief for German soldier and civilian alike. During the summer of 1945 gangs of Polish and Czech youths would board evacuation trains traveling through their countries carrying German civilians to Berlin and other parts of Germany raping any women found on board and murdering many others. The silence of the guns did not end the killing, the loss of life continued.

Professor Erickson summarized the attitude of the Russian common man at the end of the war:

> "Despite all the adversity, there certainly was a surge of patriotism, but there was also, as the war went on, a deepening feeling of revenge on the part of ordinary people. Nonetheless, some Russian civilians obviously felt caught between two fires, but one senior Soviet officer summed up the terms of the choice when he said, 'we were faced with a choice of two dictators. Hitler on one hand and Stalin on the other, but we preferred to pick the one who spoke Russian'."[353]

One of the seldom discussed aspects of war is the post-war movement of the thousands and even millions of displaced persons. This was especially the case in Germany after the fighting ended in May 1945. The millions of guest and slave workers as well as POW's in Germany made for a massive human tide of movement of these desperate people seeking their homes or a safe haven.

---

[353] *The Russian Front 1941- 1945.*

One prisoner waiting at a railway station observed some of the Soviet units returning home to the U.S.S.R. He said that it appeared to be whole villages had been mounted on trains heading east, to all points in the Soviet Union. The trains were loaded with all kinds of materials and people; demobilized soldiers, freed Russian prisoners, families, children, women, prisoners, military equipment, machinery, farm animals, pets, looted industrial equipment and the looted spoils of war.

Suffering Russia

If one takes the total Russian war casualties by the number of days the war lasted it yields the equivalent of one infantry division or 12,000 or so lost per day of the war. An enormous price to pay for the defense of the Motherland and ejecting an invader, made all the worse by mistakes, errors, waste and the shortcomings and foolishness of the worst aspects of human behavior.

When it comes to human losses in World War II no country suffered more than the Soviet Union, with arguable inclusions of Poland and China. Unfortunately the true number of casualties will never be known for certain, no doubt due to Cold War propaganda and the careless or nonexistent records maintained by the Red Army and the dislocations of government institutions. With a pre-war (1939) population of 190,000,000 the Soviets lost some 28,848,000[354] people, of which 10,000,000 were military casualties, that's one person in 6.6. Consider the following statistic, of all the men born in 1921, 90% of those who became conscripts in the Red Army were dead.

With these staggering losses to show for their struggle, few Russians in the heady summer of 1945 were in any mood to determine if the price of victory had been fair or even justified. Had the truth of the losses in men and treasure been known the celebrations in Moscow would have been more subdued. The Russian survivors of the war were just that, survivors who were hungry and homeless.

Despite the numerous quantities of medals issued and awarded, the postwar period for the veterans of the Russian Army wound up with little to show for their service to the Motherland. The deaths, wounds, amputations, emotional and psychological damage inflicted, the displaced

---

[354] Most recent estimates cite a figure around 25,000,000 one states a figure closer to 40,000,000.

[355] Conversation with museum curator, Dresden, Germany, 2007.

families and lost energy of youth does not make a nation stronger, despite the patriotic notions to the contrary.

The losses suffered by the Soviets during the war were frequently meted out by the command structure of their own forces, exacerbating the already dreadful death toll. At the conclusion of the war approximately 238 general grade officers were shot or reduced in ranks and sent to penal battalions where they were eventually killed undertaking the most dangerous tasks for failing to take assigned objectives, by an assigned schedule or at all. With such harsh consequences for the leadership of the Red Army, the lives of their soldiers must have had almost negligible worth.

In the opening scenes of a recent Hollywood movie on the subject of competing snipers in Stalingrad, one is shown, with great dramatic intensity, just what the Russian soldier was confronted with. The Russian Army was not only in desperate straits in the summer of 1942, but in the deployment and arming of its combat units, it has frequently, if not always, demonstrated a cursory level of care and protection of its human assets. Whereas most Western armies view their human assets, especially its infantry or as he is known in the Red Army, rifleman, with a level of care and concern befitting the holder or defender of terrain, whether that be native soil or captured enemy dirt. However, as most generals will admit, having a surplus of something one tends to use it carelessly, if not wastefully. Such was the fate of the typical Russian soldier in almost every war that Russia fought. One old Russian once said that we can afford to lose many men, we have plenty of them.[355] It is this simplistic brutality, its harshness, almost culturally unintended, but nevertheless used as the standard of how the common soldier was treated, valued, deployed and replaced.

As impressive as these numbers are, there are additional sources of deaths. The Germans took 5,700,000 prisoners, of these 500,000 escaped, about 1,000,000 joined the Germans and an astonishing 3,300,000 died in captivity. Compare the death rate of Russian soldiers captured by the Germans in The Great War, 5.4 percent, with the 70 percent death rate in World War II and one can not only see the magnitude of loss but the genocidal nature of the conflict. In addition, the Germans and their allies killed about 1,500,000 civilians, plus at least 5,000,000 died from starvation, freezing, war and non-war related illnesses, cross fires and air raids[356] and

---

[356] The Luftwaffe air raids in the opening days of the Stalingrad attack killed an estimated 40,000.

about 6,000,000 Jews. Thus the 29,000,000 figure that has been used in recent time to define the extent of the loss in Russia certainly has validity.[357] As lethal as the period 1939 – 1945 was for Russia, the dying did not stop when Germany surrendered in May 1945. The fighting against nationalist movements in the Baltic nations went on until 1953 and Ukrainian and Carpathian guerrillas went on until 1957.[358]

Put another way, the losses of the major combatants of World War II can be seen as follows. For every U.S. soldier that was killed in the war, Japan lost seven, Germany twenty-one and the Soviets eighty-five. No wonder the Russians believe that is was they who won the war.

[357] To give some perspective on the unidentified losses suffered in the major world wars, consider the following from the British experience in World War I. The reality of Western Front missing (soldiers) was too overwhelming. On twenty-seven British memorial walls in cemeteries spread across Belgium and France are the names of 314,234 missing men. *At one of these walls, located at Menin Gate, after chiseling in 54,360 names, the war graves people ran out of space. Close to half the British and empire dead of the Western Front have no known grave, and there is enough evidence that the true number may be higher.* (Italics added for emphasis). By way of comparison, the number of U.S. MIA's from the Viet Nam War is 2,273. Just one barometer of the horror that was The Great War.

[358] One of the chief duties of the NKVD during and after hostilities ended was the searching out and capture of German units and individual soldiers that had been bypassed in the flow of battle. One German organization in particular caused the NKVD major difficulties was the *Brandenburgers*, the special operations or special forces organization of the German Army, a combination of the OSS (Office of Special services), SAS (Special Air Service) and U.S. Army Rangers of the period. The *Brandenburgers* were flown in black painted Heinkel He-111H-23 twin engined converted bomber aircraft behind the Russian lines to attack bridges, Russian headquarters, supply depots, etc. When their tasks had been completed they were to radio a coded message to a special receiver that would arrange for a pick-up by these same aircraft. However, as the front line was pushed further and further west and the abilities of the Luftwaffe declined, pick-ups of these intrepid soldiers became increasingly difficult and in some cases *Brandenburger* units were never recovered, being told to make their own way out. These units, living off the land and the enemy fought literally to the last man as the NKVD units tracked them down and captured or killed them. Usually, due to the damage caused by the *Brandenburgers* and the effort expended by the Soviets, when captured they were promptly killed. One German Luftwaffe radio operator recalls their radio signals requesting pick-up growing weaker, increasingly weaker as, one by one they went silent. In connection with the rescue of the Brandenburgers was Operation Berezino. During Operation Bagration Russian SMERSh counterintelligence units under NKGB Fourth Directorate chief Lieutenant General Pavel Sudoplatov conducted a "radio game" known as *Operation Berezino* in which they convinced German intelligence units that a number of German soldiers were trapped behind Russian lines and if they could be provided with arms, food and equipment could be used as a potential sabotage force. It was strictly a Russian means of diverting and distracting the Germans to deliver scarce arms and equipment to a non-existent trapped force and was quite successful.

Bestial Analogies

If one seeks metaphors in the eastern war, one should look no further than the names the Germans gave their two most important and lethal armored panzers, Tiger and Panther. The enemies of these dangerous cats were the great eastern bear of Russia and his friends the American eagle and the British lion.

The Tiger, Panther, named panzers were responsible for the death of thousands of Russian rifleman and tank crewmen and the destruction of thousands of Russian tanks and self-propelled guns. The cat versus bear comparison is an apt one, and using them makes for an interesting analogy.

Germany quickly and deftly ripped into the Russian armies in June of 1941, clawing, tearing and rending the Red Army for the first three years of the war. The Russian bear went reeling backward, stunned, bleeding, dizzy, clumsy, confused but still alive. The German cats, uncertain what to do next allowed the wounded bear just enough time to gather his thoughts, focus his efforts and with the help of friends (read: Lend-Lease shipments) and with great sacrifice lunge back at the deadly cats, in the first years swinging wildly and inaccurately. In the decision year of 1943, the bear finally stopped the cats and inflicted deep wounds and stunned them. The cats had not been beaten before, never stopped before, what was this animal that dared to confront us? The battle continued into 1944, the cats continued to bite, claw and tear but the great bear, teeth and claws growing and flashing, with huge strength and stamina the cats did not possess, fought back, inflicting wounds the cats could not heal, as there was little time to seek shelter, a protected burrow, a safe haven to lick their wounds and gather strength and think what to do. Now, the bear's other friends the Eagle and the Lion were biting and nipping at the cat's tails and threatening to inflict further injury. Meanwhile, the lumbering bear came at them again and again, crushing, trashing, and mauling the now fragile, thin structure of the cats. By 1945 the cats were in desperate shape, but still dangerous, should one get too close to the still sharp, but few claws left on the bloody paws. With one final heave the bear came again, was pushed back but came on again, this time breaking into the center of the cats lair as the Eagle and Lion, now fully arrived on the field of battle from the west, sent their full fury at the cats. The cats and the children and relatives of the cats fought desperately but there was no longer room to fight, strength to defend or allies to assist. In a final gasp the cats succumbed, taking millions of innocents with them.

Total War

Many have attempted to separate the combatant and noncombatant aspects of the war. In the past this might have been possible and, indeed, if we trace back far enough the methods of warfare perhaps could be clearly, cleanly, surgically separated from each other. However, World War II was a war like no other before it, this was total war. The innocent, the weak, the young, the mothers, the children were just as much a target as a man holding a rifle. The development of indiscriminate and widespread bombing and artillery shelling of residential areas became 'legitimate' targets, the rationale being to make the enemy hurt and grieve at every opportunity. The destruction of the enemy's morale was just as legitimate a target as his factories. Nothing was off limits, nothing was sacred, it was total war in its perfect tense, and it seems safe to say that a successful invasion of Russia by land with conventional forces and weapons is an impossibility and that no one but a lunatic would attempt it.

Outside of direct contact with enemy soldiers, a significant cause of civilian casualties was the Allied bombing campaign, especially the Royal Air Force night bombing attacks. These attacks were intentionally designed to 'de-house' Germanys civilian worker population and to cause them direct harm by interfering with their domestic activities and thereby denying their use to German industry. On the other hand, the U.S. precision bombing effort which was largely directed to specific industrial and military targets, although this was the intent, collateral damage to civilian areas was almost common by 1945.

The German threat to Europe and later the world brought together the three forces that Germany could never defeat; the manpower of the U.S.S.R., the industrial resources of the United States and the global reach and might of the British Empire. Combine them all and you have the planet's unbeatable military and economic powerhouse. The real tragedy for Germany, blinded by her race based outlook of the world was that she failed to see this coming, especially after the declaration of war on the United States.

Nazi Mythology

When a German dentist, Dr. Friederich Krohn, an early member in the Nazi party suggested that the Party adopt the swastika as the symbol of its political movement in the summer of 1920, he did two things with it that none of the early cults, tribes, nations or religions did. He reversed it and tilted it. The reversing of the swastika by the Nazis clearly demonstrated that this was not just another adoption of this age-old symbol of good fortune, the reversal signified the National Socialist Workers Party was to be a new movement, the new disciple and torchbearer of the ancient Tibetan religion.

The tilting of the symbol, so as to appear to 'stand' on one of its 'legs', was also no accident or cosmetic improvement. The Party, intending to demonstrate progress, movement and action, used the 'tilting', also known in symbolic study as 'spinning', to indicate a new dynamism, a new forward motion, a new energy, a take-off of the Native American Navajo use of the swastika as a spinning bird. The colors of the new national flag were no accident or coincidence either. The colors selected; red, white and black in those proportions were selected to import the desired stimulating effect on the viewer. However, the Nazis, in their thorough research for the perfect Aryan image for their new party overlooked one interesting piece of Cabbalistic lore associated with the swastika: Chaotic force can be released by reversing it. How prophetic that was to be, indeed.

Europeans Germanicus

Let us speculate once again on an alternative outcome of the war in Europe. Let us suppose that Germany was victorious over all of Europe, Russia and England included, leaving a cowed Sweden, Switzerland and the bewildered Iberian Peninsula nations to decide what direction their probable fate lies. The task of maintaining control over and making the occupied nations produce for the Third Reich would have been an enormous task. Germany liberated no one during World War II. Germany was an invader. All during the war there was not one nation that saw its standard of living, national security or prestige rise as a result of an alliance with or occupation by Germany.

Again, from "The Third Reich, A New History",

> "Countries such as Belgium, Czechoslovakia, France, Denmark, the Netherlands and Norway were initially spared the lethal policies pursued in Poland, where on average three thousand Poles died each day during the occupation, half of them Christian Poles, half of them Jews. Nonetheless, it is worth remembering that in the case of Czechoslovakia a quarter of a

million people were killed during the war. Nazism represented a challenge to the European and global balance of power and to civilized values everywhere, blighting the lives of tens of millions of people throughout Europe. There were gross restrictions of individual freedom, and such shared tribulations as conscription for forced labor and chronic hunger, with an estimated three hundred thousand Greeks dying of starvation during the occupation as German looting of food and the disruption of normal market mechanisms took effect. In Paris, up to 270,000 people were dependent on subsidized communal restaurants for a square meal. Ersatz foodstuffs, the conversion of flowerbeds and window boxes to grow vegetables, trips to the countryside and the moral perils of the black market became the norm for those not part of charmed German-collaborator circles. In most countries, the quality of life deteriorated, with curfews, raids, blackouts, longer working hours, fuel shortages or restricted and inadequate transportations systems. The price of food soared, six fold in occupied Paris between 1940 and 1943; seventyfold in occupied Warsaw between 1939 and 1944. In Brussels, the German commander in chief noted poor people rifling through dustbins for scraps before dawn each day. Cats and dogs disappeared, and recipes abounded with inventive ways of preparing horsemeat, potatoes, swedes or turnips. Smokers combed the pavements for cigarette butts: ruining their health, but suppressing hunger more effectively than non-smokers"

"...Fuel shortages made the long winter of 1940/1 especially severe, with many people staying in bed for long periods, with rising being akin to plunging into a freezing swimming pool. Illnesses such as tuberculosis, dysentery and hepatitis were common because of poor diet, as were such stress-related phenomena as breakdowns, heart attacks, skin disease, stomach ulcers and irregular menstruation, unsurprising in societies where people could be shot for not carrying an identity card or for sheltering an unregistered person. One consequence of poor diet was that in France the average height of boys and girls growing up between 1935 and 1944 declined by respectively seven and eleven centimeters. Paradoxically, many of Germany's wartime

[359] *The Third Reich, A New History*, p. 417.

allies, such as Croatia, Italy, Romania and Slovakia, experienced lower bread rations than many occupied countries."[359]

It is hard to fathom just what Germany truly expected from its conquered nations. Did the Germans and their government think the world was going to see their annihilation of millions of innocent people, when finally discovered, would be applauded? In this *vernichtungsschlacht*, this war of annihilation did the world see the Jews and eastern Slavic people as a 'problem' as the Third Reich did?[360] German Nazism was a cancer on Europe, a cancer that had to be eradicated to ensure that Europe survived.

It can safely be stated, now as in 1945, that not one nation saw any material advantage in a permanent alliance with the Third Reich, especially with so ruthless and unstable a leader as Adolf Hitler. Germany and its conspicuous aggressive tendencies, its lack of civilized behavior, especially in its relations between nations and her lack of respect for treaties and agreements would have been a constant threat to whatever nation allied itself with her. From 1933 to 1945 Germany had demonstrated, time and again, when she saw an advantage or political desire, no matter what diplomatic, economic, military or tool of statecraft existed to the contrary she would turn on that nation and devour it. The example of the 1939 German-Russian pact is only one, but the best example.

Dear and Foot in their *The Oxford Companion To World War II* add the following:

> "Nazi ideology pointed plainly towards war. This does not mean that we should accept Hitler's *Mein Kampf* as a blue print or a program of action in foreign policy. But there were powerful and consistent elements in his thoughts and emotions: living space (*Lebensraum*) for the German people; a racial doctrine directed against both Jews and Slavs; anti-Bolshevism; and a sort of social Darwinism which saw all politics in terms of a struggle for existence. *All these pointed to a great war in the east* (italics added for emphasis), where living space was to be found, and where the Soviet Union concentrated Jewish, Slavonic, and Bolshevik enemies into a single whole. If these broad aims of Nazi ideology were seriously pursued, they would lead inevitably

[360] The noted German author Thomas Mann said in a broadcast shortly after the 28-29 March 1942 RAF Lubeck raid, "I think of Coventry, and I have no objection to the lesson that everything must be paid for. Did Germany believe that she would never have to pay for the atrocities that her leap into barbarism seemed to allow?"

to war. Moreover, we must look not only at ideological aims, but at methods. The Nazis applied in foreign policy the tactics that served them so well in their domestic struggles-intimidation, subversion, and deceit, all applied with a malevolent yet inspired boldness. For some time, such methods brought them success without war (as in Austria and Czechoslovakia), but in the long run they produced such revulsion in other countries that they made war certain. A state which behaved in such a way generated total mistrust, so that negotiation became impossible".[361]

Hitler's plans for his pan-Germanic New European Order is at once impressive as it is frightening. Again, from "The Third Reich, A New History":

"When Hitler envisaged the Greater Reich, he thought of central and Northern and north-western Europe, with the 'East' as a surrogate British India, whose inhabitants would be cowed and fobbed off with glass beads. When he spoke of future European unification, the analogy was the forging of the Bismarckian Empire from the states of Germany, a process which divided the German nation by excluding Austria. He did not even mention southern Europe: 'The immense labor involved in the welding of northern, western, central and eastern Europe into one entity will be quickly forgotten.' In other words, Europe meant nothing to Hitler, whose views were an amalgam of brutal imperialism, chauvinistic prejudice and blood-based racism. He was solely interested in absolute, permanent German dominance over the north and east of the continent, with the rest being left to his Italian ally... "[362]

"...It is also noteworthy that planning for Western Europe was both more conventional and much less systemic than for the eastern half of the continent, where the SS enjoyed de facto supremacy. There was no western European equivalent of the "*Generalplan Ost*' the masterplans for reorganizing the whole of European Russia, let alone balsa-wood models of town squares and peasant farmsteads. The west did not stimulate Nazi imaginations in the same way as the East. Whereas the Nazis

---

[361] *The Oxford Companion to World War II.*

[362] *The Third Reich, A New History*, p. 427.

imagined they had a tabula rasa, which they could draw upon at will, sometimes on the basis of having been there in mists of times disturbingly actual in their consciousness, in the West they had to tread gingerly because of collaborationist regimes and ethnic affinities, or because the West, with its advanced bureaucracies and developed skills base, could be exploited more thoroughly by leaving things relatively alone.   Moreover, planning to integrate the Franco-German coal industry was not the same as planning to move the Poles to Brazil or Siberia.   Nazi plans for Europe included realistic schemes for the efficient economic exploitation of the continent; turgid jurisprudential tracts outlining a European 'Monroe Doctrine'; works of pseudo-history extolling ahistorical versions of the medieval Holy Roman Empire; and quasi-ethnographic attempts to destroy existing nations states in favor of a patchwork quilt of sub-atomic regional particles." [363]

This Nazi utopia in Europe would require nothing less than the re-drawing of almost every border in contemporary Europe. Nations and the peoples that occupied them that did not fit into the new German European *Weltanschauung* were to be repressed, displaced, banished or exterminated. As Burleigh's description of a Germanified Europe makes abundantly clear this was to be a highly stratified construct with Germany sitting at the top and the Nazi most favored nations below in descending order of racial favoritism. Nazism rightly stands as the low-water mark in twentieth-century moral culture. No matter what the promised long term 'benefits' of the Nazi master plan, the means certainly never justified the ends.

A significant part of the inability of the Germans to muster European support and cooperation, even amongst their Axis allies, for the war against Russia and the larger campaign against Bolshevism was their lack of a sane and acceptable political vision of the future of Europe. Time and time again when pressed to provide a picture of what the German vision of a post-war Europe would look like, the question either went unanswered or was turned into an economic or military diatribe of the victories recently won.

However, life for the ordinary German or Russian was not an endless period of dread and misgivings. As was mentioned earlier, if one was careful, circumspect and lucky, life in either system could almost be described as

---

[363] Ibid, pp. 427 – 428.

normal,[364] if normal can be used to describe for their particular person or family their position, location and nationality. Richard Overy in his comparative work on Stalin and Hitler stated the following:

> "For the vast majority who were not direct victims of repression, daily life was also more normal than the popular image of either dictatorship suggests. It was possible to live in Germany throughout the whole period of the dictatorship and perhaps witness an incidence of state repression on no more than two or three occasions in twelve years – an SA bully beating a worker in March 1933, a garrulous anti-Nazi neighbor taken off for an afternoon to the police station to be told to hold his tongue in November 1938, the towns Jewish dentist sent off for 'resettlement' in September 1942. A Soviet worker could pass the twenty years of Stalin's dictatorship with only a few hours disrupted by State Security – the arrest of the technical director one day in March 1937, the disappearance of a fellow-worker with a German name in 1941, a gang of prisoners repairing the factory roads for a week in 1947. No one in either system could be unaware that State Security was out there, but for the ordinary citizen, uninterested in politics, lucky enough not to belong to one of the groups stigmatized as enemies, the attitude was as likely to be prudent respect, even approval, rather than a permanent state of fear."[365]

An Alternative Outcome?

Let us depart from the historical record briefly to explore a giant 'what if' question; a question that has been tossed about in military history texts, chat rooms, classrooms, countless eastern front board games and blogs for quite some time. Although a counterfactual history has no place in this work, the exploration of historical alternatives permits an examination of what might have been.

The question revolves around a quick, successful completion of Operation Barbarossa, just as the OKW plan envisioned it. What would

[364] The appeal of German National Socialism was deeply entrenched in the upper classes and amongst university students, some 35 per cent of all *Einsatzgruppen* commanders had doctoral degrees. See *The Eastern Front 1941-45, German Troops and the Barbarization of Warfare*, Second Edition by Omar Bartov, St. Anthony's Press, 2001, p. 50.

[365] *The Dictators, Hitler's Germany and Stalin's Russia* by Richard Overy, W. W. Norton & Company, New York London, 2004, pp 209-210.

an enlightened successful German invasion and occupation be like? How would a happy pacified and supportive western Russia respond to a gentle German occupation? What would the effects be on western Allied planning? This is an important discussion topic, as a successful conclusion to Barbarossa would have a crucial impact on what the western Allies could or could not do in the West. Although outside the purview of the impact of the German experience in Russia and its impact on the Normandy landings, it is of interest to see what might have happened, using careful, credible, thoughtful and realistic hypotheses.

David Downing in his book *The Moscow Option, An Alternative Second World War* describes what a successful invasion of the Soviet Union might look like. In his book, Moscow falls to the Germans at the end of September 1941 and the Nazis advance as far east as Gorky and Saratov. The loss of Moscow is more than just the loss of a major city, as it might be seen in the West. Moscow symbolized and was the home of world Communism, the cradle of the workers' paradise, the tomb of Lenin, the home of Stalin. There is a significant amount of Party mysticism connected to this city, and its loss, physically and symbolically, would have been difficult for the Soviets to recover from.

He shows how Moscow is also a major manufacturing location for the nation. Many of the arms and metal fabrication plants were located there as well as a host of important supporting industries as well as arms, training, and manpower distribution points. Moscow is also the nexus of the north-south rail lines of the nation. Cut them at Moscow and you have cut the rail travel from Leningrad to Rostov-on-Don; all points north and south. The alternatives for rail travel north and south are many miles and days longer. Yes, lose Moscow and the loss is a major one.

Continuing Downing's story line, while the Russians were fleeing to the east rebuilding their armies and relocating their industrial plant, the disruption permits the Germans to transfer of an entire panzer corps to North Africa, enabling Rommel to beat the British 8th Army at El Alamein in Egypt, capture the town, then move on to Alexandria, Cairo, and finally into Palestine. This was made possible by the fall of Malta in the central Mediterranean in April of the previous year due to the release of the majority of Luftwaffe transport aircraft from Russia, now that the rail connections there had been converted from the broad Russian to the narrower European gauge, allowing the Germans to bring their supplies right up to the front line by more efficient and cheaper non-transfer railroad. Although this is just a brief synopsis of part of his engaging story, one can see the consequences that a German victory in Russia might have caused. For all its appalling risk, the invasion of Russia by Germany in 1941 was a daunting task.

Lets lay out an hypothetical scenario of a German victory over the Russians in 1941. It's December; Army Group Center headquarters is safely and warmly ensconced in a conquered Moscow, Army Group North's headquarters is enjoying the ambiance of the Hermitage in Leningrad, and Army Group South's command is enjoying Caspian caviar in Stalingrad.

Moscow fell in the middle of the Rasputitsy, the slowed traffic weather caused by the rainy, muddy season after a desperate final lunge with mud encrusted soldiers, panzers and struggling wheeled vehicles. In October Leningrad was captured after a race to the Neva River that the Fourth *Panzergruppe* won, advancing a few more miles to the north to join with the Finns attacking south from the Viipuri area. Army Group South had advanced to the Desna/Donets river line and captured Rostov-on-Don after a fierce battle at the Mius River.

The capture of the cities, towns and geographical points does not imply all is well for the *Ostheer* in the newly conquered Soviet Union, soon to be renamed Greater Moscow, Greater Ukraine, Greater Belorussia and other similar labels. There is strong partisan activity in the dense forests west and south of Moscow and in the city itself hit and run attacks by the Communist Red Banner and Komsomol youth brigades and diehard commissars and remnants of Russian Army units against German soldiers, headquarters and other military facilities is a daily event.

With Moscow, Leningrad and Rostov occupied by the first snows, it was an opportune time to call a halt to the offensive for the year. The panzer divisions were almost completely worn out, and their effective strength was down to 10% in some divisions. The motorized divisions were little better off. Murmansk was in German hands by August and Allied supply convoys turned about and returned to England and Iceland. The Finns had recaptured their pre-1939 lands and now assisted the Germans in consolidating the regions east of Leningrad. The infantry had "worn out its boots" in many forced marches and was stretched dangerously thin manning the front line as well as reducing the pockets of surrounded Russian troops.

Diplomatic initiatives have resulted to a truce in place, the Germans agreeing to no additional advances in exchange for an agreement from the Russians for no hostile action against the Germans and their newly acquired holdings. The truce line ran roughly from Murmansk south on the Russo-Finnish border out to Lake Onega south-south east to the Volga Reservoir, south east to Ryazan south to the Don to Pavlovsk to Millerovo, Kamensk on the Donets followed to the Don once again and south west to Rostov.

So far, the peace was holding. The Germans expected the peace to hold for a least a year, perhaps longer based on the destruction wrought on the Red Army since June. It was estimated that the Red Army lost close to 200 divisions, 4,300 tanks, 5,000 artillery pieces and 7,000 aircraft. Although a majority of this equipment was obsolete when the war started, the Russians had not yet had time to replace much of it, so busy had they been attempting to transfer their military-industrial complex to the Ural range and beyond. Try as they might, the rail lines and bridges heading east were relentlessly bombed and strafed causing large rail backups, which the Luftwaffe destroyed at its leisure. The Russian government, seeing the writing on the wall, requested a truce as they could no longer fight due to a lack of weapons. Now their industrial areas were occupied, their attempted factory relocation failed, and the Lend-Lease aid from the Allies just starting and the ships transporting it to Russian ports were constantly attacked by German U-Boats and Luftwaffe. For Stalin it was time to call it quits and wait for a better opportunity in the future. It was rumored he and the Soviet government had fled first to Kazan, then on to the Soviet Far East.[366]

This scenario is not as farfetched as it sounds. There has been much debate on the likelihood of a Russo-German truce, especially if the Red Army had suffered catastrophic defeats in 1941 and early 1942 and Stalin was desperate enough to save his regime and determined to live on to fight

---

[366] The hypothetical Soviet retreat eastward would have much of the Russian and Siberian geography on their side. The fallback positions would have been significant obstacles for any army to overcome. A possible list from west to east: The Ural Mountains/Aral Sea/Pechora River line, the Ob River/Irtysh River line, Yenisey River line, the Lena River/Lake Baikal line and finally the smaller Kolyma River line in far eastern Siberia. In between these formidable barriers were vast deserts, frozen tundra, deep forests and trackless expanses with little or no transportation infrastructure other than the Trans-Siberian Railway.

another day. When his armies would be ready to reengage the Germans, where this would take place and how successful the re-constituted Red Army would be is too far a reach even for this scenario, save to say that it would eventually happen. With Allied support, the determination to rid Russia of the Fascist invader and the ruthlessness of Stalin, it was just a matter of time.

The German occupying forces are estimated to be about 50 divisions,[367] mostly specially formed *Sicherungs* divisions, to maintain front line security, rear area administration, and anti-partisan duties. I indicate 'specially formed' *Sicherungs* divisions, as the operations in this part of Europe will require special equipment and training due to the vast distances to be managed, climatic conditions and large populations controlled. The panzer divisions would be withdrawn to Germany for complete rest, refitting, and training and expansion. About 5 mechanized panzergrenadier divisions would remain in Russia, based in strategic locations to respond in a timely manner to any threats in the truce; to aid with internal unrest and to assist the security and border protection units in general security duties. The Luftwaffe would also return to central Europe with just a few fighter *staffeln* remaining in Russia to protect the long range reconnaissance *staffeln* needed to probe deep into the Ural range and beyond, to determine the state of the truce, monitor Russian movement and detect any violations.

Continuing our hypothetical post-truce scenario, the 50 German divisions are considered adequate for security of the conquered territory and in time could even be reduced, as the Russian and other ethnic populations begin to thrive under efficient and 'benevolent' German management. The Germans realized the necessity of securing the cooperation of the local populations to provide for their own administration, security, supply the Greater German Reich with the bounty of their country, to be the 'eyes and ears' for German intelligence and, in time, to be organized into an entirely Free Russian Defense Army to defend the new border. The importance of supporting independence movements was encouraged, as long as it did not imperil German interests and satisfied the people's desire of a say in their own futures. The "benign" German civil administration realized, as the Romans did before them, that occupying powers rule by the consent of the

---

[367] In the original planning for Operation Barbarossa, Hitler indicated that 60 divisions would be left behind in Russia for security purposes. See *The Soviet Partisan Movement, 1941-1944* By Edgar M. Howell, Department of the Army Pamphlet, No. 20-244, August 1956.

people they occupy; without it there are grave portents against a successful and fruitful relationship.

Such could have been the 'peace' in Russia, had an enlightened Germany dispensed with its repressive racial and political policies and embarked on a more rational administration of its occupied Russia. The immense amounts of raw materials from the conquered territories would be exploited by local labor and pour into the armaments factories and general industries of a "Gross Deutsch Europa", a Greater German Europe.

The newly rested and refitted mechanized and infantry units released from Russia would be redistributed throughout Europe, with an eye to consolidating the gains from 1940; also protecting any vulnerable coastal sites from Allied landings. The majority would be based in France due to its central location in Western Europe with its excellent communications and transportation network, and with the knowledge of the anticipated desire of the western Allies to return to mainland Europe. The above result would be a powerful Germany concentrated all along the potential landing areas of the English Channel to the Bay of Biscay on the Spanish border similar to the defenses built at Pas-de-Calais in 1944. With this distribution of *Wehrmacht* power all along the possible landing areas, an Operation Overlord-like landing would have been fraught with peril, enough so that any landing may have been so risky as to halt consideration of such an action and possibly require re-thinking the entire strategic picture in the West.

The above is a hypothetical scenario. Although a possibility, it is easy to see how such a close thing it might have been. A German dominated Russia would have rid the world of communism but would also have been a disaster for the Allies. This is why Russian survival and active participation in fighting the Germans were so important to the West and to guarantee the success the landings of the Western Allies in France.

Even before the start of Barbarossa in 1941, the odds of success were great against a German victory in Russia. Many have wondered why Germany attacked Russia in the first place. As Downing points out in his book, the Russians would have just kept moving farther and farther east until they had recovered their strength, and then counterattacked. This counterattack would have been directed against a front line now much farther to the east than the original plans for Barbarossa had envisioned with all the risks and difficulties that extended supply and communication lines impose. If the Germans were having trouble managing their rear areas in the historical setting, one can imagine the difficulties they would have encountered in this scenario.

The "arianization" of Europe would make for a land of cookie-cutter 'humans' that would not only look alike, but think alike, act alike and die alike. There is more to human diversity than being tall, blond, and blue eyed. The great confluence of ideas, customs, wealth, culture and people from North, South, East and West that represent the best of the Eurasian landmass would be controlled, reviewed, diverted, filtered, stopped. It would take on many of the worst aspects of Stalinism and the Communist monolithic world that came of age in the 1950's; the bland, tasteless, boring, deadening life of just enough of the minimums, including joy, happiness and fulfillment, just change the name. Nazism had to be killed, and killed quickly. The German introduction of a neo-barbarism the likes Europe had not seen since the middle ages is hardly a subject of boast. The oft demonstrated German ability to make miracles from almost nothing due to their magnificent organization, drive and will was on the cusp of making an Allied victory in the last year of the war very expensive, in lives and wealth.[368] As mentioned earlier, a Europe under Nazi German management, with all the raw materials and natural resources available to it would be a frightening thought. We can all be thankful that the Allied leaders and nations had the indomitable will to see the difficult task through to the end.

---

[368] Enzensberger points out that it is impossible to understand "the mysterous energy of the Germans... if we refuse to realize that they have made a virtue of their deficiencies. Insensibility," he adds, "was the condition of their success." The prerequisites of the German economic miracle were not only the enormous sums invested in the country under the Marshall Plan, the outbreak of the Cold War, and the scrapping of outdated industrial complexes-an operation performed with brutal efficiency by the bomber squadrons-but also something less often acknowledged: the unquestioning work ethic learned in a totalitarian society, the logistical capacity for improvisation shown by an economy under constant threat, experience in the use of "foreign labor forces," and the lifting of the heavy burden of history that went up in flames between 1942 and 1945 along with the century's-old buildings accommodating homes and businesses in Nuremburg and Cologne, in Frankfurt, Aachen, Brunswick, and Wurtzburg, a historical burden ultimately regretted by only a few." From *On the Natural History of Destruction* by W. G. Sebald, The Modern Library, New York, 2004, translated by Anthea Bell.

The Last of the Great Wars?

> "What do the old men talk about when they come back to remember? They don't talk much. They don't seem to need to. Sometimes they just stand and weep."

> *- Curator of the museum at Prokhorovka*
> *Site of the great tank battle at Kursk*

The war between Germany and Russia took a terrible toll in lives. For the Wehrmacht the total killed and missing in action from 1939 to1945 is 5,100,728[369]. Include civilian deaths of 4,400,000 and a figure of 9,500,728 is obtained.[370] Considering a 1939 population of 66,000,000 and you have a death percentage a little over 14% of the total population, that's one person in 39. Include the wounded, maimed; the psychologically and emotionally impaired and you have a nation that paid a high price for its aggressive ambitions.

The Russians, defending of their homeland against the Nazi invaders, suffered an appalling number of casualties. Krivosheev[371] states a final Russian Army figure of 29,629,200. With civilian losses of 6,700,000[372] added in the total number of deaths is truly astounding and tragic. Based on a population of 190,000,000 that brings a death percentage of approximately19% of total population.

The Fading Past

The Second World War, once so current, so recent, so awful, so all pervasive in the public consciousness is now receding quickly into the historical past. As huge as the war was, engulfing the entire planet, it is now being supplanted by more recent conflicts equally important in the minds of the combatants, just as the war in the East was, however these current conflicts are still fresh in contemporary memory. As the Confederate States

---

[369] http://www.feldgrau.com/stats.html.

[370] However, John Ellis in his *World War II, The Encyclopedia of Facts and Figures* quotes 3,250,000 and 2,050,000 respectively.

[371] *Soviet Casualties and Combat Losses In the Twentieth Century*, p. 105. Includes irrecoverable losses, sick and wounded of both army and navy.

[372] *World War II, The Encyclopedia of Facts and Figures*, p. 254.

of America found in 1865 and the Third Reich was to discover in 1945, a nation cannot be founded on the anguish and suppression of a portion of its people, no matter how high minded its aims, goals and ideals, they are only rhetoric if its peoples are divided and excluded. A nation will prevail only if all of its people are embraced and benefit.

Europe under a Nazi Germany would be a cold, sterile, artificial world indeed, bereft of all the elements that make Europe such an amazing, fascinating, rewarding and enjoyable place to live and work. The implementation of a German Nazi "New Order" would leave an intellectually dead Europe, devoid of the stimulation, diversity and joy that characterized the old, a *weltanschauungen* that was much better dead.

Memory, the memories of the soldiers, airmen, marines and sailors who fought in World War II are no longer slowly disappearing; they just as the public memory, are quickly disappearing, in the United States these men are dying at a rate of 2,200 per day.[373] Even the very youngest are in their 70's. The collective living memory of the most awful conflict of the modern era is fading away, growing dimmer, fainter with every passing day. Where will the information, the stories, the feeling, the insight, the lessons and the consequences of war come from when these gallant, desperate, marvelous and occasionally foolish warriors are no more? Who will write about those who were there, but soon are no more? The eyewitnesses, the young, the handsome, the plain, the simple, the brilliant? There is little time to waste in securing their memories, their triumphs, their tragedies, their failures and their victories. Haste, make haste to inscribe what they have done, what they have sacrificed, what they have lost, what they have saved for us, for the next generations. And when we have received their gift of experience what will we do with it? Will we squander what they so painstakingly learned? Will we redo or undo their lesson to us? The very least we can do is take heed of their message of pain and waste, or are we as humans condemned to replay this tragedy every generation or two? I fear a few more conflicts like the one in the East and there may be little humanity left to record anything.

Hitler, in his zeal to destroy communism, instead brought it to the heart of Europe. Finally, there must be an understanding why so many Germans were so enamored by and drawn to National Socialism. In the 1930s Germany began to exhibit similar patterns of behavior as was the

---

[373] Year 2008 data.

Soviet Union, the fear of the different, the outsider, the other. The fear of political decline and moral decay, physical degeneration, racial pollution, domestic role changes, social upheaval, the obsession with order and structure, a keen interest of purity and contamination, the seduction of some mythical past and the installation of a sense of duty. These personal and national preoccupations and psychological vulnerabilities made this population ripe for manipulation.

But what about the new Germany, the post-war transformed Germany? Dear and Foot in "The Oxford Companion to World War II" describes it as follows:

> "The Federal Republic escaped the Weimar's political and economic instability and its pariah status and became, unlike all previous German regimes, a functioning civilian and parliamentary democracy, feared by few. The war had wrecked German power only temporarily. Perhaps it had done more for the German mood or temper, rendering a new Germany no longer as menacing as the Third Reich or the Second."[374]

Recorded history is sprinkled with examples of characters raised from obscurity by fate and chance to influence the lives and directions of nations and peoples. Hitler and Stalin were both excellent examples of this chance happening. These beneficiaries of the hand of fate soon learn or are convinced of their uniqueness and possessed with unalterable determination, seek methods and paths to make their distinctive mark on their fellow man and, as we have seen, on nations. This mark of fate is what unquestionably drove these two men from the pit of failure to the heights of power and victory and back again. This is what must have carried Hitler along to such lengths when all around him, both man and event signaled the war was no longer winnable. However, to these men such rational thinking was for mortals, their course was determined by the stars and the benevolent hand of divine intervention. To quit, halt or stop when everyone around them pleaded for them to do so would be to do nothing less than to cast away the assured success they believed was in store for them.

The great tragedy for the Russian people during the Second World War was not only as victim of the foremost military machine in the world in 1941, the *Wehrmacht*, but also to suffer internally the ravages of its own

---

[374] *The Oxford Companion to World War II*, p. 480.

leaders and government. No other combatant nation in the Second World War, Germany notwithstanding, had to confront the external threat of destruction by an invader as well as cope with the capricious demands, punishments and perceived threats of its leadership. Stalin may have bound his nation and its disparate peoples together to fight off the invader but his xenophobia of enemies everywhere made the self-inflicted cost in lives high.[375]

So, in the end, a newly reunited Germany stands triumphant and her former archenemy, the Union of Soviet Socialist Republics, gone, replaced by a new and struggling Russia. Europe's organizational, economic and industrial colossus once again bestrides the continent from the Rhine in the West to the newly drawn borders of its perennial and hopefully permanent eastern Polish neighbor. In place of Communism a new struggling democracy is growing in Russia, battling all the difficulties of a new government and economic system while trying to banish from memory and habit the confining mindset of the old.[376]

Once again, Germany is looking east, however this time it appears to be a more benign economic gaze. What is it that so fascinates them there? The historical what-might-have-beens, the endless steppes, the limitless horizon, the beckoning of better tomorrows, of new empires, wealth, and, of course, land. This wild, uncultivated land, just waiting for German discipline and order to come and make it productive. There is a term in German for this eastern magnetism – *Ostrausch*. However, is there something more, something yet unidentified embedded in the Teutonic soul of her past, something inviting and enticing her lurking in the east?

It is interesting to compare the contemporary Germany of the last half century with its late 1930s Nazi form. The strident militaristic Germany that bestrode Europe is now one of the most pacifistic nations in Europe.

---

[375] U.S. diplomat George F. Kennan in his *Memoirs* wrote that "...a Soviet official had told me that we must teach our people that every foreigner is a spy. It is only in this way that we can train them to exercise the self-control which they should exercise as citizens of a great power. Our people must not be allowed to forget that they live in a capitalist environment, that a friend may be a friend today and an enemy tomorrow..."

[376] Developments in the new Russia are being carefully observed by the west and a worried world is concerned that a new Russia looking for its new post-Communist identity might look to the past for guidance. Although the old Russia is gone, the institutions of power that Stalin developed have never gone away. The sources of them in social, political and psychological traditions are still there, hidden in the habits of millions. As they still are there in the people they are still a threat because they are invisible and normal.

A nation that is so militarily quiet that it is occasionally difficult to get her to participate in NATO peacekeeping duties. The Germany of the 1940's, regardless what it professed to be the new leader of European culture, was hamstrung by its insane racial standards of exclusion, subjugation and extermination and would have never have been an example for the rest of Europe to emulate. As one German put it, "We have shown that if it's possible for anyone to have leadership in Europe, it must in no circumstances be us."

Despite a second bout of war with Germany in the same century it was saved from possible disassembly by the victorious Allies by virtue of becoming a confrontation state with the new enemy, the one-time Allied eastern ally, the U.S.S.R. which, by 1948 ended what wartime harmony had ever existed. The temptation to put into practice U.S. Secretary of the Treasury Henry Morgenthau's plan of a permanently de-fanged and agrarianized Germany was averted.

How will the newly rejoined Germany behave in the third millennium in Europe? The Germans are a young and dynamic race who have been seeking throughout their history to find their real identity. Will this most recent trial by fire provide them the answer they have been seeking? Only time will tell.

With unification in 1989 and the peaceful withdrawal of Soviet military units, Germany once again became its former self, with the exception of the former East Prussia, which was broken up, part ceded to Poland and part to Russia. The unification was completed with the movement of the national capital from Bonn on the Rhine in the former West Germany to the ancient capital of Berlin on the Spree in the east. Largely symbolic, the move poses the question; does it highlight the emphasis of a renewed German interest in the east? Let us all hope for the future that whatever interest the reborn and reunited Germany has in the east will be a peaceful one, dispelling once and for all that dark portion of the German soul for domination, for a future pursued gently for the betterment of all.

German winter camouflaged PzKw Mk. III L

Glossary

Abwehr. . . . . The intelligence service of OKW headed by Admiral Wilhelm Canaris.

Allies . . . . The term given to the collation of nations typically Western and Russian and their armed forces dedicated to defeating the Axis nations.

Apparat(s) . . . . Russian term for network, as in spy network(s).

Army Group Center . . . . . . The German group of armies in the center of the German-Russian front (from Vitebsk to Kovel) in the east, consisting of (from north to south in June 1944) 3rd Panzer, 4th Panzer, 9th and 2nd armies. At the outbreak of Operation Barbarossa it was tasked with seizing Moscow.

Army Group North, South . . The German army groups tasked with seizing Leningrad (Army Group North) and Kiev (Army Group South) at the start of Barbarossa.

Assault Gun . . . . Essentially a turret-less tank with a forward firing gun of limited movement and, usually, supporting machine guns, produced in large numbers by Germany, where it was known as the *Sturmgeschutz,* providing attack support in the infantry divisions and occasionally substituted for tanks in some panzer divisions.

Atlantic Wall. . . . . Also *Atlantikwall.* The series of fortifications, defensive positions, strong points built in threatened landing areas that Germany reinforced, from Holland in the north to the French-Spanish border in the south.

Axis . . . . The name adopted by the group of nations allied with Germany during the Second World War. They were Germany, Japan, Italy, Rumania, Finland, Hungary, and Slovakia.

Baltic States . . . . The three nations of Lithuania, Latvia and Estonia (west to east) on the Baltic Sea, occupied by Russia in early 1940 as part of the Russo-German Treaty of 1939.

Barbarossa . . . . German code word for the invasion of the Union of Soviet Socialists Republics in June, 1941.

Bialystok-Lvov Positions . . . . Two western 'bulges' in the Russian-German border in June 1941. Positions considered by the Russians as jumping off stages for an offensive against Germany or dangerously exposed positions subject to encirclement. The Germans saw these two positions as natural attack and encirclement opportunities, as they subsequently became.

"black radio" . . . . Foreign radio broadcasts, especially the BBC, which were forbidden to the ordinary German.

Blitzkrieg . . . . An attack combining infantry, armor and air power. Brought to high development and implemented by Germany, subsequently copied by the Allies.

Bodyguard . . . . The Allied strategic deception plans for Operation Overlord.

Brandenburgers . . . . Germanys 'special forces' unit, organized into division strength, it was parceled out in sub units as needed anywhere in Europe.

Byelorussian 'balcony' . . . . . The portion of the front line in Belorussia (now known as Belarus) in June 1944 that curved south then west approximately 250 miles.

Churchill, Winston . . . . . . Wartime Prime Minister of Great Britain. The living embodiment of English determination to save the Commonwealth and see the war through to victory.

Commissar . . . . The political representative from the Communist Party assigned to all units in the Red Army in ensure dedication to duty, obedience in obeying orders and faithfulness to the Communist Party.

Destruction of Army . . . . . The frequently used phrase to describe the two-month Group Center battle in western Russia and eastern Poland in June 1944. Also known as Operation Bagration.

Die Endlosung . . . . The Final Solution. The German program to exterminate their definition of undesirable humans, principally the Jews.

Donbas . . . . The Russian term meaning Don River basin which refers to the industrial and manufacturing region of the lower Don River.

"Dortmund" . . . . The final 'go-ahead' signal commencing Operation Barbarossa.

East Wall . . . . The series of defensive fortifications along the German-Polish border begun in earnest in 1936.

Eastern Front . . . . The theater of military operations in Russia, Poland, the Baltic states, central Europe and the Balkans during World War II.

Fallschirmjager . . . . German for paratroops.

Final Solution . . . . The Nazi master plan to put the liquidation of the Jews and other ethnically or racially undesirables on a formal footing, at the Wannsee Conference, Berlin, January 1942.

Fremde Heere Ost . . . . . . Foreign Armies East, the *Wehrmacht* intelligence gathering service on the eastern front.

Frontiviki . . . . The Russian army equivalent of *Landser* (German), G.I. (U.S) or Tommy (British).

Fuehrer Directive . . . . . . A series of orders generated by Hitler and issued to the military to carry out his wishes.

GESTAPO . . . . *Geheime Staatspolizei.* Secret State Police, the feared special police with unlimited powers of access, examination and arrest.

GKO . . . . *Gosudarstvenny Komitet Oborony.* Soviet State Committee for Defense. The supreme political body of the U.S.S.R. responsible for the overall defense of the country. See Stavka.

Great War, The . . . . This is what World War I (1914-1918) was known as until the arrival of the Second World War.

Grossdeutschland . . . . . . Greater Germany, the term used to describe Germany and her conquered nations. Occasionally referred to as the German Empire. Also the name of a German combat unit.

Guards Division . . . . A Russian Army designation applied to Red Army rifle and tank Divisions (and later larger formations) that had proved themselves reliable/capable in combat. First used in August 1941 when four Rifle Divisions had the Guards designation added to their title after the Yelnia counteroffensive near Smolensk.

Guderian, Heinz . . . . Arguably the best German panzer commander during the war, General.

GRU . . . . *Glavnoye Razvedyvatel'noye Upravleniye.* Soviet Military
Intelligence branch of the Main Intelligence Directorate.

Hauptquartier . . . . Headquarters

Heer . . . . Army, the German Army.

Himmler, Heinrich . . . . . . *Reichsführer SS* of Germany and head of the *Waffen SS*,
second most powerful man after Hitler. Was responsible
for all police and security organs in Germany.

Hitler, Adolf . . . . German dictator, Chancellor of Germany, *Füehrer* of the
Third Reich.

Hitler Jugend. . . . . Hitler Youth. The Nazi equivalent of the Boy Scouts
with a heavy military emphasis in its activities and
training. A primary source of manpower for the *12th SS-
Panzer Division* of the same name.

Hiwis . . . . Abbreviation for *Hilfswillige* or willing helpers in the east.
Wehrmacht auxiliary troops who worked in non-combat
positions.

JS-1, -2 . . . . Russia's new heavy tank series introduced near the end
of the war. JS- Joseph Stalin, also frequently referred to as
the IS-1 and 2 after the Russian spelling of Joseph, Iosef.

Jagdpanzer . . . . Hunting tank or more specifically an entire classification
of very effective anti-tank, turret-less tracked vehicles
developed by Germany during the war. They were a less
expensive alternative to the more expensive turreted
tank. Cheaper and faster to build, Germany hope to
redress the tank vs. tank balance with these machines.

Katyusha . . . . Developed in June 1938 by the Soviet Jet Propulsion
Research Institute (RNII) these 82mm and later 132mm
were unguided artillery rocket projectiles. Mounted
on clusters of 14 to 48 on the backs of Russian Zis-6
and U.S. Studebaker 6 trucks, with a range of 3 to 8
miles. Effective when launched en mass for shock effect.
Nicknamed "Stalin's Organs" by German soldiers.

Komsomol . . . . League of Communist Youth. Russian youth organization
of the Communist Party, Soviet equivalent of the
Hitler Youth.

Kremlin . . . . The old center of Moscow, a walled and forbidding
fortress where Czars lived and ruled and later where the
Communist and Russian heads of state had their offices.

Kriegsmarine . . . . Germany's navy in World War II.

Kursk . . . . A city in central Russia, the objective of the German summer 1943 campaign. It marked the largest armored engagement of the war and the last major German offensive operation of the war in Russia. (See *Operation Zitadelle*)

KV-1, –2 . . . . Russia's heavy tank(s) in the early part of the war. KVKlimenti Voroshilov, the designer.

Landser . . . . The German equivalent of the American "G.I" or the British "Tommy" or the Russian "*Frontiviki.*"

Lebensborn . . . . Meaning "spring of life," *Reichsfuhrer* Heinrich Himmler created this secret program in December 1935 for the express purpose of birthing 'racially pure' children which were then offered to SS organizations for his/her education and adoption.

Lebensraum . . . . The German concept of 'living space' for the growing, young Third Reich, usually interpreted as seeking this space in the eastern regions of Europe (e.g. Poland and Greater Russia).

Lend-Lease . . . . The economic program where the U.S. and, to a lesser extent, Great Britain shipped raw, semi- and finished military and military-related supplies to Russia and other Allied nations to help them fight Germany and the Axis.

Lucy . . . . Code name for Rudolf Rossler, chief of the Soviet spy ring operating out of Switzerland.

Luftwaffe . . . . Germany's air force.

Manstein, Fritz von . . . . . . Perhaps the best tactical commander in the *Wehrmacht*, especially in the east. Rose to rank of Field Marshal.

Marcks, Gen. Erich . . . . . . Chief planner of the German Army for the invasion of Russia.

National Socialism . . . . The German political and economic system as defined by the NSDAP

NKVD . . . . Peoples' Commissariat of Internal Affairs (*Narodnii Kommissariat Vnutrennykh Del*).

Nazi(s) . . . . The acronym for *National Socialist Deutsch Arbiter Parti* or National Socialist German Workers Party, NSDAP.

NSDAP . . . . *Nationalsozialistische deutsche Arbeiterpartei* or National Socialist German Workers Party, using the German abbreviation.

Normandy . . . . The region in northwest France that was the site for the Allied landings in June 1944.

OB West/Ost. . . . . *Oberbefehlshaber West/Ost*. Commander in Chief West/East, as the location dictates.

ObdH . . . . *Oberbefehlshaber der Heers*. High Command of the Army.

ObdK. . . . . *Oberbefehlshaber der Kriegsmarine*. High Command of the Navy.

ObdL. . . . . *Oberbefehlshaber der Luftwaffe*. High Command of the Air Force.

Oil Detachment/
  Brigade Caucasus . . . . . . The German petroleum engineering unit that was to begin exploiting the oil, if captured, in the Grozny, Maikop, Baku regions in the Caucasus in 1942.

OKH . . . . *Oberkommando der Heer*, High Command of the Army, eventually entirely concerned with managing the war in the east.

OKW. . . . . *Oberkommando der Wehrmacht*, high command of the German Armed Forces.

Operation Bagration. . . . . . The code-name given to the Soviet June 1944 summer offensive.

Operation Blue. . . . . The German summer 1942 offensive of Army Groups Center and South.

Overlord . . . . The codename for the Allied preparations for the invasion of western France.

Operation Typhoon . . . . . . The German October 1941 offensive against Moscow.

Operation Uranus . . . . The code-name for the Russian offensive to encircle Stalingrad in November 1942.

Operation Zitadelle . . . . . . The German summer 1943 offensive in the Kursk region of Russia.

Pak . . . . Short version of *Panzerabwehrkanone* or anti-tank gun.

Paulus, Friedrich von . . . . . Commander of the German 6th Army in Army Group South. Became encircled in the Stalingrad pocket and surrendered to the Russians in February 1943.

Panzer . . . . Literally translated: armor. However it has become the universal term used to describe almost any German armored fighting vehicle. Also, *gepanzert* or armored.

Panzerkamphwagen . . . . . . Armored fighting vehicle, more popularly abbreviated as *PzKw*.

Panzerwaffe . . . . *Panzer* weapon. The German tank/armored forces

Panzerfaust . . . . A single-shot, rocket propelled anti-tank weapon employed by the Germans with great effect from 1943 to the end of the war.

Panzerschrek . . . . A reloadable rocket propelledtube launched anti-tank weapon, similar to the Allied "Bazooka". Later renamed *Raketenpanzerbuchse*.

Partisan(s) . . . . The anti-German, behind the battle lines Russian guerilla movement in central Russia. There was also a Yugoslav version.

Pas de Calais . . . . That portion of France on the English Channel closest to England. Where the Germans expected the Allied invasion to land.

Pripyat Marshes . . . . The vast swamp and wetlands stretching from Pinsk in the west to Rechitsa in the east and from Bobruysk in the north to Korosten in the south, effectively dividing Army Groups Center and South for almost 200 miles.

RAF . . . . Royal Air Force, Great Britain's fighter and bomber forces.

RKKA . . . . Red Army of Workers and Farmers or in Russian, *Raboche Krestjanskaya Krasnaya Armija*.

'rasputitsy' . . . . Translation: Russian for time of no roads. More commonly used to describe the Russian spring thaw and autumn rains the resulting deep mud, bringing a halt to or severely affecting wheeled traffic.

Red Orchestra, The . . . . . . The name of the Soviet spy organization located in Switzerland headed by Rudolf Rossler, code named "Lucy".

Reichbahn . . . . The German national railroad system.

Replacement Army, The . . . The German military organization that controlled all troop activities (training, replacement, rehabilitation, transfer) within Germany and a few occupied countries.

Rifle Division . . . . The name the Russians used to designate an infantry division.

Rokossovsky, Konstantin . . . Credited with saving Moscow in 1941 and Stalingrad in 1942, Field Marshal.

Rolling Barrage. . . . . An artillery attack in which the guns are aimed and constantly adjusted to move their impact area just ahead of advancing friendly infantry.

Rommel, Erwin . . . . Best known for his exploits commanding the Axis forces in North Africa (called the "Desert Fox"), later assigned to organize and reinforce the *Atlantikwall* in western France, Field Marshal.

Roosevelt, Franklin D.. . . . . World War II President of the United States, Commander in Chief of all U.S. forces. Elected in 1933 and re-elected twice for an unprecedented third term. Died of a stroke in April 1945.

Ruckkampfer. . . . . The German term for a surviving soldier returning to the front lines or home.

SD . . . . *Sicherheitsdienst* or Security Service of the SS.

SS (Schutz Staffel). . . . . . . The armed defense force for the Nazi party, eventually replacing the SA.

Schurzen . . . . The sheets (in some cases screens) of metal skirting (hence the name) attached to the sides and turrets of German tanks to prevent shaped-charged weapons from detonating against the main armor of the vehicle.

Scorched Earth . . . . The practice when retreating of destroying anything of value that could aid the enemy.

Sicherungs . . . . Security, usually formed from battalions into division-sized units.

SHAEF. . . . . Supreme Headquarters Allied Expeditionary Force, the command responsible for the invasion of Europe under Operations Anvil and Overlord as well as the cover and deception operations under Bodyguard.

Shturmovik . . . . The nickname of the Soviet Ilyushin IL-2 ground attack aircraft.

SMERSH. . . . . The Red Army counterintelligence organization. responsible for all security in the rear of the Russian combat units. An acronym for "*smert shpionam*", meaning 'death to spies'.

Staff Oldenburg . . . . The German economic directorate that was to exploit the vast natural and productive wealth of Russia for the benefit of greater Germany.

Sturm Abteilung (SA) . . . . . The early Nazi party security detachments that battled the Communists and Socialists in the late 1920's and 1930's and defended the young Nazi party. Also known as the Brown Shirts.

Sturmgeschutz . . . . A series of turret-less, forward firing tanks the German's developed with great success. See Assault gun.

Stalin,
Joseph Vissarionovich . . . . . Soviet dictator, 1st Secretary of the Communist Party and after 8 August 1941 *Verkhovnyi Glavnokommanduyushchii* or Supreme Commander of the Soviet Armed Forces in Russia.

Stalingrad . . . . 15-mile long city on the western bank of the southern Volga River named after Stalin, formerly known as Tsaritsyn. The battle there in August 1942-February 1943 marked the eastern-most progress of the German's in World War II

STAVKA. . . . . Stalin's creation on 23 June 1941 to control all of the Russian armed forces, the complete title: *Stavka Glavnovo Komandovania* or High Command Headquarters. Stavka was both a location and an institution, housed in the Kremlin as the supreme coordinating body of the Russian military. See GKO.

T-34 . . . . The main Russian battle tank during the war. Introduced several technical innovations, such as sloped armor, wide tracks, powerful main armament and speed. Was produced with a 76.2mm main gun, later increased to 85mm.

Todt, Organization. . . . . . . Dr. Fritz Todt, Minister of Armaments and Munitions. Built the German *autobahn* road network, later with his Todt Organization, the West Wall and U-Boat Shelters and improved the roads in the occupied countries. This was a large private but state sanctioned construction company.

Timoshenko, Semyon . . . . . An able Red Army commander with a long history of service in the World War I and the Russian Civil War. He is best known for his counter offensive at Rostov in the opening months of Barbarossa at Rostov-on-Don in 1941 and the brilliant encirclement of German forces at Jassy-Kishinev in 1944.

Truman, Harry S . . . . U. S. Vice President under Roosevelt, became President upon the death of Roosevelt in April 1945.

V-Weapons . . . . The V-1 (A-1 to the Germans) was the subsonic flying bomb with a 2,000 pound payload launched from fixed and later mobile ramps along the French and Dutch coasts against London. The V-2 (A-2) was a supersonic rocket, vertically launched, also from fixed and mobile launch sites, from France, Belgium and Holland and later Germany, against London, Antwerp and Rotterdam. Both were un-aimed and were intended to terrorize the resident populations of the cities they were fired against. The "V" in the V-1 or V-2 is German for *vergeltungswaffe* or vengeance weapon.

Vatutin, Nikolai . . . . One of the more able commanders in the Russian Army, played key roles in the Stalingrad, Kursk, Dnieper River and Korsun operations. Was badly wounded in February 1944 and died two months later in April.

Volk or Volksdeutsch . . . . . Literal translation: Folk or native German people or people from German racial stock. In German it conjures a new meaning of a greater German family, an ethnic, almost tribal Teutonic identity.

Volkssturm . . . . The September 1944 militia raised and commanded by the Nazi party. Intended to inspire the German people with National Socialist zeal to defend the Reich to the last, to provide internal policing and defend against invasion if necessary.

Waffen SS . . . . This was a separate military organization, armed, organized and equipped the same as the *Wehrmacht*, but usually on a more elaborate basis, however under the command of the *Wehrmacht*. Became the elite combat force of Germany in World War II.

Wehrmacht . . . . The name used to describe the combined armed forces of Germany from 1933 to 1945.

West Wall . . . . The defensive fortifications built along Germany's western border with France, Belgium and southern Holland. Also known as the Siegfried Line.

Winterschlacht im Osten . . . The medal issued to all Germans who participated in the assault in October - December 1941 against Moscow and the consequent defensive battles afterward. Popularly known amongst the German soldiers as the or *Gefrierfleischorden*, the 'frozen meat award'.

Chronology

December 21, 1879 . . . . . Joseph Stalin is born in Gori, Russia

April 20, 1889 . . . . Hitler is born in Braunau, Austria

October 25, 1917 . . . . . . Vladimir Lenin leads the Bolsheviks to power in Moscow

April 1, 1920. . . . . The German Worker's Party is renamed National Socialist German Workers Party or NSDAP

April 16, 1922 . . . . Germany and Russia sign the Treaty of Rapallo

January 30, 1933. . . . . . . Hitler appointed Chancellor

November 1, 1936 . . . . . . Germany and Italy form the Axis

March 13, 1938 . . . . Germany annexes Austria

September 1, 1939. . . . . . Germany attacks Poland

September 3, 1939. . . . . . Britain and France declare war on Germany

September 17, 1939 . . . . . The Soviet Union invades Poland

September 27, 1939 . . . . . Warsaw falls

November 30, 1939 . . . . . The Soviet Union invades Finland

March 12, 1940 . . . . Finland seeks peace terms with the Soviet Union after Viipuri falls.

April 9, 1940. . . . . Germany invades Denmark and Norway

May 10, 1940 . . . . Germany invades Belgium and Holland

May 11, 1940 . . . . Germany invades France

June 25, 1940 . . . . France surrenders

July 10, 1940. . . . . The Battle of Britain begins

July 31, 1940. . . . . Hitler begins planning Operation Barbarossa, the invasion of Russia

September 17, 1940 . . . . . The Battle of Britain ends with British victory

April 6, 1941 . . . . Axis forces attack Yugoslavia and Greece

April 1941 . . . . German force buildup in Poland for Barbarossa gains momentum

May 20, 1941 . . . . Germany attacks Crete

June 22, 1941 . . . . Operation Barbarossa, the German attack on Russia begins

July 15, 1941 . . . . Smolensk falls

July 20, 1941 . . . . Stalin becomes Peoples Commissar for Defense

September 19, 1941 . . . . . Germans pocket 400,000+ at Kiev, city falls

September 26, 1941 . . . . . First Allied supply convoy to aid Russia leaves Britain for Archangel

September 27, 1941 . . . . . First rains fall in western Russia, beginning of the autumn 'rasputitsy' or mud season

September 30, 1941 . . . . . The long awaited German assault on Moscow begins, Operation Typhoon

October 19, 1941 . . . . . . Germans pocket 670,000 at Vyazma, city falls

December 5, 1941 . . . . . . Operation Barbarossa falters 19 miles in front of Moscow in deep snow and cold

December 5, 1941 . . . . . . First Soviet counter-offensives begin in front of Moscow

December 7, 1941 . . . . . . Japanese Imperial Navy attacks the U.S. Pacific fleet at Pearl Harbor

December 11, 1941 . . . . . Germany declares war on the U.S.

March 30, 1942 . . . . Soviet Moscow counter-offensive comes to end, both sides exhausted and spring 'rasputitsy' begins

April 5, 1942 . . . . Hitler orders planning for 1942 campaign season, later knows as Operation Blue

June 2, 1942 . . . . German general Manstein begins attack on Sevastopol in the Crimea

June 25, 1942 . . . . U.S. General Eisenhower appointed chief U.S. forces in Europe

June 28, 1942 . . . . German summer offensive to seize the manufacturing city of Stalingrad on the Volga and oil centers in the Caucasus begins

July 5, 1942 . . . . Allied arctic convoy PQ17 attacked by German sea and air units, 12 of 22 ships lost

August 19, 1942 . . . . Canadian raid on Dieppe ends in failure and 50% loss of attacking force

September 12, 1942 . . . . . Stalin orders Russian general Zhukov and Vasilievsky to begin planning Stalingrad counter-offensive

November 8, 1942 . . . . . . Allied landings in North Africa begin

November 19, 1942 . . . . . Russian forces begin counter-attack north and south of Stalingrad

November 23, 1942 . . . . . Russian forces link up west of Stalingrad pocketing 22 divisions/330,000 men

February 2,1943 . . . . Last elements of German resistance in the Stalingrad pocket collapses, total Axis casualties approximately 200,000

February/March . . . . Soviets begin general offensive in the south, retaking almost all the gains 1943made by Germany six months earlier

April 1943 . . . . Planning for the German summer campaigns begin. The salient around Kursk selected for attack to begin in May, called Operation Citadel

April 26, 1943 . . . . The Allied Combined Chiefs of Staff issue the formal order to plan the invasion of northwest Europe, code named "Cossac"

July 4, 1943 . . . . The long delayed attack north and south of Kursk Operation "Citadel" begins against strong Russian defenses, largest tank battle of the war

July 10, 1943 . . . . Allies land on Sicily

July 12, 1943 . . . . German panzers halted at Prokhorovka, high water mark of offensive

July 13, 1943 . . . . Hitler cancels "Citadel"

July 15, 1943 . . . . Soviets begin general counter-offensive against German forces north and south of Kursk

August 12, 1943 . . . . . . Stalin orders planning to begin for general offensive to retake all territory east of the Dnieper and take bridgeheads for further action

September, 9 1943 . . . . . . Allies land in Italy at Salerno

September 25, 1943 . . . . . Smolensk liberated

October 20, 1943 . . . . . . Stalin reorganizes Soviet Front armies

November 6, 1943 . . . . . . Kiev liberated

December 6, 1943 . . . . . . Eisenhower appointed supreme commander of Operation "Overlord" the code name for the invasion of Europe.

December 12, 1943 . . . . . German general Erwin Rommel appointed Commander in Chief of Army Group B, responsible for the coastal defenses of western Europe from Holland to the Bay of Biscay

January 14, 1944 . . . . Leningrad liberated

March 4, 1944 . . . . Russian forces begin spring offensive against German Army Group South and Army Group A in the southern Ukraine

March 19, 1944 . . . . Germany occupies Hungary

April 1, 1944 . . . . Finland send officials to Moscow seeking peace terms

April 2, 1944 . . . . Russian troops enter Romania

May 1, 1944 . . . . Planning for the summer Soviet offensive begins, ultimately named "Operation Bagration"

May 22-23 1944 . . . . "Operation Bagration" plan introduced to the responsible Russian commanders

May 17, 1944 . . . . Eisenhower selects 5 May 1944 as D-Day, weather permitting.

June 5, 1944 . . . . Allies liberate Rome

June 6, 1944 . . . . Operation "Overlord" begins with landings in northwest France

June 6-30, 1944 . . . . Allies build up troop strength in preparation for a breakout into greater France

June 10, 1944 . . . . Russia attacks Finish positions, resuming the war against Finland.

June 13, 1944 . . . . The first of the German *vergeltungswaffe* or vengeance weapons (V-1or A-1) is launched against England, greater London

July 17, 1944 . . . . Rommel seriously wounded by RAF air attack, general Von Kluge assumes command of Army Group B.

June 22, 1944 . . . . Russia begins its summer offensive, Operation Bagration against Germanys Army Group Center in Byelorussia

July 4, 1944 . . . . Minsk is liberated

July 20, 1944 . . . . Bomb plot to assonate Hitler at his Rastenburg HQ fails.

July 26, 1944 . . . . Russian forces reach the Vistula river near Radom, Poland

August 1, 1944 . . . . The Warsaw uprising against the German occupiers begins

August 6, 1944 . . . . Allies breakout of Normandy bridgehead

August 15, 1944 . . . . Allies land in southern France, "Operation Dragoon/Anvil"

August 21, 1944 . . . . Falaise "gap" closed, trapping 50,000 German troops and tons of equipment, however, 30,000 escape

August 23, 1944 . . . . Romania seeks peace with Russia, ends alliance with Germany

August 25, 1944 . . . . U.S. and French troops liberate Paris

September 3, 1944 . . . . . . Brussels liberated by British forces

September 8, 1944 . . . . . . The next generation of "V" weapons, the supersonic rocket bomb V-2 (A-2) is launched against England

September 9, 1944 . . . . . . Bulgaria switches sides, joining the allied camp

September 11, 1944 . . . . . First Allied troops on German soil

September 16, 1944 . . . . . Hitler gives orders to begin planning an offensive from the Ardennes region

September 17, 1944 . . . . . Ill-fated Operation "Market-Garden", the plan to end-run around the German West Wall fortifications from the north begins

September 19, 1944 . . . . . Finland ends hostilities with Russia and ends its relationship with Germany

September 26, 1944 . . . . . Operation "Market-Garden" ends, failing to seize its objective of the bridge at Arnhem

October 9, 1944 . . . . Ardennes offensive plans given name "Wacht am Rhein"

October 21, 1944 . . . . . . Aachen, Germany falls to the Allies

November 26, 1944 . . . . . American forces reach positions of the French Maginot Line

December 16, 1944 . . . . . With the help of bad weather grounding Allied airpower, German attacks "Wacht am Rhein" begin out of the Ardennes region against U.S. forces

December 22, 1944 . . . . . Running out of fuel, German forces stop short of the Meuse at Dinant, high water mark of the advance

December 26, 1944 . . . . . U.S. forces surrounded in Bastogne are relieved by U.S. 4th Armored division

January 1, 1945 . . . . German forces launch the "Balaton" offensive to retake Budapest

January 16, 1945 . . . . Russian forces begin offensive operations across the Vistula, Warsaw is liberated

January 20, 1945 . . . . First Russian troops on German soil at Namslau

January 31, 1945 . . . . Allied forces regain all ground lost to the German "Wacht am Rhein" operation

February 4, 1945 . . . . The Yalta conference begins, the eight day series of talks that determined the final fate of Germany and the future of Europe.

February 13, 1945 . . . . . . German effort to re-take Budapest fails, liberated by Soviet forces

February 23, 1945 . . . . . . Posen, Poland is liberated by Soviet forces

March 2, 1945 . . . . U.S. 9th Army reaches the Rhine River opposite Duesseldorf

March 5-6, 1945 . . . . German forces launch "Spring Awakening" offensive to retake Budapest

March 7, 1945 . . . . U.S. First Army seizes intact bridge across the Rhine at Remagen

March 15, 1945 . . . . In wet ground the German "Spring Awakening" offensive bogs down and is halted far short of Budapest

March 30, 1945 . . . . Danzig liberated by Soviet forces

April 4, 1945 . . . . U.S. general Patton seizes Kassel, Germany

April 12, 1945 . . . . U.S. President Roosevelt dies at Warm Springs, Georgia. Soviet forces begin attacks against German forces defending Berlin at Kuestrin

April 13, 1945 . . . . Russian forces seize Vienna, Austria

April 15, 1945 . . . . Main effort to take Berlin begins by Soviet forces

April 18, 1945 . . . . Ruhr industrial area of Germany taken by U.S. forces, 325,000 German troops captured

April, 20 1945 . . . . Nuremberg, Germany falls to U.S. forces

April 25, 1945 . . . . Allied (U.S.) and Soviet forces meet at Torgau on the Elbe River. Berlin encircled by Soviet forces

April 30, 1945 . . . . Hitler commits suicide

May 2, 1945 . . . . Berlin surrenders to Russian forces

May 7, 1945 . . . . German military high command surrenders unconditionally to Allies at Reims, France

Appendix:
By the Numbers

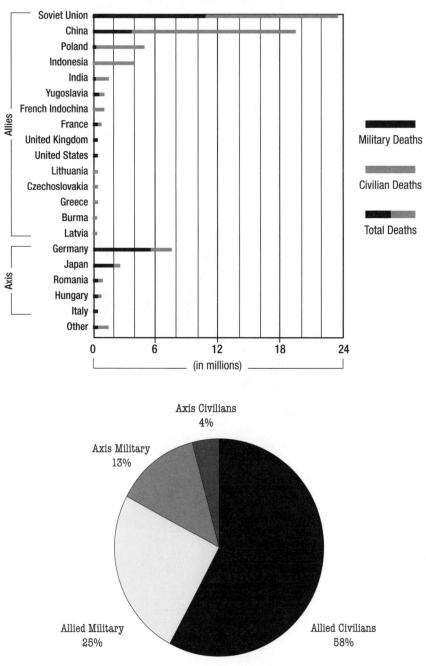

World War II Military Deaths
(Axis)

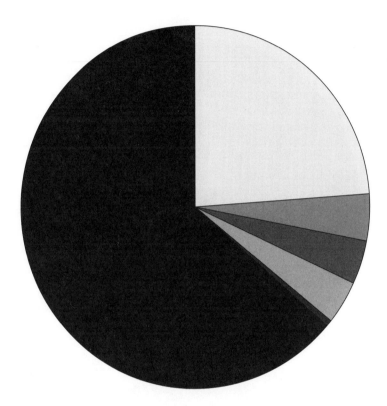

Germany 64%   Romania 4%

Japan 24%   Hungary 4%

Italy 4%   Bulgaria <0.3%

World War II Military Deaths
(Allies)

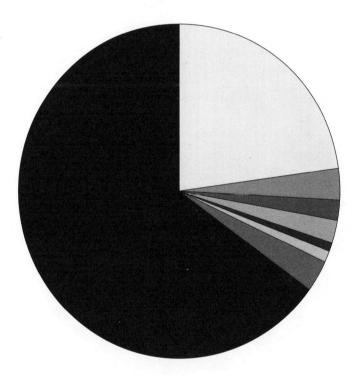

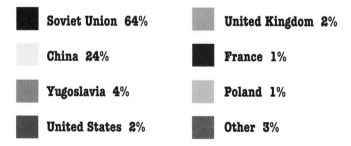

Soviet Union 64%

China 24%

Yugoslavia 4%

United States 2%

United Kingdom 2%

France 1%

Poland 1%

Other 3%

U.S.

Population
129,200,000 (1940)

No. Served in Forces
16,354,000 (16%)

No. Killed/Missing
405,000 (2%)

**Armored Vehicles
(all types)**
63,225

**Aircraft Production
(all types)**
324,750

**Artillery Production
(all types)**
257, 390

German

Population
78,000,000 (1938)

No. Served in Forces
17,900,000 (23%)

No. Killed/Missing
3,250,000 (18%)

**Armored Vehicles
(all types)**
24,450

**Aircraft Production
(all types)**
189,307

**Artillery Production
(all types)**
159,144

Russian

Population
194,000,000

No. Served in Forces
30,000,000 (16%)

No. Killed/Missing
11,286,000 (16%)

**Armored Vehicles
(all types)**
71,410

**Aircraft Production
(all types)**
157,261

**Artillery Production
(all types)**
516, 648

German Casualties by Campaign (Killed & Wounded)

Poland 1939	40,390
Denmark/Norway 1940	5,292
France 1940	154,750
Balkans 1941	3,674
North Africa 1940-1943	15,000
Italy 1943-1945	223,540
Northwest Europe 1944-1945	527,890
Eastern Front 1941-1945	5,913,750

Note: Armored vehicle, aircraft, and artillery production do not include U.K. and Commonwealth production.

Sources: *World War II, The Encyclopedia of Facts and Figures* by John Ellis, Military Book Club, 1993.
Soviet Casualties and Combat Losses In The Twentieth Century, by Colonel-General G.F. Krivosheev, Greenhill Books, London, 1997.

World War II was a war of numbers; numbers of tanks, divisions, planes, ships, guns and men. The numbers can be and in many cases staggering. What follows is an approximate comparison of the numbers of three European combatants.

U.S.

16 Armored Divisions

66 Infantry DIvisions

1 Cavalry Divisions
1 Mountain Divisions
4 Airborne Divisions
6 Marine Corps Divisions

94 Total Divisions
  69 Europe
  25 Pacific

German

67 Panzer Divisions
(Incl. Pz. Gren., Mot.
& Waffen SS Div.)
280 Infantry DIvisions
(Incl. Volks Gren. and
Reserve Div.)
5 Cavalry Divisions
13 Mountain Divisions
11 Airborne Divisions
21 Luftwaffe Field Div.:
17 Light & Jager Div.

414 Total Divisions

Russian

12 Guards Tank Corps
31 Tank Corps
9 Guards Mech. Corps
2 Guards Mech. Div.
30 Mechanized Corps
24 Motorized Div.
17 Guards Cavalry Div.
50 Cavalry Div. (Est.)
22 Mountain Divisions
121 Guards Rifle Div.
413 Rifle Divisions

731 Total Divisions

14,200 Inf. Div O&M (1943)
11,000 Arm. Div O&M (1943)
  77 Light Tanks
  186 Medium Tanks
  501 Half Tracks

17,150 Inf. Div O&M (1939)
12,300 Inf. Div O&M (1944)
10,000 VG Inf. Div O&M (1944)
14,000 Pz. Div O&M (1939)
13,250 Pz. Div O&M (1944)
  134 Light Tanks
  22 Medium Tanks ('39)
  176 Medium Tanks ('44)
  5,400 Horses ('39) Inf. Div.
  4,600 Horses ('44) Inf. Div.

9,619 Rifle Div O&M (1943)
4,600 CavalryDiv O&M (1943)
15,000 Mech. Corps O&M (1944)
9,700 Artillery Div. O&M (1944)
10,980 Tank Corps O&M (1944)
  195 T-34 Both Mech. and Tank Corps
  640 Horses ('43) Rifle Div.

Table of Equivalent Ranks

U.S.	German	Russian
General of the Army	Generalfeldmarshall	Marshal Sovetskogo Soyuza
General	Generaloberst	General Armii
Lieutenant General	General der Infanterie Gebirgstruppen Kavallerie Nachrichtentruppen Panzertruppen Pioniere Luftwaffe Flieger Fallschrimtruppen Flakartillery Luftnachtrichtentruppen	General Polkovnik
Major General	Generalleutnant	General Leytenant
Brigadier General	Generalmajor	General Mayor
Colonel	Oberst	Polkovnik
Lieutenant Colonel	Oberstleutnant	Podpolkovnik
Major	Major	Major
Captain	Hauptmann	Captain
Captain (Cavalry)	Rittmeister	
First Lieutenant	Oberleutnant	Senior Lietenant
Second Lieutenant	Leutnant	Lieutenant

Force and Loss Comparison
Operation Bagration: 23 June 1944- 29 August 1944

The Byelorussian Strategic Offensive Operation
The Destruction of Army Group Center

Russian[1]		German[2]	
2,331,700	Combat Units	400,000	
79,900	Support Units	400,000	
2,411,600	Total	800,000	(3.0 : 1)
770,888	Losses	350,000	(2.2 : 1)
	Prisoners of War	150,000	
11,337	Average Daily Losses	9,460	(1.2 : 1)
4,070	Tanks/Assault Guns	553	(7.4 : 1)
28,613	Artillery (all types)	9,500	(3.0 : 1)
6,334	Aircraft (all types)	1,151	(5.5 : 1)

[1] Source: *Soviet Casualties And Combat Losses In The Twentieth Century* edited by Colonel-General G.F. Krivosheev, Greenhill Books, 1997.

[2] Source: *German Military Operations On The Eastern Front 1943-44* by Karl-Heinz Frieser, Militärgeschichtlichen Forschungsamt (MGFA), 2007.

Effort Expanded

The chart below German combat division effort is shown in
months of effort in a given combat theater.[1]

Division Type	Theater					Total
	E. Front	N.W. Europe	Italy	N. Africa	Other	
Panzer	1,029	85	34	65	24	1,237
Motorized/Pz. Gren.	493	27	78	0	49	647
Light/Jager	277	0	27	13	122	439
Mountain	175	6	23	0	108	312
Parachute	45	66	38	7	8	164
Infantry	5,127	453	193	6	454	6,233
Total	7,146	637	393	91	665	9,032

Officers KIA (all grades)[2]

U.S.	German	Russian
31,057	71,870	1,023,093

[1] Divisions taken out of the line for prolonged period or divisions on internal security duties
are not included. From *World War II, The Encyclopedia Of Facts And Figures* by John Ellis,
The military Book Club, 1995.

[2] U.S. and German data from *The Other Price Of Hitler's War, German Military And Civilian
Losses Resulting From World War II* by Martin K. Sorge, Greenwood Press, 1986, Russian
data from *Colossus Reborn, The Red Army At War, 1941-1943* by David M. Glantz, 2005.

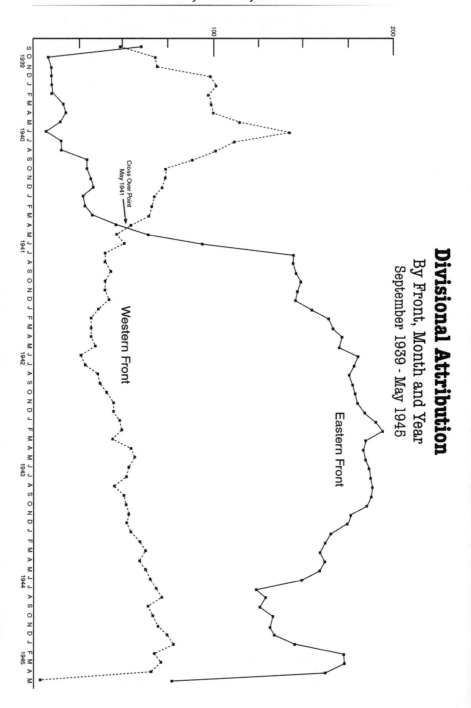

Divisional Attribution
By Front, Month and Year
September 1939 - May 1945

Cross Over Point
May 1941

Western Front

Eastern Front

The Changing Dynamic of Russian and German Military Command Independence

One of the more interesting aspects of the war in the east was the amount of independence the political heads of state permitted their military commands to enjoy. The following graph demonstrates that as the war progressed for both combatants, the amount of command independence changed, and in opposite directions. In the early months of the campaign, the German Wermacht enjoyed much greater freedom from political intervention then did their opponents, the Soviet military. However, as the war progressed and the fortunes turned against the Germans and as the Russian military demonstrated their growing tactical and strategic prowess, the amount of operational latitude permitted by the head of the Soviet government grew in almost equal proportions.

Regardless of how competent the armed forces of either nation became, they were never entirely free from, if not directed intervention by their heads of state, they at least suffered from constant scrutiny and oversight. Almost all decisions of both nations were reviewed by their political leadership and frequently these plans were changed, in some major or minor fashion. It is the nature of totalitarian nations to never loose the reigns of control over the most powerful force in their governments.

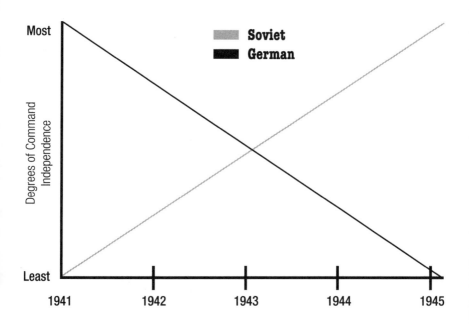

German Armored Forces 1939 - 1945

Theaters of Operation and Assignments of the Panzer and Panzergrenadier Divisions, Month and Year

To further demonstrate the effect of the war in the east on the German armored forces this bar graph is provided. This chart clearly shows where the effort and need for Germany's best and most effective combat units, the panzer divisions, were sent. The ascending vertical bars are gray scale coded by the number of panzer divisions by operational sector and by date, month and year are on the horizontal. The overwhelming number of black sections clearly indicate where Germany's "best and brightest" of the Wehrmacht were located in the period illustrated. It also alludes to the amount of panzer strength available for re-assignment to OBWest had Russia dropped out of the war.

The chart also demonstrates another aspect of the intensity of the war. It is of interest to note that from May 1942 to December 1943 not one panzer division was positioned in the Reich for any activity; whether it be rest and refit, training, or for strategic needs. With the exception of one panzer division in August 1943 in transit, Germany's most effective and powerful units were in almost constant combat or in close proximity to a combat zone. This further shows the desperate need for every combat unit to be in or near the front line, with all the stress, wastage and wear to men and machine it entails.

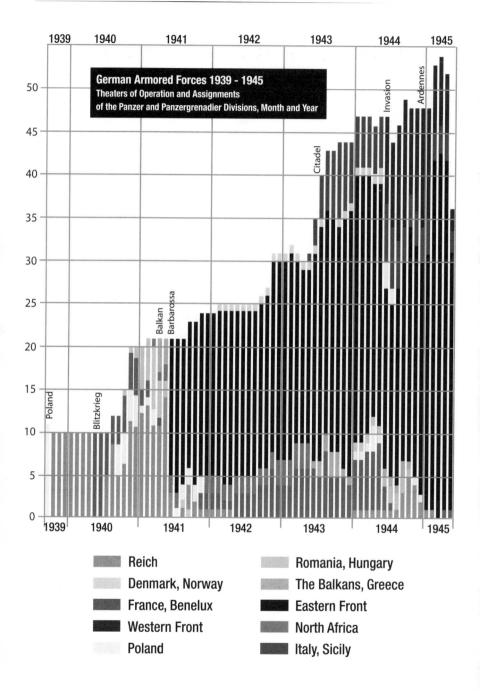

German Armored Forces 1939 - 1945
Theaters of Operation and Assignments
of the Panzer and Panzergrenadier Divisions, Month and Year

Legend:
- Reich
- Denmark, Norway
- France, Benelux
- Western Front
- Poland
- Romania, Hungary
- The Balkans, Greece
- Eastern Front
- North Africa
- Italy, Sicily

German PzKw Mk. IVH

Select Bibliography

Alexandrov, Victor, *The Tukhachevsky Affair*, Prentice-Hall, 1963.

Baryatinskiy, Mikhail, *T-34 Medium Tank (1939 - 1943)*, Ian Allen Publishing, 2007.

Beck, Earl R., *Under the Bombs, The German Home Front 1941 - 1945*, The University Press of Kentucky, 1986.

Berkhoff, Karel C., *Harvest of Despair*, The Belknap Press of Harvard University Press, Cambridge, Massachusetts, 2004.

Bessonov, Evgeni, *Tank Rider, Into the Reich with the Red Army*, Greenhill Books, London, 2003.

Bidermann, Gottlob Herbert, *In Deadly Combat, A German Soldier's Memoir of the Eastern Front*, University Press of Kansas, 2000.

Bishop, Chris and Warner, Adam, Ed's., *German Insignia of World War II*, Chartwell Books, Inc. 2002.

Bleuel, H. P. *Das saubere Reich: Theorie und Praxis des sittlichen Lebens im Dritten Reich*, Bern u. a. 1972, S. 192.

Botting, Douglas, *The Aftermath: Europe*, Time-Life, 1983.

Bradford, George, *Armored Vehicles, from the conception to the present times*, The Miniature A.F.V. Collectors Association, undated.

Burleigh, Michael, *The Third Reich, A New History*, Hill and Wang, 2000.

Caulaincourt, Armand de, *At Napoleon's Side in Russia, The Classic Eyewitness Account, The Memoirs of General de Caulaincourt, Duke of Vicenza*, Enigma Books, New York 2003.

Carell, Paul, *Invasion, They're Coming!*, Bantam Books, New York, 1964.

Carruthers, Bob and Erickson, John, *The Russian Front*, Cassell, 1999.

Cecil, Robert, *Hitler's Decision to Invade Russia 1941*, David McKay Company, Inc. 1975.

Central Intelligence Agency, *USSR Agriculture Atlas*, 1974.

Charman, Terry, *The German Home Front, 1939-1945*, Philosophical Library, 1989.

Chernyavskii, U. G. *Voina I prodovol'stve. Snabzhenie gorodskogo naseleniya v Veliuyu Otechestvennuyu voiny 1941 – 1945* Moscow: Nauka 1964.

Citino, Robert M., *The German Way of War, From the Thirty Years' War to the Third Reich,* University Press of Kansas, 2005.

Clark, Alan, *Barbarossa the German-Russian Conflict 1941-45,* Quill, New York, 1965.

Clausewitz, von, Karl, *On War,* E. P. Dutton, New York, 1918.

Department of the Army, Historical Study, No. 20-240, *Rear Area Security In Russia, The Soviet Second Front Behind the German Lines,* July 1951.

Department of the Army, Historical Study, No. 21-261a, *The German Campaign in Russia-Planning and Operations (1941-1942).* March 1955.

Department of the Army Pamphlet No. 20-234 Historical Study, *Operations of Encircled Forces, German Experiences in Russia.* Department of the Army, January 1952.

Department of the Army Pamphlet No. 20-290, *Terrain Factors in the Russian Campaign* July 1951.

Die Entstehung der Verordbung uber ausserordentliche Rundfunkmassnahmen vom 1. September 1939.

Downing, David, *The Moscow Option, An Alternative Second World War,* Greenhill Books, London, 1979.

Duffy, Christopher, *Red Storm on the Reich, The Soviet March on Germany, 1945 ,* Da Capo Press, 1993.

Dunn, Walter S., *Hero's or Traitors, The German Replacement Army, The July Plot and Adolf Hitler,* Praeger, 2003.

Ellis, John, *World War II: The Encyclopedia of Facts and Figures,* The Military Book Club, 1995.

Engelmann, Bernt, *In Hitler's Germany, Everyday Life in The Third Reich,* Pantheon Books, New York, 1986.

Erickson, John, *The Road to Berlin,* Westview Press, 1983.

Erickson, John, *The Road to Stalingrad,* Westview Press, 1984.

Fisher, John, *Why They Behave Like Russians,* Harper Brothers, New York 1946.

Fugate, Bryan and Dvoretsky, Lev *Thunder on the Dnepr, Zhukov-Stalin and the Defeat of Hitler's Blitzkrieg,* Presidio Press, 1997.

Glantz, David M., *Stumbling Colossus, The Red Army on the Eve of World War,* University Press of Kansas, 1998.

Glantz, David M. and House, Jonathan, *When Titans Clashed, How the Red Army Stopped Hitler"* , University of Kansas Press, 1995.

Grant, Michael, *Sick Caesars*, Barnes & Noble, New York, 2000.

Haller, Oliver, *The Defeat of the 12th SS, 7-10 June 1944*, Canadian Military History, Spring 1996.

Harrison, Gordon A., *United States Army in World War II, The European Theater of Operations, Cross-Channel Attack*, Office of the Chief of Military History, United States Army, Washington, D. C., 1951.

Harrison, Mark, Professor of Economics, *The USSR and Total War: Why Didn't the Soviet Economy Collapse in 1942?*, University of Warwick, 2002.

Hayward, Joel S. A., *Stopped at Stalingrad, The Luftwaffe and Hitler's Defeat in the East 1942-1943*, University Press of Kansas, 1998.

Higgins, Trumbull, *Hitler and Russia, The Third Reich in a Two Front War 1937-1943*, The Macmillan Company, 1966.

Historical Study, Rear Area Security In Russia, The Soviet Second Front Behind the German Lines, Department of the Army Pamphlet No. 20-240, July 1951, Washington, D.C.

Houterman, N. J. *Eastern Troops in Zeeland, The Netherlands, 1943 - 1945* Axis Europa, New York, 1997.

Howell, Edgar M., *The Soviet Partisan Movement 1941 - 1945*, Department of the Army Pamphlet, No. 20-244, August 1956.

Isby, David C. Ed., *Fighting the Invasion: The German Army at D-Day*, Greenhill Books, 2000.

Kantakoski, Pekka, *Punaiset Panssarit (Red Armor)*, 1998 (currently available only in Finnish).

Kaufmann, J.E. and Jurga, Robert M., *Fortress Europe, European Fortifications of World War II*, 1999, Da Capo Press, Cambridge, MA.

Keegan, John, *Intelligence in War, Knowledge of the Enemy From Napoleon to Al-Qaeda*, Alfred A. Knopf, 2003.

Kennedy, David M., *The Patient Warrior*, Time, 2004.

Kershaw, Robert, *War Without Garlands*, Operation Barbarossa 1941/1942, Sarpedon, New York, 2000.

Kreibich, Dr. Volkmar and Karin, Seeheim, Germany, conversations, summer 1990.

Lattimer, John K., M.D Sc.D, *Hitler's Fatal Sickness and Other Secrets of the Nazi Leaders*, Hippocrene Books, Inc., New York, 1999.

Lucas, James, *War on the Eastern Front: The German Soldier in Russia, 1941-1945*, Greenhill Books, 1991.

Macksey, Kenneth, *Why the Germans Loose at War, the Myth of German Military Superiority*, Greenhill Books/Lionel Leventhal Limited, London, 1996.

McNab, Chris, *World War II Data Book, The Third Reich 1933 - 1945, The Essential Facts and Figures For Hitler's Germany*, Amber Books, London, 2009.

Merrydale, Catherine, *Ivan's War*, Metropolitan Books, New York, 2006.

Montefiore, Simon Sebag, *Stalin, The Court of the Red Tsar*, Alfred A. Knopf, New York, 2004.

Mosier, John, *The Blitzkrieg Myth*, Harper-Collins, 2003.

Claus-Jürgen Müller, *Das Heer und Hitler: Armee und Nationalsocialistisches Regime, 1933 - 1940*, Stuttgart, 1969.

Munoz, Antonio J., *Forgotten Legions, Obscure Combat Formations of the Waffen SS*, Paladin Press, 1991.

Osmont, Marie-Louise, *The Normandy Diary of Marie-Louise Osmont, 1940 - 1944*, Discovery Communications, 1994.

Overy, Richard, *The Dictators, Hitler's Germany and Stalin's Russia*, W. W. Norton & Company, New York London, 2004.

Petrov, Vladimir, *June 22, 1941, Soviet Historians and the German Invasion*, University of South Carolina Press, 1968.

Pitt, Barrie and Frances, *Chronological Atlas of World War II*, MacMillan, London, 1989.

Porter, David, *World War II Data Book, Hitler's Secret Weapons 1933 - 1945, The Essential Facts and Figures For Germany's Secret Weapons Program*, Amber Books, London, 2010.

Reitlinger, Gerald, *The House Built On Sand, The Conflicts of German Policy In Russia 1939 - 1945* by, Viking, 1960.

Rempel, Gerhard, *Defeat, Chaos and Rebirth*, Western New England College.

Sebald, W. G., *On the Natural History of Destruction*, The Modern Library, New York, 2004, translated by Anthea Bell.

Shirer, William L., *The Rise and Fall of the Third Reich*, Simon and Schuster, New York, 1960.

Stephan, Robert W., *Stalin's Secret War, Soviet Counterintelligence Against The Nazis, 1941 - 1945*, University Press of Kansas, 2004.

Strategy & Tactics Magazine, Staff of, *Strategy & Tactics Staff Study Nr. 1, War in the East: The Russo-German Conflict 1941-45* by the, Simulations Publications, Incorporated, New York, 1977.

Taylor, Frederick, *Dresden, Tuesday, February 13, 1945*, Harper-Collins, 2004.

The German Campaign in Russia-Planning and Operations (1941-1942), Department of the Army, Historical Study, No. 21-261a, March 1955.

The Oxford Companion to World War II, General Editor I. C. B. Dear, Consultant Editor M. R. D. Foot, Oxford University Press, 1995.

The United States Strategic Bombing Survey, Summary Report, European War,
30 September 1945.

U. G. Chernyavskii, *Voina I prodovol'stve, Snabzhenie gorodskogo naseleniya v Veliuyu Otechestvennuyu voiny 1941 – 1945* Moscow, Nauka, 1964.

Vagts, Dr., Alfred, *Hitler's Second Army*, Infantry Journal, Washington, D.C., 1943.

Whiting, Charles, *The Home Front: Germany*, Time-Life Books, 1982.

Willmott, H. P., *June 1944*, Grub Street, 1999.

Yelton, David K., *Hitler's Volksstrum, The Nazi Militia and the Fall of Germany 1944-1945*, University Press of Kansas, 2002.

Zawodny, J.K., *Death in the Forest, Story of the Katyn Forest Massacre*, University of Notre Dame Press, 1962.

Ziemke, Earl F., *The U.S. Army in the Occupation of Germany 1944-1946* Center of Military History, United States Army, Washington, D.C., 1990.

Ziemke, Earl F., *Stalingrad To Berlin: The German Defeat In the East*, Office of the Chief of Military History, United States Army, Washington, D.C., 1962.

Internet and Unattributed Sources

Anders, Lt. Gen. Wladyslaw and Munoz, Antonio, *Russian Volunteers in the German Wehrmacht in WWII*, **http://www.feldgrau.com**, 2002.

Forging the Red Star, An Examination of Soviet Armaments Factories and Their Production, **http://members.tripod.com/~Sturmvogel/sovWarProd.html**.

Frederick I Barbarossa, **http://www.camelotint.com/world/02frederick1.html**.

Gerlach, Christian, **http://www.thirdreichforum.com** and *Kalkulierte Morde*, p. 884-895.

Geust, Carl-Fredrik, *Lend-Lease: Aircraft Deliveries to the Soviet Union*, **http://airforce.users.ru/lend-lease/english/articles/geust/aircraft_deliveries.htm**.

Gonzalez, Servando, *The Swastika and the Nazis*, 1997, **http:www.intelinet.org/swastika/swasepil.htm**.

How Uncle Joe Bugged FDR, from: **http://www.cia.gov/csi/studies/vol47no1/article02.html**.

Long, Jason, *Lend –Lease Armored Fighting Vehicles*, **http://members.tripod.com/~Sturmvogel/SovWar Prod.html**.

Origins of the Swastika, **http://www.crystalinks.com/hitler.html**.

Pravda, 29 October 2002, English language issue.

Panzerkamphwagen VI Tiger Aust. H/E Sd. Kfz. 181.

http://www.achtungpanzer.com/pz5.htm

Quesada, A. M. de, Compiled by, *The Backbone of the Der Deutscher Volksstrum: The Hitler Youth in WWII*, **http://www.adeq.net/HJ.htm**.

Quesada, A.M. de, Compiled by, *History of the German W.W. II Volksstrum, Der Deutscher Volksstrum: Organization and Military History of the German People's Militia*, August 2000, **http://www.adeq.net/volkshist.htm**.

Sieff, Martin, *When Russia Won Big in WWII*, Johnson's Russia List. **http://www.cdi.org/Russia/Johnson/6320-2.cfm**.

Skorzeny, *NKVD Troops in the Front Line*, 2003.

Vercamer, Arvo L., *A German-Soviet Military-Economic Comparison*, **http://feldgrau.com**, 2002.

Vercamer, A. L., *Supplying the Soviet War Machine*, 1951.

WWII Tech, World War II History, **http://www.geocities.com/Area51/Cavern/2941/articles.htm**

Wendel, Marcus, *The Third Reich Factbook*, 2005, **www.axishistory.com**

Index

Note: Page numbers with (n) indicate footnotes.

German PzKw V G "Panther". Germany's answer to the T-34.

Ostfront Publications, LLC,
P.O. Box 453 • Hanover, PA 1733

Quick Order Form

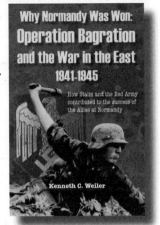

Telephone Orders:
Call (800) 247-6553.
Please have your credit card ready.

E-Mail Orders:
kweiler1@comcast.net

Postal Orders:
Ostfront Publications, LLC,
Ken Weiler
P.O. Box 453
Hanover, PA 17331

Please send me the book:
Why Normandy Was Won: Operation Bagration And The War In The East 1941-1945

Name: _____

Address: _____

City: _____ State: _____ Zip: _____

Telephone: _____

E-Mail Address: _____

No. of Copies: _____ @ $24.95 each (Paperback)

Sales Tax: Please add 6% for books shipped to Pennsylvania addresses.
Shipping by air, add:
      ❏ U.S. - $8 for the first book and $6 for each additional book.
      ❏ International - $12 for each book, $5 for each additional book.

Payment: ❏ Check - Check No: _____ Amount Paid; $_____

❏ Credit Card: ❏ Visa ❏ MasterCard ❏ Optima ❏ AMEX ❏ Discover

Card Number: _____

Name on card: _____

Exp. date: _____/_____